SMITHSONIAN INSTITUTION
INSTITUTE OF SOCIAL ANTHROPOLOGY
PUBLICATION NO. 2

CHERÁN:
A SIERRA TARASCAN VILLAGE

by

RALPH L. BEALS

*Prepared in Cooperation with the United States Department of
State as a Project of the Interdepartmental Committee
on Cultural and Scientific Cooperation*

GREENWOOD PRESS, PUBLISHERS
WESTPORT, CONNECTICUT

Originally published in 1946
by the United States Government Printing Office,
Washington, D.C.

First Greenwood Reprinting 1970

Library of Congress Catalogue Card Number 69-13812

SBN 8371-3166-9

Printed in the United States of America

LETTER OF TRANSMITTAL

SMITHSONIAN INSTITUTION,
INSTITUTE OF SOCIAL ANTHROPOLOGY,
Washington 25, D. C., June 21, 1944.

SIR: I have the honor to transmit herewith a manuscript entitled "Cherán: A Sierra Tarascan Village," by Ralph L. Beals, and to recommend that it be published as Publication Number 2 of the Institute of Social Anthropology, which has been established by the Smithsonian Institution as an autonomous unit of the Bureau of American Ethnology to carry out cooperative work in social anthropology with the American Republics as part of the program of the Interdepartmental Committee on Cultural and Scientific Cooperation.

Very respectfully yours,

JULIAN H. STEWARD, *Director.*

DR. C. G. ABBOT,
Secretary of the Smithsonian Institution.

CONTENTS

VI

ILLUSTRATIONS

PLATES

(All plates at end of book)

FIGURES

MAPS

FOREWORD

By Julian H. Steward

The Institute of Social Anthropology was created within the Smithsonian Institution to carry out cooperative research and teaching in the field of social anthropology as part of the broad program of Cultural and Scientific Cooperation under the State Department's Interdepartmental Committee.

One of the most important cooperative programs of the Institute of Social Anthropology is with the Escuela Nacional de Antropología del Instituto Nacional de Antropología e Historia of Mexico. The field research of this program will be directed toward a study of the Tarascans of Michoacán, a large group of Indians whose culture is of great interest to science and whose role in national life is of great importance to contemporary Mexico. In undertaking this work, it is the good fortune of the Institute of Social Anthropology to help further a program already extensively carried out by the University of California in cooperation with the Departamento de Antropología de la Escuela de Ciencias Biológicas del Instituto Politécnico Nacional, now the Escuela Nacional de Antropología del Instituto Nacional de Antropología e Historia, and the Departamento Autónomo de Asuntos Indígenas. The present monograph is a community study of Cherán, a Tarascan village, made by Dr. Beals in collaboration with the Mexican institutions.

This study is a basic document for understanding native American communities from the point of view both of their individuality and of their gradual assimilation to national life through economic and ideological acculturation. Although Cherán, like many other towns of the Tarascan area, is thought of and thinks of itself as Indian, it is difficult to identify anything that is aboriginal besides its language and racial type. Cherán's domesticated animals, many of its crops, its patterns of cultivation, and its general technologies and material culture are almost exclusively European. It is presumably European in its individual land ownership and inheritance, though the assumption that aboriginal America had collective land ownership needs further proof. Wholly European is its cash system, involving even a monetary standard of values, loans made for interest, and the purchase from elsewhere of most goods other than the local agricultural and forest products. It might be expected that these European economic patterns would have repercussions in other aspects of the culture; actually, the degree of Hispanicization of religious and social life is astonishing. Religion is strictly Catholic, witchcraft is European in type, and even the curers with their herbs and applications betray virtually nothing that is clearly aboriginal. Cherán's large, compact community of 5,000 persons is seemingly in the Spanish rather than Indian settlement pattern (a problem to be solved by archeology), and it may have been facilitated partly by the use of pack animals for transportation. The social configurations are likewise Spanish: the family, with a large circle of relatives by blood and marriage; the innumerable godparents; the *mayordomías* (festivals for the saints); the elaborate wedding ceremonies; and the dances, music, games, and other recreations.

With virtually all aspects of Cherán culture that can be formally categorized clearly Spanish in origin, why is Cherán considered Indian? Cherán's strong attachment to the locality, to the local group, and to traditional culture characterizes many other "Indian" communities in Mexico, Central America, and the Andes. The essential characteristic of an "Indian" would seem to be his failure to integrate emotionally and actively with national life rather than a demonstrable aboriginal content in his culture. The culture that he preserves in comparative isolation may, in fact, be far more that of 16th-century Spain than that of native America. This is not to say, however, that a pure 16th-century Spanish culture survives anywhere. In the case of Cherán, Beals suggests that the distinctive characteristics may represent the "pattern influence of native ideas" on European features, together with the effects of Bishop Vasco de Quiroga's application of Thomas More's "Utopia." For historical anthropology, these communities clearly pose important problems concerning 16th-century Spanish culture, its imposition through the conquistadors and priests on the Indians, and the subsequent long interval during which many areas stabilized their culture in comparative isolation.

Despite being considered Indian, Cherán seems to contain the potentialities for rapid acculturation. Its essential economic patterns will, so far as local productivity through agriculture or manufactures permit, facilitate further economic development as the new highway stimulates increased commerce with other areas. Its essentially Spanish social patterns and its present proletariat consciousness and political sense seem to afford a ready basis for further assimilation of national culture through the informal means of outside contacts and the more formal means of governmental programs. Its strong Catholic background will pave the way for further Church influence. One cannot predict the future of such a community in detail, for it will depend partly upon national and even international developments as well as upon Cherán's reaction to them. General trends are now observable among comparable communities; and the work that the Institute of Social Anthropology is now carrying on in cooperation with the Escuela Nacional de Antropología of Mexico among other Tarascan villages that have slightly different characteristics and degrees of acculturation and the Institute's studies in other parts of Latin America will yield data that will both clarify general trends and high-light local peculiarities.

PHONETIC NOTE

The phonetic symbols used conform to the Tarascan alphabet approved by the Congreso de Filólogos y Lingüistas of Mexico in 1939 and employed by the Tarascan Project of the Departamento de Asuntos Indígenas. The alphabet is based on standard Spanish usage insofar as possible, with additional symbols added for Tarascan and with some clarification of the Spanish symbols as indicated below.

The vowels *a, e, i, o, u* have Spanish values. The vowel ʌ is intermediate between Spanish *i* and *u*.

The consonants *b, d, f, g, j, k, l, m, n, p, r, s,* and *t* have regular Spanish values. In addition the following symbols are used:

¢ is the equivalent of English or Spanish *ts*.

č is the equivalent of English *ch*.

η is used for the sound of English *ng* in "sing."

ʌ is intermediate between Spanish *l* and *r*.

r is the equivalent of Spanish *rr*.

š is the equivalent of English *sh*.

¢', č', k', p', and t' are aspirated forms of the consonants given above.

f, l, and *r* occur only in foreign loan words in Tarascan; *b, d,* and *g* occur primarily in words of Spanish origin but occur sometimes in purely Tarascan words.

Cherán: A Sierra Tarascan Village

By Ralph L. Beals

INTRODUCTION

The study of Cherán was carried out in 1940–41 as part of the Program of Anthropological Investigations among the Tarascans, a cooperative undertaking of the University of California, the Escuela Nacional de Antropología del Instituto Nacional de Antropología e Historia (formerly the Departamento de Antropología de la Escuela de Ciencias Biológicas del Instituto Politécnico Nacional), and the Departamento Autónomo de Asuntos Indígenas. In general, the program aims at a thorough investigation of the Tarascans and their culture, both past and present.[1] An extensive program of this character is obviously the work of many persons and involves many individual projects. Consequently, a number of subjects which might have formed a part of the study of Cherán were not undertaken because they will be dealt with in other studies. The chief omission has been the lack of any general consideration of the Tarascans as a whole or any investigation of historical backgrounds. In some respects the study of Cherán would be more rounded and intelligible had fuller knowledge of the historical changes in Tarascan culture been available.

Unfortunately, the historical aspects of the Tarascan program are still little developed. Several years of documentary research would have been necessary to approach the study of Cherán with reasonably full background knowledge. Consequently, the description of Cherán is primarily a cross section of the culture of the community at the time of the study without any effort to interpret its historical development.

[1] For a fuller discussion of the Program, see Rubín de la Borbolla, D. F., and Beals, Ralph L. (1940) and Beals, Carrasco, and McCorkle (1944).

Financial support for the field work came from two sources. The Board of Research of the University of California contributed materially to field expenses and to the preparation of the manuscript. In addition, a substantial amount was made available for field expenses by the Departamento Autónomo de Asuntos Indígenas in México. Funds for a preliminary survey of the Tarascan area, which resulted in the selection of Cherán for study, were supplied by the Board of Research of the University of California and the Instituto Politécnico Nacional.

The village of Cherán was chosen for several reasons. In the first place, it is the largest of the mountain Tarascan villages and consequently offered an advantageous opportunity for several people to work simultaneously. Until about 1937 Cherán was also one of the most isolated of the mountain Tarascan towns. In that year the grade for the branch highway from the Guadalajara–Mexico City highway to Uruapan was established. Paving of this highway was completed in 1940, but little effect on Cherán had yet taken place. This situation offered an attractive opportunity for later investigation of the results of lessened isolation. Finally, Cherán is an almost wholly Indian town, a situation which is not true of most of the large mountain Tarascan settlements. Actually, in 1940 only a few families in Cherán did not regard themselves as Tarascan. The non-Tarascan families were more or less transient and occupied a low position in the social scale; most of them were the flotsam left from the highway construction crews and had neither influence nor status in the town. The majority actually left the town during 1940.

1

The exceptions were two storekeepers, both from essentially Indian towns themselves, two school teachers, a Federal tax collector, and the town Secretary.

The field work in Cherán was a cooperative enterprise, involving the work of numerous assistants. Most important of these helpers was Thomas McCorkle, of Berkeley, Calif. His greatest contribution was in accumulating the endless amount of detail necessary to the economic study, although there is scarcely a section of the paper which does not make use of data collected by him. Dr. Emmanuel Palacios, of the Departamento Autónomo de Asuntos Indígenas, is responsible for a great deal of the data on childbirth, infant care, midwifery, and medical practice in general. Sra. Silvia Rendón, of the Escuela Nacional de Antropología, worked particularly in the field of foods, but also contributed extensively on other topics, especially on matters dealing with women. She also supplied data from other towns, especially Angáhuan, Capacuaro, and Chilchota. Sr. Pedro Carrasco R., of the Escuela Nacional de Antropología, worked primarily on housing. His major contributions are included in two other papers (Beals, Carrasco, and McCorkle, 1944; Beals and Carrasco, 1944), but he also provided miscellaneous notes from Cherán, Angáhuan, Capacuaro, and Chilchota and some of the Lake Pátzcuaro towns. Some comparative notes from Patamban were collected by Ricardo Pozas, of the Escuela Nacional de Antropología, in the course of a study of pottery manufacture, the details of which are not included in this paper. Finally, some data were collected by Dorothy Beals and Margery McCorkle.

In addition to the foregoing, many persons in Cherán were of assistance. Throughout the entire period of the study two were especially helpful, Agustín Rangel and Pedro Chávez. The former, although a full-blooded Tarascan, had been born and educated in California. As a literate assistant he was extremely useful in many ways; for example, in searching the town archives and recording many important facts therefrom. Perhaps his most important service, however, was in providing an entreé into the homes of his almost innumerable relatives. Particularly to be mentioned are his parents, his aunt, Doña Feliciana Bautista, and his uncle, Don Antonio Sánchez. Agustín also afforded fascinating data himself, as we were able to observe closely the process of his assimilation into the culture and life of the community. In the course of the study, he changed from a not untypical United States high school graduate into a pretty typical resident of Cherán.

A particular debt of gratitude is also due Pedro Chávez. A native of Cherán, Sr. Chávez had been educated in a Government boarding school and was serving as a school teacher. Owing to the lack of facilities, he was able to teach only at night, and he spent his days aiding in the investigation, without compensation. No amount of pay could have secured more conscientious and faithful aid, day after day for many months. Regardless of the weather, or, I suspect, very often regardless of his personal concerns, Sr. Chávez either worked as systematic informant or accompanied one or the other of the investigators on endless visits, opening many doors to them which otherwise would have been closed. When not actively assisting, he wrote lengthy accounts of various phases of town life. A person of some eminence in the town, as well as belonging to the dominant political group, he had served as town Treasurer and was a member of the committee which administered the town's forest lands.

The hundreds of Cherán residents who aided us at one time or another cannot, of course, be listed. Many gave long hours of their time and courteous and intelligent aid on numerous problems. Essentially, this report is their report and the outsiders acted primarily as guides, recorders, and interpreters. That the people of Cherán were willing to do this was due partly to the unreserved cooperation of the municipal authorities who endorsed the study on every occasion. I am also indebted to the Executive Authority of the State of Michoacán for providing me with the proper introduction to the town.

A word should be said about field methods at this point. Obviously, working with a large group of investigators presents special problems. Perhaps the most important special technique was to arrange to have all field notes transcribed at the earliest possible moment.

Usually, field notes were classified, typed in triplicate, and filed according to a modification of the system of the Outline of Cultural Materials prepared by George P. Murdock and others for use in the Cross-Cultural Survey at Yale University (Murdock and others, 1938). In this way it was possible for all workers to find immediately what had already been collected on a subject and to discover discrepancies in accounts when these existed. The system also served to show deficiencies in the data.

Certain other problems in field methods arose. Cherán habits place some obstacles in the way of field work. The main occupations of the town are farming and forest exploitation. In the former case, men are usually in the fields all day, often at points several miles distant from town. In the latter instance, men may be away from town for 4 or 5 days at a time. In certain seasons the town is almost deserted during the day. As women will not talk with strange men in the absence of their husbands, it often took many visits to find at home a man we wished to query on some specific point. In addition, yards are surrounded by high walls and it is customary to greet visitors at the yard gate and converse with them on the street. Consequently, it is difficult to gain much insight into home life. Only women can get free access into the houses, and it is unfortunate that Sra. Rendón could not have spent full time in the field. Certain aspects of this study would then have been much better than they are.

In general, the method followed was first to discuss a topic with Sr. Chávez in detail, obtaining from him as complete an account as possible. In some cases Sr. Chávez also wrote supplementary accounts. Efforts were always made to get the names of specific people who were involved. Once we had obtained what might be considered Sr. Chávez's view of a particular aspect of the culture, this was sometimes checked with Sr. Rangel. On other occasions we started with Sr. Rangel and checked with Sr. Chávez. An effort was then made to visit and talk with a large number of the people concerned. For example, after securing Sr. Chávez' account of childbirth, a list of all the professional midwives in town was secured. These were all then visited by Dr. Palacios and interviewed intensively. Some were inter-

viewed independently by other staff members. Data were likewise taken from as many women as possible. In another instance, accounts were secured of as many fiestas and *mayordomías* as possible. Each *mayordomo* and other ceremonial official was then visited and interviewed, often several times. Finally, in this instance, as many ceremonies as possible were observed. In the case of economic life, virtually every specialist in town was interviewed and the data were checked and cross-checked. In addition, a representative sample of forest workers and farmers were interviewed. This process was facilitated by the existence of a complete roster of males of voting age for two *barrios*, together with their major occupations, given to us by the town authorities. In the case of farmers, the tax rolls of the tax collector's office were opened to us, giving some check on land ownership. Some fields were paced to estimate size (measurement was out of the question for various local reasons), and observations were made on the length of time taken to complete various farm tasks. At harvest time, the actual production of fields was determined by observing the harvest closely. In this case, data given by informants proved markedly variable from the facts. Prices of all products were established by questioning numerous producers and also by questioning buyers. Obviously procedures varied with different topics, but the examples given perhaps sufficiently indicate the general method employed.

In conclusion, acknowledgment should be made of assistance and encouragement given by persons not directly concerned with the field study. Dr. Morris Swadesh, director of the *Proyecto Tarasco*, an experiment in bilingual education with headquarters in the nearby town of Paracho, together with all the members of his staff, was extremely helpful in many ways. Scores of residents of Michoacán at one time or another rendered personal assistance. In Mexico City, Dr. Paul Kirchhoff and Miguel O. de Mendizabal were helpful, both in personal matters and in giving numerous suggestions and leads for problems to investigate. Sr. Luis Chávez Orozco, then chief of the Departamento Autónomo de Asuntos Indígenas, gave much time and effort to forward the program. Dr. Alfonso Caso discussed many problems and gave valuable advice. Numerous members of the staff of the Instituto Politécnico Nacional also gave of their time. President Robert G. Sproul of the University of California, arranged a special leave of absence to make the study possible. Above all, thanks are due to Dr. D. F. Rubín de la Borbolla, then head of the Department of Anthropology of the Instituto Politécnico Nacional and now director of the Escuela Nacional de Antropología, collaborator in the general program, who gave many days of his time in completing necessary arrangements to make the study possible.

In addition to the persons mentioned, I wish also to express my gratitude to those who have helped further the general Program of Anthropological Investigations among the Tarascans: General Lázaro Cárdenas, former President of the United States of Mexico; Dr. A. L. Kroeber, of the University of California, Berkeley, Calif.; Dr. John M. Cooper, Catholic University of America, Washington, D. C.; Sr. Luis Chávez Orozco, former Chief, Departamento de Asuntos Indígenas, Mexico; Dr. Gerardo Varela, Director of the Escuela Nacional de Ciencis Biológicas, Mexico; Lic. Gilberto Loyo, Director General of the Census, Mexico; Dr. J. B. Lockey, former Chairman, Board of Research, University of California, Los Angeles; Dr. Vern O. Knudsen, Dean of Graduate Studies, University of California, Los Angeles; and the late Dr. Charles B. Lipman, Dean of Graduate Studies, University of California, Berkeley.

The excellence of the drawings is due to the intelligent cooperation and skill of Virginia More Roediger, who worked not only as an artist but as an illustrator.

Finally, I gratefully acknowledge the assistance of the Institute of Social Anthropology, Smithsonian Institution, for editing this manuscript and for publishing it in this series, which is devoted to inter-American cooperation.

THE SETTING AND THE PEOPLE

The modern Tarascans occupy the west central section of northern Michoacán, Mexico. In prehistoric times the Tarascan area was larger, including most of the State of Michoacán, except possibly the rather abrupt and not very hospitable seacoast, as well as parts of the State of Jalisco to the northwest, Guanajuato to the northeast, and the lower end of the Balsas River basin in Guerrero to the south. This expanded area apparently represented the results of a series of conquests. Two or three centuries before the arrival of the Spaniards, the Tarascan area probably was not greatly different from that of today.

The State of Michoacán is one of the most densely populated rural States of Mexico. It lies to the west of Mexico City, and its capital, Morelia, is about 250 miles from the National Capital by road or railroad. Despite its dense population, much of the State is rugged and mountainous. Its eastern and northern parts are on the plateau of México. Level areas are often above 7,000 feet elevation, but, although it is technically a part of the Central Mexican plateau, only the northern margins of the State have large level tracts, for most of the elevated part of the State is in the so-called "volcanic axis" of Mexico. In many regions, and this is particularly true of the area occupied by the Tarascans, the characteristic sky line is a series of old volcanic cones, often surrounding basins or long depressions, in which more recent low cinder cones frequently occur (pl. 1, upper and lower left). Dozens of peaks have elevations of over 10,000 feet, but only one may exceed 11,000 feet.

To the south and southwest the terrain drops sharply toward a great basin formed by tributaries of the Balsas River. The slope is steep and so thoroughly dissected by streams that, despite the opening of many roads and truck trails in recent years, it still is not possible to reach the Balsas River by road from highland Michoacán. This great basin forms an important portion of Michoacán and is much visited by the Tarascans. Tropical vegetation and climate characterize the basin except for a semiarid section in the west.

The Pacific coast of the State is paralleled by a large range of mountains, the Sierra de

Coalcomán, which again reaches elevations of over 10,000 feet. The rain shadow of this range accounts for the subarid conditions of part of the basin area. Although these mountains are little known, apparently they rise fairly steeply on both faces and the coastal area beyond is narrow and of little use.

The drainage of Michoacán presents some peculiarities. In the north and west central region are lakes of various size, of which perhaps the best known is Lake Pátzcuaro. In common with some other lakes in the area, Lake Pátzucuaro has no outlet, but its waters are nevertheless not brackish. The high porosity of the volcanic soil may account for this phenomenon, for the lake has evidently been isolated from other drainages for a long period of time. This isolation is attested by the fact that the native fish are all very primitive viviparous species.

Moreover, despite heavy rainfall in some areas (at Lake Pátzcuaro the average annual rainfall is around 60 inches), there are virtually no permanent streams and even springs are rare. Most Tarascan towns suffer from almost constant water shortage despite the heavy precipitation. In contrast, some of the lower lands have abundant large running streams. In places, underground springs of great size emerge at elevations of about 5,500 feet. Near Uruapan, for example, a large stream is formed by a group of such springs.

The present-day range of the Tarascans cannot be defined with great accuracy, partly because of the lack of detailed studies and partly because of the degree of acculturation undergone by many settlements. Villages which outwardly differ in no visible respect from well-known Tarascan settlements often contain no persons speaking Tarascan. All around the edges of Tarascan territory occur villages in various degrees of assimilation to Mexican culture and with various degrees of physical mixture with the Mestizo population. As a result, the present-day distribution of the Tarascans can only be approximated (map 1).

On the east, the basin of Lake Pátzcuaro is definitely Tarascan, although some towns, such as Tzintzuntzan, the traditional capital of the Tarascan "Empire," are no longer Tarascan-speaking. The western edge of Tarascan territory is close to the railroad which runs through the town of Zamora to Los Reyes. The southern boundary might be defined roughly as on a line from Los Reyes to Uruapan and thence close to the railway from Uruapan to Pátzcuaro, while the new highway from Mexico City to Guadalajara in some places runs just inside the northern limits and in others, just outside. Within or near the borders of the present-day Tarascan area occur a number of old Mexican towns closely associated with the historic Tarascans and their contemporary culture, which provide the administrative centers and the major market places. These towns are Pátzcuaro, Zacapu, Purépero, Zamora, Los Reyes, and Uruapan. In some instances other towns of local importance have arisen more recently, towns which were once Tarascan but are now occupied by Mestizos and deculturated Tarascans. A good example of such a town is Chilchota.

Viewed as a whole, the Tarascan area may be characterized generally as an elevated temperate region of sufficient rainfall, deep volcanic soils, and pine or mixed pine and hardwood forests. In detail there are differences, and a number of regions may be identified.

The easternmost region is that about Lake Pátzcuaro. The lake has an elevation of slightly over 7,000 feet, and most of the villages are either on the shore or upon islands in the lake. The forests have been cleared away around the lake except upon lands too steep to cultivate with the plow. Rainfall is heavy, but is concentrated in the summer months. The climate is temperate and cool even in midsummer.

North of Lake Pátzcuaro is a large fertile valley or depression near Zacapu, ringed about by hills and mountains covered with forest. Although there is but little difference in elevation from Lake Pátzcuaro, the climate is warmer and some tropical or subtropical plants such as sugarcane are grown on a small scale.

Over a range of mountains to the west of Zacapu is a fertile valley known as La Cañada. Here the climate is warmer and more arid, as is evidenced by the frequency of irrigation and extensive cultivation of citrus fruit, bananas, and similar tropical and subtropical plants.

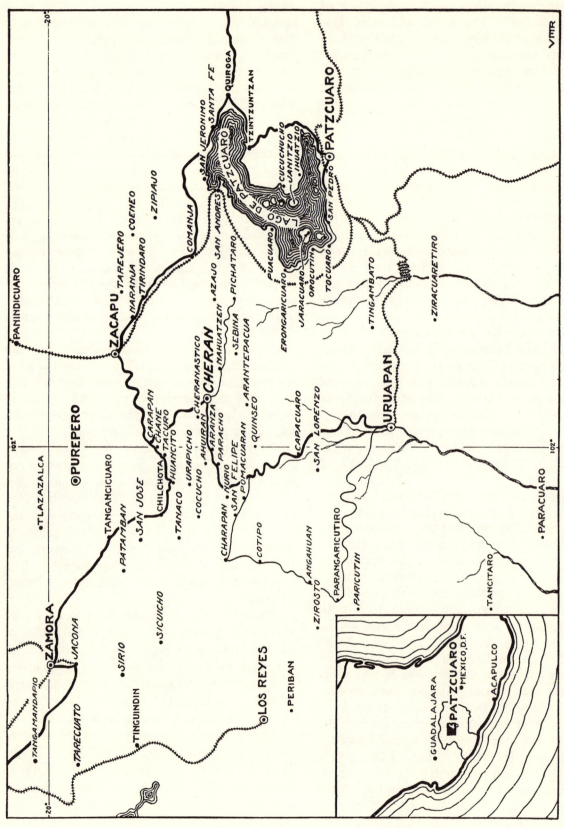

MAP 1.—Tarascan territory. Towns in italic are Tarascan in culture and speech. Towns in roman are either of Mestizo origin or are primarily Mestizo in population and culture and Spanish in speech. The list of Tarascan towns shown is complete only in the vicinity of Cherán; the inadequacies of existing maps make it impossible to show all the Tarascan towns with any approach to accuracy.

West of Lake Pátzcuaro and south of La Cañada is the rugged area known as La Sierra, extending as far west as the town of Tinguindín. This region is relatively homogeneous, with an essentially temperate climate. Although the elevation of towns varies from about 6,000 feet to about 9,000 feet, generally the temperature is cool. Heavy rainfall and the presence of numerous 10,000-foot peaks apparently combine to prevent cultivation of most subtropical plants. Extensive steep, forested slopes and lava flows are interspersed with numerous valleys and depressions in a high state of cultivation. Only in the west, where rainfall apparently is less, are a few towns favored by a milder climate. South of La Cañada and about equidistant from Uruapan, Zacapu, and Pátzcuaro is Cherán, largest of the mountain Tarascan towns and, until very recent years, one of the most isolated.

Situated on a sloping bench, Cherán looks westward over a long depression, dotted with villages and interrupted here and there by cinder cones rising as much as a thousand feet above the depression (pl. 1, upper and lower, left). North and south of Cherán, the series of peaks which bound the depression to the west culminate in two 10,000-foot cones. Eastward is another smaller basin of fertile soil, similarly marked by cinder cones and by the striking isolated volcanic peak of El Pilón, also over 10,000 feet in height.

Except for occasional marginal farm clearings, the steeper slopes, and those areas where relatively recent lava flows make cultivation impossible, are covered with forest. The predominant species are three or four types of pine, but completely pure stands are rarely found. Usually there is a fair intermixture of oak and madroña, while, beginning at the level of Cherán, fir trees occur and increase in number at higher elevations. These forest lands provide one of the important resources of the Cherán population.

Wherever the land is sufficiently level to permit regular cultivation, the forest has been almost entirely cleared away. In many places, areas hundreds of acres in extent are continuously cultivated. Maize and, to a much smaller extent, wheat, are almost the only field crops. Cultivation of these, plus exploitation of the forest resources and the breeding of a few sheep and cattle, provide the sustenance of the great majority of Cherán's population.

The town of Cherán has a population of about 5,000. The community is unique among Tarascan towns, not only for its large size—almost 2,000 more than that of any other settlement—but because the *municipio* of the same name contains only two, unimportant rancherias. Most *municipios* in the Tarascan area consist of one moderately large settlement, the *cabecera*, and a surrounding group of small settlements known as *tenencias*, and still smaller communities known as rancherias or by other classificatory terms. Usually the total populations of these *municipios* approximate the population of Cherán or even exceed it. Consequently, the unique feature of the *municipio* of Cherán is the concentration of almost the entire population in the *cabecera*.

Despite the concentration of population in the *cabecera*, the *municipio* of Cherán comprises a large area. Much of this area is mountain and forest, but there are many relatively large tracts of arable land (maps 2, 3). This circumstance, in part at least, has been the cause of numerous boundary disputes and some loss of territory. The most notable recent loss of territory has been the secession of the one *tenencia* of Cherán, the rather large settlement of Cheranástico to the northwest, which seceded in 1939 and joined the *municipio* of Paracho. The immediate cause of this secession again appears to have been a boundary dispute between the *tenencia* and the *cabecera*.

Cherán differs from the ordinary Tarascan agricultural village only in size. Throughout the area the type of settlement is the compact village. Probably in most cases the villages represent settlements of Spanish type, with a central plaza about which are the church (sometimes not actually on the plaza), the municipal building, and, more recently, the school. From the central plaza radiates a rectangular grid of streets, modified only where necessitated by the irregular terrain (maps 4, 5). In the case of a large settlement such as Cherán, there usually exists some fragmentary legend of origin of the settlement through amalgamation of aboriginal groups dispersed

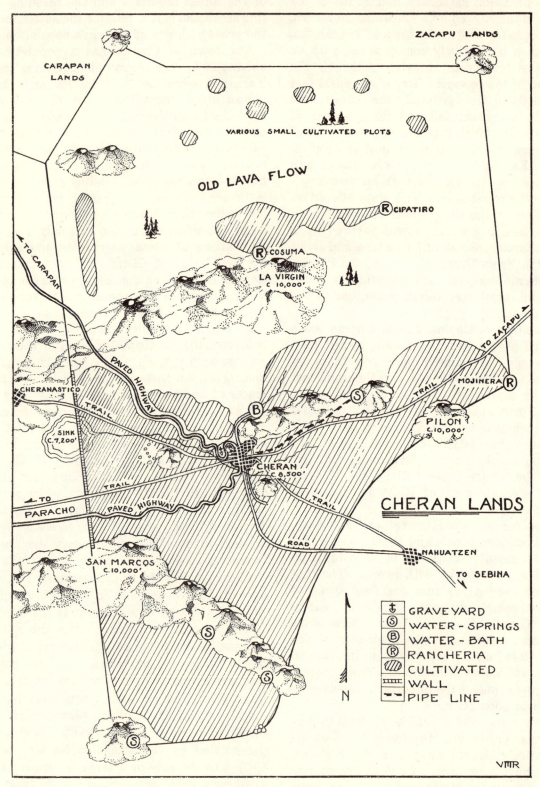

MAP 2.—Cherán lands, showing topography, principal cultivated areas, and various cultural features.

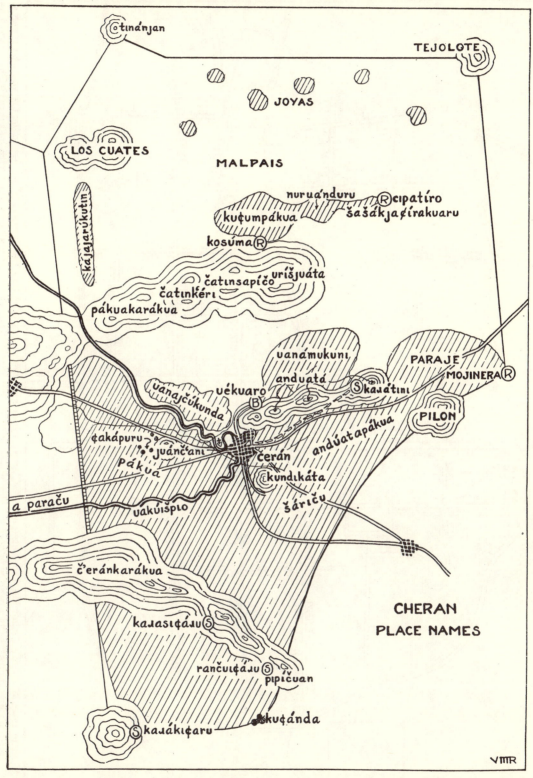

MAP 3.—The *municipio* of Cherán, showing the more important place names. See map 2 for explanation of symbols.

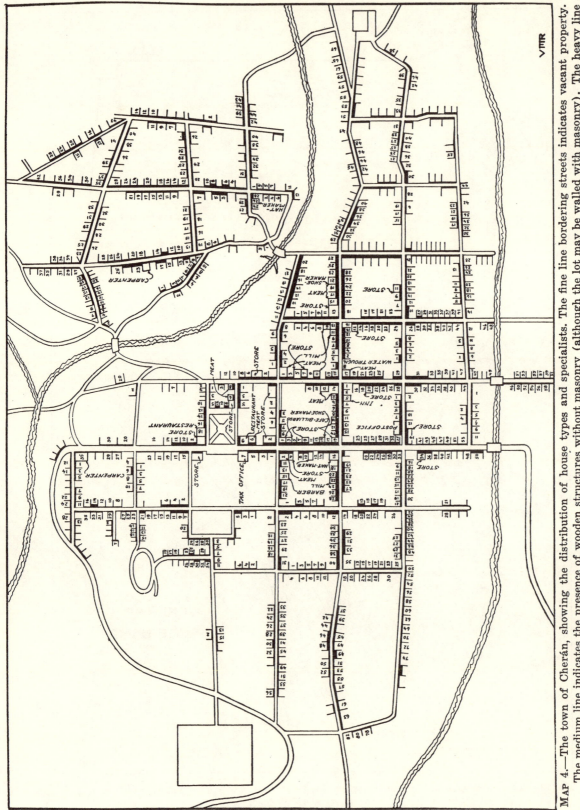

MAP 4.—The town of Cherán, showing the distribution of house types and specialists. The fine line bordering streets indicates vacant property. The medium line indicates the presence of wooden structures without masonry (although the lot may be walled with masonry). The heavy line indicates the presence of masonry or adobe structures. The majority of the latter also have one or more wooden structures on the same lot. Location of the majority of the specialized businesses or occupations is shown. The numbers refer to the house numbering system as of 1940.

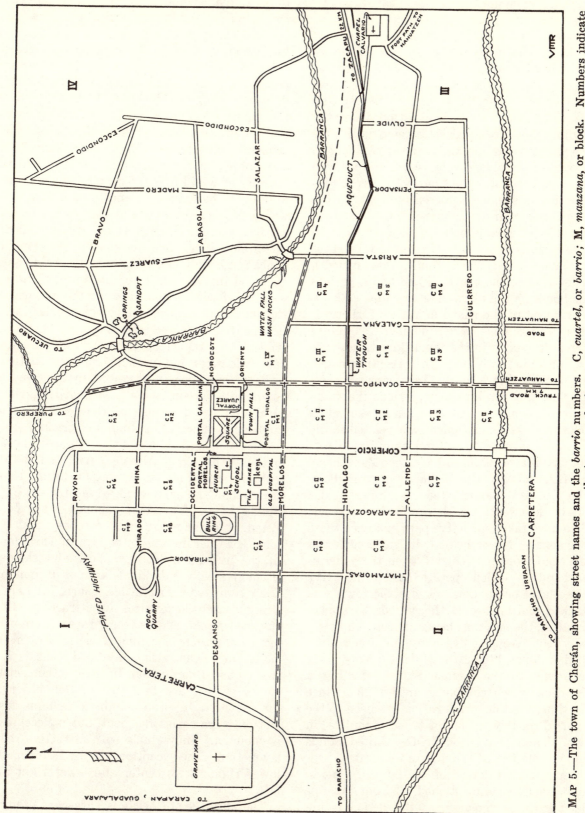

MAP 5.—The town of Cherán, showing street names and the *barrio* numbers. C, *cuartel*, or *barrio*; M, *manzana*, or block. Numbers indicate the town numbering system.

in smaller communities in the nearby mountains.

In the absence of documentary evidence, it may be surmised that Cherán is an old settlement. Archeological remains occur at several nearby places which may represent the antecedent smaller aboriginal settlements spoken of in tradition. About the period from the founding of the original settlement until 1910 there are few data, documentary or traditional. Although individuals were encountered who claimed to remember the time of the French intervention in Mexico, apparently events in the rest of the country influenced Cherán very little. Some outside settlers apparently lived in the town before 1910. Frequent references were made to a German family that owned a considerable amount of land and had a pretentious house on the plaza, now in ruins. Physical evidence in the shape of ruined structures suggests there once were a number of families of greater wealth in the town than is now the case, but apparently, with the exception noted, these families were native Tarascans.

During the revolutionary period, the town was in the center of the agrarian movement in Michoacán. This movement was related to the Zapatista movement in Morelos, and residents of other villages claim to have been Zapatistas. As Michoacán is also a Catholic stronghold, some villages participated in the religious wars of the twenties. Cherán, however, seems not to have taken an active part in any of these movements. Nevertheless, it suffered from them, and more particularly from the generalized banditry which operated under the cover of one label or another. Twice the town was attacked and burned in the period shortly before 1920, the last time being almost completely destroyed. Apparently many hundreds were killed or starved to death, while still more made their way to the United States, starting a migration which continued until 1929. Since that time, the tide of migration has been to the town. Probably a majority of families in town, though, have been in the United States or have relatives still living in the States.

Some general details of the flora of Cherán have already been mentioned. Nothing can be added to these remarks, as the region is unstudied botanically. The situation with respect to the fauna is equally unsatisfactory. Despite the extensive forests, wild life is scarce. No one in Cherán gets a living from hunting, and the amount of game taken forms an inconsiderable amount of the food supply. Deer and peccary are sometimes hunted and occasionally damage outlying fields, but they do not seem to be numerous. Squirrels, rabbits, wild pigeons, and quail are among the animals of most economic importance. Badgers are known, but are not eaten. An exception to the general scarcity of wild life is the coyote. This animal appears to be numerous and to be a danger to livestock in the outskirts of the town. Larger predatory animals, such as the jaguar and the mountain lion, are unknown. Informants could recall only one mountain lion being seen or killed in the vicinity of the town. The region is, of course, too high for the absence of the jaguar to be surprising, but smaller members of the genus *Felis* are also rare. Only the wildcat is reported. The rattlesnake and *culebrilla* occur, but are not common. As there are few handicrafts practiced in Cherán, the community is consequently primarily agricultural and the only use of the forests is for lumbering, charcoal making, and grazing.

Little need be said about the people of Cherán or their language. Although white admixture certainly exists in the town's population, there are virtually no acknowledged Mestizos. Until studies of the Tarascan population are completed, it perhaps will suffice to say that the people of Cherán seem to be typical Tarascans, on the average relatively short and slender, although stocky individuals are not uncommon. Their complexion is relatively dark, the hair is straight, and the features are attractive. Corpulence in old age is very rare. Goiter or incipient goiter is common, especially in the mountain towns, although the disease is less frequent in Cherán than in many other settlements. Teeth are bad, a condition observed for the area in pre-Columbian remains also. Not only are caries frequent, but malocclusion is common. Individuals with attractive regular teeth are the exception. (Pls. 1, upper and lower right; 2; 3, center and lower right and left.)

The language of Cherán is Tarascan, a tongue which shows relatively few dialectic differences.

Probably no group of Tarascans has great difficulty in understanding any other group. As Tarascan has not been subjected to intensive grammatical analysis, thus far no affiliations for the language have been seriously proposed.

To summarize the discussion, the Tarascans appear to be fairly typical of the plateau Indians of Central Mexico in type, but they speak a unique language. Both anciently and today they occupy a temperate to cold environment, which offers rich rewards to a farming people but which otherwise possesses relatively meager resources. In prehistoric times the Tarascans were able to utilize the present area as a base to develop a modest empire. In historic times, their empire gone, they still have maintained a degree of individuality in the face of an encroaching modern civilization.

TECHNOLOGY

EXPLOITATIVE ACTIVITIES

In this section are described the techniques of the Cherán Tarascans for the exploitation of the environment. With a few exceptions, manufacturing processes, the uses to which the products are put, and the economic system into which they enter are discussed in later sections.

COLLECTING

Plants.—No food plants are collected regularly. Recourse is sometimes had to edible greens in times of starvation or as an occasional means of bringing variety into the diet. Most useful plants, except medicinal herbs, exist in the town in virtually a semidomesticated state. This is particularly true of the most commonly used plants such as kulántro (*silantro*),[2] the most frequently employed herb for flavoring food. Similarly, *manzanillo*, probably the most generally used medicinal herb, is to be found in every garden. Discussion of these plants can therefore best be deferred to the discussions of medicine and the house gardens.

A small wild maguey growing in the mountains and in the *malpais* (lava flows) is collected from November to May. The heart is roasted in pit ovens and sold.

One minor commercial enterprise, formerly of some importance, is collecting *raiz de paja*, the roots of a coarse grass. The roots are cut off and carried to Cherán, where they are carefully laid out in rows on sunny, dry days. After drying, they are tied in bundles for sale for the manufacture of brushes. The entire family may work at this task. While some collecting of *raiz de paja* still is carried on, the market collapsed badly with the outbreak of war in 1939, depriving a number of families of an important part of their livelihood. In good times, the roots sold at 30 to 35 centavos a kilo.[3]

A root, čalankóte, is used for washing woolens and is considered superior to soap.[4] It is dug in the barrancas, both for use and for sale. In Angáhuan, Rendón found seeds of a bush called kómerame used for the same purpose, as well as leaves called apúpen and roots of the plant pačánkua.

Honey gathering.—The one collecting technique still important in Cherán is gathering wild honey. Not only are there still specialists who spend many weeks at the occupation during proper seasons of the year, but there are numerous ceremonial associations. The *panaleros* or honey collectors are divided into two groups, each with an image and a *mayordomía* of San Anselmo, patron saint of the group. There are also important ceremonial activities on the part of the *panaleros* in connection with the fiesta of Corpus Christi in June. The various ceremonies are described later.

Most gathering of wild honey takes place in the regions of old lava flows or *malpais*. The *malpaises* of Turicuaro and Tanaco are considered among the best today for honey gather-

---

[2] Tarascan words are in Roman and Spanish words are in italic unless they are in frequent English usage. Spanish words with special local meanings are in quotation marks.

[3] In La Cañada, wild gourds, *guajes* (arumbas), are collected and sold in the Chilchota market. The leaf of a wild bay (?), *baya* (hóngakua), is used in washing clothes by La Cañada Tarascans, who claim the plant is eaten by the Sierra Tarascans. Soaproot, *amole*, is used in La Cañada for bathing.

[4] The orthography used for native words is that recommended by *Proyecto Tarasco* and the *Consejo de Lenguas Indigenas* (Swadesh, 1940).

ing. The combs found here are round and hang from tree branches. They are found by observing the flight of bees; this requires good eyesight and is difficult on cloudy days. The clear weather of late spring and fall consequently is the time of greatest activity. From December until warm weather begins, the honey is sugared and cannot be extracted from the comb.

Several varieties of bees are sought. The combs found near Cherán are white and have little honey, most of the comb being occupied by brood. In the region near Tanaco the combs are red, small, and almost completely full of honey, with little brood. Other combs are described as being occupied by bees that are *muy bravo*. Only this type of bee requires the use of smoke to secure the honey. At times this bee attacks passers-by and follows until the victim covers himself with straw. Lemon juice is used to alleviate the stings. In addition to these types, wild European bees are sometimes found in hollow trees.

Once a comb is located, the *panalero* usually climbs the tree and knocks the comb down. If the tree is large, he cuts notches in the trunk with a small special-type ax, tying himself with a riata or a length of rope while he chops. The rope is not tied, but passes around the tree trunk and the two ends are held in the hands. The *panalero* holds the rope tightly while he edges up the tree. Then, with a skillful motion, he throws the loop of rope higher up the tree trunk. Once the comb is reached, the *panalero* covers his face and hands with a blanket and taps the comb until the bees leave. The procedures are regarded as highly dangerous. *Panaleros* are always careful to take a good rest before climbing a tree. They are also particularly attentive to their saint, San Anselmo, who is believed to protect them. The danger of the occupation is increased by the fact that the *panalero* always works alone and in case of accident could expect no rescue.

Honeycombs are now said to be so scarce that it is hardly worth while hunting them. Nevertheless, one *panalero* mentioned securing 19 combs on one trip which he sold for 9 pesos. Sometimes the combs are sold as collected. At other times the honey is extracted by squeezing the comb in an *ayate* or carrying net. If very clear honey is desired, it may be strained through silk. The native wild combs contain no wax. The larvae are sometimes eaten, either toasted in their cells or fried. The latter method of preparation involves picking the larvae out of the cells. Yet another method is to toast the larvae with onion, chile, and salt. The latter method is said to be especially tasty, but probably only *panaleros* ever use any of these methods very often.[5]

The larvae of another insect, the *traspanal* (*jicotera* in La Cañada), are also collected and eaten occasionally. This insect resembles the native bee but is a little larger and makes its nest in the ground to depths of 1 meter (3 ft.) or more. No other animal food is collected and the use of the eggs of wild birds was denied with every evidence of distaste.

USE OF MINERALS

Stone, volcanic cinders, and clay are the three mineral resources utilized in Cherán. Tuffs and lavas are employed for house building, foundations, and fences. The materials occur either in the town itself or in barrancas within a few hundred yards of the town. Volcanic cinders are also quarried out of the sides of barrancas, often within the town, and are employed to spread over slippery places on trails, streets, and yards. The supply of materials far exceeds demand, and the public domain affords all needed supplies.

Most of the rock used in Cherán comes from a quarry on the west face of the hill of Santa Karákua (also called Santiákujákua) within the village. Most of the rock is prised out of the upper face of the quarry in large pieces, which usually are broken up in the fall to the foot of the quarry. The broken rock is then placed in piles, which later comers will not molest. Smaller rocks and spalls are abundant and anyone may help himself to these. The rocks are usually packed by tying them on burros with ropes, while small pieces may be placed in nets or in pack boxes.

Clay is somewhat more scarce. It is used only for tilemaking and brickmaking, as no one in Cherán makes pottery. A sufficient supply of clay for all present needs is dug out

---

[5] At Sopoco in La Cañada, Rendón was told that the larvae are sometimes eaten raw.

either from the sides of public roads or from fields, with the permission of the owner. It is dug with pick and shovel, put in bags, and taken into town on muleback.

Adobes (adóbi) and adobe mortar are made from any convenient fine earth mixed with manure. In some towns dry pine needles ("huinomo")[6] or wheat or barley straw is used. The mud (adímu) for adobes is mixed in a depression in the ground. Dry earth is first mixed with manure and water is added, in the proportion of 10 loads (carretilladas) of earth, half a sack of manure or straw, and 10 five-gallon tins of water. The mud is then mixed with a spade for about 3 hours.

A wooden frame (marco or adobera), the size of the brick to be made, is now placed on carefully leveled ground. Mud is placed in the frame and pressed down well with the hands to insure complete filling of the space. The frame is now lifted off and washed in preparation for making the next adobe. The adobes are allowed to dry for 8 days, first in the original position and then on edge.

The usual size of adobes is 60 by 40 by 10 cm., or 2½ spans long. Cherán makes this size and also a brick 3 spans in length.

WATER SUPPLY

Cherán has a better water supply than most Tarascan towns, but it is still far from adequate. The larger of the barrancas through town often has flowing water, but this is used only for watering animals and washing clothes, as it is not considered pure enough to drink. At one spot, however, there are a number of small springs in the walls of the barranca. These have been improved by building cement tanks to accumulate the rather small flow, and people from the barrio of Parícutin and some other nearby residents obtain their water from the springs.

About 10 years ago an aqueduct was built to large springs near the base of the mountain, El Pilón, a distance of 15 km. (9 mi.). A 2-inch pipe line was laid, but the pipe reached only to the edge of town. From the end of the pipe the water is carried to the center of town by an arrangement of hand-hewn wooden troughs and pipes (pl. 3, upper left). Large tanks exist in the approximate center of town, and water is also piped to a fountain in the plaza. The troughs leak, however, and in some places are low enough to permit water to be dipped directly from them. In consequence, if the flow is small, water may not reach the tanks in sufficient quantity. The lower portion of the town receives no water directly and the effort of obtaining water in those sections, particularly the southwest district, is considerable.

FOREST UTILIZATION

The forests are one of the important and most utilized natural resources of Cherán. Firewood, charcoal, posts, railroad ties, shakes, and lumber of various sizes are secured from the woods. Forests cover a very large part of the Cherán lands and most of the timber is on public domain, although some forest patches may occur on privately owned land. The public domain is regarded as belonging to the town, and the Federal Government levies a nominal land tax on the community for the forest lands. Each head of a household pays a fee (rústica), usually 25 centavos a quarter, which is collected by a committee on community property (bienes comunales). This sum covers the taxes and gives each person the right to cut firewood from public lands. Persons exploiting other forest resources pay more.

Until recently utilization of other forest resources was also open to everyone. The Department of Forestry of the Federal Government is now attempting to control the exploitation of the forests, and since 1940 any use of the forest for purposes other than cutting firewood requires a permit. In 1941 an effort was being made to restrict all lumbering and charcoal burning to members of a cooperative. This is discussed later.

With the exception of a few wealthy persons, everyone who is not lazy cuts his own firewood.[7]

---

[6] Words regarded in Cherán as Spanish but which either do not appear in dictionaries or have special local meanings are placed in quotation marks.

[7] This is general even in such Mestizoized towns as Chilchota. In the latter town, however, there is some selling of firewood. During planting and harvest times the price is $0.35 a carga (burro load in this case); the rest of the year it is $0.25 a carga. Some people in Angáhuan make a business of taking firewood to Mestizo Zamora; similar cases occur in villages near Mestizo towns. Ocote (pitch pine), used principally for light, is also produced by the householder in Cherán. A long vertical cut is made on one side of a tree, which is gradually cut away as pitch accumulates. The tree is rarely cut through, but it usually dies from the operation. In Chilchota, where ocote (pitch pine) is sold,

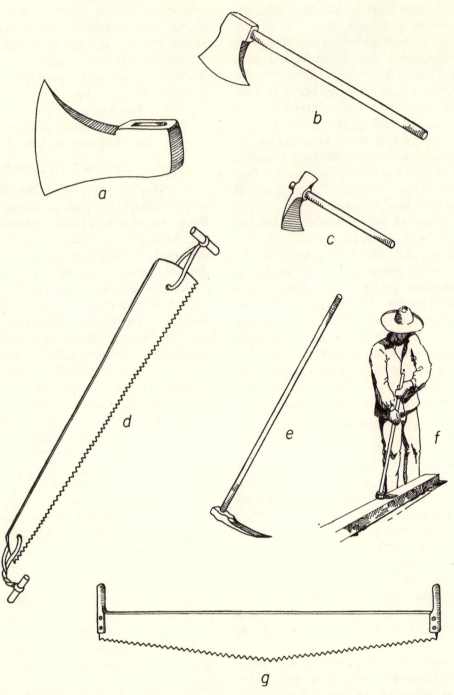

FIGURE 1.—Woodworking implements. a, Typical ax head, weighing 6 to 8 pounds. b, Same as a, with handle; total length about 3½ feet. c, Short-handled adz (angáru). d, Saw used for cutting planks (k'eréri arákutarakua), about 6 feet long; the lower handle usually is of metal and clamps over the end of the saw, engaging the saw teeth to hold it in place. e, Long-handled adz. f, Method of using long-handled adz to dress beams or planks. g, Logging saw, "sardina," used to cut felled timber into desired lengths.

Consequently, every Cherán male is a fairly competent axman and in a pinch can produce other forest products. Oak is considered far superior to other woods for burning, but it is becoming scarce near the town. The best supply is near El Pilón, several kilometers away.

With some exceptions, most skilled woodsmen work only when they have to fill definite orders. In other words, no stock of lumber or shakes is accumulated against possible future sales. Lumber or shake workers usually are farmers who supplement their income by forest products when opportunity offers. Not infrequently one or two members of a large household do lumbering but help in the fields when necessary or when unoccupied.

Pine is the main wood used for lumber, and fir for shakes. Trees ordinarily are cut with the ax (jáca). Trunks are cut in sections with a saw ("sardina") (fig. 1, g), which is operated by two persons. The trunks are cleared and debarked with the ax. The trunk is then squared by splitting off slabs ("tachones"), with oak wedges some 20 cm. (8 in.) in length driven by an oaken maul or the butt of the ax. The slabs are used for firewood or fences. Thick planks called "vigas" (anything over 2 inches in thickness) are then split out with wedges. Before use, heavy planks usually are dressed with a long-handled adz (angáru) (fig. 1, e). Thinner pieces, tablas (k'eréri), are sawed from squared sections of logs (pl. 4, upper right). The logs are elevated on a scaffolding of poles (or sometimes laid on poles across a saw pit) and sawed out by a saw (k'eréri aɹákutarakua) about 2 m. (6 ft.) long and wider at one end than at the other (fig. 1, d; pl. 3, upper right). The handle at the wide end is fixed, and that at the narrow end is hooked over the teeth of the saw. Before sawing, the block of timber is marked with a cord used like a chalk line but employing charcoal instead of chalk. All the planks from a block of timber are usually sawed about two-thirds of the length of the block; work is then begun at the opposite end. Planks customarily are about 1 inch thick, 6 to 8 feet long, and 6 to 8 inches wide. Planks cut from timber with a heavy pitch content are said to last longer.

Beams are usually squared sections of red (heart) wood. They are used primarily for foundations and joists and are split out by wedges.

An important product of Cherán is shakes, tejamanil (tasámani). The product is all exported, mostly to Zacapu. Some is also taken to Uruapan. Pine is rarely used for shakes, as the product curls during dry weather and is not as durable as shakes made from fir. However, fir shakes are more brittle. Fir trees grow only sporadically among the pine forests and must be searched for. Once a tree is found, the shake maker examines it carefully, studying the position of branches and estimating the probable straightness of the grain. If the tree does not look promising, it is left. Even after a tree has been felled with the ax, it may prove unsuitable for shakes. In this case it may be hewed into a beam, but it is more apt to be abandoned.

If the tree proves suitable, it is cut in lengths with saw or ax and the bark is removed, together with any rotten or insect-eaten portions. Each length is now split in sections (péri) with a wedge, cuña (injárukua). Each section has a width of four fingers at its outer edge, and a tree of average size will produce eight sections. One end of each section is then marked with a machete along the radii of the trunk. The section is first marked in the middle; each half is then divided in two, then each quarter, until 16 divisions are marked. At each mark the machete is driven in with blows of an oaken club to a depth of about 5 cm. The shakes are then split off with an oaken instrument called a rajador (uáŋgua). (Pl. 3, lower right and left.)

The completed shakes are thin and wedge-shaped when viewed in cross section. After drying in the sun for 2 or 3 hours they are tied into bundles of 400 called an irépita (400 in Tarascan). They are transported and sold by the bundle, the price varying according to the length. Different villages and Mexican markets have preferences for different lengths, usually 4, 5, or 6 cuartas.[8]

---

[1] centavo buys a thick piece. In Parangaricutiro, partly Mestizoized, there is some cutting of firewood as a business. In one case a father and three sons, 10, 12, and 15 years of age, cut a cord a day (16 cargas), which sold for $1.50 (all monetary values are in Mexican currency). In Parícutin two widows without grown sons buy firewood. The women are not poor.

[8] A cuarta equals ¼ of a vara (the standard measure of length, about 32 inches long).

a

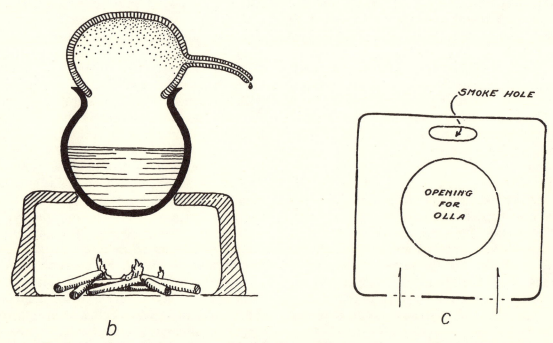

b   *c*

FIGURE 2.—Turpentine still. *a*, Perspective view. *b*, Cross-sectional view from side. *c*, Schematic view of fireplace from above.

Cherán prefers shakes 5 *cuartas* in length, called "thick shakes" (tasámani tiápiti). Shakes of 4 *cuartas* (1 *vara*) are sold primarily in Uruapan and are spoken of as *de comercio*, or "small shakes" (tasámani sapírati). Shakes 6 *cuartas* long, preferred by some Tarascan towns, are called "long shakes" (tasámani iórati). In Angáhuan, shakes 5 *cuartas* long are sold in Zamora and are sometimes called Zamorana.

Shake makers usually work from 8 a. m. to 6 p. m. A week's work routine is as follows: On Tuesday suitable trees are sought and felled. Wednesday is devoted to cutting trees in sections. Thursday and Friday the timber is split into shakes. One day is spent drying the shakes in the sun, and, if the maker is a professional, the finished product is taken to Uruapan or Zamora on Saturday and Sunday for sale. On this schedule one person might make two bundles of 400 shakes (two irépitas) in a week.

Railroad ties are usually made under contract arrangements. The workers leave town on Tuesday, usually arriving in time to cut a week's supply of logs for splitting and shaping. Wednesday, Thursday, and Friday are spent in splitting and shaping the ties with the ax. Saturday the ties are checked by the contractor, and the men are paid in time to return home that night.

A minor industry is cutting out blocks of madroña and jaboncilla wood. These are sold in Paracho, where they are made into doors, spoons, wooden bowls, and the various small wooden objects for which Paracho is famous. A few people in Cherán also make broom handles.

A considerable amount of charcoal is produced on the more distant lands of Cherán. Several men in town make their living entirely from charcoal burning. Oak is used almost exclusively for charcoal. Charcoal burners usually spend from Monday until Friday in the woods, and return home over the week end. Charcoal is usually sold in the woods to dealers, the unit of sale being a stack 8 by 7 inches by 6 feet.

In a number of Tarascan towns turpentine production is an important industry. This has been true of Cherán in the past, but, for reasons not discoverable, output at present is negligible. Turpentine is produced at any season of the year. The first cut in trees is made about 20 or 25 cm. (8 or 10 in.) from the ground, with a small ax called gúrbia. The initial cut is one-half cm. vertically and 10 cm. horizontally. At the base of the cut a small copper or pottery cup is fastened. The initial cut is lengthened upward each year until, after about 10 years, the cut is 1.50 to 1.70 m. in height. A cut is then started on the opposite side of the tree. Formerly it was the practice to leave the cup for collecting the resin at the bottom of the cut. This wasted considerable resin, and now the cup is raised as the height of the cut is increased. In order to lead the resin into the cup, a small sheet of metal is driven into the tree just above the cup. The cup is emptied every 3 days and the cut cleaned or enlarged.

The collected resin or *brea* is cooked in special stills. An *olla* of resin is placed above a firebox (fig. 2). The cover and "coil" are made of pottery (in the village of Patamban), and the turpentine is caught in another vessel. Before the decline in turpentine prices caused by World War II, a kilo of resin sold at 8 centavos in the woods and a 5-gallon tin of turpentine sold at 18 pesos. In 1941, prices were 4 or 5 centavos for a kilo of resin with a corresponding drop in turpentine prices.

HUNTING

Probably no one in Cherán derives any considerable part of his livelihood from hunting. Some men hunt casually because their farms or lumbering activities take them where game is more plentiful. Others hunt a good deal because they enjoy it. Finally, sometimes people hunt because they are poor and thus can augment their food supply or income.

The most commonly hunted animals are deer, peccary (guákin), squirrels (both ordinary, kuínike, and flying squirrels), rabbits, quail, pigeons, and less commonly, armadillos. Other local wild animals are not eaten. Heavy rifles are used for large animals, usually .30 or .32 caliber, and .22 caliber rifles for squirrels.

Deer are sometimes trapped in pits in the mountains. Squirrels are caught in snares. Horsehair threads are used to make snares to catch quail and pigeons. Quail snares are hung in the tops of bushes in which quail perch and peer about. When the bird puts its head in the noose, the hunter, who is hidden nearby, pulls a string. Pigeons are hunted mostly by boys, who set snares near watering places. The birds ordinarily water at dusk, alighting away from the water and walking toward it. The boys erect small fences by the water and hang the snares in openings left at frequent intervals.

Deer meat is sold in the village at the price of beef. It is said not to be liked very well. Squirrels are sold at 10 centavos and pigeons at 5 centavos each. Wild ducks are brought from Zacapu and sold at 50 centavos to 1 peso each, depending on size.

AGRICULTURE

Cherán is primarily an agricultural village. Many Tarascan towns have industrial specialties at which most of the inhabitants work full or part time. For example, it is fair to say that Paracho is a woodworking and weaving village or that Patamban is a pottery-making village, even though a number of persons devote part or all of their time to farming. In the same way, although there are industrial specialists in Cherán and it produces an important amount of forest products, such as lumber, railway ties, and charcoal, farming nevertheless overshadows all other activities. Most Cherán residents own land or farm on shares, and the majority engage in no other activities. In relation to all economic activities, then, farming occupies a place comparable to that occupied by pottery manufacturing in Patamban or fishing in some Lake villages.

The basic crop of Cherán is maize. Second in importance, but ranking far below maize, is wheat. Yet despite the emphasis on these two crops, Cherán farming is extraordinarily varied, as the following list of cultivated plants shows:

Maize	Cabbage
Wheat	Silantro
Barley	Mint
Oats	Fennel
Amaranth	Pears
Broadbean (*haba*)	Plums
Squash (*chilacayote*)	Cherries
Pumpkin	Apples
Bean	Peaches
Potato	Quinces

Maguey (agave)	Crab apples
Chayote	*Zapote blanco*

The above list is but a portion of the total number of varieties cultivated by the Tarascans in other villages. Plants used in Cherán but grown in other villages include onion, garlic, tomato (several types), chile (many kinds), sugarcane, sweetpotato, banana, lime, lemon, orange, guava, mamey, mango, watermelon, canteloup, avocado, *zapote negro*, and cherimoya.

TYPES OF FARM LANDS

The lands cultivated by the Cherán Tarascans all have soils almost exclusively composed of volcanic ash or cinders. However, low-lying areas which receive materials washed from the higher ground are usually more fertile and in a few specially favored spots may be cultivated annually. As a general rule, however, lands are cultivated only in alternate years.

Cherán lands are of five main categories: (1) "Plains" or valley floors, which may include some gently sloping or rolling areas but which are relatively flat; (2) patches of sloping land capable of permanent cultivation; (3) small areas of level land, usually called "*joyas*," consisting of small valleys, depressions in the midst of lava flows, which were not covered by lava, and the level depressions in the craters of cinder cones; (4) relatively level or gently sloping garden plots within the town; (5) temporary fields on the steeper slopes of the mountains.

The so-called "plains" consist of several large areas (maps 2, 3), subdivided in numerous privately owned plots. Maize and wheat are the principal crops grown. The "plains" are cultivated in alternate years under supervision of the town government. Harvest dates are fixed by the town council; after the final date, the "plains" become community pasture. Fencing of individual plots is not permitted, nor is planting in consecutive years. Therefore, men who own land in only one "plain" plant only every other year. Consequently, everyone tries to have land in at least two "plains."

The largest "plain," usually referred to simply as *el plan*, is west of Cherán, extending from the foot of the slope below the town to the boundary with Aranza and Cheranástico (pl. 1, upper left). The second most important "plain" is south and southeast of the town and extends on the east to the boundary with Nahuatzen. On the north and south the plain is bounded by hills and mountains, on the west by the slope to *el plan*. This area is usually referred to as Sharicho (šaričo). The *"plan of Arantepacuaro"* is south of the range of mountains of San Marcos, and extends to the boundary of Arantepacuaro on the south. The fourth and smallest "plain" of importance is northeast of the mountain of El Pilón.

Patches of sloping land under permanent cultivation are found scattered throughout the *municipio*. A large number of plots are found on the slope between *el plan* and the town and on the lower, gentler slopes of many mountains and cinder cones. These lands may be fenced or, more commonly, protected by deep ditches with hedges of agave on each side. Thorny crab apple or other fruit trees sometimes are also planted along ditches. Weak spots may be guarded by thorny brush and poles (pl. 4, lower left).

The so-called "joyas" are usually patches of only a few acres, often in isolated places far from town. They may be fenced or ditched to keep out animals and, like the other areas, are privately owned. Unless they are unusually fertile, *"joyas"* are cultivated only every other year.

The garden plots are within the town proper. In a few cases they may occupy an entire block, but normally they are merely part of a building lot (*solar*). Few of them are as large as half an acre. They are fenced and, unlike any other areas, they are cultivated every year.

Temporary fields are created by clearing the forest on community lands. Permission must be obtained from the Federal Department of Forestry, Hunting and Fishing. Extra forest taxes must be paid, but charges are nominal. Usually the areas cleared are steep and the soil is poor and badly leached. Frequently, serious erosion results from such fields. Although cultivated only in alternate years, these fields are short-lived and are abandoned after a decade or so. Only use rights exist for such fields and after abandonment they revert to the public domain.

THE FARMING CYCLE

A clearer picture of the agricultural cycle may be given by a monthly summary.

January: Little to do; second plowing of maize lands may begin.

February: Second plowing of maize lands.

March: Maize planting begins.

April: Maize planting; first cultivation of early maize at end of month; planting of vegetables and maize in *solares*.

May: Wheat harvest; second cultivation of maize.

June: Second cultivation of maize; some wheat threshing (continued in dry weather throughout rest of year).

July: Fairly free month; weeding of maize begins; second cultivation of maize continues.

August: Plowing for wheat.

September: Planting wheat; cutting maize fodder.

October: Plowing for maize; rains usually end; cutting maize fodder; wheat threshing nearly finished.

November: Maize harvest (if lower lands planted); plowing.

December: Maize harvest on higher lands; plowing.

SOIL PREPARATION

Land is prepared for field and garden crops (except for small kitchen gardens of cabbage and herbs) by plowing one or more times (pl. 4, upper left). The plow used is usually a wooden type (fig. 3). The Government has given some 30 steel plows to the *municipio*, which lends them to farmers; although these are all in use, they care for only a small part of the plowing.

Regardless of the type of plow, it is almost always drawn by oxen. Mules, and perhaps horses, undoubtedly are used sometimes, but not as frequently as in adjoining Aranza; in the entire season of 1940–41 no single instance was observed on Cherán lands. If the wooden plow is used, the long plow beam is attached to the ox yoke directly. Steel plows are attached to the ox yoke by a chain. An ox goad of wood, often with a chisellike metal butt (for sticking in the ground), is employed.

A great many farmers own oxen; if they do not, they must rent them at 75 centavos to 1 peso a day, depending on the demand. If drivers are hired, 50 centavos a day is usual. On the other hand, if a man has rented his land on shares, he must make sure his tenants plow at the right time. Usually land is plowed twice before planting, but the depth rarely exceeds 6 inches.

MAIZE

Except in the garden plots and a few other highly favored places, corn is never planted on the same ground on two successive years. Garden plots are more carefully cultivated and are fertilized to some extent by depositing organic refuse of all kinds and, if available, manure. Good farmers will even carry surplus manure to the fields, but some are lazy and simply throw it in one of the arroyos. It is then carried down to the "plain" west of town. As a result, a part of the "plain" where the water sinks into the ground can be farmed every year.

The basin, of which the "plain" forms a part, has no outlet. So porous is the volcanic soil that streams run only briefly after heavy rainfall. The drainage of the entire basin collects on the Cherán–Aranza boundary, where it sinks into the soil within a few hours after a storm. The entire sink area is cultivated and is highly fertile. No rotation of crops is ordinarily practiced on the plain; but in the mountains,

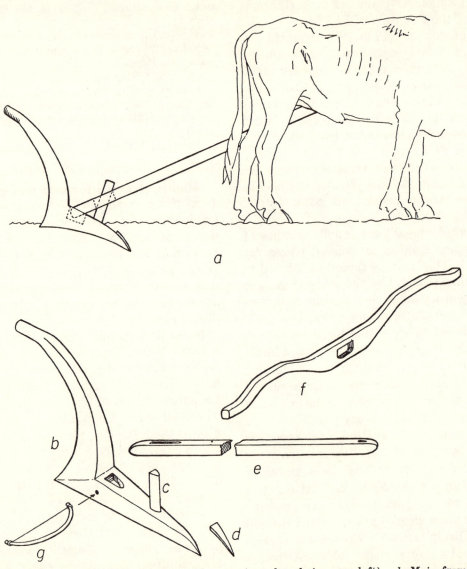

FIGURE 3.—The Cherán plow. *a*, Plow in use with oxen (see also pl. 4, upper left). *b*, Main frame, made from a single piece o1 wood. *c*, Peg over which the tongue fits. *d*, Steel plowshare fastened on the point of the main frame. *e*, Tongue which goes over peg (*c*), while the end fits in a socket on the main frame. *f*, yoke; the tongue (*e*) passes through the opening in the yoke and is held by a tapered peg (not shown). *g*, Bow used on the plow in planting to spread the dirt into the already planted furrows; the bow is inserted into the indicated hole.

when maize begins to do poorly in a field, with small stalks and poor ears, barley is often planted for 1 year. This "warms up" the soil and good corn crops are secured for a few years.

Maize lands are plowed twice, the first time in late summer or fall, the second in late winter, the furrows of the second plowing being made at right angles to those of the first. Planting takes place in the spring after danger of frost is past; on the plain this is as early as March, but at higher elevations it may be later.

Three men and two yokes of oxen are used in planting. One yoke of oxen draws a plow which opens a furrow. A man follows this furrow, dropping seed each step and pressing it down with his foot. Two grains are dropped unless worms are bad, when three or four may be planted. Maize rows are about 1 *vara* (32 inches) apart. The second yoke of oxen draws a plow which makes a furrow between the planted rows, covering the seed to a depth of about 4 inches. To aid in covering the corn, the second plow has a wooden bow fastened horizontally below the beam behind the plow point. No digging stick is ever used except to replant fields damaged by worms, and all work is done by men. There is no exchange of labor or lending of tools or animals, even among relatives.

Several types of maize are grown. Trimásion is white with a somewhat larger grain and is sown in the "plains." It has more and larger stalks and ears. Tulukénio is yellow and has small grains. It is sown in the mountains about 8 to 15 days later, but matures at the same time as Trimásion. The ears are short, ordinarily about 4 inches in length, and the stalks are smaller. The fact that Tulukénio is always sown on poorer and colder lands probably accounts for most of the differences, although it is claimed that the differences persist when the two types are planted in the same fields. However, probably because of the methods of seed selection and the isolation of mountain fields, some regressive or primitive types occur in Tulukénio which may have genetic significance. Not enough Trimásion types have been studied to define the differences.

In the garden plots a black or dark-blue maize (¢iráŋki) is planted. It appears to have some significant differences from Tulukénio,

although belonging to the same race (see Appendix 3). It is believed in Cherán that blue maize will not grow in the fields, although an almost identical genetic type is grown in the fields in Sevina and Nahuatzen. The stalks are taller and more slender and the ears are larger and longer than those of other types. Although it may be planted as early as Trimásion, the maturation time is faster and some people plant black maize late in order to have a single harvest time. In no case is black corn planted before Easter Saturday. However, much of the black maize is eaten in the milk stage as roasting ears. The stalks are also sweeter, apparently, and non-bearing stalks are cut and chewed to extract the sweet sap.

All Cherán farmers preserve a red color variant of the Trimásion and Tulukénio types. Red ears are called čóču and are considered a different variety, but genetically the type apparently is only a color variant. A few red ears are always planted in each field. The reasons are discussed below. Red maize is said to be sweeter and is used for two kinds of cookies, an S-shaped cookie called čústika and a coiled shape called tokére čústika.

No effort is made to select seed at harvest. All the maize is stored together, but as corn is taken from storage for use, the farmer's wife systematically lays aside red ears and the largest and best-filled-out ears, always taking inferior ears for food or sale. In this way, when planting time comes, the best ears remain. These are sorted and a further selection made. Grains from the butt and tip are discarded.

Maize seed selection is always done when the moon is crescent. Neither selection nor shelling is done after the full moon. This rule applies to no other seeds. Each family keeps its own seed (of all other plants as well as maize) and obtains seed from others only if its own is very bad.

Maize is subject to many plagues and animal enemies. Pocket gophers do great damage to maize (and also to wheat). Before planting, and usually before plowing, gunpowder is exploded in the runways of the animals, which is said to kill many. No effort is made to trap or kill survivors, however, even though they may be damaging growing crops severely.

While crops are small, posts are placed in the fields to provide perching places for hawks.

Worms may damage small plants to the point that reseeding is necessary, especially if there are long periods of cloudy weather without rain. Worms also damage about 35 percent of the ears. Deer damage crops badly only in isolated mountain fields. Badgers in some places are serious pests. The only remedy is to attempt to shoot the animals. Birds do little damage. Some maize is attacked by a fungus. The fungus is eaten, but it is not sold or prized as a delicacy as is the case in some parts of Mexico.

Trespass by domestic animals and theft must be guarded against. Sometimes isolated fields are completely stripped if not watched. Stray animals caught damaging corn are taken to the *municipio* and held in jail until the owner pays for the damage.

Unseasonal frost often damages corn, particularly late plantings and in fields at high altitudes. In 1940, frost, heavy enough to damage some fields, occurred on September 29.

When maize is about 1 foot high it is cultivated ("*escarda*" also "*trozando*") by running the plow between the rows, throwing dirt toward the plants. This is done a second time when the plants are about 18 inches tall. If it is delayed too long, the roots may be cut, the maize leaves will yellow at the tip, and no ears will form.

When the maize is in tassel, after the rainy season is well underway, the fields are weeded "*chaponeado*." This is done by hand with a short machete, called "*os*," with a sharp curve at the point. Also, earth is piled around such plants as were not sufficiently covered by the cultivation. If the weeds are bad, a second weeding is sometimes done, but not often. If weeding is omitted, weeds climb high up the stalks and the crop suffers considerably. The weeds removed are piled up beside the fields and are not used for feed or fertilizer.

As soon as grain is well formed on the ears, some maize is used for food, usually roasted. At this time, also, guards must be set in the fields, not only to keep animals out, but to prevent theft. Whole families may move to temporary field shelters at this time and remain until the harvest. In the "plains," usually only a few watchers are necessary. A pine tree some 20 feet high is trimmed and set firmly in the ground. The watchers climb this and spend hours standing uncomfortably in the crotches left by trimming the branches. Often several families may cooperate in watching, or several landowners may hire watchers, called *veladores*.

When the ears are well formed, but while stalks and leaves are still green, fodder ("*rastrojo*") is cut. All stalks without ears, and the ear-bearing stalks above the ears, are cut, dried, carried to the house, and stored in sheds. This forms the principal fodder for animals. The stalks remaining in the field are not cut after the harvest, but animals are allowed to graze the harvested fields.

The main work of harvesting is done by men. Women bring food to the men, and they also glean, assisted by children. At harvest each man takes two rows at a time. The ears are picked, husked, and thrown in a round cane-splint burden basket (šundis) carried on the back with the aid of a tumpline. Ears which miss the basket belong to the gleaners, who also take the nubbins. When the basket is filled, the corn is piled at convenient spots.

The harvest is the busiest time of year. Except for a few specialists, the sick, and the infirm, everyone works, either on his own harvest or as a laborer for someone else. Labor also comes from other towns. Wages are 40 to 50 centavos a day, plus the right to glean. Women and children follow the men of their own household and close supervision is necessary in order to prevent too many ears from being dropped or overlooked. The workday is about 7 hours. The larger landowners have tried unsuccessfully to eliminate gleaning by raising wages to 1 peso a day. Men refused to work without gleaning rights, despite the opinion of most objective observers that the maize secured from gleaning had less value than the additional wages. The landowners would have saved through eliminating supervisors. When the harvest is over, some farmers treat all their help to a few drinks of *aguardiente* (čaránda).

Most of the harvest is carried to town and the storehouses on burros. Nets are used to hold the ears. Sometimes other animals are used, and for some fields employment of two-wheeled oxcarts is possible, although they are rarely used. Burros usually have to be rented or borrowed; in the latter case, a gift of maize or money equal to the rent is usually made. Fifty centavos a day is the usual pay for burros, which adds considerably to the expense of bringing in the harvest from distant fields. Often pay is in maize and is subject to some bargaining.

The time of the harvest varies in different places. If the "plain" west of town is planted, the main harvest is in November, but if the "plain" southeast of town is planted, the harvest is in December. In either case, the town council, in consultation with the principal landowners, sets the dates for harvests. Where lands adjoin those of neighboring towns, usually both towns begin the same day. Eight days after the date set, anyone may turn animals into the fields. Persons who have not completed harvesting or carrying in their harvest may have difficulty protecting it from animals.

As the harvest is a time of joint work, even though not communal in character, it also is a rather festive and social occasion. Moreover, many workmen have more money than at any other time. To protect them from temptations, keep them sober while working, and avoid distractions, the sale of fruit or liquor is prohibited outside the edge of town. Actually, the "edge of town" becomes somewhat elastic, and vendors may set up stands as much as half a kilometer from town.

In 1940 the following schedule of harvests was posted:

December 5. Huanaschucun (sloping lands at the foot of the Cerro de la Virgen, northwest of town).

December 9. Eastern part of the "plain" of Sharicho and Rincon de Paso.

December 16. Western part of Sharicho.

December 19. Plain of Arantepacua.

No rules were posted for smaller isolated areas and fields which were fenced. The parts of Sharicho and other areas close to the Nahuatzen boundary were harvested beginning November 26 in order to prevent conflicts over animals crossing the boundary.

White maize and yellow maize are stored unshelled in the lofts of *trojes*. Little effort is taken to protect maize from rats and squirrels

and none at all to stop attacks of weevils or beetles. There are no mechanical corn shellers in Cherán, and bulk sales of unshelled maize are often made. Small amounts may be shelled for sale to storekeepers if there is need of a few cents in cash. One common method of shelling corn is to bind corncobs tightly with wire or cord to make a bundle about 12 inches in diameter. Maize ears are laid on the floor and rolled with this crude implement.

Black maize usually is not completely husked. Instead, pairs of ears are tied together and hung over poles in the house. The best ears are often hung on a pole on the veranda. Good field ears may also be hung in the house. Most black corn is consumed as roasting ears. Otherwise it is usually saved to make tamales in Easter week.

Discussion of land values, maize yields, and labor costs is deferred to the section on economics.

WHEAT

Wheat lands may be fertilized by hiring sheep to bed at night on wheat fields. Lands are plowed once before planting, and the seed is then sown broadcast. The land is then plowed lightly a second time, the furrows being at right angles to the first. Thorny brush, such as wild crab apple, is weighted and dragged across the furrows to break up large clods and to complete covering of the seed.

Some persons say only one kind of wheat is grown at Cherán, a type planted between September and November and maturing during the dry season. However, both bearded and beardless varieties were observed. Moreover, a few families have a so-called winter wheat ("winter" in Cherán is the rainy season, technically our summer) which is planted before the rainy season and matures in August or September. The more commonly grown wheat, it is said, would not survive so much water. Some other Tarascan towns near Tangancicuaro are reported to grow a reddish-colored wheat.

The dry-season wheat is short-stalked and often grows very sparsely. Moreover, most wheat is grown on inferior sloping lands or lands on which corn does not do well. Rains often appear to be inadequate to produce a good crop, although complete failure is rare. A little wheat is grown in town lots, where it seems to do better than in fields.

Wheat is harvested by hand with a sickle. Men do most of the work, but women and children help sometimes. The plants are cut as close to the ground as possible, tied in sheaves, and transported to the houses. One, and in 1940 two, small threshing machine is used in Cherán, but the bulk of the wheat is threshed by hand with flails. The flail used is a slender pole about 8 feet long. To this are fastened two or three heavy iron wires some 10 to 12 feet long. Threshing is done on any hard clean-swept ground when the weather is dry. One stone threshing floor exists at the end of Zaragoza Street. The owner is usually given a liter or so of wheat for its use, although it is built on public property. The straw is carefully saved, whether threshing is done by hand or by machine. Both men and women winnow the wheat on windy days (pl. 3, center). The grain is stored in sacks.

Some wheat is consumed locally. It is ground on the metate and made into bread or atole. The bulk of the wheat is sold, however, to four mills at Purépero, Carapan, Tarataro, Jacona, or as far away as Morelia (since the highway has been built). Wheat is, indeed, probably the major cash export crop of Cherán. Prices and costs are discussed later.

MINOR CROPS

Barley.—Some barley is sown in June and harvested about October. Techniques of planting and harvesting are similar to those for wheat. Barley is fed to animals or sold outside the town. It is stored in sacks. Most barley is planted to restore failing cornlands, and the quantity is not important nor is it regarded as an intrinsically valuable crop.

Oats.—Although the growing of oats is reported, no farmer was found who had planted the grain. The quantity must be unimportant.

Beans.—The soil of Cherán is said not to be good for beans; possibly the climate is also unsatisfactory. Whatever the reason, Cherán grows few beans and many are imported from the Lake Pátzcuaro region.

The principal bean grown is a small pinkish type called *criolla*. White, orange-yellow, brownish, and various spotted beans with much variation in size and shape were observed, and, in many cases, were named by informants. Until reports are received from botanists, the details of variation seem of little interest. All seem to be of climbing types.

Some people plant a few beans between the corn rows, usually in the garden. Mixing of corn and bean seed is said not to give good results. Separate planting of beans is rare, if it occurs at all. Beans are threshed by driving burros over the straw, or children may trample out small quantities.

Squashes and pumpkins.—A few pumpkins are grown in gardens for home use. The most common type is a squash known as chilacayote, although it is not grown abundantly.

The chilacayote must be planted 15 to 20 feet apart, for the plant spreads widely. Uusally it is planted in gardens. The fruit is large and green, resembling a watermelon in shape and color. The flesh is white and watery.

Some chilacayote is eaten fresh, cooked with brown sugar. Usually, though, it is cured by leaving it in the sun on roofs or wall tops for 2 or 3 weeks. Sometimes the squashes are coated with ashes mixed with water. This is believed to harden the exterior. After curing, they are stored in the "*troje*" or in the storage loft and saved until spring. Planting time is the traditional season for eating chilacayote, for this is a period when there are almost no fresh fruits or vegetables. The squashes sell for 25 to 50 centavos.

Broadbeans or habas.—Broadbeans (*Vicia faba*), a coarse variety of European vetch, are usually planted in gardens or, more rarely, in the field. They are planted in furrows, like maize, and are cultivated similarly. Broadbeans yield well in Cherán but relatively few are grown, as they are not liked as well as ordinary beans.

Potatoes.—Planting of potatoes began in Cherán only 2 or 3 years ago. Apparently they do well but only a few are planted as yet, principally for sale in Mexican communities, for they have little place in Tarascan cookery. They are planted in April and harvested in November or December.

Chayote.—The chayote is not grown abundantly. Plants are found only in gardens, usually near the house, where they spread over kitchen roofs, sheds, and fences. Planting is in the week of Candelaria. No fruit is borne until the second year.

The tubers formed on the roots of the chayote plant, called chinchayote, are dug up every third year on New Year's day or shortly after. They are found about a yard and a half from the stalk at a depth of 2 feet. They are boiled or fried and eaten. In flavor and texture they are superior to potatoes, which they resemble. If the tubers are not removed every 3 years, they rot and the plant sickens and does not bear.[9]

Miscellaneous vegetables and herbs.—Green vegetables and herbs are usually grown in small garden plots within the patio or houseyard. Most important is cabbage, of which two varieties are grown, one which heads and one which does not. The latter is the more common, producing a cluster of large leaves along a stalk a foot or more in height. Cabbage is an essential ingredient of the universal meat dish, curípo.

On rare occasions, other vegetables are grown, such as carrots, tomatoes, and onions. The latter two do not produce well in Cherán, and carrots and other vegetables have little place in Tarascan cookery.

Almost every garden has a few herbs, the most common of which is *silantro* (kulántro), used to flavor meat dishes. Two mints (kua¢itiniš and kua¢itiniš kamáta akúa) are grown for use in atoles.

Camomiles, *manzanillo,* of at least two types are grown as carminatives.

Agave.—Although agaves (akámba) are planted extensively along the ditches cut as field boundaries to keep out animals, relatively little use is made of them. There is some collection of the juice, *agua miel* (urápi). Some is consumed locally, but most of it is shipped to Uruapan. No native residents drink the juice after fermentation as *pulque.* Only wild agaves are roasted.

To secure the juice, according to description, a cavity is cut in the heart with a knife and the pulp is chopped. Three days later the chopped material is removed and the surface of the cavity is scratched with a rakelike implement. On the fourth day, collection of the juice begins twice daily. Each time juice is collected, the surface of the cavity is scratched with the rakelike implement. The juice is dipped out with a small pottery vessel and poured into a larger container. If the juice is to be shipped to Uruapan it is put in a 25-liter can. A good plant produces slightly more than 2 liters a day.

The bud of the wild agave is cooked in a round hole, 1 meter in diameter and 1 meter deep. The hole is filled with small stones to within 10 or 15 cm. of the top, and a large fire is built on top of the stones. When the fire dies down, the agave buds are thrown on it, covered with leaves of agaves and trees, and then sealed with earth. On the third day the oven is opened. The thick fleshy end of leaves of the smaller wild agave are also roasted. The season is from November to May.

Approximately 20 men in Cherán roast agave in season. They must eat sugar when the agave is cooking so that it will emerge sweet. They must also abstain from sexual intercourse during the 3 days the agave is in the oven.[10]

Pears.—The most important fruit in Cherán is the pear. It is carried by traders as far as Guerrero. Three types are recognized: *leche* (uérgamóte), *pardo* (¢arápiti), and t'ač∧ni (Spanish name unknown). The only significant difference recognized is that the three types mature at different times, although some say only the uérgamóte transports well.

Pear trees are always grafted on a rootstock of wild crab apple, *tejocote.* (This is a sloelike fruit which bears a marked resemblance in flavor and appearance to the true crab apple.) The *tejocote* trunk is cut with a saw and then split. A pear graft is inserted at each end of the split, sealed in with wax, and wrapped in clean cloth. It is believed the grafts will grow only in January, February, and March, but a school teacher with experimental tendencies claims to have grown them at all seasons.

---

[9] In Parícutin village, chayotes (apúpo) are planted in stone-lined pits to protect the seeds from gophers. The pit is about 30 cm. deep. The pulp is carefully removed from the seeds, which are then carefully wrapped in maize husks and tied with the same material.

[10] Agave is of varying importance in other towns. In Angáhuan the techniques are similar. The plant is known here as quiote; the leaves are called i¢íkua, the stalk or bud, šámaš. Mestizoized Chilchota makes mescal. The leaves are cooked in earth ovens, macerated with clubs in cement tanks, fermented several days, then distilled. The Tarascan terminology relating to the agave and its processing survives in part.

Pears and other fruit trees are not pruned, cultivated, or fertilized. Fruit to be shipped, especially pears, is picked with a special implement to prevent bruising. Three narrow pieces of shake are cut to a point at one end. They are then tied with string to one end of a long light pole, forming a triangular funnel. The funnel is placed under the fruit and raised, detaching it gently from the tree (fig. 4).

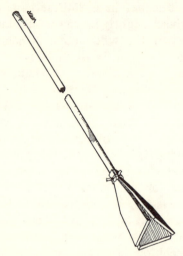

FIGURE 4.—Pear picker, made of trimmed shakes, cord, and any convenient long pole. The fruit is caught in the opening, lifted until the stem breaks, and then lowered to the ground. Bruised pears will not stand shipment.

Miscellaneous fruits.—A bitter apple, *manzana agria* or *chata*, is grown in Cherán. A larger, sweet apple is grown in Pichátaro, but only four or five trees exist in Cherán.

Three kinds of peaches are grown in Cherán: *blanco*, a type with red flesh near the pit (name uncollected), a green peach (prísku), and a yellow peach (melókuta). Relatively few peaches or apples are exported.

Two kinds of cherries, black and white, are grown in Cherán. Both are dried in some quantities and are sometimes sold in the market at Paracho.

A few *zapote blanco* are grown in Cherán, but most of this fruit consumed in Cherán is imported. The same is true of plums.

The *tejocote* is said not to be cultivated, but it sometimes is planted deliberately along field borders and its fruit is used. As, with the exception of pears, this is all the attention ever given to other fruits, it is fair to include the

tejocote as a domesticated type. It is harvested and exported for making jellies and preserves. A few are used locally.

Some quince trees are found in Cherán. They are little used, but some preserves are made.

BELIEFS AND CUSTOMS

Most beliefs and customs center about maize. Most important are the beliefs about red ears, čóču. A red ear is described as the mother, chief, and ače (ceremonial leader) of all maize. In the storage lofts, red ears are mixed in with the yellow and white to act as guardian of the rest. They are never eaten until all the white and the yellow corn are gone. Care is taken to plant seed from one or more red ears in each field; otherwise it is believed that there will be no harvest.

Red ears and black ears are both said to be used in curing, but no details could be secured.

Twin ears, *cuates* (šaninkuáte), are said to come because God wishes to send a little more. Sometimes large ears have four or five points; they are said to be the hand of the planter.

The family harvesting the first green corn in the town places two or three ears on the altar of San Francisco. Each family gives one or two *cargas* of maize on the cob to the priest.

If the rains do not come at the proper time near the end of May, the image of San Ramos is taken to the peak of San Marcos. The image is placed on a white sheet, held by a man at each corner, and tossed in the sheet. If San Ramos can be made to cry, it begins to rain immediately. During the rite a *rezador* recites a rosary, copal is burned, and *cohetes* are fired.

Every year, beginning in January, the grass is burned, causing great damage to the forests and destroying the last remnants of pasture. The burning is said to prevent heavy frosts, while the smoke hastens the coming of the rains. Town officials and officers of the Forest Service succeeded in extinguishing most of the fires in 1940.

It is said there are no beliefs regarding wheat. Nevertheless, wheat must be carried in a wooden bowl while sowing or it will be attacked by rust, "*tecolote.*" Rust is a sign the planter used his hat, blanket, or some other improper article at planting. Girls plait elaborate ornaments of wheat straw at harvest time, which are hung on the veranda or inside the house. Beliefs about these ornaments were denied.

No beliefs or customs were discovered regarding other plants except those connected with roasting the wild agave.

DOMESTIC ANIMALS

The domestic animals found in Cherán are cattle, horses, mules, burros, sheep, goats, pigs, dogs, cats, chickens, pigeons, and bees. Of these, cattle, burros, sheep, and pigs are the most numerous and of greatest economic importance. Turkeys, ducks, and geese are completely lacking, although they are found in other Tarascan towns. Sevina, for example, has a fair number of turkeys.

Cattle.—Ownership of cattle is widespread in Cherán, but accurate knowledge of the extent of ownership is impossible because of the tendency to conceal wealth. As most cattle are kept at pasture, usually in the mountains, house censuses are of no value. Possession of cattle seems to make little difference in the economic position of their owners. Wealthy men often own herds of some size which they do not appear to exploit to their fullest extent. Such men, though, probably gain some social prestige, for their bulls will be sought for use in the bull riding which forms an important part of the fiesta of the patron saint of Cherán.

Cattle are raised for several economic uses: meat, milk, draft animals, and sale outside the town. Somewhat different treatment is accorded animals raised for various purposes; consequently, separate discussion is indicated.

Relatively few cows are milked, and most families do not keep milk cows. There is no special breeding for milk cattle and a "very good" cow will not give over 2 liters of milk a day. The milk is sold in Cherán, usually for pregnant women or sick people, or it is made into cheese. Only a small part of the local demand for cheese is supplied in this fashion, however. No butter is made.

Milking is done only by men, but women clean the milk containers, make the cheese, and may care for the animals. Milking is done by primitive methods; the cow is tethered closely at the head and the hind legs are tied together.

The calf is then tied nearby while the cow is milked; it is then permitted to suckle.

The cow is milked only once a day and only from June to January or February while pastures are good. Ordinarily, the cows are kept and milked in the fields. If only one or two cows are milked, they may be pastured close to the village and driven into the house yard for milking. In this case, if the owner has feed, the cow may be milked after February.

Oxen, and sometimes bulls, are used extensively for plowing. In a very few cases they also draw two-wheeled carts to bring in the harvest, although most of this is done by pack animals. Oxen are broken to the yoke after they are fully grown, but fairly young steers are sometimes yoked together in the pastures in order to accustom them to traveling together.

Animals are not bred or raised specially for beef. Cows, bulls, and steers are killed, the main consideration being the fatness of the animal. A considerable number of the animals slaughtered are oxen considered to have outlived their usefulness as draft animals. Although specially fattened for slaughter, the beef is as tough as might be expected. Calves or young animals are never slaughtered. Animals dying of disease are not eaten in Cherán but are in other towns. The hides of slaughtered cattle are valued according to prices in adjacent Mexican markets.

Although Cherán raises more than enough cattle for its own use, cattle raising is not regarded as a very satisfactory business because of the lack of pasture during the latter part of the dry season. Usually, numbers of animals die of starvation during April and May. This is true of other grazing animals also.

When not in use, cattle are ordinarily pastured in the mountains. They are visited every third day to make sure they have not been stolen and that they are getting water. They are driven down to the farm lands and allowed to graze on the cornstalks or wheat stubble during the winter. This practice not only aids the animals over part of the dry season with its scanty pasturage, but is recognized as a means of fertilizing the soil.

Little care is used in breeding, and new bulls are never brought in from outside. If a man owning a cow has no bull, he simply drives the animal to a herd containing bulls. Sometimes he will seek a bull regarded as superior. There is no service fee. Cattle are branded when young and draft animals almost always are castrated.

Pigs.—Probably the pig is the second most important animal in Cherán; certainly it is the most common. Almost every family has at least one sow. If a family has no sow of its own, usually someone will lend a sow to be fed. In this case the litter is divided; should the animal lent be a male, the meat or proceeds of sale are shared.

The pig is raised for meat and fat or for sale, often outside the village. The skin has very little value. No use is made of the hoofs, but the entrails are prized as sausage casings. A not unimportant function of pigs is their service as scavengers.

Although some persons in Cherán were said to keep boars for breeding purposes and to charge a small fee for service (of from 25 centavos to 1 peso in Paricutin), evidently little care is taken in breeding. Most males are uncastrated until it is desired to fatten them. As the pigs roam the streets and nearby roads and woods during the day, little selective breeding seems possible. Normally, pigs are fed just enough corn to keep them returning home. At night they are placed in pens to protect them from coyotes.

Ordinarily only boars are fattened and slaughtered. Some people castrate their animals before fattening them, claiming they will fatten on less grain. Others dispute this, saying further that meat from castrated hogs has no flavor. Not every one knows how to castrate, but field notes do not indicate whether a charge is made for the operation when the aid of a neighbor is necessary. Animals being fattened are shut in small log pens with wooden floors, which are cleaned at frequent intervals. It is claimed that there are two types of pig, one of which fattens more readily than the other. At least 1 *fanega* (about 90.8 qts.) of maize is used in fattening a pig. Fattened pigs are normally sold to butchers; owners ordinarily kill their own pigs only for fiestas.

Sheep.—Although relatively few families own sheep, the number owned in Cherán is fairly large and they assist materially in fertilizing wheatfields. Wheat farmers will pay about 30 centavos a night to have an average herd bedded on their fields. This is not done for cornlands, as the return is not considered sufficient.

No sheep owner gets his living from the ownership of sheep, but in some cases individuals or even entire families live on their wages as sheepherders. Most sheepherders, however, are boys of from 8 to 20 years and old men and women. Very poor families may start their sons to learn sheep herding as apprentices as early as 6 years of age.

Ordinarily sheepherders return to town only for fiestas or when they need new clothes. Their food is taken to them by a woman in the family. If the entire family work as shepherds, the wife returns to town periodically to cook a supply of tortillas or *gordas* (thick tortilla fried in fat, sometimes made of wheat flour instead of maize).

The average wages of sheepherders are 5 pesos a month without food, but this evidently varies with the size of the flock. One of the larger owners, with a flock of about 200 sheep, pays 10 centavos a head a month, 1 *fanega* of maize, and permits slaughter of 1 sheep a month. In all cases, shepherds may eat sheep which die, if they think it safe to do so, but the pelt must be washed and dried, and given to the owner.

Shepherds watch one another to prevent misbehavior, such as secretly selling sheep, or carelessness which would reflect on the profession. Shepherds care for the flocks, protect them from coyotes, and put the ownership marks on the lambs. They are aided by specially trained dogs.

Sheep are herded in the mountains part of the year, and on farm lands after the harvest. Identification marks are made by notching or cutting the ears. Males are not castrated. During the dry season, numerous sheep die of starvation unless their owners have feed (usually wheat straw). Sheep are not dipped and in general receive little care beyond herding. Coyotes are the principal enemies, although a waggish informant listed the enemies of sheep as "First, the coyote; second, the shepherd; and third, the man who buys him for food."

Although mutton is eaten to some extent, sheep are raised primarily for wool. Sheep are sheared twice a year, in late fall and early summer. A sheep yields about 1 pound of wool in two shearings, which sells at from $1.00 to $1.25 (all monetary values are in Mexican currency). Black wool brings more than white (as it is all used locally for serape weaving).

Goats.—Only a few goats are raised. Normally they are herded with the sheep and are treated like them. In rare instances the goats are milked, and the milk is made into cheese. The most important use of goats is to sell them for food, usually outside the town, as goat meat is rarely eaten in Cherán. Goatskins are sold uncured with the hair.

Horses.—Although some horses are bred in Cherán and some care is exercised in breeding, it is said the animals deteriorate because of the cold climate. Consequently, most horses are imported, but they also deteriorate rapidly. More important than the cold, undoubtedly, is the fact that no one in Cherán understands the care of horses. They are badly fed and receive little protection from the weather. Stallions are castrated.

In any case, horses are rare in Cherán and are little used except as riding animals, especially by those with numerous cattle or pack animals. Riding and pack gear are the same as those of the Mestizos. Although in other Tarascan towns horses are used in plowing, this was denied in Cherán. A rather poor horse costs about 70 pesos. Most horses belong to well-to-do men and primarily are indicators of social position. Attitudes toward owning a horse are a weak reflection of those of the vanishing Mexican *caballero.* Women almost never ride.

Horses are fed maize, oats, maize stalks, and wheat or oat straw. Few people have any knowledge of treating illnesses of horses. Ownership is indicated by branding, and horses are given names similar to those used by Mestizos. Horse meat is not eaten, but horse hides are valued for tanning.

Mules.—Mules are even rarer than horses and have a higher value. Almost all are imported. They are used mostly as pack animals, but occasionally they are ridden or used with the plow. Care and practices otherwise are the same as for horses.

Burros.—"The poor man's mule" is one of the more common animals in Cherán. Often kept in a shed by the house, the burro is employed to bring in firewood (when he may be ridden to the woods), to bring in the harvest, carry goods on trading trips, and perform any other service of burden carrying. Burros may be used as light draft animals in such tasks as dragging brush over wheat fields to cover the seed after sowing. Often rented, especially at harvest time, burros are frequently lent to friends, neighbors, and relatives. Although hardworked, they are usually better cared for and less abused than among the Mestizos. They are often fed rather than pastured, and saddle sores and other signs of abuse are relatively uncommon.

Burros are bred in the town. Jacks are not castrated. The flesh is never eaten and the hide is regarded as of little value.

Dogs.—Usually each household has one or perhaps two dogs, but large numbers of starved animals are rare. Ordinarily a dog is fed what the family has, and if a dog is underfed, usually the family is also. Dogs are always named, usually for "pretty things or animals" such as Butterfly, Duke, Tiger, or Rattlesnake. Others are named for their coat color or because the name is liked. No effort is made to control the breeding of dogs.

Dogs are used in hunting, sheepherding, and to guard the house. In the latter capacity, the dogs of the *barrio* of Parícutin are much more aggressive than in the rest of the town. This may be because their masters are generally less friendly or may simply reflect the more rural character of the *barrio.*

Hunting dogs are used to chase deer, squirrels, rabbits, and other animals after they have been wounded. Apparently no special training is given. Sheep dogs are trained by putting them on a leash with a sheep during the day and tying them near the sheep at night. They are encouraged to bark at the right time and to attack coyotes.

Cats.—Cats are not numerous in Cherán, although they are valued fairly highly because they combat the many rats which steal stored corn. Cats seem well treated and are sometimes petted. One reason for having cats is "because they give pleasure." They are given "pretty" names or names of affection such as *Chulita* and *Negrita* ("Pretty Little One" and "Little Black One").

Cats are fed primarily on tortillas, although they usually are given a little of whatever the family is eating. Kittens are given away to friends and relatives; they are never killed, "for there are never enough cats." Strange cats may be associated with witchcraft and might be mistreated or killed, but this apparently does not happen often. Eating of cats is denied, although young fat kitten is reported to be a delicacy for really poor people in nearby Mestizo towns.

Chickens.—Many people have no chickens and no one has large flocks. They are fed, but receive little care. Fowls are sometimes eaten on special occasions, such as a baptism, when a cooked fowl may be presented to the godfather. Eggs are rarely eaten but are sold to traveling egg merchants from Mestizo towns. An average egg will sell for 5 or 6 centavos, which will buy enough beans for a whole family to have a meal, while one egg "will not satisfy even one person."

Chickens are fed whole corn or, if there are very few chickens, *nixtamal* (*masa* or corn dough for tortillas). Chicks are also fed *nixtamal*. Boxes or baskets are provided for nests. The first time a hen wishes to "set," it is not permitted, but it is the second time. Eggs from other hens are never placed under a "setting" hen. Small chicks are placed under box crates to protect them from "*onzas*" (from descriptions, *onza* in Cherán means a small weasellike animal).

Roosters are raised for cock fighting. However, organized cock fights are held only during the fiesta of Octava.

Pigeons.—Although regarded as a domestic animal, pigeons are really wild. Ownership is not clear. As the birds are not fed, but help themselves to stored grain in the lofts of the houses, ownership presumably would be felt for the birds eating one's corn. The matter seems unimportant, as the birds are rarely eaten, although they are used in connection with the San Juan fiesta. If eaten, only adult pigeons are killed.

Bees—While a moderate number of families have a few hives of bees, most of the apiculture in Cherán is carried on by a few men who may have 20 to 30 colonies. Only European bees are kept.

Beehives are wooden boxes, about 80 cm. long, 20 to 35 cm. wide, and 25 to 40 cm. high. The entrance is at one end, while the wax and honey are taken by opening the back. The hives are placed on benches or poles at intervals of about one-half meter. Lizards are believed to eat the larvae. Flowers and scented herbs are often planted in the area surrounding the hives. Wherever bees are kept, copal gum is burned in pottery censers. It is said to "feed" the bees because "the odor of copal is the odor of our Lord." It is believed it also prevents bees from leaving. No other ritual or belief could be discovered.

Honey and wax are usually taken from the hives in October or November. If delayed much after this time, the honey sugars and cannot be extracted. The honey gatherer places a net over his head and burns wheat straw to stupefy the bees. The top of the hive is smeared with honey so the bees will not leave. Should they leave the hive and not return by late afternoon, a small bell is rung to attract them.

When bees swarm, a bell is rung to make them alight in a nearby tree. A little honey is smeared over the inside of a box, which is then placed by the swarm. When a few bees have entered voluntarily, most of the remainder are brushed in and the box is closed and put in place. When it is opened, the bees usually remain. The function of the queen is known, and beekeepers can identify her.

One of the largest apiaries in Cherán contains 42 hives. The owner started beekeeping 17 years ago when he encountered a wild colony in the mountains and brought it home. He recovers 10 kilos of wax a year, which he sells in Cherán at $2.50 a kilo, and between 40 and 50 pounds of honey. Most of the latter he sells in small quantities at his home, but some is sold to stores.

All the work of caring for bees is done by men (with one exception, a widow), but if the wax is bleached, this may be done by women. Wax is used mainly for making candles.

Honey is used primarily to sweeten atole and as a treat for children.[11]

For the village of Capacuaro, Silvia Rendón reports what are probably native bees kept in sections of hollow log hung on the walls. She was told they produced "Campeche wax" (*cera de Campeche*).

Pets.—Only domesticated animals are pets. Dogs and cats are most commonly treated as pets, being stroked, fondled, picked up, or played with. However, this is not true of all dogs or cats, nor is it true of all individuals. Pigs often seem to be treated as pets, especially young animals, but they are not picked up or fondled. Kids are sometimes pets, especially if the mother had died and the animal has been reared by hand. Even more common, although by no means general, are sheep. Lambs are placed on a leash until half-grown; after this they follow their masters everywhere, even to automobiles. Many children have lambs as pets. One boy of 10 had an immaculately washed white lamb with a red sash tied about its middle. The lamb followed him everywhere and was even trained to stand on the pack pad of a burro so it could be taken to the mountains on wood-cutting trips.

Beliefs and ceremonies.—The only ceremony connected with domestic animals is burning copal for bees. Beliefs are likewise few. The association of cats with witchcraft has been noted. If a dog sits down and howls by day closeby, it is a sign something bad is going to happen. Coyotes are believed able to bewitch the domestic animals they eat, especially chickens. "Coyotes just shake themselves and chickens will go right to them."

Curing of animals.—A few men are specialists at curing animals. They are usually paid for their services. Wounds and sores are cleaned by washing with lukewarm water, to which salt is sometimes added, until all pus is removed and bleeding begins. If the wound is deep, a wick of cloth may be inserted to keep it open; sometimes peroxide of hydrogen is used as a disinfectant, but creosote is more common. If wounds are bound, carefully washed lard mixed with sugar may be applied or wet dressings may be used, dampened at frequent intervals with salt water.

Rabies is believed to be caused by the bite of some other animal, by inadequate food, or by heat. There is no cure.

Dysentery, *"posición,"* in horses and burros is believed to be caused by cold or *"salitre,"* a very salty mineral-bearing earth. The animal is fed pills of coffee, lemon, and bicarbonate of soda.

"Onia" is caused by overwork, but the symptoms were not recorded. Treatment is bleeding the side of the neck and rest. (In general, overwork is regarded as an important cause of sickness.)

Sore feet result from the feet becoming full of blood. The bottom of the foot is bled and the animal must rest until well.

"Roncha" is a disease caused by mosquito bites; if it is not cured within 24 hours, the animal usually dies. Symptoms and treatment were not recorded.

"Pirojon" is very dangerous and kills in 24 hours. It is believed to be caused by mosquitoes or flies that have bitten a dead animal already putrefying. One curer burns the bites with a magnifying glass.

Evil eye, *malojo*, may affect animals that refuse to eat. There is no cure. The best thing is to sell the animal to the man who cast the evil eye (at his price usually); the animal then recovers.

Bats are reported to bite animals at night and make them bleed. Nothing is done to prevent this. As it is said bats never bite humans, and as Cherán probably is above the range of vampire bats, the report may be folklore.

MANUFACTURING PROCESSES

In the previous sections were described the technological processes which involve the exploitation of the environment and the extraction therefrom of raw materials. The present section will describe techniques by which the raw materials are processed and made ready for consumption. Obviously, such classifications must be somewhat elastic. No doubt, good reasons could be advanced against including domesticated animals under exploitative activi-

---

[11] Beekeeping is very popular in La Cañada. Nearly every family has at least a few hives. Much of the honey is used in the household, and only the surplus and the wax are sold. Burning of copal is not practiced.

In Angáhuan and Parícutin only a few people keep bees. The largest apiary in Parícutin contained only four hives, and only three people possessed hives.

ties. Neither are descriptions of dress or house use entirely appropriate under the heading of manufacturing processes. Nevertheless, there is a certain cultural or associative logic involved which would be violated by too rigid adherence to the literal meaning of categories.

CERAMICS

No native ceramic industry exists in Cherán. Pottery is not made, but in 1940 two men, both non-Tarascans, made roofing tile and brick.

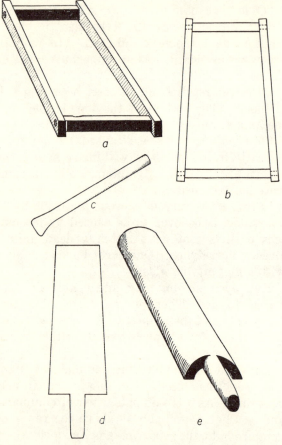

FIGURE 5.—Tilemaker's implements. a, Perspective view of the mold. b, Direct view of the mold to show proportions and the shape, which is narrower at one end than the other. c, Wooden chisel or knife used to loosen clay from mold if necessary (length about 18 inches with other artifacts in proportion). d, Outline of the form for tiles. e, Perspective view of the form for tiles. The mold is filled with clay and the top smoothed. The mold is then lifted up, leaving the clay on a bench top. The clay is then slid onto the form to receive the curved shape of the tile. After a few minutes drying, the unfired tile is slipped off the form onto the floor to complete the drying process.

Both men had arrived with the highway construction crews; neither was making what he regarded as a satisfactory living and both hoped to leave.

Tile and brick are made in an old chapel and surrounding grounds, formerly part of the *curato* or curacy. Ten percent of the finished tile or brick is given to the *municipio* as rent for the buildings and for the right to dig clay on public lands.

A grayish clay is brought to the factory in sacks by mules. It is mixed with water and manure in a board-lined pit in the patio, where it is turned with spades and hoes and trodden with bare feet. The mixed clay is pressed into a trapezoidal wooden form laid flat on a table (fig. 5). The top is smoothed carefully with the wet hand. The clay is then slipped off the table onto a wooden form resembling half of a truncated cone, but with a handle. After a few moments, the clay, now in the shape of a tile, is slipped off on the floor. When fairly well dried, the tile is moved outdoors for further drying.

Bricks are made in the same fashion but with a different wooden form. Both brick and tile are fired in a wood-fired kiln in the patio. The wood is cut and hauled by the brickmakers and tilemakers. The time required to make a thousand brick or tile is about 9 days, as follows:

	Days
Getting and mixing clay	2
Cutting and hauling wood	1
Shaping 1,000 brick or tile	5
Loading kiln	1
Total	9

TEXTILES

Mats.—Most sleeping mats used in Cherán are imported, but at least three women make them locally. The mats are made of tules imported on burros from Erongaricuaro on Lake Pátzcuaro. The mats are made in twilled technique, usually treating two tules as a single weaving element. The only tool observed was a stone fist hatchet for severing tules.

Hat making.—About four men manufacture men's hats of palm straw braid, although production does not meet the local demand. The activity involves complex trading arrangements, for palms do not grow in Tarascan territory. Palm leaf originates in Ario de Rosales, whence it is transported to the market at Paracho. Weaving of the straw into braid is done by women of the several small villages in the *municipio* of Paracho. The finished braid is sold in the Paracho market, the bulk of it going to the village of Jaracuaro on an island in Lake Pátzcuaro. The thread used for sewing the braid is an imported machine-made thread.

The tools of a hat maker include:

Sewing machine
3 or 4 hat blocks
Wooden paddle for blocking
Smooth stone for blocking
Wooden reel for thread (which is bought in skeins)
Iron punch for ventilators
Roller like a clothes-wringer for straightening and smoothing braid

The type of hat most commonly made has a low crown and broad brim. Each hat requires about three bundles of braid. The braid is sewn together in a spiral beginning at the middle of the crown. Each spiral of the braid overlaps its predecessor about three-quarters or five-sixths of its width. One man, working steadily, can make about three hats a day, but no one in Cherán works steadily every day. Essentially, hat making is a part-time occupation. Some hat makers are also farmers, while one is also a "tailor." Another also operates a *nixtamal* mill. One hat maker employs an assistant who is said to be paid 50 centavos a hat. This is doubtful in view of hat prices and the cost of materials.

Sometimes hats are whitened. They are first treated with glue, then successively coated with *oxido* (a crystalline material melted down), a white pigment (*blanco de sin*), and then a white varnish (*blanco de España*). None of these materials was further identified. The price obtained for hats varies with the thinness of the braid, fineness of the sewing, and the finish applied.

Embroidery, crochet, and drawn work.—A number of women ornament women's blouses or make crocheted petticoat borders as a part-time occupation. Women's blouses are sometimes equipped with crocheted yolks. Crocheted bands are also placed on the short blouse sleeves. Bands of embroidery for the bottoms

of petticoats are made by one woman, although this technique is primarily found in Nahuatzen. The proportion of women doing this work seems significantly smaller in the third *cuartel* or *barrio* when compared with the other *cuartels*.

The crochet may be replaced by embroidery or drawn work, especially on finer materials such as linen or rayon. Designs either come "from one's head" or patterns may be bought in market. Usually the poorest designs come from the market, but no evidence was found either to indicate preservation of traditional patterns on the part of those not using commercial patterns, or to indicate creativeness in designs. Blouses decorated with crochet involve 1 week's part-time work, and embroidered or drawn-work blouses, from 1 to 3 weeks.

Blanket weaving.—About four men in Cherán weave blankets. These men buy raw wool, and wash, clean, card, and spin the wool, and do the weaving. White, brown, and black colors are usually natural wool colors. For blue, the only other common color, the weaver dyes white wool with indigo. A urine mordant is used. To produce a gray thread, white, black, and blue wool are mixed together before carding. Raw wool is washed and cleaned, losing about one-third its weight in the process.

Carding is done with commercial steel cards which cost $8.00 a set and last about 3 years. A handful of wool is placed on one card and the other is drawn across it several times. The wool is then folded on one of the cards and the process repeated. If wool of two or more colors is being mixed, the rectangles of carded wool are torn into pieces, mixed together, and carded a second time in order to give a more uniform color.

Spinning is done with a wheel (fig. 6). The edges of a rectangle of carded wool are folded along the long side. The rectangle is then pulled apart down the middle except at one end, giving a strip of carded wool about 1½ inches wide. One end is thrown over the left arm and the other end fed into the yarn with the left hand while the wheel is turned with the right. When 6 to 8 inches are lightly twisted, the yarn is stretched to from 24 to 30 inches, given a tighter twist, and then wound on the spindle (fig. 6).

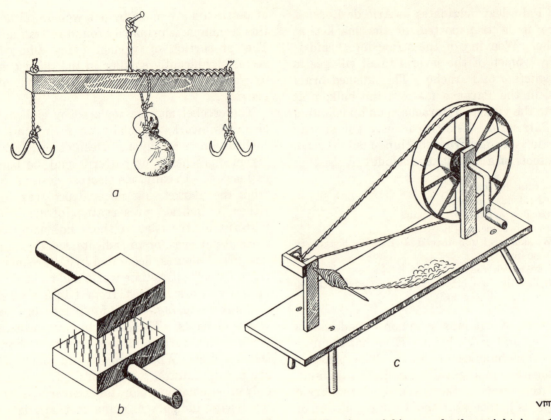

FIGURE 6.—Spinning wheel and associated implements. *a*, Scales for weighing wool; the weight is a 1-pound stone; length of the beam is 14½ inches. *b*, Carders used to prepare wool for spinning, about 9 by 12 inches; the wires are merely indicated schematically and actually are much more numerous. *c*, Home-made spinning wheel; the wheel is turned with the right hand, the wool fed into the thread with the left hand; the spinner stands to operate the apparatus.

Weaving is done on a wooden European type loom with heddles and treddle. A blanket is always woven in two strips, and then sewed together with an opening left in the center so it may be worn as a poncho. Further details are omitted pending a study of the handicraft in a town specializing in weaving.

Lace weaving.—It is probable that this technique is misnamed. In any case it is not properly a Cherán technique, the only weaver being a woman from Aranza. So far as is known, only six or eight women in the latter village know the technique.

A broadloom frame is used, about 8 feet by 4 feet. It is warped with white cotton thread. The weft, also of cotton thread, is placed with the fingers. Designs are set off by open work and consist of human and animal figures. A bedspread or tablecloth takes 2 months or more to make and sells at $75.00 and up (asking price). Often the design is

arranged to be cut up in small pieces. A 2-foot square piece in coarse thread (which weaves faster than fine thread) with figures of a man, a burro, and two deer, was purchased for $2.00.

Belt weaving.—Perhaps five or six women in Cherán weave narrow belts for women. A small belt loom is used. One end is tied to a house post or tree, and the weaver kneels on a mat. A circular warp slips freely about the yarn beams. Two heddles, a spreader, two or more shed dividers, and a batten are employed (fig. 7). The belts always have a central design with plain border. The main warp is cotton, but the central design area has a double warp, one being of wool. Sheds for intricate parts of the design are picked up with a small stick, not with the heddle. There is no shuttle; the weft threads are wound in small balls or on a piece of paper. No patterns are used for designs. Belts take about 2 days of fairly in-

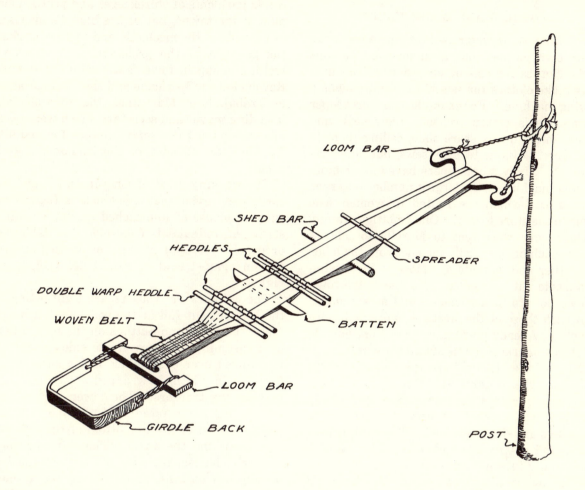

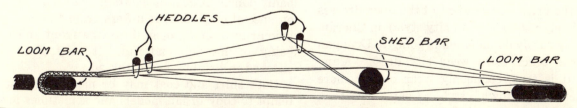

FIGURE 7.—Belt loom. Proportions are distorted to show detail; the actual width of the belt is about 1½ inches. The central part of the warp is double. The lower view shows schematically the various sheds created by the shed bar and the four heddles. Length is 3 feet 9 inches between the loom bars.

tensive labor, although the weavers usually do some housework also.

CLOTHING AND DRESS HABITS

Clothing manufacture.—Many persons make their own clothes, but a number of persons make clothes for sale or on order. Even men may make clothes for sale if the family owns a sewing machine. For example, one storekeeper makes men's cotton trousers (*calzones*) and men's shirts in his spare time, selling them in the store. His wife also sews but less frequently. Many storekeepers have one or more sewing machines—the largest number observed was three—which are rented to women who come to the store to sew. One ambitious family (whose sons were sent to Morelia to school) made much of the family income from the labor of mother and daughters. Most of the sewing is durable but not skilled. No one in the town knows how to fit a garment, and as standards approach those of the Mestizos, more and more people buy ready-made garments from outside in stores, markets, or in Mestizo towns.

Most of the "tailors" are specialists, making only one type of garment. One woman makes only men's cotton trousers. She makes six pairs a day, double-stitched. Garments for weddings are single-stitched. The cloth is provided and cut by the customer. This woman works only intermittently on order. Trousers require about 2½ m. of cloth. Men's shirts require about the same amount of material but cost more for sewing. One woman makes only aprons, while another makes only children's garments.

Men's dress.—Influence of the Mestizo world is strongly evident in men's dress. Yet, aside from the priest, no resident of the town dresses completely *catrin* (i.e., in city style) in Cherán, and only rarely do individuals going to Uruapan or some other town wear city dress. Many men, it is true, commonly wear one or more garments of "town" style. Coats, sweaters, and jackets are owned by many. Tailored woolen trousers, on the other hand, are rare, while almost none own complete suits. Ordinarily, the cotton trousers of the Mestizo countryman rather than woolen trousers replace the white *calzones* of the Indian.

The most prominent and significant change in men's dress in Cherán is not the entry of the *catrin* garments of storekeeper and professional man of the towns, but of the blue denim jeans or overalls of the mechanic and factory worker, the garment of the proletariat. As the controlling group in town is allied to the Partido Revolucionario Mexicano and the Confederacion de Trabajadores Mexicanas, the town officials, including mayor and secretary, often wear overalls, reserving their *catrin* clothes for visits to Uruapan or Morelia or for important civic events.

The working dress of Cherán males, and the exclusive dress of many, is trousers (*calzones*), shirt or blouse of unbleached muslin (*manta*), straw hat, and sandals (*guaraches*). A blanket or poncho (*serape*) is worn or carried as protection against cold or rain (pls. 3; 4, lower right).

The *calzones* or trousers are tight-fitting in the legs but cut full at the waist with a baggy seat. There are no buttons on the fly; instead of a fastening, the two ample sides of the fly are lapped over each other, and a sash, about 6 inches in width, is wrapped about the waist to hold the trousers. The lower part of the trouser leg has a piece of cloth tape attached which is used to tie the bottom of the *calzones* tightly around the ankle. The shirt, or more properly, blouse, likewise has no buttons. It usually has no tails, or very abbreviated ones, and is usually worn outside the *calzones*. It is open part way down the front and has a roll collar, but neither opening nor collar ordinarily is fastened. Buttons are never used, except in attempts to copy city garments, but strings may be provided. Such fitting as is attempted is badly done. A coat of *manta* may also be worn on special occasions; it differs from the blouse primarily in being open down the front and in being of heavier material. It may also be stitched in bright-colored thread.

Both shirt and coat may be modified by attempt to copy urban models and sometimes are purchased ready-made.

Sandals or *guaraches* have a heavy pointed double thick leather sole and leather heel. Part of the top is of leather pieces nailed to the sole, but the major portion is made of woven leather strips passing through slits in the upper sole and the nailed portions of the uppers. The toe is open. As the manufacture of *guaraches* is practiced by only a few Cherán residents, most of them recent arrivals, no detailed description of techniques is given.

An inseparable part of the costume is the straw hat. From infancy, every male is equipped with a hat, which he always wears outdoors, no matter how inconvenient the circumstances. Awkward jobs, such as carrying heavy timbers, are infinitely delayed because every time a man's hat falls off, the entire operation stops until the hat is replaced. Moreover, the first way in which a man makes an extra "luxury" expenditure in clothing is to buy a more expensive hat. The hat is frequently embellished by a bright-colored string about the front of the crown and, passing through two holes at each side, then going around the back of the head. Flowers also are often worn on the hat. Hat manufacture is described under weaving.

From the above-described working costume, many departures occur. Without achieving *catrin* styles, a gay and well-dressed man may wear a brilliant rayon blouse or shirt of blue, red, or yellow, and bright-yellow high shoes (the latter without socks). A brilliant rayon kerchief may be added, as well as a colorful *serape* or poncho, although in Cherán the latter is usually dull in color. In such a town as Capacuaro, however, Sunday or fiesta dress might consist of *calzones* of *manta* supported by a brilliant red sash, a vivid blue rayon shirt, bright green rayon kerchief, yellow shoes, a striking orange or strong pink poncho folded over one shoulder, and a large whitened straw hat with a big spray of pink gladiolus or a cluster of geraniums. Worn with an air, the ensemble is impressive.

In Cherán a good many men have shirts bought in market or in Uruapan; a necktie; a pair or two of cotton trousers, perhaps made by a tailor in Uruapan; a woolen sack coat; and a felt hat. Such a costume normally would be worn on Sunday or on trips by bus to Uruapan or some other town. Very rare, though, are individuals with a complete wool suit. Sweaters are fairly common for lounging about home or on the streets.

The dress of male children is similar to that of adults as soon as they have learned to walk and have established habits of toilet control. However, it is said that small boys formerly wore only a shirt; *calzones* for the young became common with the advent of the highway. Young boys, including even infants in arms, have hats, but until the age of 10 or 12 these are cheap woven straw hats costing 15 to 25 centavos rather than the more expensive sewn braid hats worn by men. The acquisition of an adult hat and a poncho is the principal recognition of adulthood.

Today both men and boys wear the hair short, cut either at home or by a barber. Only one boy in Cherán was observed with long hair; his mother was not a native. Still remembered, however, is the belief that to use scissors or a knife to cut hair will retard small children in learning to speak. Consequently, long hair was formerly common among small children. Although no memory persists in Cherán of long hair worn by men, in other villages it is asserted long hair was worn until a generation ago. Elderly Capacuaro informants insisted they had seen long hair worn by men in San Lorenzo, while an old man in Chilchota, now a Mestizo town, claimed his grandfather wore long hair as did many others of similar age.

Women's dress.—Probably the majority of women in Cherán wear cotton print dresses for everyday wear. However, only a few wear the styles found among Mestizo women, that is, a fairly short one-piece, rather simply cut dress of garish cotton print cloth which might be duplicated among cheap cotton house dresses in the United States. Much more common is a garment of archaic cut and usually with smaller, less colorful figures in the material. This garment is usually longer and has a definite skirt, pleated at the waistband, and a blouse, although usually the two are combined into a single garment. Flounces or ruffles are not infrequent on the skirt and the back of the waist. This garment, in some of its forms, is not essentially different from that worn by Mixe women, as well as women of other Indian groups, and probably dates back to at least the seventeenth century.

Virtually every woman in town also has a traditional Tarascan dress. This is usually worn for any formal occasion, even though only

FIGURE 8.—Women's dress. See text for description. The petticoat is made more visible than usual in order to indicate the embroidered edging. The apron commonly reaches the bottom of the skirt. The *rebozo* would normally be on the head or about the shoulders, but is shown on the arm to permit a view of details of the blouse, hairdress, etc.

for visiting or receiving guests, while a great many conservative women wear it constantly. In the latter case, if they can afford it, women have two costumes, an old one for everyday, a newer one for special occasions.

The complete Tarascan woman's dress consists of petticoat, skirt, blouse, apron, *rebozo* or shawl, and a number of woven belts (fig. 8). The greatest variation is in the blouse. This may be of cheap *manta* or even discarded flour sacking, in which case it merely has an opening for the head, short sleeves, 4 to 6 inches in length, and is unsewn down the sides. The open-sided blouse is often worn by nursing mothers, even though the materials are of better quality. No matter how cheap the materials, however, some design in cross-stitching is usually found about the neck opening.

Finer blouses may be of good cotton, rayon, or even silk, although cotton is the most common. The short sleeves may have a drawstring at the end to tie them closely about the arm. This gives a puffed sleeve appearance, although there is no fitting. More commonly, except in garments made for tourists, the lower end of the sleeve is finished with a crocheted band about 1 inch wide in a contrasting color. Often the lower seam of the sleeve is not carried to the body of the garment. The side seam of the latter is also often incomplete for about 2 inches below the sleeve. The opening left compensates to some extent for the lack of fitting. The neck opening is bound either by solid cross-stitching or a crocheted band similar to that on the sleeve. An extensive cross-stitched design usually gives the effect of a yoke, although front and back of the blouse are a single piece. The neck opening is tied together with two pieces of cord, a piece sewn to each side. Garments for sale may have a drawstring about the neck opening, which then is not extended down the front of the garment.

Cherán women's blouses are usually plainer than those worn in other villages. The decoration is usually a dull yellowish brown and is applied with restraint. No study of the designs was attempted, as it is hoped a general study of the Tarascan textile and garment industry will be made.

The petticoat is of white cotton cloth or *manta*. It reaches from the waist nearly to the ground, and the lower edge is decorated with a band nearly 2 inches wide of cross-stitched designs in blue, strong pink, or red. These designs are made in Nahuatzen on long strips of *manta* and are purchased and sewn on the lower edge of the petticoat. The garment itself is tubular with a circumference of at least 6 yards. The top edge is folded back a foot or more, giving a double thickness of cloth about the waist. It is worn flat across the front and then skillfully gathered in knife pleats across the back, forming almost a ridge of material across the back. The pleats are not sewn but are laid in place each time the petticoat is donned. The top of the petticoat comes at least 6 inches above the waist. A woven belt of wool, usually in brilliant colors, about 2 inches wide and 2 or more yards long, is then placed very tightly about the waist to support the petticoat. Only training from childhood makes it possible to endure the tightness of the belt constantly.

If Tarascan dress is worn constantly, women frequently wear the petticoat without the skirt and apron while working. This is true even when running errands on the street. Any formal occasion, however, is thought to require the outer skirt and apron.

The outer skirt is of very dark-blue or black wool cloth, either of commercial origin, or hand-loomed materials from Paracho or Nahuatzen. Two widths of the latter are required. The skirt is tubular also, and the circumference should equal or exceed that of the petticoat, the limit being the purse of the family and the fortitude of the woman. Skirts over 30 yards in circumference are known; a 15-yard circumference is probably about the minimum for a really stylish garment. The top is folded in, and the surplus material is gathered, as in the petticoat, in knife pleats across the back. The top of the skirt is well above the waist and is held in place by several narrow woven belts of bright colors and designs. Despite their elaborate designs, these belts are wrapped one on top of the other. Although one would suffice, ideally one belt is superimposed on another until they reach a thickness of as much as 2 inches (pls. 1, upper and lower right; 2, upper right and left).

The pleats of the skirt must be prepared more carefully than those of the petticoat.

When the skirt is washed, two women fold in the pleats while the material is still damp. It is then laid flat to dry or clamped between two or three pairs of sticks which project beyond the sides of the skirt and are tied together. The same device is often used when the skirt is not being worn.

When both skirt and petticoat are worn, a ridge of cloth extends across the middle of the back large enough for a small child to sit on, held by his mother's shawl. The thickness of cloth is also folded under when a woman sits on the ground, creating a seat quite as high as the low stools or chairs used by men. When walking, the skirt barely clears the ground and only glimpses may be caught of the colored band of the petticoat. In rainy weather or on muddy roads the skirt becomes wet and muddy. In the Lake Pátzcuaro region, not only is the skirt worn a little shorter, but it is often hitched up nearly to the knees by using one of the many belts to loop up part of the cloth at the back into a bustle-shaped bundle. In the same area, skirts are often of red plaid materials and the upper part is made of lighter materials, making the thickness of the folds at the waist much less.

The *rebozo*, or shawl, is an inseparable part of the costume. The everyday *rebozo*, and the only one owned by poor women, is a hand-loomed cotton fabric from Paracho or Nahuatzen. The color is dark blue with fine light-blue or white longitudinal stripes. The color is from indigo dye. A tasseled fringe some 4 inches in length finishes the ends.

For special occasions, women who can afford them wear a much finer gray or blue cotton *rebozo* from Tangancicuaro. Such *rebozos* may cost from 10 to 60 pesos or more, and the finer specimens can be drawn through a finger ring. An elaborate netted fringe 8 or 10 inches long is waxed to make it stiff. Some fine *rebozos* have a thin stripe, but the main effect is of a pepper-and-salt mixture.

The *rebozo* is sometimes worn over the head as a protection against rain, sunshine, or cold, or to hide the face partly if the wearer is embarrassed. At such times a fold may be drawn across the lower part of the face and caught in the teeth. Much of the time, however, the *rebozo* is worn as a shawl. Children or small objects are slung on the back in a fold of the *rebozo* (pl. 2, upper right and left).   The bare arms are also usually covered by the *rebozo*.   The ends may be used to lift hot objects or as a handkerchief.   The *rebozo* is worn with cotton dresses as well as with the traditional costume.

Women usually go barefooted on all occasions. Today some wear shoes, but no woman was even seen to wear *guaraches*.   Occasionally women may wear a man's straw hat over the *rebozo* when traveling in hot sun.   Usually, though, a leafly branch is plucked and held to shade the head.

Women dress one another's hair.   The hair is carefully combed and brushed, frequently with brushes from urban sources or with brushes of *raiz de paja*.   Oil or lemon juice is often rubbed on the hair to impart a sheen and preserve the hairdress for 2 or 3 days.   The hair is parted in the middle and then carefully braided in two braids.   Young women and some older women braid in pieces of bright-colored yarn or narrow ribbons.   Small girls usually have yarn or ribbon only in one braid. Very old women sometimes do not comb the hair, letting it hang in a tangled mass, possibly because they have no relatives or friends to do this.   A band or cord may, in this case, be tied around the head to keep the hair out of the face. In Mestizoized Chilchota, women still do not comb their own hair but do it for each other.[12]

Girls frequently are put in the traditional costume before they can walk.   Usually a portion of a worn-out skirt or *serape* is bound on the infant with a belt.   When the child can walk, a miniature blouse and petticoat are provided, and usually a portion of a skirt, even though ragged.   Thus, even from infancy, the girl is tightly bound about the waist and at an older age is able to stand the tight belt necessary to support the heavy petticoat and skirt (pl. 2, lower right and left).

Both women and girls wear necklaces of tubular red glass beads called *corales* (corals). Three or four to several dozen strings are worn. The strings go only part way around the neck, being attached to two ribbons which are tied behind the neck.   Earrings are also worn.

Miscellaneous cheap products of the markets may be worn, but the proper type every woman desires is a large hollow crescentic ornament with wires from each end passing through the perforation in the ear.   These are of gold or silver, gold being preferred.   A gold pair costs about $35.00.

WOODWORKING TECHNIQUES

Carpentry, including house building, is the only wood manufacturing process in Cherán except that of a single man who turns out chocolate beaters and that of a family who make broom handles.   Aside from house building, carpenters mainly make doors for houses and kitchens, gates in fences, and trap doors. While several carpenters can do other kinds of woodwork, they rarely make furniture, as Cherán carpenters do not feel they can compete with those of nearby Paracho.

The differences in the economic well-being of towns situated only a few miles apart are sharply underscored by this situation.   Paracho is a "poor" village with inadequate lands.   A considerable percentage of the population gain their livelihood as hired laborers, traders, carpenters, and weavers.   Furniture makers in Paracho receive ordinarily 50 centavos for a chair, which takes perhaps a day to make. Carpenters from Cherán, most of whom are also landowners, feel this is a quite inadequate return.   Data from Cherán indicate carpenters receive $1.50 or more a day for their labor. It may be that the traditional specialization of labor may have some influence upon the Cherán carpenter's unwillingness to make furniture, but differences in economic standards undoubtedly play a part.

Carpenters have a shop in their yard, usually consisting of a shed with one or two sides closed.   Under this is a work bench of heavy planks.   The tools are a saw, mallet, chisels, adz, hammer, and plane.   Usually the metal parts only are purchased, and handles and plane boxes are made by the carpenter.

As the majority of Cherán houses are of wood, another important activity of carpenters is house building.   Only the simplest house construction would be undertaken without the aid of a carpenter, and even the roofing of a stone or adobe structure likewise calls for a

---

[12] In Sopoco in La Cañada, women dress each other's hair after the weekly bath. The hair is "fixed" with lemon juice and the juice of an unidentified herb.

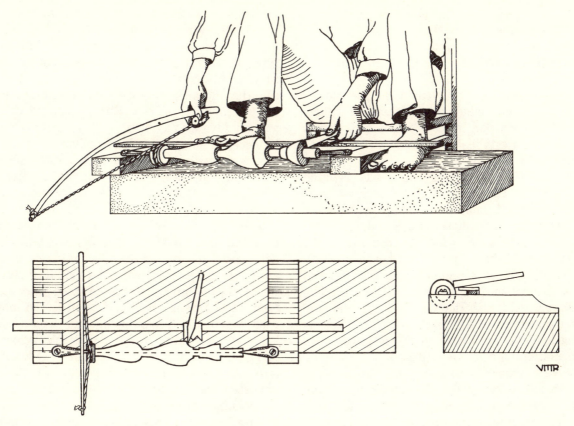

FIGURE 9.—Lathe driven by a bow. A candlestick, about 12 inches long, is in process of manufacture. The two bottom views show the position of the cutting tool.

carpenter. Inasmuch as a detailed description of houses, house use, and house furnishings has already been published, no discussion is included here (Beals, Carrasco, and McCorkle, 1944).

As mentioned previously, one man in Cherán manufactures chocolate beaters of simple type. They are made of madroño wood and are turned on a crude lathe (fig. 9). Power is provided by a bow with the string wrapped about the shaft of the lathe. The left hand is used to work the bow. The lathe rests on the ground, and both the bare feet and the right hand are used to manipulate the tools. The tools and technique are characteristic of Paracho, where a wide variety of turned wood products is made, including bowls, vases, candlesticks, chocolate beaters, salt and pepper shakers, and chessmen.

Broom handles are made by one family, as already mentioned. Pine logs are split into long staves, which are whittled into a roughly round shape with a knife. The entire product

is sold in Pátzcuaro, where there is a broom factory.

MISCELLANEOUS PROCESSES

Wax bleaching and candlemaking.—Beeswax is often bleached by exposure to the sun. Melted wax is poured into bowls so that it forms a thin shell over the inside. These shells are removed and exposed to the sun for several days until the wax becomes white. Although the wax loses weight by this process, it sells for no more than unbleached wax. The extra effort thus apparently results in an economic loss, making the motivations for the work somewhat obscure. Although men do all other work connected with beekeeping, women often bleach the wax.

Candles are made by men. Two candlemakers are reputed to live in Cherán. The only one who could be located was always so drunk at the time of interviewing that little reliability can be attached to the data secured from him. Wicks are attached to nails in a wheellike frame and are then dipped repeatedly in liquid wax until the candles reach the desired thickness. The frame is suspended from the ceiling by a rope.

Paper flowers.—The women of one rather large household make paper flowers for funerals and paper ornaments for weddings. It was impossible to establish satisfactory contacts to learn details.

Blacksmithing.—Cherán has one reputed blacksmith. The individual concerned was never found at home, nor could any details concerning his techniques be learned.

Baking.—A baker of sweetened breads (*pan dulces*) established himself in Cherán in 1943. He baked daily in a regular local oven belonging to one of the wealthier storekeepers. The bread was sold with the aid of a boy, who carried it about town in a big basket hat such as is used in Mestizo towns in the neighborhood. Information on sales was refused, but probably they were between $10 and $12 a day at three breads for 5 centavos. Expenses each day were 1 *arroba* (25 pounds) of flour, $3.62; 1 kilo (2.2 pounds) of lard, $1.50; 3 kilos of sugar, $1.08; or a cash outlay of $6.20, plus the labor of baker and vendor. This does not take into account the firewood for heating the oven. Profits evidently at best hardly justify the secrecy shown.

Fireworks.—At least one man in Cherán makes fireworks, both *cohetes* (explosive rockets) and *castillos* (set pieces built about a tall pole). The one man interviewed was born in Pichataro (which suggests he may be Mestizo in origin, although he apparently regards himself as a Tarascan) and learned the trade from his father.

Materials used in the manufacture of *cohetes* are niter, chlorate, sulfur, paper, agave fiber cord, and shakes. The worker interviewed makes *cohetes* only on order. He by no means supplies all the Cherán market.

Castillos likewise are made only on order. It is a general rule that *castillos* be bought outside the town, so the Cherán *cohetero* has never made a *castillo* for a Cherán fiesta. In 1940 he made *castillos* for San Felipe, Cheranástico, Ahuiran, and Pichataro.

Materials for *castillos* are necessarily quite elaborate, as they require fuses of various speeds, different colors of fire, and slow-burning types of powder. As handbooks exist for this type of manufacture and supply houses also furnish information to their patrons, it was felt that detailed inquiry into techniques was not worth while. The *cohetero* usually receives a small advance payment—5 to 15 pesos—when he accepts an order. He receives no further payment until the *castillo* is burned. Should there be a failure, not only may the *cohetero* fail to receive his pay, but he may be jailed and fined.

Stonecutting.—Several men do stonecutting on a part-time basis. Doorsills and bases for door posts and pillars are the major products, although some men also make grinding stones for *nixtamal* mills. A fine-grained gray lava from the barranca north of town is the most-used material. Tools include an iron-headed hammer, weighing about 2 pounds, steel chisels, and a pair of calipers. Stones for the *nixtamal* mills are made in pairs and are about a foot in diameter and 6 to 8 inches thick. About 3 days are required to make a pair.

Tanning.—The only full-time tanner of hides in Cherán is a native of Aranza, who moved to Cherán because of the better water supply. He has a house and lot on the east side of town beside the aqueduct. Most of his work is done on hides brought him by shoemakers and *guarache* makers. Such work is charged for on a fee basis.

A man and his uncle also tan hides on a part-time basis. They are primarily farmers and do relatively little of the tanning in Cherán.

Cowhides are tanned with oak bark. The process takes 20 to 30 days, mostly occupied with soaking the hides in the tanning mixture. Sheepskins, used for inner soles of shoes, must be put through a lye bath, scraped, and then soaked with oak bark. A batch of five or six sheepskins requires 2 days' labor and about 8 days' soaking.

The principal equipment consists of a number of large hollow logs for soaking the hides.

Lacquer.—One woman learned lacquer making in Uruapan. She works fairly steadily, producing a typical Uruapan black-background lacquer with floral designs in four or five colors. She sells all her product in Cherán.

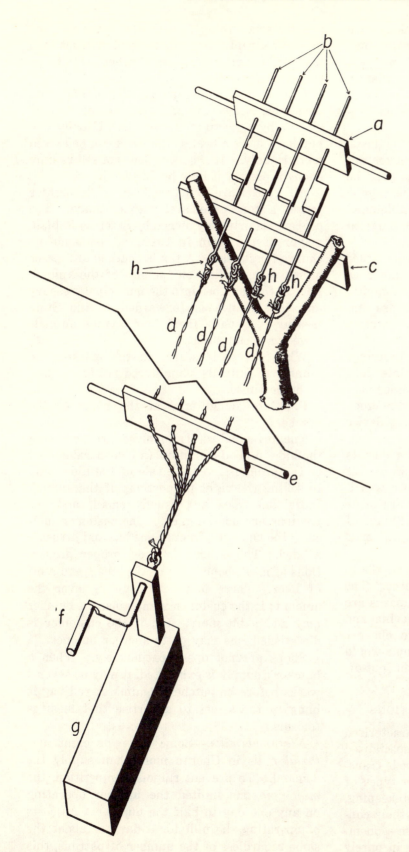

FIGURE 10.—Four-ply rope-twisting device used in making horsehair lead ropes. Three men are needed to operate the device. Four groups of horsehair threads (spun on a simple spinning device, not illustrated) are fastened at *h* and at *f*, passing through the holes in the piece of wood *e*. *c* is a second perforated piece of wood fastened to a Y-shaped stump. Crank *f* is first blocked so it will not revolve. The first operator rotates the piece of wood at *a*, causing cranks *b* to revolve and twist the four hanks of thread (*d*), into cords. Crank *f* is now released. The first operator holds the board (*a*) stationary, a second operator rotates the crank (*f*), and a third operator moves the board (*e*) toward *c* as the rope is formed by twisting the four cords (*d*) together. *g* is a heavy billet of wood, about 5 by 1 by 1 foot. As the cords and rope are twisted, the increasing tension drags *g* forward about 6 or 8 feet. *h* are short maguey fiber strings attaching the cords (*d*) to the cranks (*b*). These strings are not part of the finished rope.

Shoemaking.—One master shoemaker with two apprentices makes shoes of locally produced leather. The apprentices get no pay, working from 6 months to a year in order to learn the trade. The master shoemaker learned in the same way. The techniques present no unusual points of interest.

Equipment includes a sewing machine, lasts, knives, and awls. The master shoemaker not only must know his trade, but also he must be able to judge hides and tanning and be a good buyer. Only a portion of the Cherán demand is supplied locally, and many consider the local shoes inferior to those from outside.

At least three men make *guaraches* to order on a part-time basis. *Guarache* making does not require a sewing machine, and the capital required is small. Most *guaraches* are imported. The type is described in connection with clothing.

Rope and twine.—One man makes kite strings during the kite season in March. No interview could be secured with this man. Another man specializes in horsehair lead ropes and maguey fiber *riatas*. A fairly complex twisting device is used (fig. 10).

Hair brushes.—One family of four makes its entire living by manufacturing brushes of *raiz de paja*. The family collects its own raw·materials and dries the roots. Brushes are made by fastening bunches of root in metal rings of about 1-inch diameter, then trimming the ends off square.

Masks.—One family makes wooden masks to order, charging about 2 pesos a piece. The workmanship is very poor and most masks are bought in other towns, especially Sevina and Cheranástico. The local masks are cheaper and much easier to buy, but most people would go to considerable trouble to get the out-of-town product.

SPECIALIZED SERVICE OCCUPATIONS

A number of occupations are characterized by the selling of services requiring specialized knowledge rather than the sale of goods transformed from raw material. Certain types of trading occupations, such as storekeeping, could logically be included here, but their consideration is deferred to the section on economics. Other skilled specialists dealing in purely non-material things, such as "prayers" or *rezadores*, midwives, curers, and witches, are also left for consideration in other sections of this paper.

Butchers.—Except for *mayordomías* and large weddings, butchering of cattle and pigs is carried on by a group of specialists. Usually two butchers share a beef so the stock can be moved more rapidly. If the meat does not sell rapidly enough, part of it may be dried.

All cattle are butchered at a "slaughter house," a stone-paved area with a ramada. The property is privately owned by Seferino Fabian, mayor of the town in 1940, but he made no charge for its use. A tax is charged of 5 pesos or more, depending on the size of the animal. Part of the tax goes into the municipal treasury and the balance is forwarded to the State treasury. Usually from four to nine animals a week are slaughtered.

When cheese is scarce in the market, the number of animals slaughtered is higher than at other times.

Pigs are slaughtered at the home of the butcher.

The principal skills involved are removing the hide in good condition (a considerable part of the profit is from the sale of the hide) and in selling the right proportions of the animal. Individual sales are usually small, and the portions are not weighed. The customer indicates the amount of money she has and presents a bowl. The butcher cuts off proper proportions of meat, bone, a bit of the lungs, and a bit of liver. There is rarely haggling over the amount; if the customer complains, the butcher may add a bit more. Or, if the customer is dissatisfied, she may go to another butcher.

Shops are not open continuously. When a butcher's supply is exhausted, it may be several weeks before he butchers again. A red flag is hung in the street to advertise that meat is for sale.

Nixtamal mills.—Some seven or eight *nixtamal* mills in Cherán more than supply the demand. To prevent ruinous competition, the *municipio* has limited the number operating on any one day to half the number. As costs of operating the mill for a day are about the same regardless of the number of patrons, this arrangement guarantees an adequate number of customers each day a mill is operating.

The miller must have some mechanical knowledge as well as capital and business ability. Most of the mills are driven by an old automobile engine converted to operate on gas produced by a charcoal burner, usually made from an old oil drum. A belt drive transmits power and reduces the speed. Usually the owner (or manager in some cases) supervises the motor and the gas burner and an employee or member of the family feeds the maize into the mill and collects the charge, 1 centavo a kilo. In one case a woman occupied this post, but most of the mill operators are men.

Except for a few very poor families, everyone in Cherán now patronizes the mills. Each mill serves from about 330 to 360 customers a day.

Wheat threshing.—One wood-burning steam-driven threshing machine has operated in Cherán for several years. The machine is stationary (although it could be moved, it is too cumbersome to do so), and the customers bring their wheat to the machine. Two tenders, who feed the wheat into the machine, and a water carrier are required besides the operator. Firewood is purchased. Exclusive of interest on the investment and repairs, the operator nets about 25 pesos a day above operating expenses.

In 1940 a smaller gasoline-driven thresher, which could be moved from house to house, was said to have made considerable inroads on the trade. However, as the bulk of the Cherán wheat is still threshed by hand, there seemed to be ample business for both threshing machines.

Painters and plasterers.—This is a rare occupation followed by two or three men on a part-time basis. Only a minority of the houses of adobe or stone are plastered, and few of them are painted. The pay is fairly good, but the best worker probably does not put in more than 90 days' work a year. Brushes and stencils are used in painting.

Masons.—As the house owner normally provides all materials, the mason sells only his services. His equipment is a trowel, hammer, a board frame for holding mud mortar, a shovel for mixing mortar, an ax to cut poles for scaffolding, and string to line up the walls. Perhaps a dozen men do masonry, mostly as a secondary occupation. Work is usually charged for on the basis of square meters of wall.

Barbers.—Most men in Cherán now have their hair cut by a barber. There are two barbers in town regularly, and more come to town during fiestas. The Cherán barbers also visit nearby towns during fiestas. During the middle of the week they have little trade.

Formerly men cut each other's hair for nothing in the bull ring on Sundays, using only scissors. The barbers have clippers as well and also razors for shaving, although there is not much demand for the latter. One barber is not a native; the other learned the trade in the United States.

Water carriers.—In most households the women bring the water from the fountain or aqueduct in ollas carried on their shoulders. However, for any commercial use (nixtamal mill, masonry, the threshing machine) water is carried by men. In addition, there is one man who makes his living carrying water for storekeepers, whose wives may be too busy helping in the store, and for a few families who are somewhat Mestizoized and the husband has decided the work is too hard for the women.

Interestingly enough, the men's method of water carrying is entirely different from that of the women. Men carry water in two 5-gallon cans suspended from the two ends of a pole which is supported on the shoulder. This rigid dichotomy is observed even in families where one of the men or boys brings the bulk of the water. If the women need to bring additional water, they always use ollas and make several trips.

FOOD PROCESSING AND DIET

Consideration of food processing in this section is confined primarily to household activities. Commercial processing of food for sale, such as baking, butchering, and ice cream making, will be considered later.

The storage of food is confined primarily to maize, wheat, beans, and broadbeans (*habas*). Except for small supplies for immediate use, stores are kept in the house, usually in the loft. Maize is stored on the cob. Wheat, beans, and similar seeds are stored in gunny sacks or in baskets. Such foods as sugar, coffee, salt, lard, fruits, vegetables, herbs, meat, fish, and manufactured foods such as bread are purchased in small quantities and are kept in various covered pottery or basket containers in the kitchen.

Eating habits show considerable variability as between families. They also change with the season and the prevailing occupations. Ordinarily three meals a day are eaten, at about 10 a. m., 2 p. m., and 7 p. m. or an hour later. Very poor people may eat only twice. The major foods are tortillas and other maize dishes, meat (or fish or cheese as substitutes), and green plants. In addition to these common foods, which may be prepared in various ways, there are various occasional or seasonal foods eaten as part of the regular diet, as well as foods eaten only or primarily on the occasion of a fiesta.

Two types of morning meal exist. The most common is a meal of tortillas and either meat or greens. This is varied every 4 to 8 days with some kind of atole. Some persons have taken over the local Michoacán habit of a boiled sweetpotato or a piece of bread and a glass of milk eaten early in the morning, at 7 or 8 o'clock. Such people usually eat the midday meal a little earlier in the day, between 12 and 1 o'clock. The midday meal is almost always a beef stew with cabbage (čurípo) eaten with tortillas. Those who cannot afford meat, eat some vegetable instead, often prepared with milk and sometimes with cheese also. The evening meal is usually the same as the midday meal. Prepared food may be kept over from one day to another.

Some people may eat only two meals, at about 10 a. m. and 7 p. m. The morning meal may consist of tortillas and beans or tortillas and chile sauce, varied frequently with atole, although no one would have atole daily. At night beans may be eaten if available; if not, boiled cabbage or čurípo is eaten, depending upon economic circumstances. Meat, eggs, fish, and game are rarely eaten by really poor people. Poor people often eat atapákua (squash blossoms and immature squash) with tortillas and ground dried fish or cheese if they have a midday meal. Between meals children or adults, if they feel hungry and the foods are available,

eat cooked chayotes, chilacayotes, or boiled squash (sometimes with brown sugar).

The following are the foods most commonly eaten in Cherán:

All seasons: Tortillas, čurípo, tamales (kurúndas type), beans, beef or pork in brown mole, fish, cabbage, chiles, onions, coffee, chocolate, lemons, bananas, peanuts.
January: Cherimoyas, *zapote negro*, oranges.
February: Oranges.
March: Chilacayote (a squash stored since October).
April: Cherries, avocados, oranges.
May: Mushrooms, *nopales* (young leaves of the prickly pear), wheat breads, wheat, tortillas, avocados, watermelons.
June: Mushrooms, pears, peaches, avocados, cheese, sugarcane.
July: Cheese, immature squash, squash blossoms, pears, peaches, sugarcane.
August: Pears, peaches, green corn, sweet tamales (očepos), apples, cheese, sweetpotatoes, sugarcane, broadbeans (*habas.*)
September: Pears, apples, crab apples (*tejocote*), cheese, sweetpotatoes, sugarcane, broadbeans, honey.
October: Chayotes, chilacayotes, crab apples, honey, sugarcane, guavas, oranges, papayas, broadbeans, cheese.
November: Chayotes, chilacayotes, broadbeans, guavas, oranges, pumpkins, cheese.
December: Cherimoyas, chayotes, some chilacayotes, guavas, oranges.

Some of these foods may be available in other months, but the periods in the list represent the times of greatest use. The list does not contain a number of little-used foods. Except for a few herbs, the maguey, and wild crab apple, no wild vegetable foods are eaten in Cherán.[13]

MEAT FOODS

Čurípo is a stewed meat, almost always of beef, usually containing cabbage, a few garabanzos (chickpeas), and often a bit of carrot. Salt and a considerable quantity of ground dried chile are employed as seasoning. The thin broth is served in the same dish. One or two pieces of meat weighing about 2 ounces, a little of the vegetables, and about a cup of broth comprise the usual serving. Second servings are not usually eaten either by guests or in the privacy of the home. This food is eaten on all fiesta occasions throughout the year

[13] Some wild foods are reported by Sra. Rendón for La Cañada. Bitter prickly pear, *tuna agria* (*joconocostle*), is used as greens in čurípo and in making chile sauce (sindurakua). La Cañada Tarascans say mulberry leaves (?), *hojas de mora*, are eaten by the Sierra Tarascans "because of their poverty."

and as a daily food by all who can afford it, which in Cherán would probably constitute a considerable majority of the population. It is often eaten with tamales of the type known as kurúndas, or with boiled chayote. Meat, if not made into čurípo, usually is boiled.[14]

Mole is a less common meat dish, probably derived from the Mestizos. It consists of a stew, preferably of turkey, but if this is not obtainable, of chicken, pork, or beef in descending order of frequency as well as preference. Pieces of the boiled meat are served in a sauce made in various ways, according to the availability of the ingredients and the knowledge of the cook. The sauce may include the following ingredients: Cloves, ginger, chocolate, cinnamon, ground toasted bread or tortillas, pumpkin seeds, garlic, onion, and chile of the type known as pasíya or "chileancho." The chiles are either fried in lard or dipped in hot water, ground with the other ingredients, and cooked in the meat broth. A thick, rich, and usually rather greasy sauce or gravy is the result. Mole is usually eaten on special occasions.

Fish are brought to Cherán either fresh, broiled, or dried. Fresh fish come from Erongaricuaro on Lake Pátzcuaro only a limited part of the year, usually just after the rainy season in the fall. It is expensive compared with meat, but is much liked. During the rainy season, broiled fish are brought from Lake Chapala; in the dry season, from Erongaricuaro.

The fish are washed carefully in hot water before cooking. Fish is boiled in water with onion and silantro (a pungent herb). Some people eat the intestines, removing only the bile. Seasoning with chile and tomato, ground together, is common; sometimes the broth is thickened with maize dough and sometimes onion is added. Fish may also be fried with eggs in lard, making a sort of fish hash.

Small dry fish (čaráles), resembling small dried minnows, are on sale on market day throughout the year and also at many of the stores. They are toasted on the comal and eaten with chile and tortillas, especially for breakfast. They are also made into a broth with chile sauce.

It is believed to be injurious to eat any kind of fish when ill of the "bilis."

Game is eaten to some extent when available. Deer meat is sold in pieces or in retail quantities by the hunters in much the same fashion as beef. Squirrels, doves, and ducks are all liked. Squirrels are sold at 10 centavos, doves at 5 centavos, and ducks at 50 centavos to 1 peso. Ducks come from Zacapu. A few people eat pigeons. Only adult pigeons are eaten.[15]

Eggs are eaten to a considerable extent, fried, mixed with fish, or scrambled with cheese. But poor families, even if they have chickens, prefer to sell the eggs and buy beans.

MAIZE FOODS

Maize is made into tortillas, gordos, posole, or tamales, and is also used to thicken some types of broths and sauces. It is also eaten green, and certain foods are made from green corn. No maize foods are salted. Maize types include white, yellow, red, and black, the latter two types not being common. White maize is sold chiefly outside the village.

Methods of initial preparation vary. For tortillas and gordos the maize is boiled with lime. This softens and to some extent dissolves the outer shell of the grain. After thorough washing in a special basket, it is ground into nixtamal or dough. If economically possible, grinding is done at the power mills in the town, followed by further grinding at home. Some people are too poor to pay for the mill, and the women do all the grinding on the metate.

Tortillas are made of the nixtamal or maize dough. A quantity is scooped off the metate and shaped into a flat disk in the hands. This is then skillfully slapped between the palms until it becomes a thin sheet about one-eighth inch in thickness and 6 or 7 inches in diameter. This sheet is baked on a dry flat clay dish, the comal, with moderate heat. Usually the tortilla is turned two or three times in the process. Tortillas are served at virtually every meal, regardless of the rest of the menu, and are the main article of diet.

Gordos are smaller and thicker cakes fried

---

[14] The majority of the recipes were collected by Silvia Rendón.

[15] The people of Ichán in La Cañada are well known for their fondness for small wild birds such as kongotos, doves (huilotas), wild pigeons, torcazes, and jarrines.

in deep pork fat. Wheat is used for *gordos* more often than is maize.

Nixtamal prepared for tortillas or *gordos* is the kind used to thicken sauces or soups.

For posole the maize is cooked with oak wood ashes instead of with lime. When cooked, it is white instead of yellow, as it is when lime is used. The shell is completely removed in this process. The grain is then washed thoroughly and boiled with pork, chile, and chopped onion. Posole is essentially a fiesta dish, served especially with certain birthday celebrations.

Tamales are made from maize prepared as for posole but ground either at the power mill or on the metate. There are several kinds of tamales.

Kurúnda is the most frequently made type of tamale. The maize is prepared apart from that intended for tortillas. The dough is mixed with bicarbonate of soda, which is said to prevent the tamale from constipating the eater. The *nixtamal* is then spread on the metate with the aid of the mano or grinding stone and the cook takes a quantity in the palm of the hand, molding it into a flattened ball. It is then tightly wound with several thicknesses of maize leaves (not husks) in such a fashion that the finished kurúnda is triangular in shape. The tamale is then boiled for some time in a covered vessel. The dough is thick, compact, and heavy, retaining something of the taste of the bicarbonate of soda. Usually kurúndas are the size of the palm of the hand, but for a person who is "very refined" (*muy fino*), they may be made smaller, a delicate way of paying a compliment.

The kurúnda is an essential part of a great many special meals, such as those served at weddings, for entertainment of guests, and at fiestas. It is usually eaten with čurípo but may sometimes be eaten with atole. On such occasions, when kurúndas are served to men the wrappings are always removed but to women they are always served with the wrappings, possibly because the women frequently take them home. Kurúndas may also be eaten cold the next day, but usually they are heated on the *comal*. They are sometimes sold on the streets at 4 to 5 centavos and are always available on market days. The vendors are always women.

With čurípo, the kurúnda is one of the most typical of Tarascan dishes.[16]

There are various forms of the kurúnda, which are eaten on special occasions. The details follow.

Atápakwa kurúnda.—Atápakwa is a sauce made of any kind of chile, cooked, toasted, or raw. This is ground with green tomatoes, garlic, and onion, and seasoned with salt. Fresh or dried cheese, finely broken up, may be added. The regular kurúnda is simply dipped in the sauce as it is eaten. This dish may be served at any time, but it is most frequently used when men come home to lunch from the fields or on other occasions in the middle of the day when the family do not ordinarily have a midday meal.

Agwákata kurúnda.—Beans of any sort are cooked and ground. They are placed in layers alternating with layers of *nixtamal* until a thick cake is formed. This is wrapped in maize leaves and steamed. Agwákata kurúndas are made primarily at the time of the bean harvest (Cherán grows few beans) and are eaten at any of the main meals. They may also be given to children between meals.

Nákatamal.—This is a tamale made with maize dough filled with meat and chile sauce. Beef is commonly used, although pork may also be employed. The meat is boiled in water and cut in small pieces without bones. It is then mixed with a chile sauce made of the dry chile known as *pasiya*, which is cooked in water and ground with tomatoes, garlic, and onions. These tamales are not wrapped in maize leaves but in dry maize husks soaked in water. A small quantity of dough is spread over the leaf and on this is placed a small quantity of meat and sauce. The leaf is then doubled over and the tamale cooked in boiling water. The nákatamal must be small in size to be properly made. The name and the type suggest it is of Valley of Mexico origin. It is ordinarily made only for the fiestas of the dead on the 1st and 2d of November, although it was served to me once on an ordinary occasion. It forms a part of the offerings made to the dead and is also eaten in the graveyard by the mourners and

---

[16] In Parícutin kurúnda means "corn husks." Kurundurání means "to wrap tamales in maize leaves."

guests. A few are made for sale on the 1st and 2d of November.

Tamalito.—This is made by mixing dough with lard and salt, forming a small ball, which is wrapped in maize leaves and cooked in boiling water. It is usually eaten the following morning for breakfast, commonly with *atole blanco.*

Čarikurúnda.—This tamale is made of black maize, boiled with wood ashes, washed, and milled. The dough is allowed to stand one night, becoming somewhat bitter. Beans are cooked and ground on the metate. A layer of bean paste is laid over a layer of maize dough, covering the metate. This is cut in squares, about three fingers wide, which are then rolled up, wrapped in maize leaves, and cooked in boiling water. The čarikurúnda is about the size of the kurúnda. It is made about March, at the period in which the sowing of maize begins. The colored maize is usually set apart out of each harvest for this purpose. A little white maize is often added "to improve the taste."

Atoles (*kamáta*) of various kinds are made. The maize dough, prepared as for tortillas, is dissolved in water and cooked with various flavorings. The broth is sometimes fairly thick but ordinarily is drunk from a glass, bowl, or cup. There are also atoles made of other grains. Many are made at special seasons of the year or for special occasions. Atoles are usually eaten for the morning meal.

Nuríte kamáta.—This is the most common form of atole. It is made as is described above but is flavored with an herb called nuríte. It is usually eaten for breakfast not less than once a week. Nuríte is a wild herb greatly used for flavoring and also for medicinal purposes. It imparts a slightly bitter flavor to atole, somewhat like *yerba buena.* No sugar, salt, or other flavoring is employed. This atole is commonly eaten with tortillas and a little cheese, or squash, or *gordos* of either dry or green maize.

Kamáta urápiti.—This is said to mean "white atole." It is made of dough from either white or yellow maize cooked in water with a little thickening substance (not identified) and either without any seasoning whatever or with laurel (nurúkata). A small bite is taken from a cake of brown sugar, followed by a draft of atole, and then a drink of *aguardiente.* The atole is drunk throughout the day, even by children (including the *aguardiente*). It is made in March, April, and May.

Kágwas kamáta.—Fresh or dried nuríte is ground on the metate with three or four chiles of the type known as *cascabel* (káwas guajílyo). This is mixed with maize dough before it is dissolved in water and cooked. A little brown sugar and salt are added during the cooking. This atole is eaten in September with green corn on the cob. It is also eaten in December and January for either breakfast or supper; if the day is very cold, it may be taken during the day, for it is very "heating." For this reason it is also given to mothers for several days after parturition.

Turípiti kamáta.—This is made with maize dough and brown sugar. A quantity of corn husks is toasted until almost black; this is ground and added to the atole while cooking. The resulting atole is almost black and appears to have ashes in it. The taste is agreeable, however. Turípiti is usually eaten with nákatamales, but it is also eaten at any other time of the year, being one of the more popular atoles in Cherán. It is also sold daily at the *puestos* in Uruapan, where it is known as *atole de cascara de cacao,* "atole of chocolate bean husks," although it has not the slightest chocolate in it.

Kamáta urápiri.—This is said to mean atole of maguey (or agave). The unfermented juice of the maguey is used instead of water. The juice is cooked until foam ceases to form on top and it is a little thick. Instead of maize dough, white maize is toasted and ground into flour, then added to the juice. It is made in the period before the rainy season, April, May June.

Srímba kamáta or téri kamáta (*šrimba,* "cane," or teri, "sweet").—The sweet juice of mature green cornstalks is extracted by grinding the stalks on the metate. The juice is boiled until it no longer forms foam on top, and is a little thick. Green corn is cut from the cob, milled, and added to the liquid and cooked with water added. This atole is eaten only in the period green corn is available.

Iuɹitini kamáta.—This is a variant of nuríte kamáta, to which salt and three or four red chiles are added. Everything is passed through a colander before cooking.

Puȼiti kamáta.—This is made as is the one just described, but anis is used as flavoring and ground green corn is used instead of the ordinary maize dough. Nothing else is eaten with this.

Tamaríndo kamáta.—Maize dough and sugar are put through a colander and thoroughly boiled with 5 centavos worth of tamarind or blackberries. A small quantity of leaves of black or red maize is boiled; the liquid is added, giving the atole a blackish color. It is eaten with bread in the dry season.

Čarákata čarápiti.—According to another informant, this is made the same as tamaríndo kamáta, but with ground tamarisk or ground blackberry added. It is said this is the only occasion blackberries are used. March, April, and May, the warm season, is the time for eating this, as it is said to be a "cold" atole. When the atole has cooled and thickened, small portions are sometimes put on the colored maize leaves and allowed to thicken or harden like fruit paste. If not eaten immediately, it may be wrapped in the leaves.

Iȼúkua kámata (milk atole).—Ordinary maize dough atole is made with milk. This is one of the more common atoles. It is eaten with bread.[17]

Tóquera ičusta.—Uncooked maize tóquera (half way between green and mature maize) is ground on the metate, mixed with brown sugar and bicarbonate of soda (to prevent constipation), and fried in fat. This is a type of *gordo*.

Uačakata.—This is red or black maize which has been boiled on the cob and then dried for at least several months. This is one of the forms of maize preservation; the maize may be kept as long as 2 years. When desired, it is soaked for a day and night and then boiled. It is used ground for atole or is boiled with brown sugar.

RICE FOODS

Arroz kamáta, rice atole.—Well-cooked rice, milk, sugar, a bit of cinnamon, and a little

wheat flour or maize dough for thickening are all passed through a colander and boiled.

AMARANTH FOODS

Čápata kurúnda.—This is a tamale made from amaranth, *bledos* or *alegría* (paári), which is cultivated both in gardens and in the fields. The seed is ground with brown sugar, with water added to make a dough. It is then wrapped in maize husks and cooked.

WHEAT FOODS

At harvest time the heads are toasted on the *comal* and eaten. A kind of oval wheat flour tortilla is made just after wheat harvest, especially in May and June.

Semítas, or round wheat breads.—These are made primarily in the town, partly for sale in Uruapan or Paracho on market days. The wheat is usually ground on the metate, but there is some variation in the coarseness of the flour. Semítas are made with yeast, shaped, and set on boards to rise. They are baked in the dome-shaped Spanish oven. If the baker does not own an oven, she pays one bread for each boardful she bakes.

Tri kamáta.—Wheat is dampened and ground to flour, with water added to make a dough. The dough is dissolved in water and cooked with an herb called epazóte (*chile cascabel*) and salt. It is strained before boiling. It is eaten alone without bread or tortillas.

Gordos.—Ground wheat is mixed with water and made into flat cakes. They are fried in deep pork fat, and are pretty greasy.

VEGETABLES AND FRUITS

Cabbage is the most common vegetable. It is always eaten cooked, usually with meat. Scarcely a house in Cherán does not have a small plot of cabbage. People who do not have their own, buy cabbage from house owners who do. Cabbage is not sold in the market.

Chayotes constitute an important food during the season. Children munch on them all day. Cooked chayotes are sold on the streets at 2 to 5 centavos, depending on size.

Chayote roots, which are dug up every few years, are boiled and eaten. They resemble a very good baked potato in flavor.

---

[17] It is reported that in Zamora and Purepero, both old Mestizo towns, the favorite atole is made of mesquite. The beans are ground on the metate and cooked.

Peanuts are often on sale on the streets. They and cooked squash are the only refreshments accessible to the very poor. Generally about a handful may be purchased for 1 centavo.

Chilacayote is a member of the squash family with watery white flesh. It probably is closest to what we call pie melons in the United States. It is much liked. The young, immature fruits are boiled with a little milk and, if it can be afforded, a little cheese.

As mentioned previously, mature chilacayotes are eaten all year but mainly in the spring. If placed in the sun daily for some time during dry weather, they will keep for some months in storage. They are sometimes coated with ashes mixed in water before storage. To serve, they are cut in pieces and boiled. Usually, cooked pieces may be bought on the street for a centavo.

Atapákua is made of squash blossoms and sliced immature squash, cooked with chile and a little flour or maize dough for thickening.

Nopal (prickly pear) is used as a vegetable. The tender leaves are skinned, cut in small squares, boiled, and then usually fried very lightly in lard.

Squash greens (the tender tips of the runners on the vines), which are commonly eaten in many parts of Mexico, are rarely eaten in Cherán. An informant had "heard" that those people who did eat them boiled the greens, then cooked them lightly with lard.

Green beans are not eaten. Informants did not even know a name for them. Dried beans are boiled, usually with a very little salt. They are often not very well done because of the altitude. They are watery and tasteless to an outsider, although relished by the residents. They are scarce, as there are few suitable soils near Cherán and most beans are imported from the Lake Pátzcuaro region.

Fruits are eaten rather sparingly in season in accordance with the economic status of the family. Locally grown fruits are eaten rather more than imported fruits. Children and young people appear to eat rather more fruit than do adults. Nearly every Cherán lot will have at least a pear, peach, apple, or cherry tree. Tunas, the fruit of the prickly pear, are also eaten as fruit.

BEVERAGES

Milk is drunk to a limited extent in season by those few who have cattle. If purchased, it is used mostly for cooking.[18]

Te de naranja is sometimes drunk. It is made by steeping the leaves of a particular member of the citrus family, either fresh or dried. The leaves must be imported in Cherán. In some other villages this is a regular breakfast drink, but in Cherán it is only an occasional drink.

Coffee is rarely drunk by the Tarascans. Most stores in Cherán do not carry it at all.

Aqua miel (urapi, urápiti, "white"), the unfermented juice of the maguey or Agave americana, is liked by some but is not very popular. It is usually available in quantities only in May. It is often drunk with sections of peeled orange, pieces of chile, and sliced onions sprinkled with ground red chile and salt. Fermented pulque is not at all popular, and what little is produced is mostly sent to Uruapan.

Aguardiente (čaránda) is the most common drink. This is simply unflavored sugarcane gin.

Amargo, a popular Cherán drink, is made by putting ground cinnamon bark, sugar, lemon juice, and lemon rind in a bottle of aguardiente for 2 or 3 days. It is taken before breakfast as a remedy in certain diseases (reumas, bilis, espantos).

Honey is produced to some extent. It is used mostly in making atole blanco or white atole and also as a treat for the children.

SOME FIESTA FOODS

Čápata is made by grinding black amaranth into dough and mixing with brown sugar. The blackish paste is spread on banana leaves. It is sold without cooking.

Mole of squash seeds is a luxury dish made only by the most wealthy and by the carguero of Natividad (Christmas). The sauce is made of ground squash seeds, chile ancho, tomatoes, spices, and bread for thickening. Beef or pork is the meat served in the sauce.

Beer is sold in some stores, but it is not a common drink.

[18] In Chilchota no cheese or butter is made. Local milk is drunk or made into jojóke, milk thickened by heating. Cheese, butter, and other milk products are imported.

Carbonated drinks with artificial coloring and flavoring are sold, particularly at two stands in the plaza where the buses stop. Lemon, orange, cherry, pineapple, and banana are the common flavors. The drinks are brought from Paracho or Uruapan and sell for 5 centavos a quarter-liter bottle. Consumption is small; the stores may have six or eight bottles for 6 months.

A refreshment of water, fruit flavorings, and sugar is also sold in the plaza. Ice is usually available only on Sundays. Only men of the town buy these refreshments when they are in funds and want to try something exotic. Most of the trade is with passersby in the buses, fortunately for the health of Cherán. Water ice is sold from door to door by one or two vendors. It is made locally whenever the dealer can secure ice from Uruapan. Home-made ices are sometimes made when the water in the troughs or streams freezes in the winter.

QUANTITIES AND COST OF FOODS

A mere list of foods and recipes has little meaning unless quantities are ascertained. Potentially the Cherán inhabitant has an adequate diet, but most of the population probably suffer from some dietary deficiency, either because of poverty or because of improper distribution and preparation of foods. Vitamin deficiencies probably are subacute to acute in many individuals. Qualitative and quantitative data of great accuracy were difficult to secure, but enough were obtained to be of some value as guides to dietary problems. Below are given some diets collected:

One of the poorest families in town, consisting of 3 adults and 2 children, eats 2½ liters of maize daily, which costs 10 centavos. Once a week the family spends 5 to 10 centavos in chiles and every 3 or 4 days 3 to 5 centavos in cheese. On rather rare occasions, if the family is relatively prosperous for the moment, one-third to one-half liter of beans is purchased at a cost of 5 to 8 centavos. Eggs, meat, and some other items are almost never eaten. It is probable that some greens are eaten from time to time which were not noted by the reporter. Total food cost could average as little as 81½ centavos per week.

A poor family, but not in such desperate straits as the one mentioned above, would probably spend, in addition, 1 or 2 centavos daily for sugar, consumed in cinnamon tea, or 3 to 6 ounces of brown sugar for use in *atole blanco*. Atole would occasionally be made of milk, 3 to 5 centavos worth being bought. Such a family would drink milk only in case of illness, when a sick person might get a pint or a little more each day.

A "middle class" family, consisting of 8 persons (2 adults, 6 children aged 4 to 16), eats about 3½ liters of maize daily, about 3½ pounds of meat (a peso's worth) a week, and 10 centavos worth of cheese daily. In addition, about 25 centavos a day would be spent for other foods. (The data on the three diets given above were all collected by Sra. Silvia Rendón.)

What appeared to be two reliable quantitative records, covering 2-week periods, were obtained, the first for a wealthy family and the second for an average family. They are as follows:

Diet records of two families for 2-week period

1. Wealthy family, Don Hilaro Xhemba (10 persons in household):

Maize	111 liters
Meat	13 pounds
Cheese	2 pounds
Fruit	[1]$ 2.54
Milk	1.54
Chiles (about ½ dozen)	.03
Bread (15 pieces, whole wheat, about 4½ inches diameter, 1¼ inches thick)	.75
Beans (brown or red; little less than 3 liters)	.41
Fish (probably about ½ pound dried fish)	.21
Total expenditure	$12.50

2. Average family, Melquiades Romero (2 adults and 5 children):

Maize	75 liters
Meat	12 pounds
Fruit	[2]$0.96

[1] This amount seems high. It would be the cost of 50 to 75 oranges, small to medium size, but undoubtedly it was not all spent for oranges; in fact, it was much more probably spent for bananas, pears, and perhaps apples or peaches.

[2] Perhaps spent for 20 to 30 small to medium oranges, but probably mostly for bananas, peaches, pears, and apples.

In both cases recorded above, vegetables undoubtedly came out of the family garden and are not listed. Probably, from the distribution of purchases, this would mean cabbage daily, perhaps half a leaf per person, boiled with the meat. At this time of year there may have been a few meals with immature squash or wild herbs from the woods, stewed with perhaps a little milk or cheese and lard.

Evelyn Payne Hatcher kindly consented to attempt an analysis of the diet of Cherán. The results are full of guesswork, but they are at least suggestive. The results show that if yellow maize was used almost exclusively, the diet of a wealthy family would contain no outright deficiencies and in many respects provide more than the usual recommended minimum amounts of various vitamins and proteins and calories. A very poor family, on the other hand, would show a striking deficiency in vitamin B_1 and an inadequate caloric intake. Both diets would give a marked deficiency of vitamin A if white corn were used instead of yellow corn. Despite the inadequacy of the data, there seems little reason to doubt that in some cases, particularly among poor families, deficiencies in the diet are sufficiently large to have a pronounced effect upon behavior and cultural participation (Beals and Hatcher, 1943).

COMPARATIVE NOTES

Some interesting comparisons are afforded by data from other towns. The most complete information was secured from Chilchota in La Cañada.

Chilchota is a Mestizoized Indian town, i. e., the bulk of the population is of Indian descent but a number of Mestizos have moved in, the native language is scarcely spoken any longer, and the people regard themselves as non-Indian. Customs are closely similar to those in the nearby Indian towns, however. Following are some menus collected by Silvia Rendón (for Cherán menus, see Beals and Hatcher, 1943):

Chilchota menus

Luncheons (taken about 10 or 11 a. m.; no breakfast in this case):

Average household:

Broiled beef
Boiled beans
Black atole
Chile sauce
Tortillas

Chile sauce
Tortillas
Coffee (black)

Broiled beef
Chile sauce
Tortillas

Poor household:
Chile sauce
Tortillas

Broiled beef
Chile sauce
Tortillas

Very poor household:
Greens of wheat plants (boiled)
Tortillas

Wealthy household:
Pork cooked with chile
Fried beans
Tortillas

Fried pork
Boiled beans
Milk
Tortillas

Pork cooked in chile sauce (mole?)
Fried beans
Tortillas
Black coffee

Dinners (2 p. m. or later):
Average household:
Meat broth with cabbage (cooked)
Meat (beef) from which broth was made
Boiled beans
Tortillas

Meat broth with cabbage
Boiled beans
Rice, cooked in water

Pork broth (with rice and bitter *tunas* or prickly pears)
Rice boiled in water
Beans
Tortillas

Fried rice with tomatoes
Pork in chile sauce
Tortillas

Poor household:
Broth
Meat from the broth
Beans boiled with chile and silantro
Tortillas

Wealthy household:
Meat broth
Meat (different from that from which broth was made) cooked with chile
Beans
Tortillas

Suppers (about 7 o'clock in the evening):

    Average household:

        Boiled beans
        Chile sauce
        Tortillas

        Boiled beans
        Chile sauce
        Tortillas

        Boiled beans
        Whole-wheat bread
        Black coffee

        Boiled beans
        Tortillas
        Milk

    Very poor household:

        Beans
        Posole (hominy, probably with a little boiled
           meat)
        Tortillas

    Wealthy household:

        Boiled beans
        Tortillas
        Chile sauce
        Whole-wheat bread
        Black coffee

        Boiled beans
        Tortillas
        Chile sauce
        Broiled meat
        Milk

Fairly common suppers are tamales (with or without meat) and atole or coffee or a piece of bread (a whole-wheat bread slightly seasoned) and a cup of tea made from the herb nuríte or a type of orange leaf.

In all cases quantities are probably small, except of tortillas. Rarely would more than one piece of bread be eaten, perhaps 2 to 3 ounces at most; perhaps half a cup to a cup of beans; meat, if broiled or boiled, two pieces about 1½ inches in greatest dimension—if in sauce, perhaps a couple of tablespoonfuls with the sauce.[19]

With substitution of different foods, these would represent Cherán menus on the whole, although there would not be so much meat with breakfast-luncheon, but rather atole, while the meat broth and meat would more commonly be served together.

At the Indian town of Sopoco in La Cañada, the following midday meals were observed:

---

[19] See Appendix 1 for more data on Chilchota.

        Boiled broadbeans
        Tortillas

        Eggs cooked on the *comal*
        Fried herbs with chile sauce
        Tortillas

        Boiled broadbeans
        Boiled beans
        Tortillas

Further comparative notes (collected by Silvia Rendón)—Possibly because Capacuaro is a smaller village with extensive woods close by, more wild animals are used for food. These include doves, *huilotas*, bird eggs (kuašanda), rabbits, flying squirrels, squirrels (kuiníkes), deer, gophers (khumás), wood rats (heyáki), peccary, jackrabbits (apácis), foxes, armadillos, bee larvae, larvae of a ground dwelling bee (*jicoteras*), worms from unidentified plants (talpanal), fresh water crawfish (čapus), wild crab apple worms (kauaš), and *tlacuache* (takuače). It is to be suspected that in Cherán, where persons closely associated with the woods are not often in the town, our list of wild animal products eaten is much shorter than it should be, although it probably represents the common diet.

Two meals a day are eaten, at 11 o'clock in the morning and in the evening at varying times. In one house the morning meal was tortillas and beans; in another, coffee and bread; in a third, coffee and tortillas sweetened with brown sugar; in a fourth, atole nuríte and tortillas; in a fifth, chile sauce, boiled greens, and tortillas. The second meal most commonly consists of squash or chayotes, meat broth with cabbage, meat and chile, and tortillas.

Special dishes not already reported include the following:

Tamalitos de čápata, small tamales of black amaranth seeds (čapata; the plant is puári), made to sell in Uruapan at three for 5 centavos. The seeds are ground and cooked in maize leaves like tamales.

Ičuskata, *gordos* filled with beans, for sale in Uruapan at 5 centavos each.

Yurúričúskatas, *gordos* made of maize dough mixed with brown sugar. In cooking, a number of pebbles are put in the *comal* and the *gordos* are placed on top of these so they cook more slowly.

Toasted tortillas (harípukata), eaten frequently at meals.

Maize stalks, chewed as a sweet to a greater extent than in Cherán.

Salt-rising bread made by one baker once a week. It sells at 10 centavos a piece.

The daily adult consumption of corn was estimated at three-eighths of a liter.

In Angáhuan, a large, isolated, and conservative western sierra town, two meals daily are also the rule. The usual hours are 10 a. m. and 6 p. m. Children and sick people may also eat tortillas or cold kurúndas at other hours. Tortillas are made by only a few women, the kurúnda taking its place. The kurúnda here is not wrapped in the maize leaf (k'an) but in the husk of the ear (šarákata).

The beef broth (čurípo) is made for preference from slightly spoiled meat or dried meat. (This is also true at Parícutin.) As there are no butchers in Angáhuan, butchering is done at home. Some of the meat is sold; the rest is cut in strips, rubbed with salt, and dried on the house roofs.

The agwákata tamale is made with beans like that of Cherán. It is eaten only for the fiestas of Candelaria (February 2), Carnival, Santa Cruz (May 3), Corpus, and at weddings.

Máškuta is a posole made of boiled black maize (¢iráns), boiled beans, silantro, and chile. A little dough of ground black corn is added as thickening. This is served to guests at New Year's and at the fiestas in December and July. At New Year's the posole is accompanied by huge kurúndas weighing about 2 kilos.

Little milk is consumed. However, the town produces enough cheese for export.

Agua miel is consumed in season. Pulque is little liked. A common drink is "tepache" (čarápe), which is slightly alcoholic.[20] It is made of barley, boiled in water and left in the water for a week. Carbonate and sweetening are then added.

Papaya juice is drunk and the seeds are toasted and eaten.

Men working in the fields or woods often carry maize on the cob which they shell and toast by a fire. This is called "esquite" (guaníto). They also carry "esquite" from home already prepared and mixed with brown sugar.

In times of famine, acorns are cooked like maize for nixtamal (boiled with lye or wood ashes), ground, and made into gordos.

A special "bread" of maize is used as an offering at the house altar. This is made of maize toquera (halfway between green and mature corn) cooked like nixtamal, ground, and shaped. It is cooked first on the comal and then hardened by placing it on embers. This bread is never eaten but is hung from strings in front of the altar. The shapes include quadrupeds, both with and without horns, crescent moons, and, most interesting of all, hearts represented in pre-Hispanic style.

In Parícutin a few divergences may be noted. Most people eat atole flavored with nuríte, without sugar, salt, or chile every morning. The wild crab apple is not eaten at all. The diet of many poor people consists almost wholly of atole and tortillas with chile sauce; this is spoken of as "eating dry," "se come a secas."

In San Juan Parangaricutiro, the Mestizoized cabecera for Angáhuan and Parícutin, the favorite atole is atole de grano, made of tender green maize, seasoned with green chile and an herb called anisillo. The atole is colored green with ground squash leaves. This atole is made especially during Holy Week. (Because of the lower elevations, the region of San Juan has green maize much of the year.) Wheat bran is used to make a type of gordos. Pulque, mixed with chile sauce, is drunk during the rainy season. Agua miel without flavoring is drunk also.

EATING CUSTOMS

Eating habits seem to vary little from town to town. In Cherán food is served on tables only on special occasions by the more sophisticated, especially when an outsider is present. Usually, the persons being served sit on low stools or benches, holding the main dish in their hands. Tortillas, tamales, salt, and other foods or condiments are placed in baskets or dishes on the floor.

Generally the women eat last, but this is primarily due to the necessity of constantly warming or cooking tortillas rather than to any feeling of propriety. If there be more than one woman in the household, one or more may begin to eat with the men after the rush of

---

[20] In Oaxaca, "tepache" is pulque reinforced with brown sugar and is more than "slightly" alcoholic.

serving and preparing tortillas is over. Ordinarily, the only utensils are spoons and these are used only when coffee is served. Food is taken in the fingers or, more commonly, in a piece of tortilla.

In fiestas, separation of sexes is more pronounced. The men are seated in two rows on beams or planks. Each is served a bowl of čurípo. Tortillas, tamales, salt, and water are placed at convenient intervals between the rows. Male children are served later in the same way. All serving outside the cooking place is done by men. Women and female children eat apart with less formality, often in the cooking place.

The only possible trace of ceremonial habits relating to eating is the habit of always leaving a little water when drinking. This is poured on the ground after drinking. No reasons were advanced for this procedure.

In Mestizoized Chilchota, according to Silvia Rendón, men are always served first. At weddings, however, unmarried girls are served first, then the men, and then the married women. When in the fields or woods, Chilchota men make the fire, heat the food, and serve the women. However, they always turn the tortillas on the fire with long sticks; turning the tortillas with the fingers would be womanish.

Changes in food habits at Cherán probably have been marked in recent years. Old people say that "anciently" the major diet was cabbage and tamales. Lard was disliked so much that people could not eat it. Although the change in Cherán is attributed to the highway and the entry of Mestizos, probably the large-scale migration from Cherán to other places had much to do with the change. Although it is difficult to point out specific changes without comparative data from conservative towns, the major differences seem to be the displacement of tamales by tortillas and the eating of fiesta foods on ordinary occasions. Soft drinks, cookies, and other manufactured foods are also becoming more common.

ECONOMICS

The techniques of raw material production, manufacting processes, and utilization of products have been discussed in the preceding pages. Under the heading "Economics" I wish now to consider problems of production, consumption, and exchange of goods and services apart from the technologies involved. Such a separation is artificial, although perhaps no more so than is the segregation of any two aspects of a culture, but separate consideration is suggested both by the complexity of the subject and by the tendency in many ethnographic studies to consider discussion of technology to be a sufficient treatment of economics. Special discussion of economic problems also seems desirable in view of the present great interest in altering the basic economics and living standards of large areas of the world and the long-continued Mexican efforts to incorporate native groups more fully into the national economy.

The study of Tarascan economy is facilitated by the fact that many of the exchanges of goods and services are made on a money basis. Moreover, the convenience of money as a measure of value has so impressed the Tarascans that exchanges on a barter basis are often calculated in terms of the money values of the goods or services involved.

The fact that Tarascan economy is a money economy signifies more than ease in the study of exchange; it also indicates at once that Tarascan economy is far from primitive as that term is usually understood. Actually Tarascan economics, like the rest of Tarascan culture, is strongly influenced by European culture. It does not necessarily follow, however, that Tarascan economics is not distinctive. The long period of assimilation and reintegration that characterized all of Tarascan culture occurred also in the economic field, and the result is a hybrid. Nevertheless, Tarascan culture is more European in origin than is that of most Mexican Indian groups. Moreover, especially in recent years, the economy of the outside world has impinged increasingly upon the Tarascans so that in 1940 there were individuals whose livelihood had been seriously affected by the outbreak of war and who, furthermore, were quite aware of their relationship to world markets.

Recognition of the interrelations of various economic activities in different regions is not a new idea to the Tarascans. The economy of the region tends toward individual and local specialization with a consequent high development of trade. While undoubtedly the majority of the Tarascans are members of self-sufficient family groups so far as the bare necessities of existence are concerned, very large numbers are partly or wholly dependent upon employment, manufactures, or trade. Consequently, the internal economy of a Tarascan village not only is complex by primitive standards but also fits into tribal and extratribal patterns of even greater complexity. Quite apart from relations with the national economy of Mexico, and, through it, with international economy, large numbers of Tarascans have been traders and middlemen on a large scale. Not only have they carried local products from Tarascan village to Tarascan village, or outside the Tarascan area; they have bought goods in non-Tarascan areas to sell in other non-Tarascan areas. The study of Cherán economy, then, must be considered an incomplete picture of Tarascan economy just as the study of the economics of a single small town would inadequately describe the economics of the United States.

The following tabulation gives the units of measure used in Cherán.

CHERÁN UNITS OF MEASURE

Dry measure

1 *litro* = 1 liter, or 0.908 quart
1 *medida* = 5 *litros*
1 *fanega* = 20 *medidas*, or 100 *litros*, or 1 *hectalitro*

Weight[1]

1 *libra* = 1 pound
1 kilo = 2.2 libras
1 *arroba* = 11.5 kilos
1 *carga* = 161 kilos or 14 *arrobas*
1 burro load = ½ *carga* (approx.), 7 or 8 *arrobas*
1 mule load = 1 *carga* (approx.), 14 to 18 *arrobas*

Capacity

1 cuartillo = 1 pint or ½ liter
1 *litro* = 1 quart (approx.) or 1 liter
1 *decalitro* = 10 litros

Square measure

1 *hectarea* (hectare) = a piece of land about 10,000 sq. paces or 10,000 sq. m.

[1] The beam balance is widely used for determining weight.

Cubic measure (used in masonry)

1 *barra* = 1 yd. × 1 yd. × 16 in.
1 *metro* = 1 m. × 1 m. × 50 cm.

PRODUCTION

Production in Cherán depends more directly upon the land than it does in most other Tarascan villages. Although the land ultimately is the source of all Tarascan raw materials, some industries require relatively few of such materials. In some cases—for example, the straw hat industry—all the raw materials are imported from outside the Tarascan area. Even more numerous are instances where the raw materials are secured from some other Tarascan town.

While Cherán economy is primarily self-sufficient in character, it is less so than are most Indian economies of Mexico. Cherán does supply most of its own basic food and housing needs, but it does not supply its own clothing. Moreover, many foods every Cherán resident desires are not produced locally. Numerous Cherán families also depend on wages more than upon their own direct exploitation of the land or upon industry. Finally, Cherán produces many goods for export, although to a far less degree than neighboring Paracho.

LAND

Tarascan land is of three main types: farm, forest, and residential. To these might be added public roads, water courses, and mineral deposits. The latter are relatively unimportant. Public roads and trails of course serve communications and do not enter directly into production. Water courses are also mainly in the public domain. Virtually their only use is to supply drinking water for man and beast and for washing purposes. Public lands also supply the small requirements of sand, clay, and building stone.

All permanent farm lands are privately owned. The only exceptions are occasional temporary fields cleared from the forest on lands too steep for cultivation for more than a few years. On the farm lands the major products are white or yellow maize and wheat. Beans, squash, fruits, oats, and barley are produced only in small quantities.

The value of farm land is startlingly low, although accurate figures on either the amount of farm land in the *municipio* or the amount owned by any individual were impossible to secure. The tax rolls of the town are an inadequate guide. A very large number of lands are not listed and in many cases the area given is much smaller than actual size. A number of farmers admitted this fact. The tax rolls show only 303 farmers, although most men in town own some land. The total parcels listed number 759 with a total area of 1,943½ hectares (a hectare is 2.47 acres) with a value of $259,620. Community-owned lands are listed as 1,667 hectares valued at $100,000. This would total slightly less than 9,000 acres, or about 14 square miles. This is probably less than half the total area of Cherán.

The average holding according to the tax rolls is 2.5 pieces of land, totaling 6.41 hectares valued at $856.86. This average is misleading, however, possibly through an error on the part of the tax collector's office staff, or perhaps because a few large landowners hold high-priced lands. From $80 to $100 per hectare is the most common valuation. An average of one page of the tax roll listing 58 farmers gave 2.62 plots per person, averaging 5.1 hectares valued at $377.07 or $74 a hectare. The largest holding on this page was 32 hectares, valued at $2,560; the smallest was one-half a hectare, valued at $50. Bearing in mind that these figures represent taxable values, actual values probably average around $150 a hectare.

Data from individuals probably are even more unreliable, yet show surprising uniformity. The average value is $77.08 per hectare, Estimates from six landowners are as follows:

Area (hectares)	Value
2	$140
4	350
16	1,280
½	40
14	1,080
8	640
44½	$3,530

The surprising closeness of owner evaluations to the average assessed values suggests that farmers are well aware of the latter. Information from more individuals is desirable but is difficult to obtain. Even good friends normally either refuse information or obviously lie about the size and value of their holdings. The only further evidence available on this point is an actual sale observed in which a price of $40 was paid for about one-half hectare of wheat land. This piece was already planted to wheat and would yield about 2 *cargas*. On the other hand, $400 was being asked for a hectare of the best maize land.

Residential lands almost always include a garden plot as well as a building site. Only in the center of town is this not true. Prices of residential land, however, vary sharply with location and, to a lesser extent, with the depth of the lot and the quality of soil. In the center of town shallow lots may be valued at as much as $25 a meter frontage, while on the outskirts the price may be as low as $10 a meter. The garden plot produces blue maize, vegetables, fruit, and sometimes wheat. Probably a number of persons who were said to own land in Cherán actually own only a large residential plot, but this point was not investigated.

Forest lands are owned by the community. They serve as the source of firewood, lumber, and other forest products such as shakes and charcoal, and provide grazing for livestock; as sources of game or wild vegetable products their value is negligible.

The use of forest lands formerly was open to all who paid a small fee to aid the community to pay the Federal taxes on the land. Persons using the forest only for firewood paid less than did charcoal burners, lumbermen, or shakemakers. In recent years a permit from the Federal Department of Forestry has been required for any but household use, and efforts were being made to limit rights to members of a cooperative organization.

LABOR

The sex division of labor in Cherán bars women from most productive pursuits. Women's activities conform closely to the ideals laid down recently by a notorious central European —children, kitchen, and church. Women perform all the household duties, such as cooking, sweeping, and washing, care for the children, make most of the clothes, carry water (but not firewood unless they have no close male relatives), and take food to their men at work.

They may gather herbs, make embroidered women's garments or paper flowers for sale, do the marketing for the household, and also most of the selling. If a woman's husband hires out as a laborer during harvest time, she gleans behind him in the field. There is no strong feeling against a woman who in emergency helps at her husband's work; but women actually have very little spare time.

Most productive activity in the ordinary sense, then, is performed by men. Men do all farm work, look after animals for the most part, do all forestry, and make most of the manufactured articles that enter into commerce. Distant trade is also carried on by men, although they may be accompanied by their wives, and women may go to Paracho or even Uruapan to sell herbs, fruit, vegetables, bread, tamales, or other prepared foods.

The bulk of the population of Cherán falls into two overlapping classes, farmers and laborers. Only a small minority utilize all their labor on their own land; even smaller is the number of farmers who employ no labor. Farmers, furthermore, may be divided into landowners and tenant farmers.

Farmers may also be storekeepers, traders, forest workers, or artisans in their spare time. In addition, they may hire out as laborers when they have free time. Indeed, most laborers have land or at least a garden plot. The labor supply of Cherán, in fact, is inadequate, and laborers are hired from neighboring villages, especially Nahuatzen. The standard wages are 45 centavos a day, but harvest hands receive 50 centavos a day plus the right to have their wives and children glean behind them, apparently a not insignificant factor, as the proposal of several large landowners to raise the harvest wage to $1 a day and eliminate the gleaning privilege was rejected by the workmen. Variations in wages are discussed in connection with specific activities.

Bearing in mind that most men have some land, the list of occupations in Cherán is extensive, as shown in the following tabulation:

PRODUCTIVE OCCUPATIONS

Men

Farming
Hired labor
Shoemaking (few)
Hat making (few)
Plank making
Shake making
Cutting railroad ties
Charcoal burning
Blanket weaving (few)
Broom-handle making (rare)
Gathering *raiz de paja* (few)
Wild-honey collecting (few)
Bee keeping (few—one woman)
Baking bread (one making *pan dulce*)
Ice cream making (one)
Brickmaking and tilemaking (rare)
Carpentry (few)
Wood turning (rare)
Blacksmithing (rare)
Masonry (few)
Brush making (few)
Painting and plastering (rare)
Fireworks making (one)
Tailoring
Twine making (few)

Women

Embroidering
Belt weaving (few)
Paper-flower making (rare)
Herb gathering (rare)
Gleaning
Cloth weaving (one)
Baking bread
Tailoring
Mat making (rare)

DISTRIBUTIVE OCCUPATIONS

Men

Storekeeping
Trading
Selling at markets
Butchering
Transport

Women

Storekeeping (helpers)
Local food selling
Selling at markets

SERVICE OCCUPATIONS

Men

Grain threshing
Operating *nixtamal* mills
Barbering (few)
School teaching (few)
Billiard-hall operation (two)
Marriage managing (few)
Water carrying for pay (rare)
All political offices[1]
All formal church offices[1]
All public works[1]
Mayordomías[1]
Musician
Rezadores (men who pray)

Ritual dancing[1]
Sorcery

Women

Midwifery
Domestic service (rare)
Curing
School teaching (rare)
Minor church services[1]
Ritual dancing (pastorela only[1])
Sorcery

[1] Occupations without pay; some involving outlay of money to participate. Women's household duties are not listed. Elsewhere the distribution of women's time is discussed (p. 197).

Information from day laborers on the whole was unsatisfactory. Not only are they sensitive about their position, but there is some condescension toward them on the part of landowners despite the lack of explicitly drawn class lines. When an older man jestingly suggested that one of our local assistants should get in practice to carry a harvest basket, the young man replied that he didn't intend to carry a harvest basket, or plow either. "That is what you have *peons* for," he said.

Information about day laborers indicated a return of from 40 to 50 centavos a day, depending on season and labor. Some workers also do work by the job. Men employed to thresh wheat will sometimes get about 1½ centavos a liter. The most accurate-sounding informant, a man from Nahuatzen, estimated he could thresh 80 liters a day, a return of about $1.20 a day. This seems high, but one informant produced estimates which would have him earning $25 a day.[21]

Unemployment for laborers usually comes about the same time as the slack season for farmers, January and July. Often workers will take a vacation in this period. The more energetic will seek work at this time—bring in building stones, work in the woods, try for odd jobs about town, bring in firewood for themselves or for sale, or fatten a pig for sale. One of the storekeepers evidently will pay $2.50 a dozen for building stones delivered at his store for later resale. Pine firewood can be sold usually at four sticks for 1 centavo, oak at three sticks for 1 centavo.

[21] In Angáhuan, Rendón found similar situations. Building fences pays 50 centavos a day without meals. Other field work, however, is never paid in money. Harvest workers receive three *medidas* of maize, and breakfast and dinner. Ox-team drivers receive two *medidas* of maize and meals.

Low as wages are, Rendón collected an account which indicates that wages were only 12 centavos a day within the lifetime of elderly men. The informant stated that he preferred to work at Nahuatzen because meals were included in the wage, which is not the case in Cherán. This requires verification, as Nahuatzen normally has a larger labor supply than Cherán.

In addition to paid labor or labor for one's own account, men are required to perform certain public services. These include maintenance of the aqueduct and improvement of roads and trails. Young men may also be required to do certain work in connection with fiestas, particularly the fiesta of the patron saint and the Day of the Dead. There is also obligatory assistance of relatives in connection with ceremonials and house moving. These requirements are dealt with later.

No data were secured on the relation between labor demand and labor supply. As indicated by the presence of labor from other towns at some seasons, it is believed that at peak periods there is an undersupply of labor in the town. Much of the year, however, there probably is a labor surplus in the sense that many farmers often have time free which they could use in some other employment were it readily available.

CAPITAL

Efforts to define capital for Cherán meet with the same difficulties that are to be met with in our own society. Money used for purchasing food ordinarily is not considered capital; yet insofar as it makes the individual capable of producing additional goods or services through which his wealth is increased, such money, or stores of food accumulated for this purpose, might be considered capital. Money accumulated to buy land for the production of food for sale or export would usually be considered capital; is the land purchased to be so considered also? In the case of Cherán, I think it is, for, although most farmers would not so regard it, a considerable number of Cherán men have bought land for the express purpose of increasing wealth, not through their own efforts, but through those of a tenant farmer.

Ownership of livestock similarly poses questions. The wealthy man who keeps a considerable number of bulls whose main use seems to be to enhance his social prestige by having the bulls selected for riding at a fiesta may also sell them for beef if he needs money for productive enterprises. Sheep are capital in much the same sense that land is capital. A yoke of oxen or a burro may be used to aid production and are also rented. A horse, on the other hand, is close to a "conspicuous expenditure."

Probably the minimal capital required in Cherán is for the production of certain services. A water carrier needs only two 25-liter oil cans, a bit of rope, and a piece of wood to make a yoke. A *tabla* maker (one producing heavy hewn planks or beams) needs only an ax and some oak wedges he cuts out himself, and 10 pesos to join the cooperative (formerly he would have needed only enough to pay the tax for use of communal lands). A digging stick and a knife would suffice to gather *raiz de paja*, while herbs need only a bit of cloth to tie them in. At the other extreme are the owners of threshing machines, *nixtamal* mills, or trucks, the latter requiring a cash outlay of between 8 and 10 thousand pesos.

For the farmer, aside from land, very few capital goods are necessary. Ox teams and plows may be rented and paid for out of the crop; even land may be secured on a sharecrop basis. A special *machete* for weeding is, in fact, the only indispensable tool. Such farming, however, will bring a relatively small return, probably little, if any, more than could be earned by a hired laborer.

At the other extreme, a landowner, farming his own land, should own an ox team, yoke, plow, *machete*, burros, and nets for transporting the crop, adequate storage facilities, and sufficient cash to hire labor at crucial periods such as planting and harvesting. A man so situated will reap the best possible return from his labor.

The major investment of a farmer is in land, storage facilities, and livestock. His ox yoke and plow he may make himself, and the few metal tools needed are not costly. In general, the investment in tools and equipment is much less than that required in manufacturing or some service occupations. A sewing machine is more costly than all the farmer's tools, especially the heavy type required to make hats. Even the sandal maker's lasts, hammers, and knives probably are more expensive than farm equipment.

CREDIT, LOANS, AND INTEREST

No organized credit facilities exist in the village, but money loans are sometimes made. Storekeepers are perhaps the only group who consistently make use of credit and who also often make loans if they have capital. The major use of credit by storekeepers is to buy goods, especially cloth. Sometimes a down payment is made on cloth, the balance being paid when the cloth is sold. This facility seems to be extended primarily by wholesalers in Purépero. Most ordinary store transactions, whether buying or selling, are for cash.

One storekeeper also makes cash loans, mainly to butchers and *nixtamal* operators, who are apt to need considerable sums for a short time. The reported interest rate is 10 percent a month.

Other credit transactions are of two kinds. Most significant is the lending of money for which lands are given as security, known as the *empeño de terrenos*. In this type of transaction, the lender takes possession of the lands and utilizes them until the debt is repaid. The owner in the meantime must pay all taxes on the land. In other cases the lender does not take possession of the lands unless the debt is not repaid at the end of a term agreed upon. In either case, should the land have a standing crop at the time the lender takes possession, the crop is divided equally between the borrower and lender. There are some cases, although relatively few compared with the situation in many parts of Mexico, where lands have been held and cultivated by the lender for many years.[22] The owners have been unable to pay the debt but have continued year after year paying the taxes, in hopes ultimately of redeeming the land.

---

[22] In some parts of Mexico this is an extremely common form of exploitation. I have been told of regions where families have acquired control of large areas by encouraging small landowners to go into debt to them. The lenders have, in effect, established *haciendas*, but have been overlooked in the general agrarian reforms because the lands appear on the government records as belonging to numerous small owners. Often, ironically enough, the landowners are hired laborers working their own property in a futile effort to redeem their debts, but they never succeed in doing more than maintaining a large estate tax-free for the wealthy *hacendado*.

In addition to the above-described types of loans, there are also loans at interest for which normally no security is offered. These loans are usually made by persons within the village and rarely exceed $100 in amount. Interest is normally 10 percent per annum. In some cases it is stipulated that the debt is to be canceled upon the death of the debtor. In other instances the debt becomes a charge against the estate of the debtor. If the possessions of the debtor at death are insufficient to pay the debt, it is not transmitted to his sons. However, according to Pedro Chávez, the sons probably would make every effort to pay such a debt because of the strongly held belief that a person dying with debts cannot rest in peace until the debts are paid.

All transactions involving loans are in writing, although they are not registered at the *municipio.*

COSTS OF PRODUCTION AND INCOME

Some further insight into production problems may be gained by detailed studies of specific activities. These data throw light upon the relative profitability of such activities and also provide information on income. Not all activities are covered in the ensuing discussion, nor are the data equally reliable in each category. Such activities as witchcraft or midwifery are not included; the labor factor in beekeeping or fruit growing is impossible to ascertain. An activity followed by only a few individuals merits less attention than one followed by many.

Not only is the treatment of topics uneven, but the income data are subject to misinterpretation. It must be emphasized that virtually no one in Cherán, except a few "rich" farmers or storekeepers, has only one occupation. Consequently, any effort to establish annual income on the basis of figures in this section would be grossly misleading. Finally, it should be noted that not all the activities discussed below are productive. Because of the problem of income, I have considered a number of "service" occupations in this section.

AGRICULTURE

Maize.—Data on farm production were difficult to obtain. On no other subject is there so much secrecy or misleading information given. Three sources of information were used: (1) Data from farmers about their own activities. All this information is suspect, even after eliminating obviously false answers. (2) Data from Agustín Rangel, who was interested in establishing himself as a farmer and probably was a good and relatively unbiased observer. (3) Observation of farm practices and participation in harvests on roughly measured fields. Actual measurement of fields was undesirable and would have caused trouble.

In table 1 are given the various data collected on farm yields. The average of figures given by farmers is about the top figure given by Rangel for average land in a poor year. It is slightly above the figure for the yield of average land in a poor year as secured by participation in the harvest. The cross checks suggest the figures given by farmers are on the whole plausible although probably low. The figures given by any individual farmer, however, may be quite incorrect. This should be borne in mind throughout the discussion.

TABLE 1.—*Estimates of maize yields in Cherán*

ESTIMATE BY OWNERS

Number of hectares cultivated	Yield (per hectare) in—		Value of crop
	Cargas	*Fanegas*	
2½	40	30	....
10½[1]	180	135	....
⅑	[2]7	5¼	....
½[3]	20	15	$90–110
¼[3]	10	7½	60– 70
⅛[3]	5	3¾	25
½[3]	10	7½	65
¼[3] (early-frost area)	3	2¼	15
4	90	70	350–400
1	10	7½	40
1½	10	7½	40
½	12	9	55
½	12	9	55
Average	...	14⅗	....

ESTIMATE BY AGUSTÍN RANGEL

Type of land and year	Average yield per hectare	
	Cargas	*Fanegas*
Best land:		
Average year	40	30
Bad year	15–25	11¼–18¾
Average land:		
Average year	30	22½
Bad year	5–20	3¾–15
Poor land	.....	1½

[1] An exceptionally rich "joya," a fertile depression in the mountains fertilized by drainage from surrounding slopes.

[2] This is a stupendous yield, if true, but the land is said to be exceptionally located, with fertilization from adjoining slopes.

[3] Data in this line are typical of information from owners. One area given as ½ hectare yields a crop to be expected of a full hectare; on inspection, it proved to be nearly 3 hectares.

TABLE 1.—*Estimates of maize yields in Cherán*—Continued

ESTIMATE BASED ON OBSERVATIONS AT HARVEST

Type of land	Yield in *fanegas* per hectare	Remarks
Poor to average land........	3	Maize badly damaged by early frost.
Average land..............	12	Maize slightly damaged by frost.

In addition to securing data on yield, i.e., income, for maize, an effort was made to secure data on production costs. General statements as to the amount of time put in on farm work proved worthless. Usually the time given would scarcely provide for a single weeding. The best figures were secured by breaking down the different steps and getting experienced farmers to estimate the time necessary for cultivating 1 hectare. A summary of such data gives the following:

Labor of owner:

	Days
First plowing	10
Second plowing (at right angles)	10
Sowing..................................	3
First cultivation (with plow)	4
Second cultivation (with plow)	3
First weeding (with sickle or machete)	3
Second weeding (often omitted)	3
Harvest..................................	1
Carrying maize to house (estimated average)	5
Total	42

Hired labor:

Sowing (2 peons)........................	3
Harvesting (3 peons)	1

Costs:

Owner's labor (42 days valued at $0.45 a day outside of planting and harvesting time)	$18.90
2 peons for 3 days.....................	3.00
3 peons for 1 day......................	1.50
Total	$23.40

On the assumption that a man will own sufficient land to require hired labor, the summary given above includes 9 man days of hired labor at a cost of $4.50 or a total of 51 man days of labor worth $23.40. To this must be added $30 for hire of an ox team if one is not owned, probably $1 in taxes, and $2.50 for the value of the seed corn (one-half *fanega*), or a total of $56.90. If this is about an average piece of land, the yield will be 15 to 20 *fanegas* of shelled maize, for which the farmer should receive from $75 to $120, or a profit of $22.10 to $63.10. From this, in theory, should be deducted interest on the investment in land and equipment as well as a depreciation allowance on the equipment. If the land is worth $90 (above average), it would seem fair to allow at least $11 for these charges, which still leaves a profit of $11.10 to $52.10.[23]

As will be seen in later discussions, this makes maize farming on average or better land probably one of the most worth-while businesses in Cherán. Obviously there are elements of risk. Farmers on poor land, moreover, probably get no profits at all on this basis, for labor and expenses would be reduced very little relative to reductions in yield. The second weeding and part of the harvesting expenses might be eliminated. But if the yield is as low as 1½ *fanegas* (as has been reported) a man would get virtually no return at all. If he had his own ox team and did all his own work (with the help of sons or his wife), he might get $4 to $5 worth of maize for his effort after deducting the costs of seed and taxes. From the standpoint of our economy, there is obviously a very considerable net loss.

To view the agricultural situation in Cherán only from the standpoint of our economy, however, would be grossly misleading, for to do so does not take into account numerous cultural factors. The Cherán point of view does not reckon agricultural activity in terms of interest, profits, and wages, but in terms of maize in the storage house. I have already mentioned that harvest workers refused an increase in wages from 50 centavos to $1 if the right to glean were rescinded. Most observers agree that the amount of maize obtained from gleaning in a day is less than can be bought for 50 centavos. At $1 the workman could therefore buy more corn than his wife could obtain by gleaning. The large farmers would get a more thorough harvest and would not have to employ supervisors. On a bookkeeping basis, everyone would benefit. But the harvest hand would not have a load of maize, small though it might be, to carry home from a day's work; he would have only an inedible silver peso in his pocket.

[23] Charges for animals to carry the crop and for watchmen and storage facilities are not included.

In the case of the farmer who slaves at producing a scanty crop on submarginal land, similar considerations are important. The farmer does not count interest and wages; the measure of his effort is maize in the storehouse to feed his wife and children. It is useless to point out that he could earn enough wages for the same amount of labor to buy two or three times as much maize as he can produce, for he will not be convinced.

Even in the case of the average or somewhat better than average case cited in detail, the calculations made on the basis of our economic viewpoints are relatively valueless. Profits, interest, depreciation, and wages do not enter into the farmer's calculation (with the exception of a few large farmers). Rather would the typical farmer calculate that the maize obtained in this case would, with a family of not over five, feed the family for a year by exercising due care. If he had two pieces, each of a hectare or a little more in area, in two locations to plant alternate years, he could count with some security on feeding his family. If, in addition, he had a bit of wheatland, he would probably sell enough wheat to meet the essential cash outlays for his family. Any income from livestock, work in the forest, or as a hired laborer would then go into essentially luxury spending or savings to buy more land. It is wheat that is a money crop, it should be noted, and not maize. Only the wealthy sell maize, and only the poor or improvident buy it.

In case maize is raised for sale on any scale, however, the farmer encounters new marketing problems. The local market prefers yellow maize, as does Mestizo Purépero. Uruapan, on the other hand, prefers white maize, while the Lake Pátzcuaro region desires pink, red, or mixed color maize. As prices may vary in the different major markets, the farmer's income may be affected by the color of maize he has grown.

From the statements given above it should not be concluded that the idea of a return for land ownership, i.e., a return upon the capital investment, is lacking in Cherán. It exists, but it is colored by the local attitudes. Thus, farmers with more land than they can conveniently cultivate, storekeepers owning land, and various others may rent land on a share-cropping basis. The number of sharecroppers in Cherán is unknown, but probably is considerable. Small landowners often farm additional lands on this basis, and some fairly prosperous families are sharecroppers.

The rental paid by sharecroppers is usually one-half the crop. In the case of our average hectare this would mean the owner received 7½ to 10 *fanegas* of maize worth from $37.50 to $60.00. This might well be equal to more than a 50 percent return on the investment in land. As even the most exorbitant interest rates on cash loans from banks would not exceed 15 percent, it would appear to be a very good business to borrow money to buy land for rental on a sharecropping basis. Yet such a procedure, so far as could be discovered, is seldom if ever followed. Moreover, persons with money will lend on land as a security, receiving only interest, instead of buying land which would appear to offer a relatively larger return. (But short-term loans are at a much higher rate of interest. See p. 63.)

A number of factors still have not been treated in the foregoing discussion. It should be observed that the hypothetical farmer could still further decrease his cash outlay if he owned his own ox team. Such a team would be worth from $100 to $120, depending on size. Ownership of a team would save about $30 a year in rental in cultivating a hectare. In addition, there might be opportunities to rent the team at $1 a day for perhaps 30 days to work on maize lands and perhaps for another 30 days during the wheat season. As there is less demand in the latter time, the rental probably would be only 75 centavos a day. The returns from rentals, however, would possibly be $52.50 a year. If the saving of $30 for rentals on the farmer's own land were included the investment in an ox team obviously would be a very good one.

Ownership of livestock, however, involves the problem of feed. Mostly the feed is secured by cutting the *rastrojo* or corn fodder. Wheat straw is also fed. Part of the year animals may be grazed on the common pastures. Rarely, however, is enough feed produced, and in a bad year there is always danger of losing animals during the latter part of the dry season. Ownership of oxen also increases the amount of labor. Not only must *rastrojo* be cut, but the animals must be visited every 2 or 3 days while in pasture.

The question may be raised why horses or mules have not replaced oxen to any extent. Although horses or mules will do at least twice the amount of work in a day, owing to their greater speed and ability to work longer hours, they do not thrive on the corn fodder, wheat straw, and scanty pasturage. Grain feed is also necessary, at least during the working season. In general, horses and mules are more delicate and require more attention, greater skill, and better shelter. Finally, their initial cost is greater and they cannot be slaughtered for meat, as are oxen, when they have outlived their usefulness as draft animals.

Wheat.—Although wheat is the primary cash crop of Cherán, it is seldom grown on lands which will produce good maize. Wheat is often grown on inferior land, often on slopes, but never on really bad lands. Farmers using good land for wheat usually have a surplus of maize lands.

The cultivation of wheat takes a little less labor than does that of maize. Plowing is the same or perhaps a little less (the second plowing being shallower). Broadcasting of seed and harrowing equate with maize planting, but it is a one-man job and requires no oxen if the farmer owns a burro. The primitive harvesting with a sickle would seem to call for more labor, but estimates were fairly low. A summary of estimates for cultivating a hectare follows:

Labor:	Days
First plowing	10
Second plowing	10
Sowing and harrowing.	2 (or less)
Harvesting.	4½
Total labor	26½

Costs:	
Labor (26½ days at $0.45, value)	$11.92
Rent of oxen (20 days at $0.75, value)	15.00
Taxes.	1.00
Seed	1.00
Total production costs.	$28.92
Interest on capital investment	11.00
Total cost of cultivation. . . .	$39.92

The best wheatland produces about 2 *cargas* of wheat per hectare; lands producing less than 1½ cargas are seldom cultivated. The wheat must then be threshed before sale, and this will cost $2.50 a *carga* in the mill and about the same if threshed by hand. The wheat will sell at from $22 to $30 a *carga*, depending upon the market ($26 in 1941).

The return in cash, then, is between $33 (1½ *cargas* at $22) and $60 (2 *cargas* at $30). The net profit in terms of our calculations would vary between minus $10.67 and plus $15.08. This figure does not count the labor of carrying the wheat to the house and thence to the mill, or winnowing; neither does it include the value of the straw (used as feed). Again, however, the Cherán farmer who received $33 for his year's work on a *hectare* would count himself relatively fortunate.

The return from wheat is less than the potential return from maize cultivation on average land. In general, however, wheat is usually grown on lands giving a poor maize yield. Moreover, the demand for wheat appears to be more stable, and in days when transport was all on pack animals the greater value of wheat per volume and weight made it much more attractive as an export crop. The opening of the highway may alter the situation, as it makes bulk transportation of maize feasible. On the other hand, the highway has opened up new markets for wheat. Trucks from the large flour mill at Morelia now come to buy wheat in Cherán and even penetrate to mountain villages such as Pichataro. Consequently, a much wider market is available than the regional mills that could be reached in a day or a little more with burros. Of course, similar expansion of markets is available to maize growers and producers of other products. It is still too early to predict the effects of improved communications on the agriculture of Cherán, but some additional considerations are discussed in connection with trade.

Another way of disposing of wheat is to sell it at a flour mill in a Mestizo town or convert the wheat into flour and sell the flour. The price paid at flour mills is about $4 a *carga* above the Cherán price. Mills charge an 18 percent discount if the farmer chooses to have his wheat milled. This covers waste, bad wheat, and the milling charge. A *carga* produces about 14 *arrobas,* or about 250 pounds of flour, of which the mill takes 2½ *arrobas,* or 62½ pounds. The farmer receives 187½ pounds of flour. Either of these procedures involves the labor of transporting wheat to the mill and, in case the farmer has no burros, the rent of pack animals or trucking charges. Mills are at Jacona (regarded as the best), Purépero, Tanátaro, and Carapan.

Yet another way of disposing of wheat is to grind it at home or in a *nixtamal* mill and bake bread for sale in the market towns and at fiestas. Only relatively small quantities are used in this way.

One agricultural activity for which few data were obtained is fruit growing. No information was secured on yields of trees or on labor. The main labor cost is harvesting, usually done by the family at a time when there is little other agricultural activity. Fruit may be carried to markets, or it may be sold to traders.

Another view of farming activity may be gained by examining the income of individual farmers. These data are probably somewhat unreliable, for, as previously indicated, there is a tendency to minimize wealth and income. Table 2 summarizes the available information.

Case 1 is a school teacher with a small family who rents his land. Probably his share in good years supplies most of his family requirements of maize. Case 2 is a storekeeper who also rents his land. In years when his land lies fallow, he must have to buy a little

maize. Case 3 owns a store run by his children, but he regards himself as a farmer by preference. Even without his store, he would be well off by Cherán standards, although not a "rich man." In 1940 he produced nearly enough maize for his family and sold over $300 worth of wheat. In 1941 he probably was able to sell not less than 35 *fanegas* of maize above his family's food needs (less if he raised pigs or fattened beef for butchering). Case 4 is a widow. Her land is cultivated by a nephew, but under what circumstances is not known. If the nephew lives with her, the amount of maize is a little inadequate; on the other hand, if she lives alone, the quantity is more than enough for one person.

ANIMAL HUSBANDRY

It is virtually impossible to secure useful data on labor costs or profits in relation to animals. Under agriculture I have mentioned some of the facts about oxen. No data were collected on chicken raising; probably no one in Cherán knows how much grain he feeds chickens or how many eggs a year he gets. Prices vary from 2 to 6 centavos per egg. The situation about pigs is little better.

Virtually everyone keeps pigs; no one has any idea of the total amount of grain fed except during the fattening period. Shoats have little value and are frequently given away. Data on labor are lacking, yet the labor cost cannot be negligible when the animal is being fattened and its pen is cleaned frequently. A

TABLE 2.—*Data on farm income*

[Data for 1940, claimed; for 1941, estimated.]

Case No.	Land cultivated			Yield			Value of crop[1]		Total income for year		Combined income for 1940–41
	Number of parcels	Number of hectares	Value	Crop	1940	1941	1940	1941	1940	1941	
1[2]	2	2	$140	Maize	20 fanegas......	....	$100–140	....	$100–140	....	} $150–240
	1	....		do	....	10–15 fanegas...	....	50–100	....	50–100	
2[2]	1	4	350	Maize	35 fanegas......	....	175–200	....	175–200	....	175–200
	1	Town lot	....	Pears	10–100's........	8–100's........	....	....	....	....	
3	1	8		Wheat	17½ cargas.....	....	[3]358–571				
	1	1		Maize	7½ fanegas....	....	40	}	448–561	....	
	1	1½	1,280	do	7½ fanegas....	....	40				} 733–1,231
	1	Town lot[4]		Peaches	25–100's........	25–100's........	10	10			
	1	5½		Maize	....	55–110 fanegas...	....	275–660	....	} 285–670	
4	1	½		Wheat	1 carga.......	....	25				
	1	½	120	Maize	9 fanegas......	....	55	....	} 80	....	} 135
	1	½		do	....	9 fanegas......	....	55	....	55	

[1] Values of fodder or wheat straw not included.
[2] Land rented; crop values represent owner's share (one-half).
[3] Cost of threshing deducted.
[4] Value not included in $1,280.

pig takes from 1 to 2½ *fanegas* of maize to fatten, valued at from $5 to $7. According to size, the animal may bring from $30 to $75, a gross profit on the fattening process of from $12.50 to $70.00. This would be 5 to 7 pesos less if the pig was bought. If an adequate market were developed, or if sales and transport facilities at a distance were to be developed, pig raising might be a more important activity, although an increase in the number of pigs would decrease the amount of foraging possible and would require more feeding.

Sheep raising is engaged in by only a few. The reliability of the major informants is suspect, but the evidence suggests that sheep raising is profitable. The major expense is the initial cost of the flock and the wages of a shepherd. Sheep are worth $2.50 to $5.00 apiece. Shepherds' wages vary with the size of the flock, but probably rarely exceed $20 a month plus a *fanega* of maize and one sheep for food; most shepherds receive considerably less, often only $5 a month without food. Often several small owners merge their flocks and hire a single shepherd.

Income from sheep is mainly from wool and payments to have the flocks bedded on farm land. Sheep average a pound of wool a year (this seems low but the sheep are of poor quality), which sells for $1 to $1.25. A fair-size flock of sheep would bring 50 centavos a night for fertilizer. A few sheep are sold for meat outside the village; almost no lamb or mutton is eaten in Cherán. No data were secured on prices. Mortality on sheep is high, but again no usable data were obtainable.

A flock of 200 sheep studied represents an investment of $750 in theory although it probably was built up by natural increase from a smaller flock. The shepherd receives $20 a month, 1 *fanega* of maize worth at least $5, and a sheep worth, on an average, $3.75, or a total of $28.75 a month ($345 a year). Wool would produce $200 to $250 a year. Bedding on farm lands would produce probably 50 centavos a night for this flock for 110 days (estimated) or $55. Total income from these sources would be $255 to $305 a year. The natural increase may safely be assumed to be 75 head. Sold at $2.50 apiece, they would bring in $187.50 a year, or a total of $442.50 to $492.50 a year. Deducting expenses of $345 leaves a return on the investment of $107.50 to $147.50. As indicated before, these figures are suspect. The owner of this flock is not believed to be very truthful on financial matters. For example, he claimed to own 20 sheep; Augustín Rangel said he had over 200. He is, though, a hard-headed storekeeper and farmer who would not keep sheep if they were not profitable. The most suspect item in the calculations is the amount of wool per sheep.

The evaluation of the role of the burro is as difficult as in the case of oxen. Burros reduce the cost of numerous operations by saving the rental of animals, they facilitate such tasks as bringing in wood (which otherwise would be carried in by the woodcutter rather than on rented animals), and they may be rented. Burros involve little investment—$30 to $40—but they do require attention while in pasture and the provision of feed when kept at home. Although burros not in use are often lent, they sometimes are rented. Information on rentals is contradictory; at the harvest season, when demand is highest, rentals are probably about 50 centavos a day plus feed for the animals.

The ensuing topics are dealt with in summary form to bring out the essential factors of capital, labor costs, cost of materials, and income.

WOODWORKING

Shake making:
> Tools:
>> Ax, wedges, machete, splitting tool
> Product:
>> ½ irepita (an irepita, or bundle, is 400)
>> a day at.......................... $5.00
> *Profits* (return on labor, less interest on
>> capital, etc.) $2.50

Comment: Shake making is a well-paying occupation, but profits are less than the data above suggest. Shakes are made either only to order or are sold in Uruapan or some other Mestizo center. In the latter case the man may work regularly, but must spend 1 or 2 days a week taking his product to market. Neither does the estimated result for a day's labor include the time spent searching for a suitable tree. Usually only a 5-day week or less is worked and the season is confined to the rainy period. As a result, shake makers must shift to other work, such as plank making, tie cutting, farming, etc. The term "profits" is loosely used throughout, as wages are often included.

Plank making:
   Tools:
      Oak mallet
      Oak wedges
      Ax
      Two-handled saw
   Expenses:
      Haulage (ox team, horse, or even burros)
      Forest use tax (now 10 pesos for membership
        in cooperative)
   Production (with good workmen):
      3 dozen planks per week
   Gross profits:
      $0.85 to 1.25 per day per person

Comment: Sawing planks requires two men, hence work is done by teams. The gross profits probably are very nearly all net, as deterioration of equipment is slight. Maintaining an average income of the larger size indicated would require 6 long work days a week for the most skilled workers.

Firewood cutting:
   Some men at times cut firewood for sale. A burro load brings $0.25 to $0.30.

Tie cutting:
   Data on this subject seem unreliable and are omitted.

Charcoal burning:
   Beyond the fact that charcoal burners work a 5-day week, no economic data were secured. The little charcoal used in Cherán is sold at 2½ to 3 centavos a kilo delivered.

Carpentry:
   Tools:
      Mallet, saw, chisels, hammer, ax, adz, plane;
        value about $20–$30
   Products, labor, value:
      As each carpenter's job is unique, only a series
        of cases can be given, as follows:

(a) Large door takes 4 days (10 to 12 hours daily), lumber cost $4, selling price $17, gross profit $13, daily return (not allowing for interest on capital, etc.) $4.25.

(b) Average door takes 4 days (6 to 7 hours daily) lumber cost $4, selling price $12, gross profit $8, daily return $2.

(c) Average door takes 6 days (but this carpenter has rheumatism and cannot work steadily), selling price $5 a door if lumber is furnished, daily return less than $1.

(d) House building or house moving, $1.50 daily (if done under contract, as usual).

Comment: As only carpenters with other members in the family to get wood, do chores, look after animals, etc. can work more than 6 or 7 hours a day, probably $2 a day is top income. Moreover, as work is not steady and as all seem eager to take house building or house moving jobs at $1.50, it may be assumed that average wages the year around are less than $1.50.

Wood turning:
   Equipment:
      Lathes
      Saws
      Chisels
   Product:
      Chocolate beaters
   Cost of materials:
      No data; the small quantity of madroña
        wood used is probably a minor factor.
   Labor:
      About 25 to 30 beaters are made in a day's
        work. Sale price at 50 centavos per
        dozen.........................$1–$1.25

Comment: Considering the costs of materials and the time involved in selling the product, returns for labor probably are under $1 a day. Only one man in Cherán follows this trade.

MINERAL PROCESSING AND USE

Brickmaking and tilemaking:
   Labor (per 1,000 tile or brick):

	Days
Getting and mixing clay	2
Cutting and hauling wood	1
Shaping	5
Loading kiln	1
Total	9

   Other costs (in kind):
      Rent of building and right to dig clay on
        public lands (paid to *municipio*), 10 per-
        cent of product value:

Tile, per 1,000	$3.00
Brick, per 1,000	3.20

   Sales prices:

Tile, per 1,000	$30
Brick, per 1,000	32
Gross profit, tile, per 1,000	27
Daily profit per worker	3

Comment: While brick bring a slightly higher price, there is a greater loss in firing. Consequently, profits are about the same as for tile. The demand for brick or tile is not sufficient to employ two men full time. The wage return is hence misleading, indicating what might be possible if demand provided steady labor. The fact that both tilemakers took jobs on highway construction crews whenever possible at $1 a day suggests that income over a long period of time is much less than is indicated. On the other hand, the tilemakers probably average a higher annual income than do unskilled landless farm laborers in Cherán.

Masonry:
   Equipment:
      Trowel ("*cuchara*")
      Short shovel
      ½-pound iron mallet ("*marro,*" maso)
      2-pound sledge with pointed ends ("*picadera*")

Production:

Less than 1 meter to nearly 2 meters a day

Price:

From 80 centavos a meter to $1.25; about $1 a meter seemed most common

Average return:

From 80 centavos to $1.50 seems common

Comment: Essentially the mason's wage is clear profit. Replacement of tools is undoubtedly a minor factor. Attractive as the wage is, a mason is idle much of the time. It is doubtful if masons earn enough to live on without also farming or working as laborers. Some masons are also butchers, plasterers, or *tejamanil* makers.

Stonecutting:

Tools:

2-pound iron mallet
Chisels
Calipers (value unknown)

Labor:

Nixtamal grinding stones (pair) ... 3 days
Door bases (pair) .... 1 week

Sales price (gross profit):

Nixtamal grinding stones (pair) $9
Door bases and sills (each) 10

Comment: The figures suggest a $3 a day gross income, but stonecutters work only to order and do not work regularly.

TEXTILE MANUFACTURE

Tule mats:

Costs:

Tules at Erongaricuaro, per bundle $0.25
Rent of burro, 3 days 1.00
Total cost of 10 bundles of tules (1 burro load) 3.50

Labor:

	Days
Getting tules	3
Weaving 13 mats	6½
Selling mats	2½–3
Average total time	12

Sales price at 60 centavos each $7.80
Gross profit 4.30
Daily profit per worker .... .35 plus

Comment: Except for one woman, mat making is a side line and only one a day is woven. The figures given above represent the single case where a woman spends all her time at mat weaving. Actually, this woman has a slightly higher income, as her mother buys the tules. On the other hand, two people are supported by the work, for the weaver has to rely on the mother to perform most of the household duties.

Hats:

Cost of materials:

Braid, 3 to 4 bundles at $0.30 to $0.40
.... $0.90–$1.60
Thread, per hat .... .15
Sizing materials for white hats .... Unknown

Total .... 1.05–1.75 (?)

Labor, per hat .... 3–9 hours (approximately)
Selling price, per hat $1.25–4.00
Gross profit, per hat $0.20–2.10
Return for labor, per hour ... $0.06⅔–0.23 plus (?)
Return for labor, per day $0.60–2.10

Comment: The apparently wide range of returns for labor is misleading. Few men could work 9 hours a day every day, owing to the need of getting firewood, repairing the house, caring for farm lands, etc. The more expensive hats, giving a much larger return, require much more skill and are in very slight demand. Ordinarily they are made only on order.

In addition, hatmaking requires a large capital investment. A sewing machine of the type required costs $40 to $50 second-hand, or rents at $10 a month. Hat blocks last indefinitely, but do involve initial outlay. Metal eyelets also must be provided for the ventilating holes. If depreciation, interest on investment, and minor expenses not calculated were taken into account, the income of the average hatmaker would shrink still more.

When it is considered that two skillful hatmakers claim only 1 dozen hats apiece a week, obviously the returns must not greatly exceed those for ordinary field labor. Only men who consistently produce and sell hats above the $1.25 price gain real economic advantage from their trade as compared with other activities. On the other hand, if the trade is a supplement to farming and is followed at times when similarly situated farmers are at leisure, then they realize a very positive economic gain.

Embroidery, crochet, and drawn work:

Materials, thread from stores, cloth (estimated) $1.00
Labor (part time) .... 1–3 weeks
Selling price .... $4.00–$12.00
Gross profit .... $3.00–$11.00
Return for labor, per week $3.00
Return for labor, per day .... $0.40–$ 0.50

Comment: For part-time work, the daily return seems, and probably is, high. In most cases the cost of materials is probably higher than the estimate.

Blanket weaving:

Equipment:[1]

Cards, life 3 years $8.00
Spinning wheel, life indefinite 12.00
Loom, life indefinite .... ?

[1] Spinning wheel and loom might be made by almost any man with moderate skill in woodworking. Weavers usually make their own looms.

Cost for 6-pound blanket:

Wool, 9 pounds (varying with year and
    season) $11.25

Labor: *Days*

Purchase of wool 1
Cleaning and washing, actual labor
    (covering 2 or 3 days' time) 1
Carding 2
Spinning 2
Weaving 2

        Total 8

Asking price $25.00
Average sales price 20.00
Gross profit 8.75
Return for labor per day .... 1.09 plus
Return per day for total days spent on
    part-time basis .... .58 plus

Comment: Although involving only 8 days' actual labor, the work would be spread over about 15 days. Weavers usually would have to take 1 or 2 whole days off to get wood and some days or parts of days when the weather might be unpleasant. In addition, repairs to equipment and houses must be made, perhaps an animal must be looked after, and so on.

Belt weaving:

    Equipment:
        Loom, home-made

    Costs:
        Materials, thread and yarn .... ?
        Labor, part time .... 2 days
    Asking price $1.25
    Actual selling price 1.00
    Gross profit, estimated .... .80–.90
    Daily labor return (part time, probably
        5–6 hours) .... .40–.45

Clothing manufacture:

    Capital investment:
        Sewing machine $40.00–150.00

    Expenses:
        Materials (for work on order) .... None
    Returns per day (from various workers'
        statements) .... $0.75–$1.30

Comment: Most workers, especially men, are part-time operators; many work only on order, when daily income for elaborate garments may be much higher. Income figures are hence misleading, as they are based on steady work on low-priced garments.

Clothing made for exchange at weddings usually is only single-stitched; regular clothing is double-stitched. Prices for sewing men's cotton trousers vary from 10 to 15 centavos for single stitching and 15 or 25 centavos for double stitching. Men's shirts vary in cost from 25 to 40 centavos (or more for fancy rayon shirts). Women's aprons cost 12 centavos.

Some persons make and sell finished garments. Men's trousers or blouses require about 2½ meters of material, at an average cost of about 30 centavos a meter. One woman specializes in children's garments. She claims to make 3 to 4 dozen children's garments a week, selling them at 80 centavos to $2.50 apiece (including materials). Her profits vary. A child's rayon dress requiring $1.50 worth of material she sold for $1.75, while for a cotton dress requiring $0.40 worth of material she charged $0.80.

All fitted or tailored garments, which are growing in popularity, are imported. A widely heard comment was that anyone in Cherán who could make and fit garments, especially men's shirts, would make great profits.

MINOR ACTIVITIES

Candlemaking:
    Cost of wax (per kilo) ....
    Sales of candles from 1 kilo of wax ... $2.25–$2.50
    Possible profit (excluding labor and
        equipment) .... $0.50–$1.00

Rope making (horsehair):
    Horsehair $0.50 per kilo $0.37½
    Labor .... 1 day
    Sale price $1.50
    Gross profit per day $1.12½

Comment: Only one man was found who made ropes. No data were secured on agave fiber ropes made by the same man, nor on the time taken in marketing and securing raw materials. As all the equipment is home-made and very little capital is needed, the gross profit probably is close to net profit except for the factors mentioned.

Shoemaking:
    Equipment:
        Sewing machine $55.00
        Lasts .... ?
        Knives .... ?
    Labor:
        1 cheap pair of shoes per day is produced by a
            shoemaker and 2 unpaid apprentices
    Value of product (per pair) $3.00–7.00
    Estimated gross income:
        Per day 1.50
        Per pair of shoes 1.50–3.50

Comment: No clear picture of the economics of this industry was secured. The selection and purchase of hides involves knowledge of tanning, size, and quality of the hide. Guarache makers apparently earn as little as 20 centavos a day, but there are no full-time professionals in town. All local manufacturers make guaraches to order and in claiming they make only one pair a day, they probably mean they do not attempt to make more than one pair a day.

Tanning:
    Charge per cowhide .... $5.00–$10.00
    Charge per sheepskin .... .50
    Average daily return 1.25

Comment: The average daily return is an estimate, based on the assumption the tanner is busy all the time. The only full-time tanner buys hides, tans them on his own account, and sells them outside the village when he is not occupied with commissions. Consequently, his income is probably fairly steady.

Lacquer:

Weekly income about $5

Comment: Only one woman lacquer worker is found in Cherán. Her entire output is sold locally. The figure given is her estimate of her weekly income. Some of the lacquer materials are fairly expensive and the wooden trays used as a base must be purchased. Probably net income is much less than $5 weekly. The main lacquer industry is in Uruapan and is mostly in the hands of Mestizos.

Bakers (commercial):

Cost of materials (per week):

Flour, 1 *arroba* (25 pounds)....	$3.50–$3.62
Lard, 1 kilo...................	1.50
Sugar, 3 kilos................	1.08
Total.....................	$6.08–$6.20

Labor:

No precise data; bakings per week, usually.......................	3

Sales:

Gross returns per week, estimated.................	$10.00–$12.00

Profits:

(Estimated after deducting any rental costs for use of oven)..	$3.80–$5.92

Comment: Sustained sales at the reported levels would produce slightly better than average wages. Despite the lack of definite data on hours of labor, a baker certainly works fewer hours and less strenuously than a laborer. Much time is probably consumed in selling; this may be done by a wife in the case of professional male bakers. Selling time is not included in the estimates. It should be remembered that a number of women bake occasionally; some bake regularly for the Sunday market in Paracho.

Bakers (home):

Aside from the professional baker of *pan dulce* recently established in the village and from whom no satisfactory information could be secured, there are a number of women who bake bread. Salt rising bread (*pan de sal*) is sold at two for 5 and one for 5 centavos, depending on size. If *pan dulce* is made, it sells at 1 centavo or at three for 5 centavos, depending on size. In most cases the baker owns her oven, but in some cases an oven is rented. The rental is usually one bread for each "board" (on which the bread is placed to rise).

Threshing machine:

Equipment:

Woodburning steam-driven threshing machine. Cost unknown, but probably several thousand pesos.

Charges for wheat threshing (a *carga*)...	$2.50
Capacity daily	12 *cargas*
Income daily	$30.00

Operating expenses (daily):

Wood.........................	$2.00
Hired labor	2.00
Water carrier	1.00
Total........................	$5.00

Operating season (June 20 to Oct. 25, period worked in 1940 estimated):

	Days
June......................	8
July......................	25
August....................	25
September.................	20
October...................	15
Total.....................	93

Total business (1,116 *cargas*, estimated, at $2.50 a *carga*).....................	$2,790
Net profit annually before deducting repairs, wages for owner, interest and depreciation, approximately	$2,365

Comment: Probably the threshing machine has the largest peso volume of business of any enterprise in Cherán, although one of the *nixtamal* mills probably is a close second. The threshing machine also represents the greatest capital investment except for some individual investments in real estate. High repair costs probably reduce the true net profit considerably, while depreciation in this case cannot be ignored. Add to this the time and skill required of the owner, and it is probable that this is not the most profitable enterprise in town even though it be the largest. Certainly, other families of farmers or combination farmers and storekeepers show more outward signs of prosperity.

Nixtamal mills:

Cost of equipment.............	$300.00–$1200.00
Costs daily:	
Gasoline and oil for gas engines........	2.00
Charcoal for producer gas equipped engines	1.20
Labor, 1 man.............	.80–1.00
Gross income at 1 centavo per kilo of maize ground (daily)	13.00–15.00
Net income (daily)	10.00–12.00

Comment: Mills work only half time; i.e., by agreement only half the mills operate any one day, so net income should be halved. Even so, this gives a sizable income, but probably the life of the equipment is short. Cost of repairs and the replacement of grinding stones

($9 every few weeks) is also an item not included. Some engines are equipped to saw wood, when not driving mills; pine logs are cut in lengths suitable for splitting into box lumber. The blocks are shipped in trucks to Uruapan, where they are split to make crates for shipping fruit. No data on costs or sales were secured on this minor business.

Barbers:

Prices:

Haircuts:

Weekdays	$0.15
Sundays	.20
Shaves	.10–.15

Number of "jobs" daily:

Except Saturday	4–8
Saturday	10–15

Income (a week)	$6.00–$7.50

Comment: Average income is probably under $1.00 a day. One of the two full-time barbers (with the smallest income) supplements this by card playing. One barber works only on Sundays and makes shakes during the week.

Musicians:

Wages:

For 2-day fiesta	$10
For wedding	2

Number of engagements (individual cases):

(a) 6 fiestas, 15 weddings, in 9 months	90
(b) 5 fiestas, 5 weddings, period unknown	60
(c) 10 fiestas in 1 year	100

Comment: The musicians obviously do not make a living from music. All have other sources of income; some are farmers, storekeepers, barbers, etc.

Painters, plasterers:

Daily wage	$1.75–2.50

Comment: Painters and plasterers have only occasional demands for their skills. Only a few stone or adobe houses are plastered, and fewer still are painted. Most jobs are by contract.

Billiard parlors:

Equipment	$1,500–$1,700
Rent (monthly)	10–20
Charge per game	.05

Comment: No estimate of the amount of business was received. It is evident, though, that the enterprise is profitable, to judge by dress and other characteristics of the owners.

Butchers:

Prices paid for beeves on hoof	$80–$150

Prices reported paid at wholesale for beef weighing:

15 *arrobas* (375 pounds)		$90
14 *arrobas* (350 pounds)		65
16 *arrobas* (400 pounds)		92
Retail price (per kilo)		.70
Gross profit on beef (per kilo)		.40–.45
Price of pigs		30.00 and up
Gross profit, per week		7.00–8.00
Gross profit, per pig		3.50–8.00

Comment: Returns to butchers are slight on the basis of meat sales. Generally the profit consists of: (a) Meat for the family at no cost, and (b) sale of the hide, usually for $10.00. Most butchers handle beef only, but one who specializes on pork, butchering one or two a week, claimed a profit of 7 or 8 pesos. An item unaccounted for in the figures for beef is a tax of $5.00 on each animal killed. It is also widely believed that some butchers deal in stolen cattle at a considerable profit. Few butchers lack other sources of income, however, which argues against great profits. Butchering also varies in profitableness at various seasons; when cheese is abundant the demand for meat falls off, and the butcher may have to dry part of his meat and sell it at a lower price.

Field watchers:

Wages:

In maize	1 row in 30
Average income for 6 weeks to 2 months (cash value of maize)	$60–$65

Comment: Field watchers (*veladores*) must be men of good reputation. Usually they watch 20 to 25 pieces of land. Although wages seem high—$1 a day or more—the work is seasonal and involves staying day and night in the fields.

Water carrying:

Charge for two 25-liter cans	$0.06

Comment: Only one man engages in this work regularly. He works fairly steadily, but no data were secured on his income. Presumably it is as good or better than he could earn as a laborer.

Beekeeping:

12 hives produced:

15 liters of honey at $0.60	$ 9.00
3–4 kilos of wax at $2.25–$2.50	6.70–10.00

Wax:

1 kilo makes 10–centavo candles worth	3.00– 3.25
3–4 kilos make 10–centavo candles worth	9.00–13.00
Potential income from 12 hives if owner makes candles	18.00–22.00

Comment: In all cases bees are kept as a profitable, but not extremely important, sideline to other activites.

Fireworks making:

Figures from the one fireworks maker in Cherán proved inconsistent upon analysis. The following facts seem reasonable.

Materials and prices: *Per kilo*
   Nitrate.. $1.70
   Chlorate....................................... 5.00
   Sulfur... .80
   Fiber string................................... 1.00
   Shakes, cane, etc..........................Nominal
      (Shakes are $5 a bundle of 400, but the
      number used is small; 3 or 4 per dozen
      cohetes, for example.)

Comment: Cohetes are made to order and sell at $3.00 to $4.00 per dozen. *Castillos* or set pieces are done on contract. Gross income from this source was at least $400 in 1940. Between times *cohetes* were made fairly steadily. Probably the fireworks maker's income is above average.

DISTRIBUTION

The problem of distribution affects primarily those goods which are exported from Cherán and those things which are imported. Only a small fraction of the materials produced locally are sold locally; in the main each family produces the local products it consumes and sells its surplus for export.

The export goods of Cherán consist almost wholly of forest products and farm products. The first are usually sold on contract or are transported by the producer to market. Railroad ties, for example, are always cut on contract. Charcoal is mostly sold to dealers from Zacapu and is delivered to the nearest spot where it can be picked up by trucks. However, there is some small local sale, mostly for operation of producer gas generators for *nixtamal* mills, and a little is carried on burros to such a town as Uruapan. Similarly, planks and beams are mainly sold, either to dealers who pick them up in trucks for export or locally on contract to someone building a house. In towns close to Uruapan, Zamora, or other centers, much of the sale of such products as charcoal, planks, and beams is direct, the maker carrying the goods to town on market day.

The major exception to the marketing methods for forest products described above is tejamanil, or shakes. For the local market, the shake maker usually works on order. For the export market he usually takes his product on burros to some nearby Mestizo town. These expeditions may be combined with other trading operations. Thus, shakes may be taken to Turetan via Nahuatzen, Tingambato, and Ziracuaretiro, a full-day trip with burros from 5 a. m. to 8 or 9 p. m. As Turetan is considered the source of the best bananas in the region, a return load of bananas frequently is purchased. Tejamanil may also be taken to Uruapan, Zamora, or Zacapu.

Marketing of farm produce follows several patterns. Bulk crops, such as maize and wheat, are today sold mainly to dealers who come to town with trucks to carry off their purchases. Maize and wheat are sold as far away as Morelia. While large farmers may sell quantities directly to such dealers, the storekeepers also play a considerable part by their purchases of small quantities of corn or wheat. Most of the purchases in this case are of one or two *almuds* at a time when the family happens to need a few centavos. Nevertheless, some wheat is carried to the mills by the owner on burro back, and corn may be taken to one of the larger markets. Individual small-scale buyers also occasionally visit the town, mainly to purchase eggs, chickens, or even small pigs. Today they arrive by bus, as a rule, and put in the day going from house to house, generally taking their purchases to Uruapan for sale.

Some local vegetables and fruit are also taken for sale to Paracho or, more rarely, to Uruapan. Bread, atole, or tamales may also be carried to market by the women. The most important fruit export, pears, is often carried considerable distances into Colima or into Guerrero. Sometimes the owner will carry his own pears, but more frequently a regular trader or *viajero* will buy the fruit. Other exported fruits include tejocote, cherries, apples, and quinces.

Another aspect of distribution, naturally, is concerned with the supplying of imported goods to the inhabitants of Cherán. Practically all manufactured goods used in the village are imported. This applies not only to machine products but to household industries as well, for the specialists of Cherán in no field supply all the local demand. Three principal agencies of distribution exist: First are the stores, specializing primarily in machine products; second, are the local markets, although for everything but foodstuffs the principal occasions are when fiestas occur; third, are the *arrieros* or *viajeros*, the traveling traders of Cherán who bring back products from as far away as the Balsas Basin in Guerrero or even from the Pacific Ocean. Even men who are not regular traders will go on local market. Finally, it should be noted that individuals often visit markets, especially those in Paracho or during fiestas at nearby towns, and make purchases of needed goods. Especially since the highway has brought bus service to the town, for important purchases a man may even go to Uruapan. It is not uncommon for well-to-do men, for example, to have garments made to order by the tailors in Uruapan.

It is impossible to compile from present data a complete list of the products imported into Cherán. The list extends from chile and beans to horses and sewing machines. Many articles are available only on special occasions. For example, the almost universally used type of water jar in Cherán is made only in Patamban, and is offered for sale only on the occasion of the fiesta of the patron saint in October. Householders must anticipate their yearly needs of these fragile (but quite long-lived) articles at this time; otherwise they are forced to attend a fiesta in some other town and pick up a different plain style of jar made in Uruapan or La Cañada.

Nearly all goods sold in the stores are imported (except occasional local products such as clothing). A considerable list of these goods is given in the discussion of price (p. 88). Tarascan products imported include fish and tules from the Lake area; hat braid of palm straw, chairs, tables, beds, and various wooden objects from Paracho; pottery from Santa Fe, Quiroga, Patamban, La Cañada, and the "hot country," or *tierra caliente* (the last is non-Tarascan); axes from Tingambato; knives, machetes, plow points, and jewelry from Nahuatzen; oils, garlic, spices, and vegetables from Zacapu and the Lake region; *rebozos* and cloth from Paracho, Nahuatzen, and elsewhere; pigs from La Cañada; beans from the Lake region; chiles from various places; and a variety of fruits. The latter include bananas, coconuts (from non-Tarascan sources), sweet and sour lemons, oranges, guavas, mameys, plums, mangoes, watermelons, cantaloups, avocados, zapotes of all sorts, and cherimoyas.

From non-Tarascan sources, but still outside the more conventional commercial channels, are

to be mentioned pottery from Guanajuato (and even from Oaxaca), dried meat from *tierra caliente*, cattle, and horses. Machinery and tools made in industrial establishments include axes, saws, hoes, hatchets, plow points, engines (for *nixtamal* mills), sewing machines, flat irons, and, quite rarely, radios, phonographs, typewriters, and trucks. The functioning of the principal distributive agencies will now be examined in some detail.

TRADERS

A fair number of men in Cherán who engage in trade are known as *arrieros* or *viajeros*. Whether there is any distinction between the two is uncertain. The impression received—and it is no more than an impression—is that originally the *arrieros* traveled to distant places outside of Tarascan territory, while the *viajeros* traded among the local villages. At present the two terms seem to be used as synonyms.

In the town voting register a number of men are listed as *arrieros*. Nevertheless, so far as could be learned, none of them dedicates all his time to trade. At the same time, there were numerous other men listed as farmers or laborers, yet who make fairly regular trading trips. The main distinction seems to be that a man listed as an *arriero* ordinarily makes about three long trips a year, while other men may make only one. Some men who make fairly regular short trips are not listed as traders. For example, one man who carries palm leaves regularly to the Paracho market is not included.

The main season for trading is from late fall until June, that is, the dry season. The principal routes followed for long trips are to Guerrero, Coalcomán, and Colima. A good many shorter trips may be taken to local fiestas, especially the great fiesta and market at San Juan Parangaricutiro. In addition, some men go to Guadalajara and Celaya for goods to carry to Guerrero. Finally, a long trip usually involves a number of short local trips around Cherán, either to purchase goods for transport to the *tierra caliente* or to dispose of merchandise brought back.

The *arrieros* are all men, with a single exception (reported but not seen). Wives, however, frequently accompany their husbands. Sickness is the greatest hazard. Women are believed to be more resistant to the illnesses of *tierra caliente*, and tales are told of women who saved their husbands by nursing them or by bringing them back to the healthful highlands. For this reason, traders rarely go alone, although large parties are rare. The major disease appears to be malaria. Insects, especially one attacking the feet, are mentioned as a great bother.

Robbers are also a source of danger; however, the most traveled route—that to Guerrero —is said to be entirely safe. Some of the greatest dangers on the route to Coalcomán or Colima seem to have been in Tarascan territory. The village of Capacuaro had a particularly evil reputation at one time.

Goods are ordinarily transported by burros. A poor man may have to carry goods on his back. The *arrieros* never ride except when seriously ill. An exception is that journeys to Celaya are made on the train, while nearby trips may sometimes be made by bus since construction of the highway.

The first step in a trading expedition is the assembling of goods for the trip. These may consist of pears from Cherán; apples from Pichataro; wooden products ("*tornillo*") from Paracho; sweetpotatoes from San Francisco; fine pottery (not cooking ware) from La Cañada, Guadalajara, or Quiroga; oils and spices from Pátzcuaro; dolls, pottery, and other goods from Celaya. Most of the goods carried by Cherán traders, however, are local in origin, i.e., within the Tarascan area. In such cases, trade goods either are assembled by one or more short preliminary purchasing trips or are bought en route. Guadalajara pottery requires a 7- or 8-day trip each way with burros. Celaya goods, as stated, involve a trip by train.

On the return trip various products are brought. From Guerrero come dried fish, dried beef, gourds, gourd containers, coconuts, and cheese, the last being most important. Few data were obtained on the products brought from Coalcomán, as few Cherán traders make this trip, but cheese and dried beef are probably the most important items. However, the one trader to give specific information bought beeswax. Chiles are brought from Colima.

Generally the goods brought back are not sold until Cherán is reached. Then they are sold locally (usually a minor part) or taken to the weekly Paracho market or to fiestas in nearby towns. Often goods are kept some weeks if there is a prospect of a scarcity developing, or an important fiesta is scheduled.

The majority of the long trips are to Guerrero, usually to Petatlán, where the fiesta of Holy Week attracts the greatest number of Cherán traders. The length of the trip taken depends to some extent on the rapidity with which goods are sold; once stocks are exhausted, traders turn back. One trader reported having reached Acapulco on one of his trips.

Some typical trips follow:

M. F. goes on Sunday to Paracho, where he awaits his trading partner from another town. Monday the two go to San Francisco and buy sweetpotatoes. Thursday they arrive in Tepic (Colima) and sell the sweetpotatoes. Friday they go to Guajuya (Jalisco) and buy chiles. Monday they return to Tepic and Saturday M. F. reaches Cherán. The trip involves 12 days' traveling and 2 days' resting, buying, and selling.

The schedule in detail is as follows:

Sunday	Paracho
Monday	San Francisco
Tuesday	Periban
Wednesday	Buena Vista
Thursday	Tepic
Friday	Guajuya
Monday	Tepic
Tuesday	Buena Vista
Wednesday	Periban
Thursday	San Francisco
Friday	Paracho
Saturday	Cherán

Some traders go to Colima proper by way of Zaragoza, but details were not obtained. It is 17 days' travel each way.

M. F. also goes to Coalcomán, carrying pottery from La Cañada which he buys in Cherán or Paracho. The route is the same as far as Tepic. Thence he stops at Obregón, Las Parotas, and Coalcomán. The round trip takes 3 weeks, of which 18 days are spent in traveling.

On his trips to Petatlán, Guerrero, M. F. buys wooden toys from Paracho and pottery from Santo Tomas. Starting on a Thursday, he goes to Pichataro. On Friday (market day) he is in Pátzcuaro and buys garlic, oils, and spices (*marjoram, pincente,* etc.)   The trip to Petatlán takes a total of 18 days (see itinerary below) ; San Gerónimo is 5 days farther.   A round trip usually takes about 6 weeks.

J. G. also leaves on a Thursday.   Leaving his burro at Pátzcuaro, he goes to Quiroga to buy pottery (probably on the bus, as he does not take his burros).   Returning to Pátzcuaro, on one trip he bought 500 strings of garlic, 15 liters of oils at $1.50 a liter (salad oil, olive oil, *aceites de razar, malza mantequilla, canaldo, mastral,* and *verbena*), and spices (*pimiente,* rosemary, *mandruje, flor de azalco,* and *manzanilla boraja*), and 2½ dozen wooden spoons of assorted sizes.

At Paso de la Vaca, J. G. began to sell a little, but only enough to buy food (he had run out of money).   His itinerary is similar to that of M. F., but he made one more stop.   On his return he loaded one burro with dried meat and rode the other because he was sick.   For the same reason he spent 8 days at one place. The two itineraries follow:

Arrive	*M. F.*	*J. G.*
Pichataro	Thursday	Thursday
Pátzcuaro	Friday	Friday
Santa Clara	Saturday	Saturday
Ario de Rosales	Sunday	Sunday
Alinonzita	Monday	
Corral de Piedras		Monday
Cayaco	Tuesday	Tuesday
Guadaloupe	Wednesday	Wednesday
Río de las Balsas	Thursday	Thursday
Paso de las Vacas	Friday	Friday
		(began to sell)
Limón	Saturday	
	(began to sell)	
Zopilote		Saturday
Tepehuaje	Sunday	Sunday
Colmenaros	Monday	Monday
La Unión	Tuesday	Tuesday
La Onía (close to Pacific from here on)	Wednesday	Wednesday
Pantla	Thursday	Thursday
Puerto Sijuatanejo	Friday	Friday
Cuicuayul		Saturday
San Geronimito	Saturday	Sunday
Petatlán	Sunday	Monday

San Gerónimo is 5 days' traveling beyond Petatlán; Acapulco is 6 days' traveling from San Gerónimo.

Another example is C. S. C. who makes only one trip a year, a visit to Holy Week in Petatlán, Guerrero.   He carries woodwork from

Paracho and brings back coconuts and dried meat.   He normally travels only a half day. (However, his half day would mean a dawn start and continuing normally until midafternoon.)   His stops are as follows: Pichataro, Sirawén, Ario, Las Palmas, La Playa, Cayaco, Guadaloupe, Las Balsas, Corcoles, La Limón, Tepehuaje, Colmeneros, La Unión, Pantla, Puerto Sijuatanejo, San Geronimito, and Petatlán.

Arrieros probably have superior techniques for handling burros.   *Criolina* is carried for treating saddle sores, and burros are shod "when the burro catches cold in his feet." Dysentery (*"posición"*) is the most frequent cause of loss of burros on trips.

Arrieros also observe special ceremonies.   A candle and prayer are offered to San Antonio before going on a trip, and thanks are rendered on return.   The *arrieros* also maintain a *mayordomía* for San Antonio, which is described elsewhere.

In general, knowledge of the economics of the *arrieros'* activities is unsatisfactory.   It would be extremely difficult to gain an accurate idea of the amount of goods exchanged by this method or to discover the monetary or other rewards obtained by the *arriero.*

The importance of the *arriero* class undoubtedly will wane rapidly with the extension of highways and truck trails.   Already the importance of the *arriero* in the Coalcomán region has greatly diminished as a result of truck trails opened up in recent years.   When a direct connection is made between the highland and the developing truck trail system in the Balsas Basin, the *arriero* probably will rapidly disappear.

TRANSPORTATION

As has been indicated at various points in the preceding pages, the burro is the most common means of transportation still, supplemented occasionally by horses or mules.   Poor traders may even make long journeys carrying their goods on their backs.   Nevertheless, a revolution in transportation is under way in Cherán.

One alteration in the transportation picture is the truck which picks up bulk goods in Cherán for markets that formerly were closed to these items.   As much as 4,000 kilos of wheat has left in a single load. As yet, though, the most important influence of the highway is the frequent bus service. The regular buses, connecting with buses for Guadalajara, and going directly to or from Morelia, and Mexico City, pass through to and from Uruapan about once an hour during the day. In addition, smaller buses from Uruapan to Purépero and Nahuatzen pass by several times a day. As a consequence, individual vendors often go to market by bus. Women take foodstuffs or herbs to Uruapan for the Sunday market regularly. Others may visit the market at Paracho merely as a recreation. Not a few in the village have made a trip or two to Mexico City.

Modern transport has even reached into Cherán itself. Three of the more well-to-do men in the town have purchased a 1½-ton truck, which carries freight to Uruapan or Morelia at 1½ centavos a kilo. On Sundays it also operates as a "wildcat" (i.e., unlicensed) bus to Paracho. The fare is 25 centavos plus a charge for bulky bundles; for example, 20 centavos for three bundles of palm leaves. Although trucks are not supposed to carry passengers, a satisfactory working arrangement has been made with the traffic police.

STOREKEEPERS

Cherán is unique among large Tarascan towns in that virtually all storekeepers are natives. A few of the storekeepers are large farmers whose families run a store on the side, but most of them made their start as storekeepers although they may now also be farmers. As one of the successful storekeepers explained, less capital is required to start a store than is needed to buy adequate farm lands. According to this same informant, if a man has fifty pesos, he can get a hundred pesos worth of goods, and if he has a place to operate, he is established in business. Moreover, the work is not as hard as farming. In addition, as people in Cherán have the same idea of living standards, business volume in most stores is small, so small that it is said not to have attracted the Mestizos. It is asserted that only those accustomed to Tarascan living standards and ways can succeed in making a living as a storekeeper in Cherán.

The more able storekeepers not only sell goods, but may make buying trips in person to Purépero for cloth or to Uruapan for groceries. Some storekeepers make clothing in their spare time or have sewing machines for rent. In addition, storekeepers may add to their income by buying corn, wheat, or eggs in small quantities. It is no uncommon thing in some stores to see a small girl arrive with some wheat tied up in one end of her *rebozo* and perhaps one egg, and bargaining with the storekeeper for some small purchase. It is noteworthy, though, that the transaction is not on a barter basis. First the sale of wheat or eggs to the storekeeper is completed and the money paid over. The seller then indicates what she desires to purchase.[24]

Time did not permit the making of a detailed study of the functioning of Cherán stores. It would be of considerable interest to do so, and if the cooperation of the wholesalers in Uruapan and Purepero could be secured, probably a fairly accurate idea of the movement of goods into the Cherán market would be possible. In the discussion of price some idea of the range of goods carried is given (p. 88).

Although not forming an important item in Cherán trade, it should be observed that women, children, and occasionally elderly men, sell some goods on the streets, usually at a street corner. Perhaps half a dozen corners always have one to three vendors selling such things as cooked squash or sweetpotatoes, fruit, peanuts, and other things which are purchased primarily as *golosinas*, or between-meal snacks. Similar vendors appear in some numbers at harvest time, often out in the country, at which time their stock also includes *čharanda* (sugarcane alcohol and water).

MARKETS

An important mechanism of exchange among the Tarascans is the market. In a great many towns markets are held only on the occasion of a religious fiesta or, if present at other times, are small and relatively unimportant. Taras-

---

[24] An hour in the store of M. S. is typical. A small girl brought 1 liter of shelled maize, two ears of maize, and one egg for which she received 11 centavos. Several other persons came in, bringing single liters of wheat or corn. One person brought 20 liters of beans (this is unusual as Cherán raises less beans than it consumes). In addition to a number of sales of less than 5 centavos, the following sales at 5 centavos were made (there were none larger): one cake of soap, *criolina*, castor oil, lime.

can economy is also linked with the national economy through the markets. The Sunday market at Uruapan, for example, is an important occasion for the disposal of Tarascan goods and for the purchase of supplies. The Uruapan market, however, is primarily a Mestizo market, and the Indian part in it is minor and far from obvious.

Quite otherwise is the market at Pátzcuaro. Although it is perhaps even more of a Mestizo town than Uruapan, the markets at Pátzcuaro on Fridays and Sundays are predominantly Indian markets. The Pátzcuaro markets are probably the most important agencies of exchange to be found in Tarascan territory. They would well merit intensive study.

The Sunday market in Paracho is the only large, regular market in the Sierra Tarascan area. While numerous Mestizos participate, the bulk of the vendors and almost all the buyers are Tarascans. Although subject to fluctuation in size from week to week, the Paracho market compares favorably at any time with the occasional large markets held in other towns on the occasion of a fiesta.

Cherán does boast of two weekly markets in addition to the infrequent affairs on the occasion of important fiestas. These markets, however, are merely insignificant reflexes of the Paracho market. Traveling salesmen or *viajeros* whose route to Paracho leads through Cherán often set up shop in the Cherán plaza on Saturday afternoon. In the evening or early the next morning they move on to Paracho. If they have not sold out their goods in Paracho, they may stop Monday morning in Cherán for a few hours. The number of vendors and the amount of goods sold, then, are relatively insignificant. Fresh vegetables are the main items, and housewives who do not expect to go to Paracho the following day may stock up for the week.

The Saturday market at Cherán usually gets under way about 1 o'clock in the afternoon. Vendors continue to arrive, however, until as late as 4 o'clock, and the main activity of the market is between 5 o'clock and dusk. The market occupies the street on the south side of the plaza in front of the municipal building. The vendors form two facing lines on opposite sides of the street. Only on unusually busy days do the lines extend the full length of the plaza. The Monday morning market is much smaller.

TABLE 3.—*Products sold in the Cherán market, 1940*

Product	Number of vendors selling product on Sept. 7	Product sold on—	
		Nov. 9	October 6 (fiesta)
Agua fresca (sweet water)			X
Anillos (rings)			X
Ajo (garlic)		X	
Aretes (earrings)			X
Atole			X
Ayates (carrying nets)			X
Bateas (wooden bowls)			X
Cacahuates (peanuts)		X	
Cahetes (jellies)			X
Calabazo cocido (cooked squash)			X
Camotes cocidos (cooked sweetpotatoes)		X	
Camotes (sweetpotatoes)	5		X
Canastas (flat baskets)			X
Carne seco (dried meat)			X
Cebollas (onions)	4	X	X
Changungas			X
Chayotes cocidos (cooked chayote)		X	
Cherimoya		X	X
Chiles	13	[1]X	X
Chiquihuites (baskets)		X	
Cocos (coconuts)			X
Col (cabbage)		X	
Cucharas (spoons)			X
Čundas (harvest baskets)		X	X
Dulces (sweets)		X	X
Dedales (thimbles)		X	
Dardenistas			
Fajas (sashes)			X
Frijoles (beans)	1	X	X
Guayabas (guavas)		X	X
Habas cocidos (cooked broadbeans)		X	
Helotes cocidos (cooked green corn)		X	
Higos (figs)		X	X
Jicamas			X
Jitomates (tomatoes)			X
Juguetes (playthings)			X
Leña (firewood)	1		
Lenteja (lentils)	1		
Limas (sweet lemons)	1		X
Loza de Oaxaca (pottery from Oaxaca)			X
Loza (pottery)	2		X
Manos			X
Manzanas (apples)	3	X	X
Mecates (ropes)			X
Morales (bags)			X
Muñecas (dolls)			X
Naranjas (oranges)		X	X
Nieve (ice cream)			X
Pan, blanco y moreno (bread, white and dark)		X	X
Pan dulce (sweet bread)			X
Pan de horno (cookies)		X	
Pastura (fodder)		X	
Peras (pears)	2		X
Pescado (fish, several kinds)[2]	3	[2]X	X
Petates (mats)		X	X
Platanos (bananas)		X	X
Pitsekuas[3]		X	
Papas (potatoes)	1		
Queso (cheese)	1		X
Rebozos (shawls)			X
Religion (crosses, medals, etc.)			X
Ropa hechó (clothing)			X
Sanhorias (carrots)		X	
Silantro			X
Serapes (blankets)			X
Sombreros (hats)			X
Tascales (baskets for tortillas)		X	
Tela (cloth)			X
Tomates (husk tomatoes)	2	X	X
Tunas (prickly pears)		X	
Velas (candles)			X
Vidrio (glass)			X
Yerbas (herbs)			X
Zapatos (shoes)			X

[1] Black and red chile from Querendaro; green chile, large and small; red chile, large and small; chile pasilla ancha; chile guajillo; chile mirasol; chile verde ¢irápsi.

[2] *Chara* (kuéřepo—small, dried, from Pátzcuaro; turuči—large, fresh, from Pátzcuaro).

[3] Small, black fruit like green tomato in taste.

On the occasion of a fiesta, the market occupies the entire plaza and overflows onto side streets. The variety and quantity of goods on such occasions exceed that at the regular Paracho market. Table 3 shows this clearly in the market held for October 6, 1940, the fiesta of the patron saint. Only two weekly markets were checked in any detail, as the fluctuations in the market simply reflect those occurring at Paracho the following day. Table 3 gives a list of the articles on sale in Cherán on three different dates, and for September 7 the number of vendors of each article is given.

TABLE 4.—*Place of origin of products and vendors in the market at Cherán, Saturday, Sept. 7, 1940*

Origin of vendor[1]	Article	Origin of article
Chapala	Fish	Chapala.
Cherán	Pottery	Huancito.
Do	Apples	Pichataro.
Do	Pears	Cherán.
Do	Pottery	Huancito.
Cherán (4)	Wood	Cherán.
Cherán	Apples	Do.
Do	Apples	Pichataro.
Do	Pears	Cherán.
Do	Cheese	Tierra caliente.
Pátzcuaro	Green chile } Onions }	Pátzcuaro.
Cherán	Chile	Uricho.
Uricho (2)	Yellow chile	Do.
Pátzcuaro	Onions, chile } Tomatoes }	Do. Pátzcuaro.
Uricho	Yellow chile } Tomatoes }	Uricho.
Pátzcuaro	Onions, cabbage	Pátzcuaro.
Do	Onions, cabbage, tomatoes	Do.
Uricho	Chile, onions, tomatoes	San Francisco.
Zacapu	Onions, tomatoes	Zacapu.
Pátzcuaro	Potatoes, beans, tomatoes	Pátzcuaro.
Pandicuaro	Sweetpotatoes (purple)	Zipiajo.
Villa Jimenez	Beans	Villa Jimenez.
Zunapario	Chile	Zunapario.
Cherán	Bread, peaches	Cherán.
Caranco	Chile	San Gabriel, Jalisco.
San Francisco	Chile, tomatoes	San Francisco.
Zacapu	Onions, tomatoes	Zacapu.
Do	Tomatoes	Do.
Cherán	Tomatoes	Cherán (?).
Pandicuaro	Sweetpotatoes	Pandicuaro.
Cherán	Chile	Cherán (?).
Etucuaro	Lentils	Etucuaro.
El Tigre	Chile	El Tigre.
Zacapu	Tomatoes	Zacapu.
Lasalga	Sweetpotatoes	Purépero.
Pandicuaro (2)	do	Zacapu.
Chucandiro	do	Zacapu (San Simon).
San Pedro Caro	Dried fish	Hacienda de la Luz.
Carapan	Lemon	Carapan.
Chapala	Cooked dried fish	Chapala.

[1] Numbers in parentheses indicate number of vendors if more than one.

Tables 4 and 5 show the places of origin of products and vendors in the market at Cherán and at Paracho in September, 1940, and table 6 gives the products and number of vendors at the Paracho market on various dates in 1940.

About 70 to 80 percent of the vendors in the Paracho market on September 1 (table 5) were

TABLE 5.—*Places of origin of products and vendors in the market at Paracho, Sept. 1, 1940*

Product	Origin of product	Vendor		
		Place of origin	Number from each place	Total number selling product
Agua fresca (sweet water)	Paracho	Paracho	1	1
Aguacates (avocados)	Cañada	(1)	1	1
Anillos (rings)	Patamban	Paracho	1	1
Aretes (earrings)	Nahuatzen	do	1	1
Bagas (burden ropes)	Paracho	do	2	2
Bordada (strip of embroidery)	Nahuatzen	Nahuatzen	1	1
Caldo (broth)	Paracho	Paracho	1	1
Camotes cocidos (cooked sweetpotatoes)	La Azarca	La Azarca	1 }	6
	Cañada	Cañada	1 }	
	Purépero	Purépero	2 }	
		Paracho	2 }	
Cebollos (onions)	Paracho	do	2	2
Cerezas (cherries)	Kinseo	Kinseo	2	2
Cestas (baskets)	Pandícuaro	Zacapu	2	2
Chabacanos (apricots)	Pichataro	Pichataro	1	1
Chalecos bordados (embroidered vests)	Nahuatzen	Nahuatzen	1	1
Changungas	Tierra caliente	Uruapan	1	1
Chiles (peppers)	Paracho (?)	Paracho	5 }	9
	Cherán (?)	Cherán	1 }	
	Pátzcuaro (?)	Pátzcuaro	3 }	
Col (cabbage)[1]				
Coliflor (cauliflower)[1]				
Dulces (candy)	Paracho	Paracho	1	1
	Pichataro	do	1 }	
	Cherán	Cherán	6 }	
Duraznos (peaches)	Pichataro	Pichataro	8 }	20
	Kinseo	Kinseo	2 }	
	Cheranástico	Cheranástico	2 }	
	Uruapan	Uruapan	1 }	
	Tierra caliente	Cherán	2 }	
Fibra de palmas (palm leaves)	(1 woman, maybe all, carried it up)	Paracho	1 }	7
		Pátzcuaro	1 }	
		Barsi	3 }	
	Pátzcuaro	Pátzcuaro	1 }	
	San Gerónimo	San Gerónimo	2 }	
Frijoles (beans)	Carapan	Carapan	2 }	8
	Tirindiro	Tirindiro	1 }	
	Cañada	Cañada	1 }	
	Tangancicuaro	Tangancicuaro	1 }	
Guitarras (guitars)	Paracho	Paracho	1	1
Habas (pulse or broadbeans)	Cañada	Cañada	2 }	3
		Carapan	1 }	
Helotes (cooked green corn)	Paracho	Paracho	1 }	3
	Cheranastico	Cheranástico	1 }	
	Cherán	Cherán	1 }	
Higos (figs)	Cañada	Paracho	1 }	2
		Cañada	1 }	
Huaraches (woven sandals)	Purépero	Purépero	1	1
Jicamas (root)	(1)	Paracho	1	1
Lechuga (lettuce)[1]				
Limas (sweet lemons)	Chilchota	Chilchota	3	3
	Paracho (?)	Paracho	1 }	
Limonas (lemons)	Chilchota (?)	Chilchota	3 }	5
	Tierra caliente	Guanajuato	1 }	
	Guanajuato	Purépero	1 }	
	Huansito	Huansito	1 }	
	Patamban	Patamban	3 }	
Losa (pottery)	do	Nurió	1 }	9
	Quiroga	Zacapu	1 }	
	Paracho (?)	Paracho	1 }	
	Quiroga	Tzintzuntzan	1 }	
Manta	Nahuatzen	Nahuatzen	1	1
Mandils (aprons)	Paracho	Paracho	4	4
	Pichataro	Paracho	2 }	
Manzanas (apples)	do	Pichataro	13 }	18
	Cherán	Cherán	1 }	
	Pichataro	do	1 }	
	Kinseo	Kinseo	1 }	
Manzanas-chatas (crab apples)	Pichataro	Paracho	1 }	4
	Uruapan	Uruapan	3 }	
Mostacillos (?) (beads)	Guadalajara	do	1	1
Muebles (furniture)	Paracho	do	2	2
	(1)	Paracho	1 }	
Naranjas (oranges)	Uruapan	Uruapan	1 }	5
	Limon	Limon (?)	1 }	
	Chilchota	Chilchota	2 }	
Nuezes (nuts)	Cherán	Cherán	1 }	2
	Pichataro	Pichataro	1 }	
Pan (bread)	Tanaco	Tanaco	2 }	6
Pan dulce	Cherán	Cherán	4 }	
Papas (patatas) (potatoes)	Nahuatzen	Paracho		1

[1] No data.

TABLE 5.—*Places of origin of products and vendors in the market at Paracho, Sept. 1, 1940*—Continued

Products	Origin of product	Vendor		
		Place of origin	Number from each place	Total number selling product
Paraguas de paja (straw raincoats)	Arantepacua	Arantepacua	3	3
Peras (pears)	Pichataro	do	4	
	Cherán	Cherán	4	18
	Pichataro	Pichataro	9	
	do	Cherán	1	
Pescado seco (dried fish)[1]				
Platanos (bananas)	Tierra caliente	Paracho	1	5
		Uruapan	4	
Queso (cheese)[1]				
Rebozos	Paracho	Paracho	4	4
Serapes	do	do	2	2
Sigras (large, lemonlike citrus fruit)	Chilchota	Chilchota	1	1
Silantro seeds	Cañada	Cañada	1	2
	Chilchota	Chilchota	1	
Sombreros (flat-top, white hats)	Paracho	Paracho	1	1
	Pátzcuaro	Pátzcuaro	1	
	Paracho (?)	Paracho	5	
Tomates (husk tomatoes)	Nahuatzen (?)	do	1	10
	Cherán (?)	Cherán	1	
	Morelia (?)	Paracho	1	
	Cherán (?)	do	1	
Toronja (grapefruit)	Chilchota	Chilchota		2
Tunas (prickly pears)	Tanaco	Tanaco	3	4
	Purépero	Purépero	1	
Uakinikin (a long nut)	Chilchota	Chilchota	1	1
Uikumu (yellow fruit?)	Los Reyes	Paracho	1	2
	Cimotlan	Cimotlan	1	
Tela (cloth)	Paracho	Paracho	2	2
Violin	do	do	1	1
Yerbas (herbs)	Cherán	Cherán	1	
Yerba buena (mint leaves)	Chilchota	Chilchota	1	2
Zapatos (shoes, orange; also white)	Paracho (?)	Paracho	1	1

[1] No data.

interviewed. The number of vendors and the articles sold, by classes, are as follows:

Articles:	Number of vendors
Fruits	52
Vegetables	26
Prepared food (including bread)	12
Wearing apparel	21
Baskets and pottery	15
Furniture	2
Ornaments and musical instruments	3
Palm fiber for hats	7
Total	138

Most vendors not interviewed were engaged in the sale of fruits or vegetables, mostly vegetables.

Another example of an unimportant market is given by Rendón for San Juan Parangaricutiro. The main articles sold were small quantities of tomatoes, chile, jicamas, onions, cabbage, silantro, garlic, limes, oranges, guavas, cherimoyas, peanuts, and sugarcane. Two persons sold candies from Zamora, two booths sold sweetpotatoes, one each sold pottery and shoes,

TABLE 6.—*Products and number of vendors in the market at Paracho, 1940*

Product	Number of vendors on—					
	Sept. 1	Sept. 29	Oct. 20[1]	Nov. 3	Nov. 24	Dec. 29
Agua fresca (sweet water)	1	4	2	1		
Aguas gaseosas (pop)		3	8	3		1
Aje (pigment)					2	
Ajo (garlic)						6
Aguacates (avocados)	1		1			
Anillos (rings)	1					
Aretes; collares (earrings; necklaces)	1	1				3
Atole (maize gruel)					2	2
Ayates (nets)			2	2	2	
Bagas (burden ropes)	2					
Batea para lavar ropa (washtray)				1		
Bateas (wooden bowls)		1	1			
Bordada (strip of embroidery)	1			2		
Borrega (mutton)		3		3		
Cacahuates (peanuts)		4	5		9	2
Cal (lime)					2	
Caldo (broth)	1					
Calabacitos (small squash)				3		
Calabazo cocido (cooked squash)		4	5	14	12	1
Calses (cakes)				1		
Camas (beds)	1			1	7	
Camotes (sweetpotatoes)	4	8		2		1
Camotes cocidos (cooked sweetpotatoes)	2	2				
Caña (sugarcane)			3	1		
Canastas (flat baskets)				1		1
Carne de puerco cocido (cooked pork)		1	1	2		3
Carne seco (dried beef)		1		6	12	6
Cebollos (onions)	2	15	11	12	18	15
Cerezas (cherries)	2		1	5	1	
Cerezas secas (dried cherries)			1		2	1
Cestas (baskets)	2	3	1	4		
Chabacanos (apricots)	1					
Chalecos bordados (embroidered vests)	1					
Changungas (a fruit)	1					
Chayotes			3	1	7	
Chayotes cocido (cooked chayotes)		3		4		
Cherimoyas (a fruit)					4	
Chicahuites (harvest baskets)				1	3	
Chicharos (peas)		4	3	4		
Chicharos cocidos (cooked peas)				1		
Chiles (peppers)	9	53	32	15		
Chiles, large wide, red				7		
Chiles, large long, red				15		
Chiles, small, red				20		21
Chiles, verdes (green)				8	25	18
Chile, negros (black)				2	5	7
Cintas (belts)						1
Ciruelas (plums)		2				
Cocos (coconuts)				3	1	
Col (cabbage)		14	10	2	6	7
Coliflor (cauliflower)		1			2	
Corbatas (neckties)			1			
Cucharas (spoons)		1		2	1	
Cracklings					1	
Custard						1
Dibujos y arte, flores			1			
Doughnuts				1		
Dulces (candy)	1	6	4	7	4	2
Dulces de membrillos (fruit paste)		1				
Duraznos (peaches)	20	22	1	3		
Escobas de palma (brushes of palm)	1					
Escobas de paja verde (brushes of green straw)						1
Espinaca (spinach)			1			
Fajas (sashes)		2	2	2	1	3
Fibra de palma (palm leaves for hats)	7	5		1	11	
Floreras (flowerpots)						1
Flores (flowers)					2	
Flores de papel (paper flowers)						2
Frijoles (beans)	8	13		6	24	
Gorditos (fried maize cakes)					1	
Granadas (pomegranates)		6		31	30	2
Guavas					1	2
Guitarras (guitars)	1					
Habas (broadbeans)	3	1		1	4	
Habas verdes (green broadbeans)					1	
Helotes (green corn on cob)	3	1	4	6	1	
Higos (figs)	2					
Hoja de betabel (chard)		3				
Hoja de limones (lemon leaves)		2				
Hoja de naranja (orange leaves)		1		2		
Huaraches (woven sandals)	1	1	4	1		
Ixtle (maguey halters)		11				
Jalatina (jelly)				1		
Jicamas (a turniplike root)	5			3	6	
Jitomates (tomatoes)					6	
Juegos de naipes (card games)				5		
Juguetes (playthings, e.g. dolls)		5	2		2	

[1] Fiesta of Santa Ursala.

TABLE 6.—*Products and number of vendors in the market at Paracho, 1940*—Continued

Product	Number of vendors on—					
	Sept. 1	Sept. 29	Oct. 20[1]	Nov. 3	Nov. 24	Dec. 29
Jugetes de losa (pottery figurines)...	.....	3	8	13	1	....
Lana (wool).........	.....	.....	.....	.....	1	....
Lechuga (lettuce).........	.....	1	.....	.....	.....	....
Limas y limones (lemons and limes).	8	17	7	16	13	7
Loquats.........	.....	.....	.....	1	.....	....
Losa (pottery).........	9	1	.....	64	5	2
Macate (maguey fiber string).....	.....	.....	1	.....	.....	....
Mandils (aprons).........	4	.....	.....	.....	.....	....
Mantas (blankets).........	1	.....	.....	.....	.....	....
Manzanas (apples).........	22	37	5	16	2	....
Maize (corn).........	6	.....	1	.....	2	....
Macetas (flowerpots).........	.....	.....	.....	.....	1	....
Madroño berries.........	.....	.....	.....	.....	.....	1
Mamey (a fruit).........	.....	.....	.....	.....	1	....
Mascaras (masks).........	.....	2	1	.....	.....	....
Maza (maize dough).........	.....	1	.....	.....	.....	....
Mazorca (maize ears).........	.....	.....	.....	1	.....	....
Medias (stockings).........	.....	.....	.....	.....	.....	2
Miscelanea (cheap jewelry and notions).........	.....	1	19	4	8	1
Molineros (chocolate beaters).....	.....	.....	.....	1	.....	....
Morales (bags).........	.....	.....	.....	1	.....	....
Mostacillos (beads).........	1	.....	.....	.....	.....	....
Muebles (furniture).........	2	.....	.....	.....	.....	....
Naranjas (oranges).........	5	11	1	22	21	3
Nieve (ice cream).........	.....	1	1	1	2	2
Nuezes (nuts).........	3	.....	.....	.....	.....	....
Orange plum.........	.....	.....	.....	1	.....	....
Palma tejida (hat braid)[2].........	.....	.....	.....	.....	1	....
Pan (bread).........	6	26	28	29	28	17
Pan de huevo (cake).........	.....	.....	.....	.....	.....	2
Pan con miel (bread with honey)...	.....	.....	10	.....	.....	....
Pan dulce (cookies).........	.....	.....	.....	1	1	....
Papas (potatoes).........	1	8	6	2	5	2
Paraguas de paja (straw raincoats)..	3	.....	.....	.....	.....	....
Peluqueros (barbers).........	.....	.....	.....	6	.....	....
Peras (pears).........	18	14	.....	.....	.....	....
Pescado (fish).........	.....	12	5	1	13	6
Petates (mats).........	.....	1	.....	2	4	1
Plátanos (bananas).........	5	4	1	19	3	2
Plumas (pens).........	.....	.....	.....	3	.....	....
Pulque.........	.....	.....	.....	.....	1	....
Queso (cheese).........	1	17	9	3	8	2
Rebozos (shawls).........	4	11	15	.....	21	11
Redes (nets).........	.....	1	.....	.....	.....	....
Serapes (blankets).........	2	4	2	1	7	8
Servietas (napkins).........	.....	.....	.....	.....	1	....
Sigras (a fruit).........	1	.....	.....	.....	.....	....
Silantro semilla (seed for flavoring).	2	5	1	4	4	....
Sillas (chairs).........	.....	.....	.....	3	.....	....
Sombreros (hats).........	1	2	1	1	2	2
Sopladores (fire fans).........	.....	1	.....	.....	.....	....
Sweaters.........	.....	.....	.....	.....	.....	1
Tamales.........	.....	19	.....	23	.....	1
Tejecotes (wild crab apples).........	5	5	.....	.....	.....	2
Tela (cloth and clothing).........	2	.....	.....	2	.....	2
Tela de lana (wool yardage).........	.....	.....	7	.....	.....	....
Tesquisquite.........	.....	1	.....	2	.....	10
Tomates (small husk tomatoes).....	10	36	26	19	8	....
Toronja (grapefruit).........	2	.....	.....	.....	.....	....
Tortillas.........	.....	.....	.....	.....	5	3
Tortilla baskets.........	.....	.....	.....	.....	3	1
Tunas (prickly pears).........	4	.....	3	.....	4	1
Uakinikin (nut).........	1	.....	.....	.....	.....	....
Violina (violin).........	1	.....	.....	.....	.....	....
Velas (candles).........	.....	.....	3	.....	.....	....
Yerba buena (mint leaves).........	1	1	.....	.....	.....	....
Yerbas (herbs).........	1	.....	.....	.....	1	....
Yellowfruit.........	.....	1	.....	1	.....	....
Yams.........	.....	.....	1	.....	.....	....
Zanhorias (carrots).........	.....	1	2	.....	.....	1
Zapatos (shoes).........	1	3	8	3	9	7

[1] Fiesta of Santa Ursala.

[2] An obvious error. Braid vendors were present every Sunday, but had no stands.

and three sold dry goods. A line of women sold atole and kurúndas, the yellow Tarascan tamale.

The Mestizo town of Chilchota has a market on Sunday which is not notably different from a medium-size Tarascan market. Indeed, as this is the market town for La Cañada, prob-

ably a majority of the attendants are Tarascans. Rendón, who collected the data, observes that there is a fairly clear sex division in market activities. Prepared foods are always sold by women. Sugarcane, medicinal herbs, pulque, and *ocote* (pitch pine) are almost always sold by men. Such things as lime, sweetmeats, and pottery are usually sold by women, although men may sell them. Vegetables are usually sold by women, while fruits may be sold by either sex. In general, selling is done mostly by the women. Buying, on the other hand, seems equally divided between men and women. Merchandise sold on two different market days (dates not given, but probably in February 1940) is shown in table 7. The organization of the market is shown in figure 11.

TABLE 7.—*Goods sold at two markets at Chilchota*

Goods sold	Number of vendors in—	
	Market A	Market B
Sugarcane............	15	12
Cooked agave (mescal)............	8	0
Green tomatoes............	2	5
Ripe tomatoes............	6	0
Green chile............	0	3
Dry chile............	7	7
Cabbage............	3	4
Cooked chayote............	8	6
Cooked chayote root............	10	8
Cooked squash............	3	8
Cooked sweetpotato............	3	0
Dried meat............	1	0
Greens............	0	2
Limes and oranges............	3	2
Cherimoyas and other fruit............	6	8
Peanuts............	6	0
Lemon-leaf tea and nurite............	1	1
Sweets............	2	3
Pulque............	0	6
Sweet tamales............	12	10
Flour tamales............	6	4
Regular tamales (kurúndas)............	12	6
Medicinal herbs............	1	2
Soaproot............	1	1
Salt and lime............	4	4
Pitch pine............	2	0
Pottery............	8	11
Total............	130	123

CONSUMPTION

The most important type of consumption in Cherán is that occurring in the family. Obviously, the consumption of raw material and semifinished goods in manufactures is significant, but the essential data regarding this have already been presented in the previous discussions. Likewise, there are many aspects of consumption related to various cultural activities dealt with in later discussions. Special types of consumption occur in connection with the life crises, especially marriage, and to a lesser extent with birth and death. A very significant consumption of goods occurs in connection with religious activities, particularly in relation to the *mayordomías* Less important, perhaps, is consumption in connection with governmental activities. All of these, nevertheless, are subordinate in importance to consumption by family groups.

tities may be consumed in connection with any festal occasion. Consumption of any other items will depend upon the amount of money available.

The major food consumption of the family has already been analyzed (Beals and Hatcher, 1943). In monetary terms it has been shown that great differences exist. Food expenditures

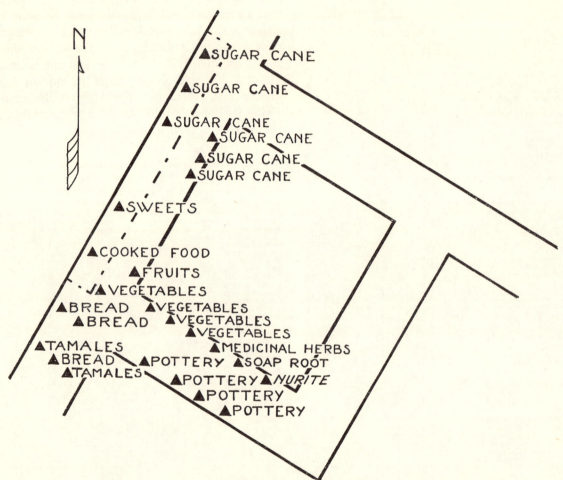

FIGURE 11.—Market at Chilchota, showing the location of the vendors.

The major product consumed by the family is maize. In the vast majority of cases most of, if not all, the maize consumed is produced by the family. The same is true of a number of supplementary items in the diet such as fruit, cabbage, and other vegetables. On the other hand, beans, meat, cheese, and fish, important constituents of the diet, are usually purchased. Maize consumption is about one-half liter a day per person (averaging the consumption of all ages). Much greater quan-

vary from 11.6 to 17.8 centavos a day per person. In general, a very poor family with its own maize supply will spend 5 to 10 centavos in chiles a week, 3 to 5 centavos in cheese every 3 or 4 days, 1 or 2 centavos in sugar or brown sugar daily, and perhaps occasionally 5 to 8 centavos in beans. Unless the family is quite poverty-stricken, about 2 centavos a day is spent in having the maize ground in a *nixtamal* mill. Among families in slightly better circumstances, about a peso a week is spent on meat. Families not regarded as poor might spend as little as 60 centavos a day on food for a family of six (two adults and four children). Checked in several ways, although obviously the quantitative data are inadequate, it appears that most prosperous (but not wealthy) families with sufficient land to produce all their own maize may spend less than 1 peso a day. It is estimated by some that this amount also includes the cost of all clothing and some maintenance of buildings but would not include special expenses, such as replacing animals, giving fiestas, holding funerals, etc. Frankly, this seems hard to believe.[25]

An approach to consumption (in terms of peso values), based on such quantitative data as it was possible to collect, indicates a much higher consumption rate for the normal Cherán family. Taking, for convenience, a family of five, the following seems a reasonably close approximation of consumption and expenditure:

Home-produced goods consumed:	Per day	Per year
Maize, 2½ liters daily	$0.15	$54.75
Vegetables and fruit	.10	36.50
Firewood	.08	29.20
Total value		$120.45

Goods requiring cash expenditure:		
Expenditures at store and butcher shop	$1.00	$365.00
Man's clothing (a rough estimate of minimum requirements for work clothing plus some "dress" clothing)		27.00
Woman's clothing (one typical woman's outfit of Tarascan type clothing, plus a couple of cotton dresses a year)		60.00
Clothing for 3 small children		15.00
Total cash expenditure a year		467.00

Total value of goods consumed a year $587.45

In addition to the above ordinary expendi-

[25] In Mestizo Chilchota, Rendón collected the following data: For a family of two adults and four children, 6 to 22 years, food expenditures were said to be 75 centavos to 1 peso daily, mostly for meat, the remainder for beans, lard, pitch pine, chiles, tomatoes, salt, lime, and other things. The maize consumed is grown. Another family of four adults and one child of 5 years spent about a peso a day. Another family of four adults and three children, 8 to 14 years, spent a peso to a peso and a half daily. In all cases the major expenditure was said to be for meat, with beans coming second. All grew their own maize. Unlike those in Cherán, all these families consumed coffee once and sometimes twice a day.

tures, there will also be less frequent ones. In the life time of the average family, a house and kitchen will have to be bought or built. By usual Cherán standards, this will mean a capital expenditure of $170 to $450. Animals must be replaced from time to time, an item difficult to estimate, but probably involving capital expenditures of around $200 every 10 years as a minimum.

Periodic expenditures will also include a blanket every few years at about $20, reroofing of house and kitchen every 10 years or so at a cost of about $40, an occasional mayordomía, and the expenses of weddings, births, and deaths. Finally, there are taxes on property and contributions to the church. All these are impossible to estimate accurately with the available data. A mayordomía, for example, may vary from an outlay of perhaps $15 or $20 for Mass, candles, and ornaments for the altar in the house to a cash expenditure of about $500 for the mayordomía of Nochebuena plus extensive use of maize and butchering of animals etc. belonging to the mayordomo. Weddings likewise may vary enormously according to economic resources, but may run up as high as $500 in cash outlay. In addition, there are the innumerable occasions when one must participate in weddings, roofing or house-moving fiestas, etc., each of which involves more or less expensive gifts aside from possible contributions of labor.

The above factors suggest that a Cherán family of five in about average circumstances makes a total outlay on consumption goods of not less than $500 a year if such capital expenditures as housing are allowed for. This does not include the value of home-produced foods. Many families unquestionably have a much smaller cash outlay than the amount suggested, but, equally certainly, some families spend more. Furthermore, these estimates assume that the family has inherited all the land it needs and is not making any expenditures for land purchases.

The preceding considerations suggest that insufficient attention has been paid to the quantity of exports and the movement of money in Cherán economy. Such data are difficult but not impossible to secure, although a considerable margin of error must be expected.

The motivations of consumption appear several. Primary is the need of food, shelter, and clothing. For very poor families, this is virtually the only type of consumption. Food requirements are intimately linked with productive efforts. The basic necessities by Cherán standards are mostly produced by the family unit, and the processes are apart from the system of commerce and exchange. Any family unit regarded as meeting Cherán standards of living will also have other consumption motivations. Participation in the social and religious life of the community is perhaps the second most important consumption motive. Crisis periods, especially marriage, and the possession of a *mayordomía* are occasions for consumption of goods, often on a very large scale. Such consumption, however, comes not entirely in the category of "conspicuous expenditure" but rather as the fulfilling of a social duty. It is true that the wedding ceremony is designed to emphasize public display of the consumption involved; nevertheless, failure to give as elaborate a wedding as the means of a family justified would suggest to the inhabitants of Cherán either that the family was stingy or that the family disapproved of the match. Yet another interpretation might be that they did not regard the girl as socially acceptable, either because of the poverty of her family or because of her reputation. In one case observed, the bride's mother, a poor widow with few relatives, prepared to finance part of the wedding herself when she found the wealthy family of the groom was planning a modest ceremony. In this case the threatened action of the bride's mother precipitated so much gossip and unfavorable comment that the groom's family at the last minute greatly increased its expenditures for the wedding (and the bride's mother, incidentally, did not have to carry out her threats).

In general, wealthy people do not display their wealth ostentatiously except through undertaking the more expensive *mayordomías* and giving the most elaborate weddings. Often the houses of wealthy persons are less pretentious than are those of the middle class. A man of the latter class with a large family may well operate a much more elaborate establishment than the wealthy man with a small family. The wealthy are apt to be envied in Cherán, it is clear. Memories of the more violent revolutionary days are close enough that people conceal their wealth rather than display it. That this was not always the case is evidenced by the considerable number of ruined stone buildings, homes of the wealthy before the revolution. Today wealthy men live modestly. Their table differs primarily in quantity rather than in quality from that of the poor. Wealthy men dress like others, unless they are going to Uruapan or Zamora. Their wives wear better quality clothes, as a rule, than do other women, and on special occasions they display more and better jewelry. There are few servants in Cherán, and their place is taken by dependent relatives or orphans who are members of the family.

The major methods of conspicuous expenditure acceptable in Cherán are quite stereotyped. Perhaps most common is to be sponsor of a moro dancer or to be responsible for some phase of a fiesta, posts assigned by the *municipio* rather than sought after by the individual. The ownership of cattle which can be used for cattle riding in the town fiesta is another socially approved method of ostentation. Ownership of a horse is also permissible, but it is considered that only a few wealthy men really need horses—men with distant lands or herds that must be visited frequently. The man who buys a horse without really needing it is considered to be "showing off." In the main, the methods of ostentatious consumption not only are communally recognized and approved but are restricted to specific social occasions. In ordinary life there is little to distinguish one Cherán man or family from another, if one except the very poor.

VALUE AND PRICE

The values of the major commodities and services in Cherán are expressed in monetary terms. Perhaps the only significant exceptions are the services rendered by relatives and *compadres* in connection with house moving and various fiestas, services rendered the community, and the goods which are exchanged at betrothals and weddings. In the latter case, wholly fictitious values are placed on the goods exchanged, but even here the equation is ultimately made to money values. With these exceptions, it may perhaps fairly be said that prices are the expression of Cherán values with respect to goods and services. Moreover, the major price determination at Cherán is not by local standards but in terms of fluctuations in Mexican economy as a whole. It is not supply and demand in Cherán which determines most prices, but supply and demand (and Government controls) in the surrounding regions. The extent to which this is true is a measure of the degree to which Tarascan economy is linked with that of Mexico, a relationship that is much closer than is ordinarily recognized by Mexican students.

The prices of the most important commodities produced in Cherán, corn and wheat, are determined by what will be paid by purchasers from outside the town. In similar fashion, the prices of most imported goods are determined by the wholesale prices existing in centers such as Uruapan, Purépero, and Pátzcuaro. The price of labor is likewise determined, although to a somewhat lesser degree, by the price labor can command in markets outside of Tarascan territory.

It is interesting to observe, however, that this influence does not extend far out of Michoacán. The Government, in building the highway with local labor, is reported to have paid only a peso a day, somewhat less than the legal minimum wage. As it was, the high wages (by Michoacán standards) tended to disrupt the local wage structure.

Within this major framework of price determination, of course, there are subsidiary exceptions. The price of pears, for example, will fluctuate somewhat in relation to local supply and demand, and the same is true of other fruits which have not yet found wider markets. Similar conditions obtain with respect to cheese and fish. Land prices in general seem to bear little relation to productivity and yield, although here our analysis may be at fault.[26] The preference for exercising gleaning rights in the corn harvest in place of higher wages also shows that in some areas of Cherán economics, nonmonetary values operate.

In general, the coming of the highway is bringing higher prices for local products.

[26] It is possible that a more adequate analysis of labor costs might show our estimates of net yields from farming are too high.

Tables 8 and 9 give the prices of some goods and products. Although little evidence is yet visible at Cherán, at Chilchota in La Cañada, where the highway has been in use longer, it was said that the price of chickens had risen from 50 centavos to $1.50 with corresponding rises in other products.

TABLE 8.—*Prices of some important goods and products in Cherán*

Goods or products	Number or quantity	Price
Maize (shelled)	Liter	$0.04–$0.07
	Fanega	5.00– 7.00
Wheat	Medida	.55
	Carga	23.00–27.00
Beans	Liter	.15– .26
Squash	Each	.25– .50
Cabbage	do	.03– .08
Pears	Per 100	2.00–¹3.00
Peaches	do	.40
Honey	Half liter	.30
Wax	Kilo	2.25– 2.50
Bread	2, small	.05
	1, large	.10
Raiz de Paja	Kilo	2.25– 2.50
Beef	do	.70
Pig (fattened for butchering)	1 (live)	40.00–75.00
Sheep	do	2.50– 5.00
Charcoal	Kilo	.02– .03
Planks	Dozen	6.00– 7.00
Railroad ties (Oak, pine, or fir)	Each	.60
Shakes (5 *cuartas* long)	Bundle (400)	5.00 and up
Handwoven wool cloth	Yard	1.00

¹ In Zamora or *tierra caliente*.

WEALTH AND PROPERTY

The major wealth of Cherán is forest and agricultural land. As has been indicated previously, all lands capable of permanent cultivation are privately owned, the remainder belonging to the community and being open to the use of all community members. One informant mentioned a possible exception to this statement, saying that the one large land holding of prerevolutionary Cherán has been taken by the Government and offered for sale to Cherán residents. The informant believed some lands in this holding were still unsold, but no further information was secured. In any case, the incident does not alter the fundamental pattern of Cherán land holding.

In terms of individual wealth, the basic Cherán concepts are those of rural Mexico. Wealth is primarily land and silver. Cattle loom less important, partly because they are not owned in large numbers, partly because the revolutionary period taught the people of Cherán that cattle are a less stable form of wealth. The man who owns sufficient land, however, has an essentially inalienable resource by which any losses of less stable types of property may be made up. Even silver is less safe, for someone may find the buried hoard and steal it. In addition, it is not productive. He who harvests from 50 to 100 cargas of maize is wealthy; while the man who harvests from 8 to 15 cargas may regard himself as a typical Cherán citizen.

them, houses are essentially portable property like furniture, tools, or cattle.

Little exists in the way of incorporeal property in Cherán. Perhaps the most important instances are the possession of knowledge of dances or of the texts for the dialogue in such performances as the pastorela. Theoretically

TABLE 9.—*Prices in Cherán stores in winter of 1940*

Commodity	Amount spent or quantity usually purchased	Unit upon which price is based	Price of commodity in store—			
			A	B	C	D
Salt	1¢; kilo	Kilo	$0.15	$0.14	$0.14	$0.14
Maize	1-10 liters	Liter	.06	.06	.05½	.06
Beans	¼-1 liter	do	.18-.26	.23	.23	
Sugar	1¢; kilo	¼ kilo	.36	.36	.36	.36
Chocolate	Cake	Cake	.05			
Rice	5¢-8¢	Kilo	.36	.36	.32-.36	.38
Lard	2¢; ¼ kilo	do	1.60	1.60	1.65	1.65
Cookies	1¢-5¢			[1].01-.05		
Cheese	1¢-4¢	Kilo	2.80			
Coffee (milled)	1¢-4¢	Ounce	.01			
Soap	Cake-5¢		.03-.20	.03-.20	.03-.15	
Brown sugar	1¢; ½ kilo	Kilo	.36	.35	.36	
Spaghetti	2¢-5¢	do	.60			
Cigarettes	Package	Package	.07-.12	.07-.10	.07-.14	
Lime	[2]1¢-4¢		.01-.15	.05-.10	.05-.10	
Candles	3¢-5¢	Each	.09	.08	.08	
Paraffin lights	1					
Chiles	[3]3¢-5¢					
Canned chiles	[4]1¢-5¢					
Vegetable oil	[3]1¢-4¢					
Olive oil	[3]1¢-2¢					
Creosote	[3]1¢-5¢		.01-.05		.03-.05	
Wax matches	3¢; box	Box				
Small dried fish	[3]2¢-5¢					
Soda pop		Bottle	.05	.05	.05	
Orange drink		do	.10	.10	.10	
"Spool" thread:			.05	.05	.05	
White			.06			
Colored				.05		
Small fine, colored				[5].01-.08	[5].01-.08	
Ball thread				.03-.08	.01-.10	
Cords (mecates)		Kilo		.90		
Rope						
Hats:						
Children's				.30	.35	
Men's				1.60	1.55	
Nails	3¢-5¢	Kilo		.70		
India ink		2 ounces				.05-.10
Aguardiente	Glass	Glass		18.00	18.00-20.00	
Ponchos					5.50	
Blue jeans				.10		
Brooms						
Ribbon:						
1-inch		Piece			1.00	
2-inch		do			2.00	
Cloth (unbleached muslin):						
No. 40		Meter		.30	.25	
No. 50		do		.35	.30	
No. 60		do		.40	.35	
No. 70		do		.48	.40	
No. 80		do		.55	.45	
No. 90		do		.60	.50	
No. 100		do		.65	.60	
Indian Head					.30	
Boreado				.70-.90	.65	
Anzulas					.60	
Ganital (for shirts)					.50	
Telas					.35	
Tonos (for shirts)					1.40	
Flat silk						

[1] Depending on type and quantity.
[2] Price per weight not ascertained.
[3] Quantity not ascertained.
[4] Quantity not ascertained; probably 1 per centavo from opened can.
[5] Depending on size.

Houses and buildings are also a form of wealth. The traditional type of house is owned apart from the land and is frequently bought and sold apart from the land. This is not true, of course, of stone or adobe buildings. Except for the somewhat greater difficulty of moving anyone might pick up this knowledge, but there seems a tacit understanding that this should not be done without the permission of the owner. Such knowledge is valuable, as such persons are paid by the mayordomos to teach the performers.

Other types of incorporeal property possibly are the knowledge of the herb gatherers, midwives, and witches. However, there is no sense of property in Cherán concerning this knowledge, and the idea of buying or selling it was not encountered. Such knowledge seems not to be differently regarded from the knowledge of how to farm or to care for animals or make bread.

A unique type of property right is the ownership of certain images of saints and of *mayordomías*. Two cases were encountered. One is the ownership of the *mayordomía* of the Three Kings (*Los Tres Reyes*), January 6. Several men were instrumental in starting this *mayordomía*, formerly celebrated only by the dance of the Europeans (*danza de los Europeos*). Not only did these men put on the first *mayordomía*, they put up funds, aided by contributions, to secure a fine set of images for the *mayordomía*. In subsequent years they decided who should receive the *mayordomía* each year. As one of them said to me, "It looks like this *mayordomía* is going to be a good business." However, he spoke in figurative terms, for, so far as could be learned, the "owners" of the *mayordomía* expected to receive only spiritual rewards and perhaps community approbation.

The second case is the ownership of a miraculous saint. The owners found the saint, erected a chapel, and receive contributions from worshippers. The owners claim that all gifts go to clothe the saint properly and care for the chapel, a statement that is open to doubt although there is no evidence to the contrary.

The distribution of wealth in Cherán appears to be relatively equitable. Certainly there are no really wealthy men in Cherán and there are relatively few impoverished individuals. So long as wealth is measured in land and most families in Cherán have a reasonable amount of land, this condition will continue. It is true that people in Cherán talk a great deal about *los ricos* (the rich men). In practice, almost no one can readily identify the rich men. Partly, of course, this is because rich men, in order to avoid envy, are careful not to flaunt their wealth. But it also is an indication that really wealthy men are probably scarce, if not absent. One of the regular assistants, Pedro Chávez, talked constantly about the rich. Repeated efforts to pin him down resulted in the identification of not a single individual as a *rico* and the assertion that anyone who harvested 50 to 100 *cargas* of maize is a rich man. As this means a cash income from this source of around $300 to $600 or $700 a year, the standard is not high, although probably wheat, cattle, and other sources add to such income. It is worth observing that almost no storekeepers are classed as wealthy—they usually do not have much land.

The inheritance of property in Cherán is normally from parent to children. Should an individual die without formal disposition of his property, the municipal officials would endeavor (subject to whatever influences might be brought to bear on them) to divide the property equally among children without regard to sex. Normally, however, the heirs would make the division, and it would merely be submitted to the *municipio* for approval. In this way inequalities often creep in through domination of one heir by another and the desire to avoid a fight.

It is quite common in Cherán for the property to be disposed of by the owner before death by making a will or, more commonly, by making a statement of intention to a reliable and trusted friend before witnesses. Such decisions will be respected and enforced by the *municipio*.

Property owned by women will ordinarily go to their children. However, should a couple be childless, the spouse does not inherit. There are numerous cases in Cherán of well-to-do couples where the bulk of the property is owned by the wife. Although the husband uses and administers the property, he has no rights in it unless it is formally made over to him by his wife during her life time. Similarly, a widow does not inherit except in special cases. This, again, involves a will or making over of the property during the life of the owner. Usually such an act is taken by a man only when his sons are rebellious and unfilial.

There are frequent cases where men do not leave property equally to all children or where they leave it to some other relative. In rare cases, there may have been some assignment of property to children before death. Then the child, usually the youngest, who has cared for the parent in old age, receives all the remaining property, a form of ultimogeniture. Such cases are understood and usually cause no friction. Other instances sometimes give rise to bitter feelings. Cases were recorded where children had broken away from parental authority and had become established through their own efforts. Sometimes the elderly persons were cared for by a niece or nephew, or even by some person not related at all, who received all the property. Resentment is generally felt by the children, even though they may have well deserved such treatment.

If properties are small, the daughters are sometimes slighted. If a lot, for example, is too small to divide and there are a son and daughter, the son will get the lot. On the other hand, if the lot is large, it will be divided between them. Often, however, the brother will take advantage of his sister, who, to avoid a quarrel, will accept an unfair division but will lose no chance of getting even. An example that came to attention was a division of a lot in which the brother took the part containing most of the fruit trees. When the brother went on a 3-day trip during pear season, his sister and her husband cut all the pears and sold them. The brother hesitated to do anything about it because it would have brought out the unfairness of the original transaction.

Frequently, the division of personal and movable property is unfair. Children who are away from home are apt to get nothing. However, their land rights are usually more or less respected. Even so, on their return, they may appeal to the *municipio*, which will force the other heirs to make a proper settlement.

Various adjustments are made to meet special situations. Often an expert in property values is called in to make the division. For example, a man with two children may have left a lot and a piece of farm land too small to divide. The expert decides the value of each and the one receiving the least valuable parcel is recompensed through sale of personal property. Where a lot cannot be divided, a piece of land may be sold from the estate to buy a lot for one of the children.

Conflicts also arise from transactions entered into by the owner before death without informing the heirs. For example, Agustín Rangel's father bought a house from his own father.

The grandfather died while the Rangels were living in the United States, and a brother moved the house onto his land. The Rangels returned some 27 years later and claimed the house, producing papers to show that it had been purchased. This was the first the brother had known of the transaction, and he was not only angry but refused to surrender the house until forced to do so by the *municipio*. This did not smooth family relations.

Other instances illustrate and bear out the assertion that most of the conflicts in Cherán are over inheritance. For example, a woman on her death bed divided her property as follows: A lot and certain lands to each son, three lands divided among her three daughters (one married, two small), and a house (*"troje"*) to be sold to pay the marriage expenses of the unmarried daughters. A few years later a brother tried to sell the house, and the girls appealed to the witnesses. The witness spoke to an uncle, who forced the brother to give up the idea.

Even in those few cases in Cherán in which sons remain in the family group and which function as joint families, the group dissolves immediately on the death of the father. Informants were unanimous and positive on this point, despite the fact that before the father's death the elder brother usually will have been handling the communal treasury and acting as head of the family.

All inheritances are supposed to be registered at the *municipio*. This is certainly done where an outsider is called in to make the division. Then each heir is required to sign (or someone signs for the heir before witnesses) a statement that he accepts the division. Evidently most property transactions of any sort are so registered. It should be noted that registration of a property transaction in the *municipio* is quite apart from registering lands with the tax collector and there is no connection between the two offices. Land not registered for taxes may be sold and the sale recorded by the *municipio*.

Even though many details of the economic system of Cherán are still not known in detail, some observations seem possible. The Cherán economic system has important relations within a general Tarascan economic system and also with the larger national economy. Some of the deficiencies of this report spring from the fact that study of these larger economic systems has not yet been made. It is apparent that the Cherán system functions in considerable part as a money economy and that in many respects it is essentially a European type economy.

Nevertheless, there are some differences of possible significance. Despite the fact the economy may be studied in monetary terms, wealth concepts do not revolve wholly about money and its values. Land itself has a surprisingly low money value, yet it is the major basis for evaluating individual wealth. Maize also occupies a higher position than its money value would indicate. Money is valued after maize, not before it, and the man who has money but no maize is apt to be regarded as poor indeed if there should be a maize shortage. Even in normal times, the man who has to buy maize is pitied, even though he has plenty of money.

Although further analysis might be desirable, it also seems that the emphasis on nonproductive expenditures is higher in Cherán than in our own culture. The outlay in cash and goods involved in religious festivals, weddings, and similar events, seems much higher proportionately. Men often forego material advantage also for the spiritual rewards of offices connected with the church, an aspect which has not yet been discussed but which will be described later in detail. It seems doubtful if the motivations in these cases correspond entirely to those of the "conspicuous expenditures" of our own society.

THE COMMUNITY

The community of Cherán may be viewed in several ways. There are, first of all, the physical attributes of the town, its layout, subdivisions, and boundaries. There are the objective characteristics of the people who occupy the area, their numbers, demographic characteristics, and groupings. Yet other aspects of the community are the bonds which hold it together and the groupings within which the individual functions as a part of the larger entity—the family, the kinship group, the various institutions such as the compadrazgo. The organization of the community politically is also of great importance: the structure of government, its management, organization, functions, and obligations. Finally, there looms important in Cherán the ceremonial and religious organization. Although logically forming a part of this section, discussion of the latter is deferred for a separate treatment.

THE MUNICIPIO

Cherán is, first of all, a municipio, an administrative unit, smaller than the usual county in the United States but having somewhat similar characteristics. The ordinary municipio in Michoacán consists of a cabecera or head town, somewhat similar to our county seat in functions. In most Tarascan municipios about half the population live in the cabecera. Subordinate to the cabecera ordinarily are a number of tenencias, villages of several hundred to more than a thousand population, and rancherias or other small units. All these subordinate units are administered from the cabecera through local, appointed delegates, the jefes de tenencia. Theoretically the residents in the tenencias and other units play an equal part with the inhabitants of the cabecera; in practice, government is controlled from the cabecera.

Cherán differs from the usual pattern in that the municipio consists of the cabecera and one small rancheria. Cherán, the town, is thus about twice as large as most Tarascan cabeceras, although the municipio has about the same population as others. Formerly the situation was somewhat different, with the tenencia of Cheranástico forming part of the municipio. As the result of circumstances to be related later, the people of Cheranástico withdrew from the municipio of Cherán and now form part of the municipio of Paracho. Had the population of Cheranástico been sufficiently large, it might even have become a separate municipio. The withdrawal of Cheranástico emphasizes the fact that cabeceras and tenencias have their respective boundaries within the larger limits of the municipio.

The general situation of the *municipio* has already been discussed in the first section of this paper. That discussion and maps 1, 2, and 3 indicate the main features, and no further amplification seems necessary.

The *municipio* has fairly well defined boundaries, although there are usually disputes with neighboring communities. Thus Cherán currently has disputes with Cheranástico and Arantepacua. The boundaries are marked in various ways. In the cultivated areas the boundaries are marked with stone walls. Where water courses form the boundaries, no markers are placed, but in the woods, a strip 4 or 5 meters wide is cleared along the boundary. This is done by communal labor, and when the line needs clearing again an assembly is called and a day fixed for the work. Every male is supposed to go. The Municipal Representative (described later) is supposed to lead the party.

THE TOWN AND ITS SUBDIVISIONS

Cherán is a compact and essentially urban settlement with a population of about 5,000. Few North Americans, unfamiliar with the concentrated settlement forms of Mexican towns, would imagine it contained anything like this population. There are no suburbs and very little straggling out of houses from the main center. Around the outskirts the lots are a little bigger and the density of population is less but the transition from town to open fields is nevertheless abrupt.

The layout of the town is undistinguished. A central plaza with a fountain, *portales* or sidewalks covered with arches about it, the municipal building, school, priest's residence, and church may be duplicated in hundreds of Mexican towns. The plaza is not today the center of the settlement geographically. Undoubtedly the town has grown since the time of its founding, and because of the deep *barranca* to the north, expansion has been in the other directions, leaving the plaza north of the present center of town by two or three blocks.

Radiating from the plaza is a network of streets laid out in a rectangular grid which makes only minimal concessions to the irregularities of the terrain. The enclosed blocks or *manzanas* are utilized as administrative divisions of the town. This feature will be discussed later.

A larger subdivision than the block is furnished by the *barrio* as indicated in maps 4 and 5. These divisions function in relation to elections, office holding, and certain municipal and ceremonial obligations. *Barrio* No. I is to the northwest and is known as Jalúkutin, or in Hispanicized form Urúkutin. This name is said to mean "something on edge" or "something in a small corner," apparently referring either to its position on the edge of the largest *barranca* or its position against the small hill on the northeast edge of town. *Barrio* No. II is called "Keíku," "down," or the lower *barrio* (*barrio de abajo*), and is the southwest *barrio*. The southeast *barrio*, No. III, is "Kalákua," "up," the upper *barrio* (*barrio de arriba*). *Barrios* II and III are usually known by their Spanish terms, and not everyone knows the Tarascan names. The fourth *barrio* is Parícutin. This means "to pass to the other side" and refers to the position of the *barrio* on the other side of a *barranca*.

The *barrios* show very few differences. Parícutin is less populated, has larger lots, and is said formerly to have been more isolated and backward, with fewer people speaking Spanish. The staff of the investigation all had the impression that this is still true to some extent, although little concrete evidence could be secured. Certainly, as the staff can well attest, the dogs of Parícutin are far less socialized than those of the remainder of the town.

Membership in the *barrio* is based entirely on residence. Property owners who reside in another *barrio* have *barrio* obligations only in the place of residence. There is no rivalry between *barrios* nor any instances in which *barrios* act as units on their own initiative. All the functions of the *barrio* appear to be derived from the *municipio*. There is no evidence whatever that the *barrio* has anything to do with regulating marriage or other social relationships. Even *barrio* chapels are lacking. In all probability the subdivisions are of Spanish origin and the only reason for suspecting otherwise lies in the mention of *barrios* by early Spanish writers in nearby areas.[27]

---

[27] On the other hand, as Silvio Zavala has shown fairly convincingly, Bishop Quiroga, first bishop of Michoacán and great

THE POPULATION

The total population of Cherán in 1940 was about 5,000 as indicated by voting lists. Data from other censuses follow:

1900 4,395
1910 3,908
1920 3,552
1930 . . . . Not available

Information concerning the age composition of the Cherán population is limited. The only source of adequate information is provided by the voting lists for the 1940 election for two *barrios* and interviews. This information applies only to men of voting age. A summary of this information is given in table 10. The

TABLE 10.—*Age and occupational distribution of Cherán males*

Age and occupation and other classifications	Distribution of males in *barrio*—				
	I (partial)	II (partial)	III	IV	Total
Age group:					
18–30 (17–30 for *barrio* III)..	29	16	62	86	193
31–40....................	24	13	85	35	157
41–50....................	17	15	62	62	146
51–60....................	15	10	27	18	70
61–70....................	7	12	26	15	60
71–80....................	7	0	0	0	7
Age not listed...........	2	6	5	1	14
Total..............	101	72	267	227	647
Unmarried................	3	6	2	0	11
Able to read.............	25	40	51	29	145
Occupation:					
Agriculturalist..........	73	47	124	63	307
Laborer..................	6	5	119	133	265
Merchant (traders and store-keepers)	10	5	7	1	23
Hatmaker.................	......	2	......	1	3
Mason....................	1	......	3	2	6
Carpenter................	2	2	3	3	10
Barber...................	1	2	......	......	3
Musician.................	1	1	2	......	4
Maestro..................	1	......	......	......	1
Shoemaker................	......	1	6	1	8
Tilemaker................	......	......	1	......	1
Various or none given....	4	7	2	3	16

data on ages is probably more reliable than that from most primitive groups but still is not completely accurate. An analysis of the original data shows that a very great majority of the ages given end in "0" or "5," clearly indicating that they are guesses. Interviews showed the presence of a tendency to increase the ages of young men, and a decrease in the ages of elderly men is suspected.

Additional incomplete but interesting data on the population are provided by the study of

the municipal records, which probably are relatively complete and moderately accurate. The data have been worked up into tables 11 and 12 by Dr. Emmanuel Palacios, of the Departamento Autónomo de Asuntos Indígenas, one of the collaborators in the study.

TABLE 11.—*Births in Cherán, 1936–39*[1]

Year and month of birth	Total births	Boys	Girls	Percentage of boys	Percentage of girls
1936					
January...........	9	6	3	1.7	0.9
February..........	15	7	8	2.0	2.3
March.............	9	4	5	1.2	1.5
April.............	10	4	6	1.2	1.7
May...............	11	3	8	.9	2.3
June..............	26	11	15	3.2	4.4
July..............	23	11	12	3.2	3.5
August............	21	12	9	3.5	2.6
September.........	15	7	8	2.0	2.3
October...........	9	2	7	.6	2.0
November..........	12	7	5	2.0	1.5
December..........	6	1	5	.3	1.5
1937					
January...........	3	2	1	.6	.3
February..........	......	......	......	......	......
March.............	15	5	10	1.4	2.9
April.............	15	7	8	2.0	2.3
May...............	9	4	5	1.2	1.5
June..............	19	13	6	3.7	1.7
July..............	21	9	12	2.6	3.5
August............	13	6	7	1.7	2.0
September.........	10	4	6	1.2	1.7
October...........	12	6	6	1.7	1.7
November..........	13	7	6	2.0	1.7
December..........	22	9	13	2.6	3.8
1938					
January...........	13	8	5	2.3	1.5
February..........	18	11	7	3.2	2.0
March.............	6	3	3	.9	.9
April.............	24	14	10	4.0	2.9
May...............	9	4	5	1.2	1.5
June..............	5	3	2	.9	.6
July..............	11	5	6	1.4	1.7
August............	22	10	12	2.9	3.5
September.........	10	7	3	2.0	.9
October...........	12	5	7	1.4	2.0
November..........	10	3	7	.9	2.0
December..........	18	11	7	3.2	2.0
1939					
January...........	14	8	6	2.3	1.7
February..........	13	5	8	1.4	2.3
March.............	20	9	11	2.6	3.2
April.............	23	13	10	3.7	2.9
May...............	24	13	11	3.7	3.2
June..............	18	16	2	4.6	.6
July..............	22	13	9	3.7	2.6
August............	18	11	7	3.2	2.0
September.........	15	4	11	1.2	3.2
October...........	16	9	7	2.6	2.0
November..........	17	7	10	2.0	2.9
December..........	14	8	6	2.3	1.7
Total.......	690	347	343	100.0	100.0

[1] Data prepared by Dr. Emmanuel Palacios, Departamento Autónomo de Asuntos Indígenas, Mexico.

Birth records are probably correct for all live births. There is some possibility that many stillbirths were not reported either in the birth statistics or the death statistics. Although a fine is levied against persons known to have buried a still-born child without registering the fact in the *municipio*, the fine is nominal, and municipal authorities believe that probably the majority of stillbirths are not reported.

evangelist of the Tarascans, was much influenced by Sir Thomas More's Utopia. The Utopian cities were divided into four divisions which served administrative purposes (Zavala, 1937; More, 1923, p. 54).

For the years 1936–39, inclusive, there were 690 registered births in Cherán. The sex ratio was very nearly 1:1, with 347 male births and 343 female births. The distribution is shown in table 11. It is of interest that great excess of female births occurred in 1936, reaching a peak in June of that year, while a considerable excess of male births occurred in 1939, also reaching a peak in June.

TABLE 12.—*Marriages in Cherán, 1937-39*[1]

Age of married person	Married men		Married women	
	Number	Percent	Number	Percent
13	......	......	3	2.0
14	1	0.7	23	15.4
15	2	1.3	49	32.9
16	12	8.1	26	17.4
17	8	5.4	9	6.0
18	32	21.5	6	4.0
19	12	8.1	2	1.3
20	15	10.1	3	2.0
21	5	3.4	......	......
22	10	6.7	......	......
23	5	3.4	2	1.3
24	......	......	2	1.3
25	9	6.0	5	3.4
26	5	3.4	1	.7
27	1	.7	......	......
28	5	3.4	3	2.0
30	3	2.0	2	1.3
31	1	.7	......	......
32	2	1.3	......	......
35	4	2.7	2	1.3
37	2	1.3	1	.7
38	1	.7	......	......
39	......	......	1	.7
40	4	2.7	2	1.3
45	3	2.0	3	2.0
47	1	.7	......	......
48	......	......	1	.7
53	1	.7	......	......
55	1	.7	1	.7
60	2	1.3	2	1.3
80	1	.7	......	......
82	1	.7	......	......
Total	149	100.0	149	100.0

[1] Data prepared by Dr. Emmanuel Palacios, Departamento Autónomo de Asuntos Indígenas, Mexico.

Data on the 149 marriages for 1937, 1938, and 1939 are shown in table 12. The age data are subject to the same probable inaccuracy in age estimates as is the case with the data on adult men. However, inasmuch as many Cherán residents are today sensitive about the early age of marriages and it is known that the ages given for young persons about to be married are often exaggerated, the data underscore the early age of marriage. In round numbers, 2 percent of girls married were only 13, 15 percent were 14, 32 percent were 15, 17 percent were 16, and 6 percent were 17. Only 2 percent of girls married were aged 20. It is significant that no marriages were recorded for girls aged 21 or 22. In all probability all, or nearly all, marriages recorded after this age were remarriages.

The earliest age recorded for married males is 14, this age group comprising 0.7 percent of the total male marriages. However, there is reason to believe that the age of males is falsified at marriage more than that of females. Most marriages, according to the statistics, take place at 16 or after; 8 percent of males marry at the age of 16. Five percent were married at 17, 21 percent at 18, 8 percent at 19, and 10 percent at 20. None were married at age 24, but 6 percent were married at 25. Some marriages listed at this age are probably remarriages, and certainly few first marriages take place after 25. The emphasis placed upon marriage as a normal state is indicated by the considerable age of some persons married. Two women and two men are shown as married at 60, while one man is shown as married at 80 and another at 82.

No particular season of marriage preference is evident if marriage frequencies are analyzed by months, despite assertions that most marriages take place in the winter after harvest. Evidently marriages take place when people have resources, regardless of the time of year. The fluctuations from year to year probably could be accounted for in terms of variable economic conditions. It must be remembered that the month of marriage reported is the time of the civil registry and church wedding. Probably the majority of marriages are consummated before these events.

In addition to the statistical data, even earlier marriages are believed to take place. One girl, whose age was alleged by several people independently to be only 15, had four children. Gossip told of another case of a girl of 10 years who was "half married," that is, the groom's parents did not yet permit him to sleep with his wife. But at the age of 14 the girl was said to have had two children. Before the Tarascans are censured for the practice of such early marriages, it should be born in mind that Bishop Quiroga, who had so much influence on the Tarascans, in his ordinances authorized the marriage of boys over 14 and girls over 12 (Arriaga, 1938).

Data on family composition and fertility were obtained by interviews with 53 families where the wife was 47 years of age or older and had not borne children recently (table 13).

TABLE 13.—*Fertility of Cherán women* [1]

Number of births per woman	Number of women	Living children per woman	Number of women	Deceased children per woman	Number of women	Male births per woman	Number of women	Female births per woman	Number of women	Male children living per woman	Number of women	Female children living	Number of women
1	1	0	2	0	4	1	4	1	13	1	17	1	18
2	5	1	15	1	14	2	14	2	7	2	15	2	15
3	6	2	7	2	12	3	12	3	17	3	6	3	3
4	9	3	16	3	5	4	5	4	5	4	1	4	1
5	10	4	8	4	9	5	6	5	2	5	1	5	0
6	10	5	3	5	3	6	6	6	1				
7	4	6	0	6	2	7	1	7	0				
8	3	7	1	7	2	8	4	8	0				
9	0			8	1								
10	4												
11	1												

(Average) 5.2 per woman | (Average) 2.7 per woman

[1] Based on interviews with 53 women past child-bearing age. In the data on male and female births, the sex of 3 children was not remembered.

TABLE 14.—*Deaths by age groups in 1936, 1938, 1939, and 1940*

MONTHLY DEATH RATE

Age in years	1936 Jan	Feb	Mar	Apr	May	Jun	Jul	Aug	Sep	Oct	Nov	Dec	1938 Jan	Feb	Mar	Apr	May	Jun	Jul	Aug	Sep	Oct	Nov	Dec	1939 Jan	Feb	Mar	Apr	May	Jun	Jul	Aug	Sep	Oct	Nov	Dec	1940 Jan	Feb	Mar	Apr	May	Jun	Jul	Aug	1936	1938	1939	1940	Total
Under 1 year	.	.	2	2	1	2	1	1	1	.	1	.	1	3	4	4	1	1	.	2	.	2	8	8	.	1	5	4	.	1	.	3	.	4	.	3	.	5	.	.	1	.	2	.	8	40	23	12	83
1–9	2	3	1	1	1	2	1	1	1	2	2	.	.	5	5	1	.	1	1	1	3	9	8	10	5	2	2	3	2	1	2	3	3	4	1	1	.	5	1	3	1	1	3	4	15	50	18	15	98
10–19	.	1	1	.	1	.	.	.	.	.	.	.	.	1	1	1	.	.	.	.	.	.	1	3	.	.	.	.	1	.	.	1	2	1	2	.	.	1	1	.	1	.	.	1	4	6	4	2	16
20–29	1	1	1	2	4	.	2	.	1	1	.	.	5	1	2	1	.	1	.	1	2	1	1	3	3	.	1	2	3	.	.	1	2	1	1	1	1	.	1	1	.	.	3	1	8	6	7	3	27
30–39	.	1	.	1	2	1	1	1	.	.	.	1	.	.	2	1	1	2	.	.	.	.	1	3	1	.	1	2	4	.	.	1	3	2	.	1	.	.	1	1	1	.	.	1	10	13	14	3	38
40–49	.	1	1	.	2	.	1	.	.	.	.	.	5	1	.	.	.	.	.	.	3	.	1	.	1	.	.	1	1	.	.	.	.	.	.	.	1	.	.	1	2	1	.	1	8	9	3	4	18
50–59	1	.	1	2	1	1	.	.	1	1	1	2	5	1	1	1	.	.	.	3	.	.	1	1	1	1	1	1	1	.	2	1	1	.	1	1	.	1	1	.	1	.	1	1	3	9	10	4	16
60–69	.	1	.	1	.	.	1	.	.	.	.	.	.	1	1	1	.	.	.	.	.	.	4	3	1	.	.	1	1	.	.	1	1	1	1	.	1	.	.	.	1	1	.	1	7	9	10	4	30
70–79	.	1	1	.	.	.	1	.	.	1	.	.	.	.	1	1	1	.	1	1	.	.	3	1	.	1	.	1	1	.	.	2	1	2	1	1	.	1	1	.	1	.	.	1	2	4	9	3	16
80–89	.	.	.	.	1	.	.	.	.	.	.	2	.	.	.	.	.	.	.	2	1	1	4	1	.	.	.	1	.	.	.	1	1	1	.	1	.	1	.	1	.	1	.	1	0	5	9	2	13
90+	.	.	.	1	.	.	.	.	.	.	.	.	.	.	.	.	.	.	.	.	.	.	2	.	.	.	.	.	.	.	.	1	.	.	.	.	.	.	.	.	.	.	.	.	2	1	2	3	8
Total	3	6	6	8	6	7	5	3	4	4	6	6	9	11	12	7	1	5	2	17	12	16	29	26	10	5	11	15	9	2	8	9	10	12	5	7	3	10	6	4	5	9	9	8	60	147	103	53	363

TABLE 15.—*Deaths according to sex in 1936, 1938, 1939, and part of 1940*

MONTHLY DEATH RATE

Sex	1936 Jan	Feb	Mar	Apr	May	Jun	Jul	Aug	Sep	Oct	Nov	Dec	1938 Jan	Feb	Mar	Apr	May	Jun	Jul	Aug	Sep	Oct	Nov	Dec	1939 Jan	Feb	Mar	Apr	May	Jun	Jul	Aug	Sep	Oct	Nov	Dec	1940 Jan	Feb	Mar	Apr	May	Jun	Jul	Aug	1936	1938	1939	1940	Total
Male	1	3	4	3	3	3	4	2	2	3	2	3	5	4	6	5	1	3	1	7	5	8	8	12	5	3	5	8	7	1	5	7	2	4	4	5	1	4	5	1	3	3	3	3	33	69	56	23	181
Female	2	3	2	3	5	4	1	0	1	1	2	3	4	7	6	2	0	2	1	10	7	8	17	14	5	2	1	7	2	1	3	2	8	9	1	2	2	6	1	3	2	5	6	5	27	78	47	30	182
Total	3	6	6	8	7	5	3	4	4	6	9	11	12	7	1	5	2	17	12	16	29	26	10	5	11	15	9	2	8	9	10	12	5	7	3	10	6	4	5	9	9	8	60	147	103	53	363

TABLE 16.—*Causes of death in 1936, 1938, 1939, and 1940*

Cause of death	Totals 1936	Totals 1938	Totals 1939	Totals 1940	Total
Pulmonía (pneumonia)	11	14	11	6	42
Difteria (diphtheria)					1
Decrepitud (senility)	6	4	5	3	18
Fiebre (fever)	9	3	5	3	20
Tos ferina (whooping cough)	5	59	7	0	67
Bilis (bile)	11	11	18	13	47
Herida (wounds)	5	12	4	0	18
Disentería (dysentery)	27	17	10	9	33
Paludismo (malaria)	4	0	0	0	4
Bronquitis (bronchitis)	3	2	5	5	12
Viruela (smallpox)	0	15	4	1	20
Parto (childbirth)	1	3	2	1	7
Accidental (accidents)		1	4	1	6
Gripa	2	0	6	1	9
Congestión alcohólico (alcoholism)	1	3	3	1	8
Tifo (typhus)	1	0	0	0	1
Reumatismo (rheumatism)	1	0	1	1	3
Cardiaco (heart trouble)	1	8	8	4	13
Cólico (colic)	1	0	2	0	4
Envenenado (poisoning)	1				1
Estriñimiento (intestinal obstruction)		1			1
Apoplejía (apoplexy)		1			1
Enfermedad (disease)		1			1
Dolor (pain)		3			3
Arma de fuego (shooting)		2	1		3
Erisipela (erysipelas)		1			1
Desconocido (unknown)			2		2
Tumor (tumor)			2		2
Quemadura (burns)		1			1
Tuberculosis (tuberculosis)			2		2
Aborto (abortion)		1	2		2
Neumonía fulminante (fulminating pneumonia)			1		1
Cancer (cancer)				1	1
Vómito (vomiting)			1		1
Hinchazón (swelling)			1		1
Alferecía (epilepsy)			1		1
Ahorcado (hanging)				1	1
Diarrea (diarrhea)			1	1	1
Deposisión (colitis etc.)			1	1	1
Sarampión (measles)				1	1
Purgación (gonorrhea)				1	1

TABLE 17.—*Death causes by summation groups of causes in 1936, 1938, 1939, and 1940*

MONTHLY DEATH RATE

Cause of death	1936	1938	1939	1940	Total
1. Accidents, injury, firearms					35
2. Pulmonary diseases					55
3. Intestinal diseases					35
a. Bilis					46
4. Fevers					52
5. Heart					13
6. Whooping cough					66
7. Infectious disease					33
8. Unknown					1
9. Old age					8
10. Childbirth					8
Total	60	147	103	53	363

Monthly totals — 1936: Jan 3, Feb 6, Mar 6, Apr 6, May 8, Jun 7, Jul 5, Aug 2, Sep 3, Oct 4, Nov 4, Dec 6 = 60.
1938: Jan 9, Feb 11, Mar 12, Apr 7, May 1, Jun 5, Jul 2, Aug 17, Sep 12, Oct 16, Nov 29, Dec 26 = 147.
1939: Jan 10, Feb 5, Mar 11, Apr 15, May 9, Jun 2, Jul 8, Aug 9, Sep 10, Oct 12, Nov 5, Dec 7 = 103.
1940: Jan 3, Feb 10, Mar 6, Apr 4, May 5, Jun 8, Jul 9, Aug 8 = 53.

The data again are not entirely reliable because of a tendency not to count deceased children until urged. Almost always emotion was manifested upon recalling a specific child. Women were more commonly able to supply the names of deceased children. It is the impression of the interviewers that the data presented are fairly accurate for all children baptised but that stillbirths and perhaps death before baptism were not counted.[28]

Although most Cherán informants believed families were small through the small number of childbirths, the data indicate an average of 5.2 births per woman. No case of a childless woman was encountered in interviewing, although some exist in Cherán. If the failure to report stillbirths is taken into account, it is probable that Cherán women would rank fairly high in fertility. The small family size consequently is due to deaths rather than to lack of births. Data from the same families indicated only 2.7 children living at the time the data were collected, indicating nearly half of all children born had already died. The data are summarized in table 13.

Data on deaths for the years 1936, 1938, 1939, and part of 1940 are given in tables 14, 15, and 16. As might be expected, the highest death rate is in children under 1 year of age (probably higher than shown when unrecorded stillbirths are taken into account). The second highest rate is in the period from 1 to 9 years of age. For adults, the periods from 30 to 39 years and 60 to 69 years appear to be the most critical. Again, however, ages are only estimates and must not be considered as accurate.

The table of deaths by causes (table 16) should be considered primarily of interest in showing the disease concepts prevalent in Cherán. There were no doctors in Cherán at the time these data were collected. Generally, the cause of death was provided by the relative registering the death, at the insistence of the Secretary that he had to put down something for his records to the State authorities. Epidemics of whooping cough and smallpox are clearly recorded, however.

[28] In taking a house census at Sevina, a neighboring town, the interviewers called attention to the fact that a babe in arms had not been included in the household total. Said the grandfather: "That one is too new. One hardly knows yet whether it lives or dies, so we do not count it."

Possibly (although not necessarily) of more significance is the summary in table 17. This summation was prepared in the belief that the general class of cause was perhaps more accurately known; in other words, diphtheria as a cause of death very likely is an incorrect diagnosis, but very possibly a pulmonary disease was involved. Particular attention is called to category 3a, *bilis*. It is not at all certain that an intestinal disease is involved. *Bilis* is the catch-all of Cherán medicine. Whenever one is "under the weather," he is apt to say he has *bilis*, and very possibly the concept is a receptacle for whatever beliefs of supernatural disease causation still exist in Cherán. The problem will be elaborated on in the discussion of disease and curing.

Knowledge of emigration is necessary to understand the Cherán population situation. Virtually all the emigration has been to the United States; relatively few persons appear to have emigrated either to other parts of Mexico or to other Tarascan towns. Impressionistically, it would appear that a very considerable portion of the Cherán population has been in the United States. Probably very few families either have not been in the United States or do not have some fairly close relative who is or has been in this country. Too small a sample was taken for statistical data on this point to be valid, but of 28 males interviewed specifically with reference to emigration, 25 had been in the United States. Discussion of the motivations, character, and personal significance of this migration will be given later.

Although many Cherán residents have emigrated, few persons have immigrated. A tanner from Aranza and a butcher from Chilchota, two tilemakers, two school teachers, the secretary, and the tax collector are the only persons known to have settled in the town in recent years. Of these, only the first two regard themselves as permanent residents. Most outsiders are treated as citizens, and there is no bar to purchase of land by outsiders. However, if land is for sale, owners are expected to offer it first to local residents.

If the Cherán population continues to increase to the point that land becomes scarce, it will be interesting to observe whether an emigration pattern again develops. The present war may well have caused a new migration to the United States, for many persons were eager to return if they could be sure of employment. Such a movement, however, would not have the sociological significance of a movement arising more directly out of local conditions. There is no tendency as yet to develop primogeniture in farm holdings. Should farm holdings become so reduced in size as to be indivisible from the Cherán viewpoint, though, it is possible that some such pattern as that of the Irish peasant or the French Canadian might develop the more readily, in view of the already existing tradition of migration.

Class or caste stratification is almost unknown in Cherán. There still remains much of the tradition of town unity so characteristic of Mexican Indian and, to some extent, of rural Mestizo towns. There is much talk of rich and poor but, as indicated in the discussion of economics, a rich man is one who harvests 50 to 100 cargas of maize. A list made out by a "radical" informant contained 14 names, and several people to whom the list was shown agreed that it was approximately correct. Fourteen "ricos" in a town of some 5,000 is hardly a class, particularly when the standards are so low. Formerly these wealthy men would have tended to occupy most of the town offices, but today this is not the case. As one informment put it, "We now elect moderately poor people as persons who know work and necessity better and who will thus better discharge the work of their office." Wealthy men are still accorded a modicum of respect and relatively little envy. Only two of the rich men are considered to have inherited all their property, and the others are believed to have reached their present state either wholly or partly by their own efforts. This fact also probably limits envy and dislike. The only occasion when the wealthy form a group is at State and national elections, when, with the storekeepers and a few others, they are apt to be on the more conservative side.

The most influential group at present in Cherán is probably not the wealthy, but the middle class—people who were valiant in fighting against the psuedo-agrarians who once dominated the village, who help the village with money when things are needed, and who "think and speak better." As a matter of fact, the leader of this group is relatively poor.

The informant who was most class-conscious admitted in casual conversation that the divisions existing in the town were essentially the result of individual likes and dislikes and personal ambitions. In this unguarded conversation, he admitted that class and ideological differences were of very little importance.

To the outside observer, however, the situation is not so simple. Even though class distinctions are of little significance, nevertheless persons with little or no land who work as laborers or sharecroppers receive much less respect in conversation. It must be admitted, however, that so far as our information and observations went, they are never disparaged to their face. In addition, there are two men who seem to be pariahs to whom no one pays attention. They work as professional water carriers and porters for the most part and seem very poverty-stricken, sometimes begging at

houses for food. Little could be learned about them either in conversation or from others. Nevertheless, their isolation may not be intentional. One of our assistants had apparently never paid attention to them; after we pointed out their peculiar position, the assistant always made it a point to speak to them whenever he passed them on the street, although no one else did so.

The nearest approach to class groupings is that persons seem to associate mostly with individuals who are their own age mates and of the same economic class. Circumstances were not favorable for detailed studies of association, but there is little doubt that this subjective impression would be verified by such a study. Across this class grouping are at least two others. One centers about the division into progressives and conservatives, words not used in the town, but quickly adopted by our aides when we explained their significance. There seemed little difficulty on the part of anyone,

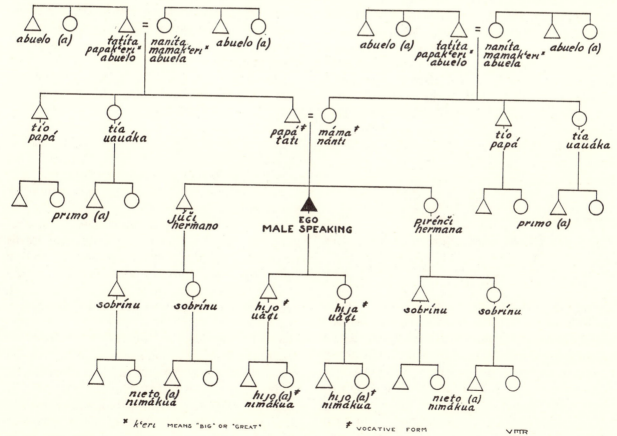

FIGURE 12.—Cherán kinship, male speaking. In general, the first form given is that most frequently used except where the form is vocative.

once he understood the words, in classifying the people he knew in these categories. The second major division is a relatively new one, that between the *cabildo* or *ačes* in charge of the church *mayordomías* and their followers, and those who oppose this group. The details of this dispute will be given later. Other classifications are essentially those of kinship and the *compadrazgo* system.

KINSHIP TERMINOLOGY AND BEHAVIORS

Spanish kinship terms are in common use in Cherán, with very little difference from standard Mexican usage. Many of the Tarascan terms have been forgotten entirely. The few Tarascan terms still remembered are rarely used and no one person knows all these. The terminology secured was obtained by getting several genealogies. After these had been compared and collated, Pedro Chávez spent several weeks in casual inquiries, as a result of which he added several Tarascan terms, most of which are used with the same meaning as the more commonly employed Spanish term. In the charts of the terminology, both terms are given. In a few instances, different terms are employed in the vocative and in indirect discourse. In this case, the vocative term is indicated by (‡). The Cherán Tarascans have very little interest in kinship and the data are presented with little confidence in their significance (figs. 12 (see p. 99), 13, 14, 15).

mími
hermano

EGO
FEMALE SPEAKING
(OTHERS AS MALE)

jingónikua
hermana

FIGURE 13.—Cherán kinship, female speaking. This chart shows only the differences from the terms used by the male. For all relatives not shown the female uses the male terms.

The nomenclature as it exists today is absolutely bilateral. There are also no distinctions based on relative age. In the Tarascan terms a few distinctions are made in the sibling group based on the sex of the speaker. The brothers of parents are occasionaly called *papá;* this was once more common. No such practice was recorded for the sisters of parents. The term "abuelo"(a)[29] is extended to the brothers and

---

[29] The "o" ending is masculine, the "a" feminine.

sisters of grandparents, but the other grandparent terms appear to be confined to the actual grandparents. Of some interest in the descending generation is the fact that ego's own grandchildren are called by the same terms as ego's children in Spanish discourse, while the children of nephews and nieces are called by the Spanish grandchild terms. In Tarascan discourse, however, ego's grandchildren and the grandchildren of ego's brothers and sisters are all called by the same term regardless of sex.

In the affinal terms, survival of a Tarascan term for sister-in-law (woman speaking) may be noted. Puzzling (and possibly incorrect) is the reappearance of the term for brother (man speaking) in the term for daughter-in-law. The parents of a child's spouse are referred to as *compadre* and *comadre;* in this connection it should be observed that they actually become *compadres* and *comadres* as a part of the wedding ceremony, along with most of the other close relatives of the spouse. The terms *páli* and *máli* applied to brothers and sisters of a child's spouse are simply terms of respect or appreciation which may be applied to one's own children or to a completely unrelated person.

Two terms not appearing in the charts should be mentioned. Tarámba refers to the daughter-in-law of a third person, that is, of neither the person speaking nor the person addressed. Similarly tarámpiri refers to father-in-law of a third person. In Spanish discourse, first cousins (children of parents' brothers and sisters) are sometimes referred to as primo(a) hermano(a).

In addressing or speaking of any person beyond the range of the charts, usually the terms tio(a) and primo(a) would be used, depending upon age. All persons with whom kinship obligations are recognized would be so called, even though neither person could remember the degree of relationship or trace the connection. In general, an individual regards the cousins of his uncles and aunts as pretty remote relatives, although he will call them tio(a) and their children primo(a) and usually will be able to trace the relationship. It would be unlikely for the children of such distantly related cousins to maintain the kinship address, even though of the same family name. How-

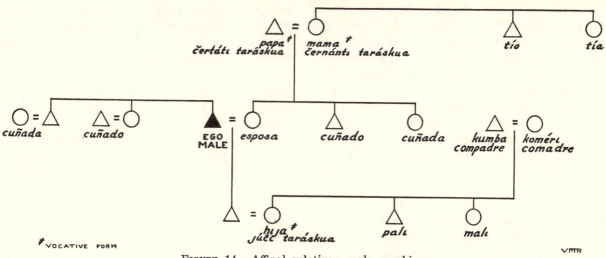

‡ VOCATIVE FORM

FIGURE 14.—Affinal relatives, male speaking.

ever, should the parents happen to have been close friends, they might continue to call each other primo(a) and continue to observe the appropriate behavior.

The major kinship obligation is to attend at certain functions and to assist with labor under certain circumstances. All close relatives must be greeted by relationship terms when encountered on the street or in the house, but this greeting may not be given to persons who still have reciprocal obligations such as distant cousins.

Parent-child behavior.—Parents are expected to look after the material needs of children, provide the necessary education, seek the proper godparents for them, and aid them to have a proper wedding. Children are expected to be respectful and to aid parents in their old age. If they do not conform to expectations, they may be disinherited.

Behavior of siblings.—The ideal pattern of Cherán evidently expects siblings to be close friends and to help one another. To a certain degree this behavior exists. Only for brother or sister would a man give monetary aid or give free labor at any other time than a house moving. Nevertheless, numerous cases were

encountered of bitter quarrels between siblings, usually over inherited property or property transactions. In some cases this extended to refusal to assist in traditional ways in which the aid even of remote relatives is expected.

Avuncular-nepotic relationships.—Data on behaviors in this category are inadequately documented. Evidently boys often have close relationships with their uncles. This relationship is evidenced most clearly in the fact that a boy often tells an uncle when he has "stolen" a girl and may take his fiance to live in his uncle's house, while the uncle first breaks the news to the boy's father. In general, boys seem to turn to their uncles in crisis rather than to their fathers. There likewise seem close relations between girls and their aunts and uncles. Cases are known where a niece rather than a child has cared for old people (and in some cases inherited the property). Comfortably situated families with few children may care for a niece from a poor family with many children, feeding the child well and often buying new clothing. In return, the child will help, running errands and doing housework. In at least one case, the niece really took the initiative. Invited to spend the day,

FIGURE 15.—Affinal relatives, female speaking. This chart shows only the differences from the terms used by the male. For all affinal relatives not shown, the female uses the male terms.

she simply did not go home except to visit. She said, simply, that her aunt fed and clothed her better than her parents and there was less work. The girl's parents fully approved the step; friendly, and possibly affectionate, relations continued.

General behaviors.—All more distant relatives are expected to take part in any "labor." This refers not to ordinary activities, but to such affairs as a wedding, house moving, death, or *mayordomía*. For such affairs each family wishes to have as large a crowd as possible, for prestige values are involved. On such occasions the husband's relatives attend, but only the closer relatives (and the *compadres*) will ordinarily assist actively. The one exception is in a house moving where the husband's male relatives do all the labor. Relatives of the wife also are expected to attend all functions. The males do no labor, but the wife's female relatives assist in the cooking and serving. Attendance at such affairs is expected even of relatives so remote that they are not called by kinship terms. If they cannot come, they must send an adequate excuse (illness or business out of town alone are adequate) and send a small gift such as they would have brought had they attended. Failure to appear would cause bad feeling and refusal to attend "labors" of the offending relative. Roughly speaking, the obligation extends to anyone addressed or referred to as *primo* or *prima* and to any children or parents of such persons. It also extends to all *compadres* and their children.

Another occasion in which kinship obligations are apparent is when a family returns to the town after a long absence. Then all the relatives and friends come and spend a day with the family (usually at the house of a close relative). There are also many invitations to meals. Augustín said when his family returned to Cherán he ate scarcely a meal at home for several weeks.

THE COMPADRE SYSTEM

Fully as important as kinship in Cherán is the system of *compadrazgo*. Ordinarily this could be translated as simply the godparent system, but at Cherán the relations between parents and godparents are often as important as those between godparents and children and

may be entered into in some cases without children being involved. In many parts of Mexico, both Indian and Mestizo, the *compadrazgo* is an extremely important aspect of social relationships and it has taken on many special localized forms. As yet, the only adequate study of the institution is that made by Spicer for the Arizona Yaqui.[30]

The following account of the *compadrazgo* was written by one of the Tarascan assistants, Pedro Chávez. Additions to the original Chávez manuscript are in parentheses.

The *compadrazgo* is very common among the Tarascans and is highly respected. All *compadres* and *comadres*, when they meet on the street, must salute each other with the phrase "*Buenos dias compadre*" (good-day) or "*Buenos dias comadre*," or its equivalent in Tarascan "nájeranku kumbáo (or koméri)." This obligation is especially strong between *comadres* or *compadres de pila*, as are called the *compadres* of baptism of a child. In this case it is obligatory to shake hands in sign of a certain mutual respect the two maintain. (These obligations endure for life, even though the child may have died long since.)

Classes of *compadres*: Among the *compadres* exist the following classes:

1. *Compadres* of baptism.
2. *Compadres* of confirmation.
3. *Compadres* of the crown (*corona*) or circumcision.
4. *Compadres* of marriage.

The degree of mutual respect and appreciation between *compadres* is approximately in the order in which they are given. (It should be noted that there are really two classes of *compadres* of marriage. There are the godparents of the bride and groom, usually a married couple, and the relatives of the bride and groom who become *compadres* as described below.)

Duties: The main duties are those of *compadres* of baptism. Immediately after the act of baptism (in which the infant is carried to church and the small fee paid by the godparents), they say to each other "*comadre*" or "*compadre*" or "*koméri*" and "*kumbá*," which are the same as the Spanish. This is the first duty and the first occasion it is said. From this arises the duty to care for the godchild, for example, to treat it as nearly like a son as one's resources permit. The godparents have the duty of giving the godchild some kind of clothing, such as a hat, shirt, or trousers, whenever they can afford to do so. This can be done as often as the godfather wishes. The father of the boy or girl has the duty of educating the child, telling him that he has the obligation to speak to the godparents with the words "pagrínitu" or "magrínitu." (If the godchild dies before the age of 10, the godfather must provide the burial clothing.)

[30] Spicer, 1940, p. 91 ff.

The *compadres* both have the duty of visiting one another when one of them is sick or has encountered some difficulty and, if it is possible, help him in some form. When one of the *compadres* has a duty (that is, a wedding, funeral, *mayordomía*, house roofing, house moving, or fiesta duty), it is the duty of the other to accompany him as many days as may be necessary. (The same mutual obligation exists between godparents and godchildren.)

When a godson kidnaps a girl with intention of marrying her, it is the duty of the father of the youth, before all else, to go to the house of the godfather of the youth, that is his (the father's) *compadre* and give him the news so that they may present themselves together in the house of the bride. This is a duty of the godfather. This duty (the father) has toward the three godfathers, of baptism, confirmation, and crown.

The duties of the marriage *compadres* are limited solely to accompanying each other when one has some obligation (such as wedding, *mayordomía*, etc.), the moving or termination of a house, and the duty of saluting each other with the name of "*compadre*."

Method of selecting *compadres*. In selecting the *compadres* some of the following characteristics are taken into consideration:

1. When a family wishes to have *compadres*, in general if it is rich it endeavors to find *compadres* in the same category.

2. If the family is poor, it tries to have a *compadre* in its same category, as it has been seen that sometimes when a poor person seeks a rich man as *compadre*, the latter accepts but afterwards he is ashamed to say "*compadre*" to the other who is somewhat poor. For this reason the latter (rich *compadres*) are not common.

3. Many times they (the parents) try to find a *compadre* who knows how to read. They say this is with the object that the infant will also be intelligent and know how to read. This is a belief among many, but it is not universal.

4. On other occasions efforts are made to find a *compadre* who is distinguished as a valiant person, in the sense of having bravery or, better, to be bold to fight when occasion offers—this, in general, indicates what among us is meant when a person is called "valiant"—with the object that the child will grow up and may be equally valiant as his godfather.

5. There are also cases in which a godfather is selected because he has done a favor on some past occasion or because of hope to receive some favor in the future. In general, this is the method of selecting a godfather. All usually try to find their *compadre* in an equal (social) category with these exceptions already noted.

The marriage *compadres:* In order to recognize one another as *compadres* of marriage, it is necessary to perform a certain act or ceremony in the moments when the last act of the marriage is about to terminate. This act takes place in the house or the kitchen (usually the latter) of the bridegroom. Present are the t'árepiti diosv uandari (marriage manager), the parents of the bride and groom together with all their brothers, sisters, and first cousins, in short, all the people the bride or groom may call aunt or uncle. Only these have the right to become *compadres*. Inside the building a mat is spread on the floor. The parents of the bride and groom enter first and kneel on the mat, where they remain during the ceremony. The others follow. They also kneel, but before kneeling they embrace one another, saying "In the future you will be my *compadre* (*comadre*) of Heaven and I pray God that we never offend one another. *Buenos tardes, compadre.*" One after the other repeats the same words. Sometimes they are in Tarascan: "Kumbéskari ka auándaɹu anápueskari ka uéke diósʌ éskaksʌ no méni ambé arijperoka. Na čúskuskiá kumba." Meantime the t'aɹépiti is iterating that all have the right to be *compadres*, that is to say, the aunts and uncles. (The language used by the marriage manager is not a fixed speech.) When this act is completed, all have the right to call each other *compadres* in the future.

To the preceding account a few additions must be made. Relatives may be sought as godparents of a child, especially of baptism, but only rarely is this done. The reason usually is a desire to save money, as between relatives there need be no ceremony or expense. *Compadres* of confirmation are selected to accompany the child to church at the time of confirmation. *Compadres* of the crown or circumcision are normally sought when the child is between the ages of 6 months and 10 years. The child is taken to the image of any saint wearing a crown (the *mayordomía* saints kept at private houses are used, not those of the church), and the godmother places the saint's crown on the child. She says an "Our Father" and burns a candle. When she has finished, she hands the crown to the *mayordomo* or his wife to replace on the saint and pays from 6 to 25 centavos. Normally only one *compadre* of the crown is sought.[31]

In some parts of Mexico—for example, among the Mayo of Sonora—if a child dies, the same godparents are sought for the next child born. The Tarascans are more apt to seek another godparent, believing that the death of the child was from the "luck" of the godparents. Any request to be a godparent may be refused.

In view of the fact that the duties of god-

---

[31] In other towns, a godparent of the crown may be sought at any time, especially if a child has been sickly for some time, or merely because the parents like someone. I received requests to be godfather of the crown in other towns where I visited very briefly; I never received a request to be a godfather of any type in Cherán.

parents and *compadres* are taken seriously in Cherán, it is obvious from the description given above that the *compadrazgo* obligations are nearly as important as those of kinship, if not more so. Scarcely a person in Cherán does not have at least 10 or 15 *compadres*. Most people have 20 or 25 or more. Don Luís Velasquez, the oldest of the marriage arrangers, who also says prayers at funerals, stated that he had more than 100 *compadres* of baptism alone. When it is considered that usually one acquires most of his *compadres* through weddings, the total number possessed by Don Luís must be enormous. He declined even to make a guess at the number of *compadres* he had of all classes. The obligations of *compadres* of baptism are as great or greater than those of relatives, with the exception of the immediate family (parent–child and possibly sibling obligations), while those of other classes are at least equal to those of cousins.

Some use of the *compadrazgo* is made by the church on special occasions. When a new image is blessed in church, for example, people are invited to become godparents of the image. They kneel behind the image when the priest blesses it. For this they are expected to pay from 1 to 5 pesos. In such cases the participants do not call each other *compadres,* nor do they have any relationship with the owner of the image in case it is a household saint.

GOVERNMENT

The governmental system of Cherán on the surface and in its organization is not obviously different from that of any other Michoacán *municipio.* In its functioning, however, it possesses many unconventional features. Even elections, ostentatiously conducted according to legal forms, may actually be conducted very differently beneath the surface.

The major governmental agency is the *ayuntamiento* of five persons and five alternates or *suplentes.* These serve a term of 2 years and are alternated in office, two being elected one year and three the next. Elections are made by *barrio.* Formerly Cheranástico elected one of the five; since this *tenencia* has become associated with Paracho, I could not discover what device was used to elect the fifth member. Whether the situation is still not resolved or whether there was a purposeful vagueness about

procedures I could not discover. One of the members of the *ayuntamiento* automatically serves as mayor, the office rotating from one *barrio* to another each year.

In addition to the *ayuntamiento,* there are a secretary and a treasurer, both chosen by the *ayuntamiento;* a *síndico,* who is one of the members of the *ayuntamiento;* an elected judge and *suplente* and a secretary of the court.

Certain other duties are performed by *comisionados,* that is, persons commissioned by the *ayuntamiento* or by the mayor. These include the 4 *barrio* chiefs and the 45 block chiefs. *Comisionados* may also be named for special duties in connection with fiestas or public works.

In addition to the above officials, there are other groups with special duties. The representative of the people, *representante del pueblo,* and two assistants are named by the town. The representative is confirmed in office by the Governor of the State and stays in office until deposed. His main duties are looking after the public lands. Finally, there is the *reserva,* headed by the *jefe de defensa.* The *reserva* is a group of armed men, 11 in number, authorized by the State military authorities, and, at the time of the study, headed by the real political boss of the town.

The nature of these offices will now be described in more detail.

Ayuntamiento.—Five *proprietarios* and five *suplentes* make up the group, serving 2 years. Those from odd-numbered *barrios* are elected one year, those from even-numbered *barrios* the next year. Cheranástico was classed as an odd-numbered *barrio;* what is done now is not clear. One of the members of the group serves as mayor, the other as *síndico.* The remaining members participate in policy decisions and in the naming of certain officials. Otherwise they have few duties. The *suplentes* apparently sometimes participate in discussion, but they have no real function except in case of the death or absence of their *proprietario.* Members of the *ayuntamiento* receive no pay. Normally they meet once a week to discuss municipal affairs.

Mayor or Presidente Municipal.—In years the odd-numbered *barrios* elect, if the mayor is to come from *barrio* I, the *síndico* comes from *barrio* III. Cheranástico, when classed as *barrio* V, apparently never filled either office. Similarly, if the even-numbered *barrios* elect, the mayor will be from *barrio* II, the *síndico* from *barrio* IV. The following 2-year period the situation will be reversed. Although the mayor is elected for 2 years to the *ayuntamiento*, he serves only 1 year as mayor. The second year he is merely an ordinary *municipe* or *regidor*, that is, an ordinary member of the *ayuntamiento*.

The mayor has the most important duties in the government, for upon his ability and initiative depends most of the success of an administration. It is he who initiates most activities, the *síndico* who carries them out. Not only does the mayor preside at town meetings or *juntas* and meetings of the *ayuntamiento*, but he settles minor disputes and levies fines of less than 1 peso, orders temporary imprisonment, supervises and orders most municipal expenditures, appoints most of the *comisionados*, and sees that public works are initiated. The mayor alone of all the officials must be present daily in the *municipio*. If not present, he must have his *suplente* present. (In 1940, the mayor rarely was in the *municipio*, leaving administration to the *suplente*. If anything of crucial importance arose, however, the mayor would be called in.)

As a minor judicial official, the mayor settles many small cases involving thefts, drunkenness, minor assault, rape, debt, or fraud. In some cases, brief jail sentences are imposed; in others, fines are assessed, all fines below a peso going into the pocket of the mayor as his only salary. The mayor also gives orders about minor improvements, such as cleaning the plaza or painting the benches. In case expenditures are involved, he may advance money out of his pocket for supplies or labor, later getting a receipt which he presents to the treasurer for payment.

Síndico.—The *síndico* supervises most public works and may initiate minor work. He is in charge of streets and the repair or reconstruction of bridges, and sees that many undertakings ordered by the mayor are carried out. With the help of a *veedor*, he oversees community affairs, such as the adequacy of the water supply and clandestine illegal activities.

He is in charge of the slaughterhouse; the collection of proper taxes and prevention of "black market" slaughtering are his responsibility. He supervises all questions of inheritance and the properties connected therewith, seeing that the heirs receive their due share of property. In cases of quarrels over inheritance, wounds inflicted with knives or pistols, and murders, the *síndico* makes the initial investigations and prepares the papers for submission of the cases to the judge. The *síndico* receives no pay.

Secretary.—The secretary is named by the mayor with the approval of the *ayuntamiento* without a fixed term being set. His duties are to make all classes of documents and to maintain the municipal archives. These include the birth, death, and marriage records of the town. The secretary is paid $1.50 a day. He may augment this sum by preparing private documents for a fee. The office is fairly new; in the childhood of fairly young men there was no secretary. The present incumbent is not a native of the town.

Veedor.—The veedor is named by the *síndico* with the approval of the mayor. He is supposed to see that the water supply is functioning properly and to report any illegal acts. Apparently he receives no pay.

Treasurer.—The treasurer receives all the town funds from various sources, including fines above 1 peso, taxes, assessments, and funds from State and Federal sources. He is responsible for the collection of the small tax on vendors at the markets. He pays all bills of the *municipio* and must keep detailed accounts which are inspected by State officials. The office of treasurer is also new. His pay is 25 percent of the income. There is no term to his office.

Judge.—The judge and his *suplente* are usually elected every 2 years but if the office is satisfactorily filled, the election may not be held for 3 or 4 years. The judge hears all cases certified to him by the *síndico*. He may order brief imprisonment or fines, which are paid to the treasurer, but all serious cases are referred to the district court at Uruapan after a preliminary hearing. This is particularly true of murder cases or serious crimes. The judge reviews all cases of inheritance in which quarrels arise, and all land sales must be authorized before the judge. In such cases he may discover falsified documents, and will levy fines against the guilty party. Disputes over land ownership may come before him also and usually will be settled without reference to higher authorities. An example of the latter type of case occurred where a person occupied lands belonging to Aurelio Ceja S., which the latter had registered for 20 years. The intruder was sentenced to return the land, pay the owner 10 percent of the value, and all costs of the litigation.

The judge receives no pay, but he is assisted by a secretary who is paid $1 a day by the *municipio*. The secretary may collect fees for preparing private documents. More detail on judicial cases will be given later.

Police.—Two (later three) men were employed as police in 1940-41. Their main duties were not actually police functions, however, but rather the running of errands and carrying messages for the mayor, *síndico*, and judge. Most real police functions are carried out by the *síndico*, *veedor*, and the *ronda*. The police receive 75 centavos daily; all are persons incapacitated in some way for heavy work.

Comisionados.—There are many kinds and classes of *comisionados*. Perhaps most important are the four *barrio* chiefs, the *jefes de cuartel*, appointed by the mayor each year. These men, together with the previous officials, are exempt from any other service during their year of office. The *barrio* chief commands the block chiefs and also the *ronda*. He transmits instructions of the *ayuntamiento* to the block chiefs when necessary.

The block chiefs are also appointed by the mayor for 1 year, and they have no other duties. On instructions from the *barrio* chief, the block chiefs notify the residents in their block if any communal labor is necessary, such as repairs to the water system, road or bridge work, clearing of town boundaries, or work in connection with a fiesta etc., and they see that each person does his duty. Special block chiefs may be named for unusual events such as the taking of the census. Such special block chiefs serve only for the time necessary to complete their special assignment.

The *ronda* is a "voluntary" night watch. The town is patrolled every night by a group of 8 to 12 men under the orders of the *barrio* chief. The latter has the duty of notifying individuals when they are to serve. Each *barrio* provides the *ronda* for a week in turn, and each individual serves a week every time he is called. Theoretically, every adult male is expected to perform this service, but the men over 40 or 50 years and persons of some distinction are seldom if ever asked. One of the assistants in the project, member of the committee in charge of communal property and a school teacher, had not been asked to serve for several years. Neither do the storekeepers serve; instead, they give a package of cigarettes or some 10 centavos to those who do serve. There is no obligation, nor any regularity, about this gift. The average man who is asked to serve probably is called on four or five times a year.

Comisionados may also be named if funds are to be raised for some special municipal purpose. The purpose may be to send a delegation to Morelia or Mexico City to look after the interests of the town in some affair, or to purchase material for some public work for which funds are not available in the treasury, such as the materials for the water tanks. This may happen twice in a year or may not occur at all. The *comisionados* are charged with collecting the money in their *barrio* or whatever area is designated.

There are many *comisionados* in connection with fiestas. For the fiesta of the patron saint in October, some 70 *comisionados* are named to raise funds for music, fireworks, and other expenses of the fiesta. A group is named by the mayor for each *barrio*, and it has the responsibility of raising money through taking up a collection (or members paying out of their own pockets), conducting negotiations with musicians or fireworks makers, and seeing that the work is completed. In addition, four men are commissioned each to provide a moro dancer. The *comisionado* has to seek out a dancer, pay for his food and costume, and take care of him during the fiesta. Finally, at least 40 young men (10 or more from each *barrio*) are commissioned to provide poles for building the bull ring. The total for this fiesta is not less than 114 *comisionados*.

For the fiesta of Corpus, eight *comisionados* are named for each *barrio* for each occupation represented in the fiesta. Each major traditional occupation is required to hire a band, and the *comisionados* must raise the money by taking up a collection or by paying out of their own pockets. A separate set of *comisionados* is named to take up another collection to hire music for the celebration of the Octava. Voluntary service is also given by the bee hunters. The total *comisionados* for this fiesta probably reaches 250. *Comisionados* for a fiesta often put in many days of labor.

One final type of *comisionado* should be mentioned, the men named to do communal labor. Probably every eligible man has to put in 2 or 3 days a year on such work. This may be for work assigned to a *barrio*, or it may be some community-wide program such as cutting poles for the erection of an electric light system.

At a rough estimate, probably each man eligible for commissions gives about 14 days or nights of service a year to the community, if it be taken into account that about half the adult males are exempt for reason of age or service such as office holding, school teaching, store keeping, etc. However, the work is probably very unevenly distributed, for there is no systematic method of assignment. A person who raises many objections or who is not in proper economic condition may evade many commissions. For example, no right-minded mayor would commission a poverty-stricken man to bring out a moro. Consequently, persons who are conscientious and do not complain are apt to receive many more commissions than others.

Reserva.—The *reserva* consists of 11 men armed by the Government (State or Federal?) with modern weapons and, in 1940, captained by the real political boss of the town, Moisés Valencia. Although all were agreed that the 11 were chosen by the people, no one seemed to have any idea of the mechanism of choice. In all probability the group was chosen in the same way Valencia was chosen political boss, through aggressiveness in defense of town interests and personal popularity. Even a town the size of Cherán does not need formal elective machinery at times in order to express popular will, as will be seen in the discussion of elections. During the disturbed period in Michoacán during the installation of President Camacho, the reserve received instructions from the military

district commander to arrest all strangers and send them to Uruapan. So far as I could learn, nothing was done.

Representative of the people.—The representative of the people or *representante* is named by the people at a town meeting along with two other persons, forming an administrative committee. The representative is the *presidente* of the committee, another is a secretary, and the third is an ordinary member or *vocal*. The appointments are confirmed by the Governor and last until the people elect new ones at another *junta* or town meeting. None of the members receives any pay but the work is not onerous. Usually signing a few papers is the major duty. The reward, according to one member of the committee, is in being selected as one of the best "elements" in the town.

The collection of funds for use of the forest lands is done by the inevitable *comisionado* system. With the approval and, if necessary, the backing of the mayor and *ayuntamiento*, the committee names the *comisionados* who collect 28 centavos from each householder every 2 months for the right to cut firewood on public lands. This money is used to pay the Federal taxes.

At present no one is supposed to cut wood for lumber, charcoal, posts, etc., without securing a permit from the forestry service. (As indicated elsewhere, efforts were being made to concentrate all activity in the hands of a cooperative. The description here is of conditions before organization of the cooperative.) To prevent unauthorized exploitation of the forests by Cherán residents, or poaching by persons from other towns, a forester is employed to patrol the woods. The source of pay of the forester is obscure, but he is entitled to make use of a certain amount of fallen timber on his own account and if he encounters poachers from other towns (such as Zacapu, Carapan, and Purépero), he may either confiscate their products and sell them or charge the poachers 20 or 25 centavos for each burro load. The proceeds are kept by the forester.

The institution of the *representante* is reasonably old; at least it has been in existence as long as men now living. While the representative apparently has no official responsibility, if things go wrong he is blamed. In 1939, a forest fire damaged a considerable area and the forestry engineers called the representative down severely for not having been more efficient in fighting the fire. This attitude was hardly justified in view of the strong Tarascan tradition of burning the pastures in the winter.

Illegal exploitation of the forests is also blamed on the representative. Two major cases occurred during the period field work was under way, one involving illegal cutting of railroad ties, the other, illegal sale of lumber. Responsibility for failure to prevent both infractions was laid to the laxness of the *representante*. In connection with one of these cases, a town *junta* was called to discuss what should be done, but no decision was reached and the matter was finally dropped.

It was evidently felt that the *representante* would be involved in boundary disputes if they affected public lands. The two disputes existing in 1940, however, apparently affected only lands in private ownership. The dispute with Arantepacua was in process of settlement with a compromise being made between the two claims. As there was only a question of which town would get credit for the taxes paid, the dispute was not bitter. The quarrel with the former *tenencia* of Cheranástico, however, was much more prolonged and bitter. Apparently Cheranástico claimed some of the best agricultural lands of the lower plain as community property. It was, however, owned in individual holdings by owners who all had registered titles. Consequently, Cheranástico has accomplished nothing, but every time there was a new governor or other governmental change, the people of Cheranástico made another attempt.

BARRIO FUNCTIONS AND COMMUNAL IMPROVEMENTS

In addition to the function of the *barrio* or *cuartel* as an administrative device as described above, certain public improvements are made through the *barrio* mechanism. In this the *barrios* do not act independently but merely as instrumentalities of the *municipio*. No informant had ever heard of a *barrio* doing anything on its own initiative.

The major duty performed by the *barrio* is the maintenance of the water system. Each *barrio* has a section of the aqueduct within the town (not the pipe line to the edge of town but the system of hollowed logs which conducts water to the center of town) for which it is responsible. Upon notification that repairs are needed or that logs must be replaced, the *barrio* chief notifies men in his *barrio* of the work needed and the time. This notification may come from the *síndico* (or his *veedor*), or any person noticing something wrong may report it to the *municipio*. The *barrio* not only provides labor but must raise funds if equipment or materials are needed. *Barrio* I is responsible for the section from the cement water tanks to the street called Arista. *Barrio* II is responsible for the section from Arista to Pensador, *barrio* III for the section from Pensador to Olvide, and *barrio* IV for the section from Olvide to the pipe line.

The work is done under the direction of the *síndico*. Usually 24 *comisionados* are named for each log trough needed. Eight men are responsible for cutting the log and hollowing it out; 8 more bring the log down from the mountains, and 8 others put it in place.

In addition, each *barrio* has responsibility for certain other public works. For example, *barrio* III is responsible for maintaining two bridges on the road to Zacapu.

Still another *barrio* duty is cleaning the graveyard of weeds and brush in preparation for the Day of the Dead. The cemetery is divided into four squares corresponding to the four *barrios*, and the young men from each *barrio* are assigned to a section. In 1940, in *barrio* III, having the most numerous population, each youth had a strip 4 paces wide by 65 paces long to clear, while youths of other *barrios* had strips from 6 to 8 paces wide. *Barrio* IV, although having a population as large as *barrio* II and larger than *barrio* I, took a half day longer to do its part and the young men were teased about it.

The maintenance of the pipe line is a sore point, evidently. The original pipe line was installed by the State or Federal Government. Some maintenance is done by the *municipio*, but the line was in bad condition in 1940 and needed replacing. Even more interest, however, was shown in replacing the present wooden aqueduct with a pipe line and perhaps extending it to some other parts of town. It was estimated that the project of merely replacing the wooden aqueduct would cost between $2,500 and $3,000, and efforts were being made to get the Federal Government to provide the money. Actually the job could have been done by an assessment little larger than that called for by the two main fiestas of the town, but such an idea had not occurred to anyone. This feeling that major improvements should be made by outside agencies is a common one in Mexico.

This attitude was somewhat reinforced by the action of the Federal Government in extending a power line to the town and supplying it with street lighting. In this case, it is true, the town was required to provide the posts for the power system. *Comisionados* were named who cut the posts and charred the ends under the direction of the *síndico*. However, this involved expenditure of labor rather than of money.

A number of road repair jobs are undertaken from time to time. In 1940, in preparation for the harvest, the community repaired part of the road toward Nahuatzen. A new entry into town was made which avoided the necessity of crossing a bridge over the southern *barranca*. The existing bridge was in bad repair, and replacement was thus postponed.

ELECTIONS

Elections in Cherán ostensibly follow regular legal forms. Extensive and nearly complete lists of voters are prepared by the municipal officials. Some 2 or 3 weeks before the election the mayor calls a town meeting to nominate candidates. The mayor asserted that everyone was invited in 1940 but that very few attended. Most of those, he insisted, had been rounded up by the police. Others felt that only the most influential people in town were invited. In either case, apparently only about 50 persons attended. As at the 1940 election *barrios* II and IV were to elect members of the *ayuntamiento*, two tickets were nominated. These tickets were forwarded to the State offices of the PRM (*Partido Revolucionario Mexicano*) in Morelia, and the second of the two tickets was approved as the official PRM ticket. This must have been an act of prestidigitation on the part of the State officials, for there was nothing to choose between the two tickets and the State

officials could have had no basis for selection. Actually, the *suplente* in *barrio* II was one of the reactionary members of the community, leader of the *ačes*. He was chosen solely to stop his constant criticism of the administration.

The election was held on December 1, 1940. In theory, the first Sunday of December is the usual day. A commission, named by the mayor 15 days before, conducted the elections. Two ballot boxes were placed at opposite ends of the *corredor* in front of the *municipio*, one for each *barrio*. Only 45 votes were cast in *barrio* II and only 25 in *barrio* IV. The result of the election was to select the official PRM ticket in *barrio* II and the "opposition" ticket in *barrio* IV.

The procedure resulted in the mayor for the succeeding year, the successful candidate for *barrio* II, being elected by the majority of the 45 votes cast in that *barrio*. The mayor-elect promptly got very drunk and paraded from saloon to saloon for 2 or 3 days, shouting, "*Yo y Avila Camacho*—I and Avila Camacho." (Camacho was about to be installed as President of the Republic.) Murmurs of protest about the new mayor began to be heard on every side, becoming louder and louder. By the end of the month rumors of violence at the installation of the new *ayuntamiento* on January 1 were heard on every side. Loudest to complain were those who had attended neither the nominating *junta* nor the elections.

On January 1 very few people attended the installation of the new officers. The new officials went at the head, the new mayor in the middle, on his right the new *síndico*, and on his left the judge. The mayor carried a *bandera*, a round disk with the national colors in three vertical stripes, while his two companions carried ribbons hanging down from the *bandera*. Behind the new officials came the *reserva*, then a relatively small group of males. At the rear came the band. The procession made a circuit about the plaza and streets of the central part of town. *Cohetes* were fired off as the procession started and at each corner where it changed direction.

On the return to the *municipio*, the new mayor made a speech, received with a scattering of handclaps. The *jefe político*, Moisés Valencia, made another speech, urging cooperation with the new officials and the betterment of the town. He stressed especially fixing up the plaza and planting trees. His remarks drew more handclaps than did those of the mayor. This concluded a remarkably tame and peaceful affair.

On the surface, all the rumors had come to nothing and an uninformed visitor might have thought the talk had been nothing else. But the mayor who was inducted at this ceremony was not the elected mayor. In fact, he had not even been a candidate. The same was true of the *suplente* for the *síndico*. Obviously, explanation is called for.

Actually, the matter was simple. The talk and complaints had resulted in action. Apparently no one, on sober thought, wanted the elected mayor. So the *ayuntamiento* picked out someone they thought would be satisfactory and installed him as mayor. The choice seemed actually an excellent one. The new mayor was one of the best-educated men in town, a sober, honest, and conscientious man, fairly prosperous but not rich. None of the investigators found any objection or any tendency to question the action. According to the retiring mayor, one man, an *Almazanista* (that is, a follower of Almazán, the defeated presidential candidate) with little following had raised some objections. But the retiring mayor pointed out that the objector had never bothered to come to the nominating *junta* or to vote, although the mayor had personally invited him to do so and had asked him to make a house-to-house visit to all his followers, urging their attendance. Legality was to be maintained, however, and the State authorities received proper election returns certifying the election of the men installed.

Did this represent corruption and the breakdown of democratic methods as would be the interpretation of legalistic minds deeply steeped in the proprieties of parliamentary procedure? None of the staff of the investigation in Cherán felt it was. The persons finally inducted into office were capable men. They seemed highly acceptable to the bulk of the population, whereas the duly elected candidates were not. Rather, it seems that a truly democratic result had been obtained for a people who are unfamiliar with and distrustful of parliamentary procedures.

Persons who are shocked at the procedures at Cherán should seriously contemplate the difficulties in carrying out a formal election with written ballots with a population which is very largely illiterate. In this case economic limitations and lack of imagination prevented carrying out the system used in national elections where the candidates each select a color and separate ballots are printed in the different colors. The voter then asks for his ballot by color and drops it into the ballot box. Not secret, and lending itself to ballot box stuffing, the method is at least an attempt to deal with the problem of an illiterate electorate. In a town such as Cherán the method followed in the election described seems equally efficacious—as long as the officials are responsive to public opinion.

That unconventionalities are frequent in elections is further illustrated by the presidential elections earlier in the same year. Many months before the election a group of Almazán followers organized and began an active campaign in the town. The followers of Camacho (the PRM group) remained inactive. At the end of 2 or 3 months a PRM delegation waited on the Almazán followers and pointed out that there had been no interference with their campaign but that nevertheless the bulk of the town favored Camacho. The facts were apparently indisputable, and when the PRM group stressed the fact that further campaigning could only result in creating divisions and dissensions in the town, the Almazán group ceased its campaign. At the election, Cherán cast a unanimous ballot for Camacho.

Two things of interest emerge from this account. The first is the power of the argument against disunity in the community. Particularly in the Indian community, unity is prized almost above all else. Sophisticated in some ways as Cherán is, this argument is still one of the most potent that can be made. The second point of interest is the bearing this sequence of events has on interpretation of the national election returns in Mexico. What happened in Cherán probably happened in hundreds of other towns in Mexico and helps partly to explain the one-sided results usually reported in Mexican elections.

In relation to external politics, most Cherán inhabitants have little interest. There are many people who are willing to take a free ride to some big rally for one or another presidential candidate, eat heartily of the free meal, and cheer the candidate's speech enthusiastically. The following week they are quite as ready to accept the hospitality of the opposing candidate, and at election time be too disinterested to vote. Not only is interest lacking, but there is considerable cynicism about the external Government agencies. As one humble farmer remarked, *"Almazán o Camacho, ¿que nos importa? Aqui siempre estamos en la riata—* Almazán or Camacho, what does it matter to us? Here we are always in the noose."

Some interest is also awakened by the discovery of the Indians as a colorful adjunct to ceremonials. At the inauguration of Camacho as president, some Federal agency (probably the *Departamento Autónomo de Asuntos Indígenas*) took the town officials, the band, and a group of moro dancers to Mexico City. The Cherán citizens lucky enough to get such a trip are always pleased, but it is doubtful whether they are much interested in the reasons.

FISCAL SYSTEM

Just as the economy of Cherán in general is partly a money economy, the governmental system is also based partly on money. The presence of hired officials immediately requires some form of cash income for the town. This income is derived from the following sources:

1. Taxes on each beef slaughtered.
2. Taxes of $1.15 on each bill of sale for an animal.
3. Fines.
4. Business licenses. These are collected by the State tax collector, who remits 40 percent of collections to the municipal treasury.
5. Registration of brands. Every cattle brand must be registered and the registry renewed in the first 3 months of each year. This is the biggest source of income for the *municipio*. Three pesos are collected by the *municipio*, which also collects and remits 30 centavos to the State government and 15 centavos to the Federal Government for each brand.
6. Market tax (*piso de plaza*). Every vender in the plaza on Saturdays and at the fiestas (except Corpus) must pay a small tax based on the amount of space occupied. Income from this source averages $5 or $6 weekly.
7. Certification of documents. This is rather rare, consisting of charges for copies of documents, marriage or birth records, etc.
8. Taxes on forest products. All forest products sold outside the community are taxed by the Federal Government and must be accompanied by a certificate of origin. Dealers in the large centers pay the tax, surrendering the certificate of origin. The Federal Government then remits 30 percent of the tax to the State government and 20 percent to the municipal government.

It should be noted that real estate taxes in Mexico are a monopoly of the Federal Government and there are no local taxes. Ten percent of all local collections other than the registry of brands is paid to the State government and 5 percent to the Federal Government.

The income from all these sources varies. In the first 3 months of the year it may exceed $300 a month. At other times it may be as low as $125 a month. In the year Pedro Chávez was treasurer it totaled about $1,800. In 1940 it must have been considerably higher, but the investigators were already sufficiently on sufferance to be unable to demand access to the current town records.

Expenditures against income are as follows:

	Per month
Two policemen at $0.75 (a third policeman was added in 1941)	$45.50
Municipal secretary	45.00
Court secretary	30.00
Treasurer (25 percent of income at an estimated $150 monthly average)	37.50
Monthly average	$158.00

In addition, there are some occasional small irregular expenditures, for instance, painting the plaza benches for a fiesta etc. These are small, for the regular expenses pretty well use up the regular income. The treasury usually has only 2 or 3 pesos in it at the end of the year and often shows a small deficit of 10 or even 20 pesos. For this reason, unusual expenditures are financed by a collection.

The treasurer is required to make three types of reports, one to the Federal Treasury Department, one to the State treasurer, and one to the general accounting office of the State. The first two deal with income payable to Federal or State government, while the third deals with all the municipal accounts.

UNOFFICIAL ORGANIZATIONS

The functioning of government in Cherán is often affected by unofficial organizations and informal groups. At the time of the study, the most influential of such groups was one affiliated with the CTM (*Confederación de Trabajadores Mexicanas*). Probably this same group also functioned as a local branch of the official government party, the PRM (*Partido Revolucionario Mexicano*).

The actual functioning and organization of these groups was quite informal. Considerable difference of opinion existed in the town as to the desirability of such organizations, many. holding that they are disruptive in character. Others, the so-called progressives, felt that such organization is necessary if the town is to receive its fair share of Government aid. Between these conflicting viewpoints could arise violent disagreement. With great reasonableness, however, the "progressives" organized only informally. Those who felt the town should be organized in the fashion mentioned, named officers and got themselves recognized by the State branch of the CTM. When documents arrive which need action or signature, the members of the group talk them over informally in house-to-house visits and send the necessary replies. There are no meetings or overt evidence of the organization. From the standpoint of union and party officials in the State capital, the town is organized; from the standpoint of the majority of the inhabitants of Cherán, it is not.

The development of this informal organization grew out of another and earlier organization that had gotten the town a bad name. In 1940–41, within a short time any investigator soon heard of the *zafarrancho*, the disorder or riot. Evidently a landmark, many events were dated by reference to this affair. To learn about it, however, was not easy. Many people refused to talk about it at all; others suggested that it was unwise to talk about it. Only after many months was the story finally secured in

confidential talks, and even then it is doubtful whether all the details were abstracted from unwilling witnesses. The story as learned does not seem to call for all the secrecy involved, and this gives weight to the suspicion that the truth of the underlying factors was not secured and that these factors are more operative today than anyone would admit.

At the height of the agrarian movement in Michoacán, the control of the *municipio* was secured by a group of some 30 men calling themselves "agrarians (*agraristas*)." Everyone seemed agreed that there was no genuine agrarian problem in Cherán and that the members of the group had no desire for land but only for power. Perpetuating themselves in office, members of this group at first were tolerated but gradually became more and more overbearing in their attitude. When people finally began to show signs of discontent, the "agrarians" asked the State authorities for aid on the grounds that the people were rebellious. As a result, a detachment of soldiers was stationed in Cherán under the command of a lieutenant to enforce order and the authority of the municipal officials. The young lieutenant apparently soon saw that his troops were perpetuating an illegal and unpopular group in power and tried to get his superiors to make a real investigation, but with no success. The tyranny of the ruling group now became unbearable.

The climax came when a drunken member of the group began firing his revolver on the main streets and threatening people. One of the soldiers endeavored to arrest the man and was shot and killed. The lieutenant now succeeded in having the situation thoroughly investigated, and as a result the detachment of soldiers was withdrawn. The following day occurred the *zafarrancho*. Some 10 to 12 of the "agrarians" were killed and the rest fled the town. In 1940, they were still living in exile in nearby towns.

For a time following this, Cherán was governed by a *presidente militar*, an appointed army officer. Technically, this was true in 1940, but the commander rarely even visited the town and all troops had been removed some time before. The present "progressive" government has effectively been in power since the affair. This is also the group which has organized the local branch of the CTM, no doubt a factor in securing the withdrawal of the always unpopular military garrison.

The leader of the progressive group is a man who has not held any official office in the town, Moisés Valenzuela, commander of the *reserva*. An orphan as a child, Valenzuela was aided by a woman he calls his aunt. According to Valenzuela's own story, he left Cherán at 16 and tried to go to the United States. Refused admission for some reason, he fell into bad company and became involved in smuggling liquor across the border during prohibition. Eventually the activities of the group extended to narcotics, Valenzuela was caught and held about 18 months in a Texas jail, after which he was deported. He then entered an army school, learned to read and write and received some further education, eventually becoming some sort of officer. Returning to Cherán during the time of the agrarians, he organized and led the resistance to them, and quite informally arrived in the position of being, as one informant put it, "head man" of Cherán. Locally he is regarded as an influential person over an area extending as far as the State capital, Morelia.

So far as evidence could be found, Valenzuela is an honest man, well-liked in the town. He talked several times of the necessity of going away and earning some money. According to his story, he did not mind giving most of his time for the town, but the time had come when he should look after his wife and children better than he was able to do in Cherán. Certainly he did not live in a pretentious house, and his customary clothing was overalls. His dress, of course, could be assumed for political reasons, but when he made trips to Morelia or Uruapan on community or private business, he certainly dressed little better. It is, of course, quite possible that persons with a different view of Valenzuela were afraid to talk freely. He himself deprecated his position and seemed somewhat amused that the townspeople accorded him as much respect as they did. His own story of his arrest and jail sentence in the United States was told with a somewhat rueful and artless good humor. On the many occasions he was seen with others, he always seemed ready to listen to other points of view and to advance his own without any attempt at domina-

tion. It was, indeed, difficult to imagine him as the leader of a bloody riot.

As a final footnote on the affair of the "agrarians," one of the first acts of the new government installed in January, 1941, was to send letters to all the members of the agrarian group, inviting them to return to Cherán and guaranteeing their safety if they refrained from political activities. This was done with the approval, if not at the actual instigation, of Valenzuela.

An entirely different type of organization is the cooperative. Essentially an economic organization, it deserves treatment here because it potentially might yet have important political repercussions. Although not openly opposed by anyone in hearing of the staff of the study, comments made by several men while drunk implied great bitterness on the part of some of the people in the town. The cooperative, still in process of formation in 1941, was organized under the leadership of one Valentin Velásquez. Velásquez was not dressed in typical Cherán fashion, and he had spent several years in the United States. He speaks typically Cherán Spanish, however, somewhat in the manner of the famous screen comedian, Cantinflas—he never finishes a sentence and only after several sentences is it apparent what his ideas really are. He is an orphan who has bettered himself economically at the cost of terrific effort, according to his own story, and his interest in the cooperative, he claims, is merely that of a good citizen who feels it his duty to aid others to better their lot. By his own admission there is a good deal of opposition to the cooperative, and he has been threatened with death several times. He lays this opposition to ignorance.

The organization of the cooperative would give it a monopoly on all exploitation of forest lands except for cutting of firewood for personal use. The cooperative would charge a membership fee of 10 pesos, and members would be required to market all their products through the cooperative. Only the cooperative would be licensed by the Forestry Department and all work would have to be done in areas designated by the Forestry officials, using care not to destroy young trees. Members would receive better prices for their products through the bulk marketing and better bargaining power of the cooperative. In 1941 it was claimed that a considerable number of the individuals working in the woods had signed up, as well as some men in the town who wished to indicate their support of the idea although not themselves forest workers.

Two things were said to be holding up the completion of the organization of the cooperative. The first was the necessity of raising enough capital to pay advances to the members when they deposited their products with the cooperative for marketing. The second was the refusal of the *representante* to sign the necessary papers. According to Velásquez, this refusal was not because the *representante* disapproved of the idea, but because he felt many people in town were opposed and he did not wish to sign the papers counter to their wishes. As the signature of the *representante* was not absolutely essential, the organization probably was completed without his approval.

It may be noted that the cooperative had nearly come to grief in its early days through an action by the *presidente militar* imposed after the 1937 *zafarrancho*. The military governor had ordered posts cut for the installation of the electric lighting system without securing a permit from the Department of Forestry. The Forestry officials had blamed this on the cooperative, levied a thousand peso fine, and threatened to revoke the permit of the organization. This had been cleared up, and it was rumored that the former military governor was going to have to pay the fine—which may very much be doubted.

A number of other organizations of a religious nature exist and will be dealt with later. Potentially most influential in political matters are the church societies such as those of the Sacred Heart, the Third Order of Saint Francis, and others. In Cherán in 1940, it was difficult to learn much about these. The meetings were private, and secrecy had been impressed on the members. There is very little doubt that a new priest who took over the parish late in 1940 was utilizing these organizations to undermine the existing liberal political order in Cherán. Trouble was brewing in Cherán on the religious and political front and there is little doubt that it was being con-

sciously fostered by some elements in the Church, probably the same groups fostering the Sinarquista movement in the adjoining region of the Bajío north of Tarascan territory.[32] Additional data on the change in attitude of the church in Cherán will be presented under religion.

CONFLICT AND LAW

The people of Cherán are very reticent about conflicts within the town. Efforts are made to convince the outsider that the town is a harmonious unit, and it is very difficult to secure data to the contrary. The impression, after many months in Cherán, is that a great deal of hostility underlies the apparent harmony. In part, this is apparent in the prevalence of witchcraft and some of the evidence is presented under that heading. Interfamily and intrafamily jealousies and conflicts, however carefully concealed, cropped up time and again in casual remarks. Nevertheless, little definite information could be secured. Any efforts to pick up the small leads occurring in conversation were usually adroitly countered. Consequently, the material presented in this section consists primarily of the more overt conflicts which, under certain circumstances, lead to official interference.

A great variety of minor conflicts constantly reach the office of the mayor. Many of these never pass the stage of discussion and informal settlement. For example, a man had been drunk all week, insulting people indiscriminately. One man finally struck the drunkard. The case was discussed at length. Some argued that the drunkard should be arrested. Others claimed that both should be arrested. Ultimately, nothing was done, but as anyone present in the *municipio* could enter the discussion, word probably got around to both parties. The drunkard's relatives probably restrained him and the man giving the blows kept out of sight.

Another case illustrates the handling of minor offenses. A woman was brought before the acting mayor (the mayor's alternate), charged with stealing a blanket from a man while he was drunk. The woman was accused vigorously by the acting mayor but denied the charge with equal vigor. Finally the acting mayor ordered that she be locked up, and, despite voluble protests against injustice, the woman was conveyed forcibly to the jail. The whole procedure seemed very high-handed, but when the woman was out of earshot, the acting mayor turned to me mildly and remarked that he would not have acted that way on the man's word alone but there had been two witnesses and there was no doubt of the woman's guilt. He was trying to frighten the woman into a confession and restitution of the blanket, with which he would be content to dismiss the case.

Several drunks on the morning of October 3 created a commotion. Two got into a fight and were locked up. The rest were not molested.

On another day, two women were noticed in the jail. One said the other had thrown a gourd at her head. The second accused the first of stealing something from her lot. They were both thrown in jail to cool off.

A little girl was "horsing around"—to use the phrase of Augustín Rangel—near one of the street-corner vendors. The woman told her to go away, but the girl's mother did not interfere. In the mother's absence the girl broke some pottery. The two women began to quarrel and finally went to the mayor's office. After discussion, the woman with the pottery was advised to be more careful of her goods when there were children around.

Three men walked down the street, in various stages of drunkenness. Two began to quarrel and the drunkest of the three picked up a rock and threatened one of the men. The third man interposed himself, talked soothingly, eventually got the rock away from the drunken man, and they continued their walk.

One drunken man kept saying to another "You are rich and can do everything you want and I have nothing." The second man ignored this. After a while the first man said, "I don't care if you are rich, you —— —— ——," and then began commenting on the man's mother. The second man said, "Take back what you said about my mother." The first man said, "Never." Then they began to fight. Nothing was done about this.

The cases given above represent conflicts which resulted in no official punishment. Con-flicts and illegal acts which brought official action were few (outside of property suits, which are not considered here). The following is the calendar of cases placed on the records from October 9 to December 3.

October 9. A man knocked down a child and hurt her head. He was placed in jail overnight.

October 12. A man was drunk and disorderly. He was placed in jail (no term indicated).

October 15. A man was drunk and disorderly. He was placed in jail overnight.

October 16. A drunken man broke onto a house. He was placed in jail until the eighteenth.

October 22. A woman was "disobedient" (probably disorderly conduct of some sort). She was placed in jail overnight.

November 3. A man raped a young woman, his second offense. He was placed in jail until the 10th. It should be observed that according to Cherán ideas a properly brought up girl whose parents looked after her as they should would never have been in a situation where rape would be possible.

December 3. A man "abused confidence" by trying to register a piece of land as his own which actually belonged to his mother-in-law. He was put in jail overnight.

The above cases do not include those which involved fines of less than one peso nor cases which came before the judge.

Despite the fact that Cherán has a bad reputation in other towns for violence, there seem to be relatively few serious fights. Drunks often fall to fisticuffs, usually ineffective, but knife fights are rare and the use of firearms is even more unusual. In ordinary times there is probably not more than one killing a year. However, a very serious affair occurred shortly before the close of the study.

At a wedding the new priest appeared after the drinking was well under way. He reproved the people soundly for their excessive drinking and urged them to go home. One of the men, who was already very drunk, took the priest's words to heart and started home. Crossing the bridge to the *barrio* of Parícutin, he was shot from ambush and killed. That night the *ronda* went from house to house asking for certain persons, but up to the time the study closed nothing had been done. Probably more than personal motives lay back of the killing, but it was impossible to discover them.

Marriage customs are another frequent source of conflicts reaching the mayor. Ordinarily a boy "kidnaps" the girl he is going to marry. The kidnapping is public and usually nothing is done about it, but the boy may be forced to marry the girl if he does not go through with the ceremony in a reasonable time. Occasionally, though, the girl's relatives make so much commotion that the mayor has to act. If the kidnapping has been "legitimate," that is, the boy intends to marry the girl, usually the men participating in the kidnapping are thrown in jail for 2 or 3 hours and released with an admonition, almost certainly given with tongue in cheek.

In other cases the matter may become more serious, especially if it is exploited by the girl. One example will illustrate the situation.

A boy stopped to talk with a girl of dubious morals. When he left, she followed him, saying she was going home with him. The boy ran away and hid. Later in the day the girl's parents came to the mayor and claimed the boy had kidnapped the girl. The boy was ordered

to marry the girl by a certain date. He failed to do so, as he wished to marry another girl and knew also that the girl laying the charges visited a house of assignation. He was thrown in jail. Later, his mother went his bond and he was released. The boy fled town and had not returned several months later. His mother was put in jail overnight but was released the next day.

The preceding discussion is a very unsatisfactory treatment of conflict situations and law. Information on the unformalized personal and familial conflicts is very scanty. Intimate day to day knowledge of households which would produce such information is extremely difficult to secure in Cherán. On the other hand, not enough detailed material was secured on the types of conflicts reaching the *municipio* to make possible any adequate statement regarding legal concepts. In theory, the law in Cherán is Mexican law. Enough examples have perhaps been given to indicate that much of the justice dispensed in the *municipio* is according to informal and generally accepted rules. Only observation of a very large number of cases would permit abstracting the principles on which action is based.

RELIGION AND CEREMONIAL

Religion in Cherán revolves about the church and the formalized practices and beliefs associated with it. In addition, there is a lively belief in witchcraft, plus a body of miscellaneous and unorganized beliefs and customs. In the main, the organized ceremonials, aside from those associated with life crises, which are dealt with in another section, are linked with the church and are group or community affairs. The ceremonials and rituals connected with witchcraft and miscellaneous beliefs are primarily individual in character and are not organized in any way, although there is a certain gradation between the two types of ceremonial with respect to organization.

The church ceremonials and rituals are of four types. Central to the system are those church rituals and ceremonies which follow more or less conventional Mexican Catholic lines and are wholly under the direction of the

priest. The Mass, Rosary, confession, baptism, confirmation, and so on all fall in this category. A more or less conventional church organization headed by a priest is almost solely responsible for these ceremonies. Associated with this part of the religious organization are the various societies, such as those of the Sacred Heart, Daughters of Mary, Apostles of Saint Joseph, and the Third Order of Saint Francis. Linked with the church organization in part is the *cabildo* or the *ačes*.

Forming a mixture of church and community ceremonials are the fiestas. The organization of fiestas is related to the political organization and, aside from the Mass and strictly church rituals, the fiestas are essentially secular celebrations centering round a religious object.

The *mayordomías* are the third important type of religious ceremony and are connected with the church through the *carguero* system and dance groups dominated by the *cabildo* or the aċes. Although a Mass in church is involved, the ceremonies are conducted primarily by laymen. The aċes are related to the church organization proper on the one hand, and control the *carguero* system on the other.

The fourth and final type of ceremonial consists of *mayordomía* and dance groupings which are not under the control of the aċes. In some cases connection with the church is maintained to the extent of paying for a Mass, but neither the priest nor the aċes have any real control.

THE CHURCH

The physical aspect of the Church is represented by the church building, the priest's residence, and a chapel called the calvary. Formerly the physical structures were more extensive, including a second chapel at one side of the church, an extension of the priest's residence, and the hospital, now in ruins. As all the church property today belongs to the State, under the administration of the *municipio,* parts of these buildings and associated grounds have been taken over for other uses. Part of what was formerly the priest's residence now is used for the Federal rural school. The second chapel is used only in emergencies. It was employed as the church at a time when a new roof was being put on the church. At the time of this study it was rented to the tilemakers. The church building is reverenced to some extent: men lift their hats as they pass in front of it on the street.

Maintenance of the structures still used by the church organization and the priest depends upon voluntary contributions by the faithful. The municipal organization spends no funds on repair or maintenance of the church structures, although it may spend money on the parts used for the school. Some of the extensive patios formerly associated with the church are used for recreational areas; others are still used by the priest and are cultivated by him. Two wooden structures occupy part of the grounds, one used as a storehouse for certain ceremonial equipment and one used by the kéŋi, an official of the *cabildo* or aċes, as a residence.

The church building has obviously undergone a number of major alterations in its history. Originally the church did not front on the plaza but upon an atrium facing the opposite direction. The change of entrance probably was made more than 50 years ago. At about that time the walls of the church were raised considerably and a row of windows placed near the top of the walls. During the revolution the roof was destroyed when the town was burned and was replaced sometime during the 1920's.

The cost of these changes and repairs, as indicated, is borne by voluntary contributions. The labor is paid for and there is no voluntary labor for the upkeep of church structures and property, although there is considerable voluntary work in connection with the ceremonials and the care of the altars and images. In the case of small improvements, the priest asks for donations of some 10 centavos, usually making an announcement from the pulpit. For larger and more extensive repairs or improvements, *comisionados* are named by the priest who go from house to house soliciting larger contributions.

A new idea was introduced, however, by the priest who left Cherán in 1940, an idea which has had interesting economic repercussions. With the completion of the reroofing of the church, many other necessary improvements still remained. With some funds at his disposal, the priest succeeded in rebuilding the pulpit. The priest then announced an inaugural ceremony and issued invitations to become godparents of the pulpit. The invitations were written or printed and stated that the persons were being invited as honorable persons who led good lives. Acceptance involved a payment of not less than 1 peso nor more than 2 pesos. Practically all those invited accepted the invitation. The priest had prepared a large quantity of pottery banks in the shape of pigs, made of the attractive Black ware of Quiroga and Santa Fe. At the inauguration, the priest announced that additional improvements were being planned and that each person should take one of the banks and put a 20-centavo piece in it every 15 or 30 days. Moreover, the person who first "fattened" his pig, that is, filled it with 20-centavo pieces, would be put in a position of especial sanctity. With this incentive, many people filled their banks rapidly in order to be the first and even those who did it more slowly accumulated a substantial contribution without feeling the drain on their finances. In this way the priest accumulated enough money to rebuild the altar and the choir loft as well as make other improvements.

This procedure would have amounted to little more than a clever money-making scheme had not the priest projected it much more deeply into Cherán life. At the same time he gave the pig banks to the adults, he gave smaller banks to all the children. The children he instructed, not to save money for the church, as one might expect, but to accumulate their centavos so that when a fiesta came along they would have money to buy what they wanted and have a good time. The result of this procedure was that today the majority of Cherán residents, both adults and children, each has his bank, in which he accumulates small change, and the habit of saving, usually for some specific end, has become quite common in the town. A regular part of the pottery stocks brought to Cherán at fiestas are pottery banks, now made not only in the shape of pigs but in the shape of many other animals, with a frequent touch of the fantasy and caricature which characterize Tarascan modeled pottery.[33]

THE PRIEST AND THE CHURCH ORGANIZATION

The priest, of course, is appointed by the Bishop in Zamora. At the time the study began, the resident priest had been some years in Cherán and evidently was popular and well-liked. Shortly afterward he was transferred to another parish, and considerable efforts were made to persuade the Bishop to change his mind about the appointment. A petition was also circulated and taken to the Bishop. Considerable feeling was generated by the Bishop's adamant stand on the matter, and for several weeks no request was made for a new priest in hopes of getting a return of the former priest. When the old priest returned for a visit and to settle some business affairs, the entrance to the residence was ornamented with flowers and pine

branches, and large numbers came to visit him. Despite these efforts, a new priest arrived some 2 weeks after the departure of the old priest.

The household and assistants of the priest vary somewhat. The mother of the old priest served as his housekeeper, and there were several servants. The old priest relied primarily on the *cabildo* or *ačes* for his aides in church. The new priest brought a household whose exact composition I did not learn. In addition, he brought a sacristan and one or two other assistants, who took over several of the functions of the *cabildo*. In general, the new priest adopted a much more aggressive attitude. Not only did he immediately get into a bitter quarrel with the *cabildo* (to be described later), but he interfered with customs on every hand, wore his priestly dress in public and permitted people to kneel in public and kiss his hand, and mixed in political matters. Considerable numbers of Cherán residents resented his attitude bitterly, including many of the devout members of the community.

The support of the priest is based on voluntary contributions, but in Cherán the priest is aggressive. Formerly, the *cabildo* kept the priest informed as to the amounts of harvest, and the priest, often personally, at other times through one of his assistants, directly asked for "alms." The amount suggested is the traditional tenth; in some cases people give him this amount, but many give less. The payments are mostly in kind, usually wheat or corn, which is brought to the priest's residence and placed by him in a storehouse in charge of the kéηi. It was reported that the priest normally sells corn and wheat to needy local residents at about 1 peso a bushel below the market price. The facts in the case at the time of inquiry were somewhat obscured by the quarrel with the *cabildo*.

The functions of the priest in Cherán are numerous. Not only does he say the obligatory Masses, but he also celebrates special Masses in connection with every fiesta and *mayordomía*. All weddings are also celebrated with special Masses. He also arranges for such special events as visits of the Bishop for confirmation.

The Bishop paid one visit to Cherán during the time of the study. The priest appointed four *comisionados* in each *barrio* to gather con-

---

[33] The pig bank, as is well known, was introduced to Mexico by the wife of the late Ambassador Morrow. Those interested in making anthropology a predictive science might well be somewhat nonplussed by the devious, even fantastic, route by which the pig bank and the savings idea were transmitted to Cherán and became a part of Cherán culture.

tributions. For some time before this visit, rockets were fired off at noon and at 3 p. m. and the church bells were rung about 3:45 p. m. This was to call people to confess in anticipation of the Bishop's visit.

Another activity, about which little is known, is in connection with the various societies. As indicated previously, there seems to be a degree of secrecy about the functions of these groups; undoubtedly they are primarily religious. For example, on January 3, the day of the Sacred Heart, members of the Society of the Sacred Heart spent the day in church. They wore red bands about their necks with ornaments of red ribbons and spent much of their time kneeling and in group prayers led by a maestro or lay reader. There is also reason to believe that the new priest, at least, used these groups for political purposes. Scarcely a day passed without one group or the other being summoned to a meeting at church by means of special signals on the church bells.

The majority of the people in town belong to one society or another. Rarely or never do they belong to two. The societies of Saint Joseph and of Mary are for boys and girls, respectively; when they marry they are dropped from membership. Adults belong to the other societies. Membership is by invitation only. Each society has a board of directors (mesa directiva) which issues the invitations. All meetings are held in the church or in the priest's quarters.

There can be little doubt that Cherán is a strongly Catholic community. During the height of the conflict between the Church and the Government, when priests were forbidden to officiate and the churches were closed,[34] Cherán residents underwent considerable risk to bring a priest to the town periodically. Many of the services were held in a private house belonging to a certain Cherán resident who was later in bitter conflict with the new priest who arrived in 1940. The minority in the town who were opposed to Church domination in political affairs did not dare to speak openly. Quotation of a statement given me by one of

these men illustrates the situation clearly, particularly as it came to a head in 1940. That the informant had no violent anti-Church sentiments is indicated by the fact that he previously deprecated the rumors that a school was to be established, pointing out that it would merely be a sort of religious seminary primarily for the girls, who were not being sent to school in Cherán anyway. His statement was as follows:

The priest (referring to the new priest in 1940) is entering into political matters and speaks from the pulpit about them. In the meetings which he calls, he speaks much more directly. In one which I attended, he said he was sent to put himself in front of the people to guide them on the road they should follow. No one, he said, could molest him nor interfere with him. Even though there were some misguided persons in the town who spoke against him, he would not permit them to prevent his arriving at his ends, and if it proved necessary, he himself knew how to manage pistol and rifle and knew how to fight in the forefront of his people for their rights.

This speech was received with great enthusiasm and applause and I had to remain silent. That is one of the unfortunate things here that no one can say anything against the priest or practically the whole town turns against him. As the people have always the idea that the priest is a sacred person and that a town without a priest is not a town with a complete life, the priest has only to say that a certain person is against him and the whole town will attack the person.

I believe that this priest is very disruptive (muy divisionista) for the town. He wears his clerical garb in the town very proudly, receiving homage in the streets, a thing that the priests have not done before. The priest who left here was somewhat that way when he arrived, but when, as a friend, I indicated to him that he had spoken of political matters from the pulpit, he said it was a slip which he would not repeat. With the old priest one could speak reasonably about anything and discuss the affairs of the town and the attitude he should take, but with this one it is impossible to say anything. He will not permit the slightest criticism.

Some of the minority faction in the town who are inclined to be anticlerical are undoubtedly affected by their experiences in the United States. A former mayor was very outspoken in his objections to the behavior of the local priests. Many of the priests, he said, are guilty of much opposition to the Government and especially to the schools. He asserted that the priests seem not to wish people to read and write and are responsible for many fathers not sending their children to school. For this reason there is much unnecessary ignorance in

[34] It will be recalled that this restriction was imposed when the Church refused to permit priests to obey the new laws requiring them to register. The real point of the conflict, of course, was in those aspects of the laws which prohibited Church schools and stripped the Church of all economic rights.

the town. Continuing his remarks, the former mayor also said that the priests seem not to want people to understand the prayers and rituals. He then went on to point out how different conditions are in the United States, where he had spent some years, and entered into a discussion of the reasons for the differences.

RELIGIOUS FIESTAS

The most important rituals and recreational events at Cherán are the fiestas. They are not, however, intimately connected today with the Church. It might be fair to say that the saints' days are the excuses for holding the major fiestas. All the large fiestas are accompanied by special Masses, but the extent of church connection is perhaps less than that involved in the *mayordomías*. Essentially, the fiestas are secular events with religious overtones. All the major fiestas are conducted by the municipal authorities, rather than by the church. They are important commercial events in the town, especially the fiesta of the patron saint. They also provide a great deal of entertainment. In general, they offer occasions for making the major purchases of the year, showing hospitality, overdrinking, and for the excitement of large crowds and release from routine. Only a few people find the religious aspects of importance, even though they may attend the Mass.

In some towns the fiestas are in disrepute and have been abolished. In Cherán there is no opposition to the fiestas on religious grounds, but primarily on grounds of drunkenness. As one solid farmer remarked—

The bad part of the fiestas is that people get so very drunk; you have seen how the women become more disorderly than any (I had not observed this as a general thing, by any means). The worst is where the fiesta is too large, as in Cheranástico, where three bands are employed although the town is small. People there have to pay 13 to 15 pesos per family. Also bad is when *cargueros* have to pay the entire cost of the fiestas. Here the fiesta costs only 1 or 2 pesos per person (family).

Such views are unusual in Cherán and, except for efforts to introduce such novelties as basketball games, the progressive administration takes pride in perpetuating the conduct of the fiestas on a grand scale.

FIESTA OF THE PATRON SAINT

The fiesta of the patron saint, San Francisco, is held for 4 days, beginning the first Sunday after October 4. Usually after the Fiesta of San Luís in Nahuatzen August 25, *comisionados* are named by the mayor (on August 20 in 1940) and are notified by formal letters delivered by the police. Only persons out of town or those providing very good reasons may refuse to accept the post. The major duties are distributed by *barrio*, and for each *barrio* a head commissioner is named who selects a group of from 5 to 15 assistants. The duties in 1940 were distributed as follows: *Barrios* II and III each had to provide a band, *barrio* I provided the fireworks or *castillo*, and *barrio* IV provided the wax (*la cera*). The *barrio* IV duty really meant that it paid for the Mass and for the special candles burned. These duties are rotated so that in the course of 4 years, for example, each *barrio* will have provided the fireworks. The commissioners collect a sum varying from 80 centavos to perhaps a little more than a *peso* from each householder in the *barrio*, which they may use for their expenses. Anyone refusing to pay may be thrown in jail. The costs are not entirely equal for the different *barrios*, and, owing to the discrepancy in size of the different *barrios*, the individual contributions demanded also vary. The commissioners seem to have complete responsibility for collecting and expending funds, but if expenses are greater than the amount collected, the commissioners must make up the sum out of their own pockets.

In addition to the commissioners named for the above purposes, young men are commissioned for each *barrio* who have to provide poles and posts and reconstruct the bull ring or *toril*. Finally, four commissioners are named for the moros or dancers connected with this fiesta. Each commissioner has to find a dancer, provide him with his costume, and feed and look after the dancer throughout the fiesta. The duties of the commissioners will now be discussed in more detail as they functioned in 1940.

The commissioners for the *barrios* in 1940 were Mateo Ocampo, *barrio* I, fireworks; Florentín Rafaél, *barrio* II, music; Fernando

Durán, *barrio* III, music; Marcelino Guerrero, *barrio* IV, wax. Each of these men had a number of assistants. Marcelino Guerrero, for example, had eight. This group first estimated their expenses at about $125 to cover the cost of candles and the Mass. As late as September 17 they were not sure how much the wax would cost, because they had not yet talked with the new priest to find out what he would think necessary. Ordinarily in the past about 14 kilos of wax had been used, made into candles weighing a half kilo each. Smaller candles are also provided. The large candles have decorations of white paper. Formerly the candles were taken to church in a procession with music, but now there is no ceremony.

In addition to estimating expenses, the commissioner and his assistants made up a list of all the men in the *barrio* and set a quota for each contribution, varying from $0.50 to $1.25 per person, according to their economic conditions. About September 17 the commissioners visited all the houses to inform people what the quotas were and to warn them to be ready to pay their contribution. The following Sunday they made their actual visits for contributions. In 1940 they had some difficulty, because maize was scarce at the time and numerous people were having to buy maize.

Mateo Ocampo, commissioner for the fireworks, and his group had made up their accounts by September 12. At that time estimates were that the main *castillo* would cost $150 and would be 20 yards high. The individual contribution averaged $1.25. (On October 1, Ocampo was still collecting money.) The fireworks maker had been engaged from Paracho. In addition to collecting money, the commissioner and his assistants had to cut and bring the poles for the *castillos*. The commissioner also had to feed the fireworks maker and his assistant for about a week.

The commissioners for the music functioned similarly. Their task was more onerous, for the musicians are the most expensive of the obligations. Fernando Durán, for *barrio* II, had arranged for the band of Nahuatzen at a cost of $270 for 4 days, Sunday to Wednesday. In addition to this, the commissioners had to feed the musicians for this time. If any funds were collected more than the amount needed to pay the musicians, these might be employed to help pay for the meals. Usually the commissioner and his assistants were each responsible for serving one meal at his house. When a band is invited, usually 5 or 10 pesos are paid in advance and a written contract is signed, stating the amount to be paid and the time the music is to play. It is customary always to invite a band from outside, although sometimes the local band is hired. In 1940 the two bands were from Nahuatzen and Pichataro.

One commissioner for the moros is named from each *barrio*. He has no assistants and does not collect money, paying the entire expense out of his own pocket. The commissioner finds a young man who knows the dance and persuades him to dance. He does not ordinairily pay the dancer (who receives gifts from storekeepers and others during the fiesta), but he must feed him breakfast and dinner (but not supper) throughout the fiesta. The commissioner also must assemble the costume, usually renting the more expensive parts, provide a horse with a good saddle, and attend on the moro all the time he is dancing, looking after his needs and making any necessary adjustments or repairs in the costume. The shirt, trousers, and shoes are bought and are presented to the moro.

In 1940 only three moros appeared. The fourth commissioner was a forest worker away from home during the week. On investigation, it developed that the policeman delivered the letter to the man's wife, who claimed she mislaid the letter and forgot to give it to her husband. No one believed her, but nothing could be proved otherwise. Certainly the family's prestige in Cherán went down, for everyone was annoyed that only three moros appeared.

The four commissioners for the bull ring are all younger men. The commissioner for *barrio* I, Plácido Romero, had four assistants. None of these had to provide services but aided in seeing that the other young men complied with their obligations. Each *barrio* had to provide 18 long peeled pine trunks and 7 stout posts. In most *barrios* each young man had to bring either a post or a pole, but in *barrios* with small population, such as No. I, it was necessary to bring two. When the materials are all assembled, the young men have to rebuild the bull ring. Anyone not doing his part or providing his materials, as Romero put it, "rests in jail."

The bulls for the bull riding are sought by the mayor or by a member of the *ayuntamiento*. Different persons provide bulls for each of the 3 days they are ridden. On the Sunday the fiesta begins, the mayor or one of the councilmen takes a bottle of *charanda* to the house of the person to be invited to provide bulls. If the person accepts the bottle of *charanda*, he is obligated to provide his bulls for riding (only a few people in town have suitable bulls). The owner of the bulls then invites others to help him bring in the bulls or, if they own bulls, to bring theirs as well. If they accept, he gives them a drink of *charanda*. The same routine is followed for the bulls to be ridden the other 2 days.

Sometimes bulls are brought from another town. If the relations between the towns are friendly, usually the bulls will be lent, if not, it may be necessary to pay rent for the use of the animals. The rent is paid from the municipal treasury, using some of the money collected from vendors in the plaza.

One other obligation exists which should be noted. The one rancheria of Cherán, Cosúmo, provides a *chirimía* band each year (the *chirimía* is an oboelike wind instrument). In 1940, the band was said to be from Carapan. The men from the rancheria also act as policemen during the fiesta.

The sequence of events leading up to the fiesta and the fiesta itself will now be described. As already indicated, the first preparations began with the naming of the commissioners by the mayor on August 20. Obviously, the actual notifications on this date were preceded by discussion of suitable persons and the preparation of the letters. The commissioners then sought their assistants, began estimating costs, making up the lists of contributors, and collecting money, at the same time making arrangements with fireworks makers, musicians, and candlemakers. The commissioners for the moros began hunting for dancers. Meanwhile, every Sunday, the young men practiced bull riding on the tame bulls kept near town. They also began to bring in logs

during September. Each *barrio* piled its logs somewhere in the *barrio* as they were accumulated and took them to the bull ring only when the number was complete.[35]

On September 27 lengthy discussions took place concerning the erection of a grandstand for spectators. This is usually done, but there appear to be no set arrangements. In the discussion, it developed that one year the seats had collapsed because the posts were not well set and no cross bracing was employed. One person was hurt; the only reason more were not hurt was that the entire stand went over as a unit instead of one end collapsing. It was agreed that cross bracing should be used (but it was not).

It was finally decided to persuade individuals to take responsibility for putting up the seats. There was some difficulty about this, as the persons approached were suspicious that they would be taxed so heavily that any profits from admission charges would be wiped out. When told that the *municipio* would not tax the concession, the builders at first refused to believe it and kept asking to be told in advance what the tax would be. Moisés Valencia, the town "boss," finally had to persuade them. Intense activity now started on the part of the builder (one man finally undertook the task of erecting all the stands) and his assistants, collecting materials and hauling them to the bull ring behind the church. Boards were borrowed from some dealers in town for making the actual seats, but logs had to be cut and hauled for the framework.

On September 28 carpenters began erecting the first stand or booth on the plaza. Several wooden booths were erected in the following days, mostly for selling soft drinks or ice cream.

On October 1 the transportable parts of the *castillo* or fireworks were brought in two lots. Rockets were fired off upon their arrival. The fireworks maker and an assistant set up shop in part of the old chapel used by the tilemakers. Later, when the pole for the big *castillo* or set piece was brought in, part of the operations

---

[35] About 3 weeks before the fiesta a great deal of activity began in painting, plastering, and furbishing up houses, especially those on the plaza and on nearby streets. This went on right up to the time of the fiesta. The mayor took some part in suggesting improvements, but most of the householders made them on their own initiative.

was transferred to the arcade on the north side of the plaza.

On October 3 (Wednesday in 1940), men brought their ox teams and plows into town, and all agricultural work ceased until at least Tuesday of the following week. On this day, also, people began arriving in numbers for the fiesta, including the first of the vendors.

Three or four, indeed, had arrived the day before, including three women with "a little religion"—medals, rosaries, votive offerings, pictures of saints, etc.—who had expected to stay in the house of the priest, but after learning of the change of priests, had to seek lodging in a private establishment. In addition to these women, there were the following: A street vendor, shouting "*Milagros, milagros de plata, muy barata,*" who offered votive offerings of various parts of the human anatomy made of what he claimed was silver; a seller of Guanajuato pottery; a few sellers of cloth; another seller of religious articles; and a number of hard-faced women preparing to open food and drink establishments. These were all placed together on a street a long block from the plaza. Some or all of the women evidently make a business of following fiestas, as I recognized some of them from fiestas at other towns. Their reputation in Cherán was very bad.

Some street cleaning began on this day. Trash was burned in the streets and the streets were swept. This is done voluntarily by the owners of property on the streets. The municipal authorities had the plaza swept and all surplus dirt and rocks from recent construction activities carried out of sight. The borders of the plaza walks were whitewashed and the benches painted a bright green. The benches were also repaired and set more firmly. The paid police did most of the work.

October 4, Friday, was the actual Saint's day. Rosary and Vespers were celebrated together the evening before from 7:30 to 9 o'clock. The big bell of the church was rung for about an hour afterward. At midnight of the 3d the Cherán band began to play and continued intermittently through the night. The members either were calling at the houses of persons named Francisco, who had to feed all visitors, or were hired by such persons to play a piece

or two. The big bell also began to ring about midnight and was rung intermittently all the rest of the night. Early in the morning there was a Low Mass and at 9 a.m. a High Mass. These were performed by the priest as part of his duties and were not the special Masses paid for by the town. About noon a few members of the Cherán band gathered in front of the priest's house and played for a time, continuing intermittently the rest of the afternoon.

Much activity was under way in the plaza, although the main market day would not be until Sunday. Vendors of shoes, clothing, cakes, candles, candy, apples, peanuts, chiles, dried fish, and painted wooden bowls in Quiroga style were added to those already present. A gambling game was set up. The booths for the liquor and food shops were mostly set up on this day. Comments implied that the girls running the booths were all prostitutes, but all the booths were completely open. In any case, the booths are the center for most of the drunkards and most of the fights and disorder associated with the fiesta. The *castillo* was nearly complete (pl. 6, upper left). On this day also, the church was cleaned up and decorated. A few began working at the bull ring, digging up old posts and clearing away weeds, while others transported new posts and logs from the various *barrios*.

All day Saturday vendors arrived. Most of them merely located their space and unpacked their animals, but did not unpack their goods (pl. 5, upper left). A great many people arrived, and the plaza and nearby streets were crowded. A large carousel or merry-go-round was set up in a patio behind the *municipio*, while a smaller one was placed on one of the side streets.

In the evening, shortly before dusk, the commissioners and their assistants went to the calvary, the chapel at the east edge of town, to meet the bands coming from Nahuatzen and Pichataro. The bands had not arrived by dark, when one of the most violent thunderstorms anyone could remember deluged the party. It was said there were no ceremonies of greeting ordinarily and that the commissioners merely greeted their band and led it to one of the houses for supper. Certainly, there were no ceremonies that night.

Somewhat later, after the storm had subsided, the *chirimía* band arrived. Four or five players on an oboelike wooden instrument (with a double reed mouthpiece and a number of finger stops) played in unison, accompanied by a drum. They played for some time in the arcade before the municipal building. The shrill music, played with great verve and noise, seemed vaguely familiar and finally became recognizable as the "Beer Barrel Polka." It remained the favorite and almost only piece played by the *chirimía* band throughout the fiesta.

Sunday the market was in full operation, and the plaza and adjoining streets were jammed with people (pl. 4, lower right). Not only were most of the residents of Cherán on the streets, in some cases making extensive purchases (this is the only time of the year that pottery is sold in Cherán, for example), but there were hundreds of visitors. The bands played early in the morning. The young men were busy working on the bull ring.

The High Mass was celebrated about 10 o'clock, with the church filled to overflowing. About 12 o'clock the first moro appeared on horseback, followed in a short time by the other two. They rode slowly around the plaza, followed by one of the bands. After a short time the moros went to lunch without dancing. Many people invited guests home to eat with them at this time, often issuing invitations well in advance. To a lesser extent, guests may be invited on other days of the fiesta. About 3 o'clock the moros returned and sat on their horses in the plaza in front of the church while the bands played. The moros then went to the *municipio*, dismounted, and danced in front of the building. Remounting, they returned to the church and danced in front of the church. Many people were openly critical of them for not dancing first in front of the church. After the performance in front of the church, the dancers went on foot down the main street, dancing in front of various stores until about 6 o'clock, when they went to eat again. During the afternoon a basketball game was played between Cherán and Paracho. It aroused little interest.

In the evening the big *castillo* or fireworks set was to be burned. Not until after dark were attempts made to raise the structure, various volunteers working under the direction of the fireworks maker. The commissioners for the fireworks had kept their promise to bring in a 20-meter pole, and great difficulties were encountered in trying to raise it. The climax of several abortive efforts came when the pole snapped about halfway up. By some miracle no one was hurt, although it appeared to fall in a dense crowd.

The collapse of the pole cast a damper on the whole fiesta, for the burning of the *castillo* is one of the high points of any Mexican fiesta. Some violence was threatened the fireworks maker, so he was promptly arrested by the authorities, partly to protect him from the crowd. He pointed out that he was not responsible for furnishing the pole and that the commissioners had brought a pine pole instead of a fir pole of similar size. The fireworks maker also argued that there was a smaller *castillo*, planned for the following night as a surprise; if he were arrested, he would be unable to put the finishing touches on that *castillo* and there would be no fireworks at all. Finally, he promised he would salvage a large part of the damaged *castillo* and the following night it would be possible to have two *castillos*. When the crowd quieted down, the fireworks maker was released and succeeded in carrying out his promises.

The threats of the crowd were not idle, by any means. The fireworks maker is always held responsible for any failures and cases are known where the maker has been badly mauled. In any case he is usually jailed and often heavily fined. In the present instance the municipal officers were all reasonable men, and no drastic measures were taken. The fireworks maker did not, however, receive the full price.

Monday morning the market continued. The first band appeared and began to play about 11 o'clock. The second band appeared with the moros about an hour later. The moros dismounted in front of the church and went into the priest's residence, dancing before him. Then they went down the street dancing before the stores again, finally stopping for dinner. About 2 o'clock it was rumored that the bulls were about to be brought in. Actually, they were being held in a meadow in the *barranca* below town and were waiting both for the proper time and for the last finishing touches to be put on the bull ring.

About this time the *chirimía* band appeared again and played in front of the *municipio*. It then started on a round of the stores, with special attention to the saloons.

The bulls were brought in about 3:45. This was a high point for many of the crowd but it was somewhat of an anticlimax, for the animals seemed a somewhat cowed and meek lot. The moros followed the bulls down the street on horseback, accompanied by a band. When the bulls were finally in the ring, the moros departed to remove their costumes. A band was placed in each grandstand. The municipal officials were seated in a special reserved section of one of the band stands, each carrying a bunch of flowers. The grandstands were soon filled. Those who did not have the admission price or who could not find a place, sat on the railings of the fence or peered between them.

The man in charge of the bull ring is always the owner of the bulls being used that day. He is assisted by a number of volunteers, some mounted and some on foot. The first act is to clear the ring and get the bulls in a pen at one side. Then one bull is let out into the ring and the performance starts.

The object of the performance is not to fight the bull but to ride him. For this, a front foot and a hind foot of the bull must be lassoed and the animal thrown (pl. 5, lower left). Before this is accomplished the bull is teased and played for a time. A few men and boys imitate the actions of bullfighters, using blankets instead of capes to persuade the bulls to charge. Several men on horseback also try to lasso a foot; they usually fail and often the bull is goaded into charging. This is mightily pleasing to the audience. Usually the lassos are actually placed by men on foot.

When the bull is thrown, several men hold him down while a rope is wound tightly several times about the bull's chest and knotted securely. The volunteer rider has heavy spurs fastened to his feet and mounts the bull while it is still held down. He takes a firm grip on the rope and hooks his spurs under the rope also. When he is ready, the bull is released. It rises and endeavors to throw the rider (pl. 5,

upper and lower, right). By the end of 2 or 3 minutes either the rider is thrown or the bull gives up. In the first case, men with blankets rush out to attract the bull's attention so he does not gore the rider. In the second case, the crowd cheers lustily and the band plays the bullfighter's triumphant flourish, the "Diana." The performance is then repeated until the bulls have all been used or darkness puts a stop to the performance.

The bull riding at Cherán is carefully supervised, and drunken men not only are forbidden to attempt to ride the bull but are excluded from the ring. If they manage to get in, they are quite literally thrown out by a couple of husky helpers. In this respect Cherán differs from many places. I saw bull riding at the Paracho fiesta, and not only were drunken men permitted in the ring but were permitted to ride. Serious injuries are said often to result in such cases, although I saw no mishaps. Even at Cherán it is not uncommon for two or three persons to be injured, although serious injuries are fairly rare. One boy's front teeth were knocked out on the third day of bull riding in 1940.

The procedures described above were repeated on Tuesday and Wednesday. In theory this ended the fiesta, but the musicians by now were so much in the spirit of things that they did not go home Wednesday night. Thursday a group of young men got permission from the municipal authorities for another day of bull riding and paid one of the bands an extra 10 or 15 pesos to stay and play for the affair. On this day, the good bulls all having been ridden, the young men borrowed bulls from residents who had more or less tame bulls nearby. Bulls are not ridden at any other fiesta.

While the market continued to some extent throughout the 3 days of bull riding, some people left even by Monday. By Wednesday the majority of the vendors had departed. There were no special closing ceremonies for the fiesta.

THE FIESTA OF CORPUS

The fiesta of Corpus in May is apparently the most interesting of the Cherán fiestas. It was not observed, and the notes which follow are based on accounts of informants. There is no bull riding and the market is unimportant. In place of the market there is a mock market conducted by the persons who have some special occupation.

While all the occupations in the town are represented in the fiesta, only the more important ones take official part. These are the *arrieros* or muleteers, the traveling merchants and storekeepers, the agriculturists, the shake makers, the board makers, and perhaps others. For each of these groups, eight commissioners are named for each *barrio,* or a total of 32 for each occupation involved. The commissioners are obligated to provide a group of musicians for their occupation. They are privileged to take up a collection from other members of the occupation, but contributions are strictly voluntary and payment is not enforced by the *municipio* as is the case with the fiesta of the patron saint. The merchants usually nominate their own commissioners, transmitting the list to the mayor; this may be true of other occupations also.

Other occupations, such as the breadmakers, the weavers, the butchers, the storekeepers, and the honey collectors, are also participants in the fiesta, but they are not obligated to provide a group of musicians, although they sometimes do so. The honey collectors, however, have special duties.

Some 15 days before the fiesta, the honey gatherers take the two images of their patron saint, San Anselmo, to the rancheria of Cosúmo. They usually make a camp in the woods, where they have music and drink a great deal in the evenings. During the day they collect bee nests or *panales.* These are brought to Cherán shortly before the fiesta, and two structures, katárakua, are prepared. These are made of two poles crossed at one end to form a V Cross pieces are fastened to these and the whole well covered with shakes. To the shakes are fastened the honeycombs collected, held in place with a large net similar to the fish nets of Lake Pátzcuaro. The two largest honeycombs are placed at the top of each structure. In this fashion they are paraded around the plaza on the days of fiesta (some say only on Tuesday). After the fiesta they are sold.

The *panaleros* or honey gatherers also stage a greased-pole climb near the calvary on the east side of town. At the top of a smooth, well-greased pole are placed cigarettes, handkerchiefs, etc. These are called the *panal* or "honeycomb" and form the reward of the first man to get up the greased pole. The honey gatherers also often hire musicians, but this is voluntary on their part.

The fiesta begins on Monday and ends on Saturday, but the main events take place on Tuesday, Thursday, and Friday. On these days all the persons following different occupations assemble in the plaza, and there is a mock market. Each person exhibits the type of goods he has made or the occupation he follows. Shake makers split shakes on the plaza and the plank makers saw planks. In addition, miniature shakes and planks are made and offered for sale. The carpenters make miniature houses. The farmers (and possibly the restaurant keepers) set up tiny tables with miniature dishes and serve miniature portions. They offer tiny tortillas about 2 or 3 cm. in diameter and other things, including the dishes, in proportion. When people partake of the food they ask, "How much?" The reply is "One hundred pesos" or some fantastic sum. The purchaser, however, usually gives a piece of chewing gum, candy, or some other small object. The blanket weavers and belt weavers offer miniature blankets and belts for sale as well as tiny woven wrist bands. Agriculturists exhibit all the seeds they grow, and in processions scatter seeds over the crowd. The *arrieros* or muleteers exhibit the goods they carry, such as salt, rice, brown sugar, and other basic necessities. They also make atole in the plaza, with a man grinding the maize on a metate. The traveling merchants and storekeepers exhibit notions such as thread, chewing gum, and dry goods. The breadmakers make quantities of miniature breads about an inch and a half in diameter. These are used as money by everyone.

About 2 o'clock in the afternoon of Tuesday, Thursday, and Friday, those exhibiting their wares carry them about the plaza, giving a special high-pitched cry used on no other occasion. At first they say nothing, but then they use special Tarascan words, also employed on no other occasion. "Aríjeta," they shout, meaning "Come quickly everyone," followed by

"Šéjeta (look at it)" and "Piájeta (buy it)." Mock trade is carried on, using the small pieces of bread as money. This procedure continues until about 7 o'clock in the evening.

Often a group of young men will ask permission of the municipal authorities to collect the *"pisos de plaza,"* that is, the tax on merchants for using the plaza (which is not collected by the *municipio* on this occasion). No one pays the young men in money, but instead in produce—miniature breads, miniature planks, a few bananas, etc. Other young men may secure permission to be the "bandits," *los asaltadores.* Both groups then arm themselves with wooden pistols and rifles. When the first group has collected the "tax," it is assaulted by the second and the two pretend to fight, "shooting" at one another until the bandits have taken away part of the things secured by the tax collectors.

The Mass for this fiesta is celebrated on Thursday. I could not find out definitely who pays for the Mass, most informants hazarding the guess that there is a *carguero* or *mayordomo* for this. On Monday, Wednesday, and Saturday there are no public functions. The musicians play in the houses of the different commissioners. There is no *castillo,* nor is there any bull riding.

FIESTA OF LA OCTAVA

The Octava occurs a week after Easter Saturday and is held on Saturday and Sunday only. It is primarily a commercial fair, resembling the fiesta of the patron saint on a smaller scale and without *castillo,* dancers, or bull riding. Five to eight commissioners are appointed for each *barrio* and they raise enough money to hire one band. The cost of the band is divided equally among the four *barrios.* No data were secured on the way in which Mass is paid.

The major feature of the fiesta is cock fighting. Usually a group interested in cock fighting hires a house near the center of town, puts up a ring and some benches, and conducts fairly organized matches. However, there are many other fights on street corners and in the patios of private houses. Bets are placed on the fights. Cocks are specially raised for fighting, but the Octava is the only time there are any organized fights or any considerable amount of betting. During 8 months I neither saw nor heard of cock fighting except in connection with the fiesta.

CARNIVAL

The Tuesday before the beginning of Lent, everyone fasts until noon. After breaking the fast, the young men go about the streets, some with musicians and some without. The girls sit at the doors of their houses with baskets of elaborately painted eggshells filled with confetti which they have been saving for several months. The boys buy the eggs from the girls and then break them over the girls' heads. The boys and girls also throw confetti at one another and sometimes the boys get such things as oranges and throw them at one another. This is repeated on Wednesday and is the only celebration of carnival.

LENT AND HOLY WEEK

Most of the population fast part of Lent. Some people fast until noon every day. Others do this only two or three times. On Fridays most people abstain from meat but otherwise do not fast especially.

Before Palm Sunday, the collector (an official of the *cabildo*) visits the fathers of boys of suitable age and selects a boy from each *barrio.* When the boy and his father have accepted, the boy picks a girl to assist him, usually his sweetheart. The collector then visits the girl's father and gets his consent. The boys now make a trip to the hot country to bring back green palm leaves for use in the church on Palm Sunday. Before leaving, each boy gives the girl about half a hectoliter of maize, 5 liters of black maize, and some brown sugar. The girl toasts the regular maize well, grinds it, and makes large balls of the ground maize, or pinole, and the brown sugar. These are wrapped in leaves painted with many colors with analine dyes. The black maize she makes into *gorditos,* a sort of fried tortilla.

The boy also provides a wooden cross some 5 feet high. To this are fastened the balls of pinole along the upright and the arms of the cross. At the top of the cross and on the arms are also hung many fiber bags (*morales*) and small cloths used to wrap up tortillas. The latter are given to the girl by her relatives. Her father and mother present her with 1 bag and 1 cloth, but the rest, as many as 20 of each, are presented by her grandparents and cousins. At the top of the cross and at the end of each arm are fastened small sprays of green palm. On Palm Sunday this cross is carried by the boy.

The girl carries a stick, usually of oak, about 2 yards high. Hung to this is every kind of fruit, especially tropical fruits, all provided by the boy. These may include a bunch of bananas, some coconuts, and perhaps a watermelon. Or the girl may carry a watermelon, together with some honeycombs, on her back. Often she can scarcely carry the load.

There is much competition between the *barrios* in this regard (the only hint of *barrio* competition secured). Each looks to see which girl is most laden with things, which girl has been able to make the largest balls of pinole and decorate them best, and which has the most grandparents and cousins (and hence the most bags and tortilla cloths).

On the afternoon of Palm Sunday all go to the little rise in the road toward Nahuatzen (the road to the hot country) beyond the bridge at the edge of the town, and from there all go together to the church. The boy and girl from each *barrio* have their companions, all relatives. Those relatives of the girl who have given a bag or a cloth and those relatives of the boy who have given a honeycomb for the girl to carry are adorned with the *gorditos*. The four boys together will have hired musicians, and many others come to see and hear. About 4 o'clock they all reach the church; they go inside for a moment and then return home, where they divide the things among the relatives who have helped them or accompanied them. There is no special ceremony in the church on this day.

During Holy Week a Mass is held every day in the church. The Tenebrae are also represented. All the candles are put out. Sulfur is burned and bombs are exploded to represent the lightning. Then the candles are relighted with an ordinary wax match.

Thursday the image of Christ is placed in a cage of bars. It is guarded by a number of persons representing the Jews, who are dressed in common-colored women's dresses and hats of *catucho* (a word I have not identified) and are carrying spears.

On Friday, the three times that Christ falls with the cross are represented with a cross and the image of Jesus of Nazareth. The cross is very large, but it is made of light materials, so it weighs little. The figure carrying the cross is put on a table, and it is manipulated from beneath the table to make it fall slowly and rise again. While the figure falls, the Jews pretend to beat it and mistreat it.

The Crucifixion is represented at a *velorio*. Three crosses, one bearing a crucified Christ, are placed upright in a corner of the church. The Jews pretend to beat the figure and injure it with their lances. Later in the same service the figure is lowered from the cross and placed in a special box. This represents the Holy Sepulcher and is guarded by the Jews.

On Saturday morning, 12 boys are placed in a corner near the altar. One of these washes the feet of the others. This act (obviously out of place in the chronology of events) is the only representation of the Twelve Apostles.

Some 20 years ago a somewhat more elaborate representation was given which included the portrayal of the garden of Gethsemane. Persons representing Pilate, Herod, and the Jews went about the plaza asking for Jesus. One, representing Judas, went up to a Christ image surrounded by branches and kissed the image. Jesus now answered, and the whole group fell down. Then they tore down the branches and took the image prisoner. Judas went around showing people the money he had received. On two occasions in the past the apocryphal incident of Veronica was also represented in connection with the three falls of Christ. After one of the falls, a girl pretended to wipe the face of the image with her handkerchief.

The activities in connection with Easter week are carried on by the persons attached to the church and the various societies. Nurukáta, laurel, is brought from the mountains in large quantities and is used to decorate the church during the week. After it has been "sanctified" it is taken home and kept in the houses. It may later be used for medicinal purposes. A special food for Easter week is tamales of black corn mixed with layers of boiled beans milled on the metate.

MINOR FIESTAS

A number of calendrical church affairs receive minor attention. The day of San Juan, June 24, boys ride about the streets on horseback. Girls fasten live pigeons with cords, and men of the family raise and lower them from the housetops. The boys try to catch the pigeons. If they succeed and the pigeon survives, they take it home. If pigeons are not available, chickens of similar size are used. Christmas, New Year's, and the Day of Kings also receive special attention. As these functions are carried on by *cargueros* or *mayordomos*, their description is left until later. The Day of the Dead is also in some measure a community celebration. As has been noted, the *municipio* requires the young men to clean up the cemetery for this occasion. The actual· ceremonies, however, are individual and are described in connection with the death rites.

SECULAR FIESTAS

A number of minor fiestas appear to be celebrated which have no religious motivation connected with the church. These are patriotic affairs and are not taken very seriously. On May 5 there is a procession with the band. The bells of the church are rung and *cohetes* are fired. On September 16, Independence Day, there are usually a parade, music, and perhaps a speech or two. A great many people get drunk over the week end, but there is little formal celebration. In 1940 the Cherán band went to Chilchota for the fiesta, and there was even less celebration than usual.

HOUSE-ROOFING FIESTA

Although most private fiestas are described elsewhere, the fiesta celebrating the roofing of a house is described here because the data on house construction have been published in another paper (Beals, Carrasco, and McCorkle, 1944). A house-roofing fiesta is celebrated whenever the shakes are put on a new house. The following account describes the fiesta held by Pedro Chávez.

The house-roofing fiesta is virtually an obligation on the part of the house owner. He is always assisted by various relatives, who also put pressure on him to hold the event. For the Chávez fiesta one of the wife's cousins provided the music. A relative of the husband provided atole; other relatives of the husband supplied *charanda* or *aguardiente*, as did one of the *compadres* of the husband.

A day or two before the fiesta, the house owner gives cigarettes and matches to the master carpenter. The latter offers cigarettes to various relatives and *compadres* who agree to come and help with the roofing. During the actual work, the relatives of the house owner hand up shakes and nails to the workmen but do not put any shakes in place. The shakes are put in place and nailed by the master carpenter and his relatives and *compadres*.

In the morning of the house-roofing day, two *cohetes* are fired to notify people that the fiesta is to take place. The guests assemble in the late forenoon. The men go to work at the roofing; the wife's female relatives assist in the cooking. When the roofing is nearly finished, *charanda* is circulated among the workmen. The women also· make an arch with flowers. This is placed over a cross placed on the ridge pole when the roof is finished. The relatives and helpers now eat, the men eating first. *Compadres* of the husband assist in the serving, the host merely supervising. The men sit on two long logs, and baskets of tortillas, dishes of salt, baskets of tamales, and jars of water are placed on the ground between the two logs. Each man is served a bowl of čurípo, beef stew with cabbage and chile (pl. 7, upper left). After the men have finished, the small boys are fed in the same way. The women eat in the part of the yard where cooking is going on.

After the meal was over in the fiesta observed, the musicians (a stringed orchestra) arrived. They should have arrived before the meal, but the cellist was sick and it was necessary to send to Nahuatzen for another, who was late in arriving. The musicians are served before they begin to play. The women relatives of the host now bring fruit, which they present to the female relatives of the wife. Everyone is then served a bowl of black atole and a piece of bread. The female relatives of the master carpenter now arrive. They are seated on a mat near the space cleared for dancing, and are served. While all this is going on, a few women start dancing.

Before the last arrivals finish eating, most of the women leave with the musicians to bring the *cuelgas* and to bring the relatives of the wife who had been preparing them. The *cuelgas* are women's narrow belts to which are tied pieces of bread in the shape of animals, mostly bulls, thin tortillas made of wheat, and paper flowers. There are also some figures of animals, such as birds and mules, made of painted corn husks and filled with *pinole* (parched corn flour). The house owner is decked with several of the *cuelgas*. Single *cuelgas* are also put on some 20 men present, including the master carpenter and various uncles and cousins of the house owner. (At the Chávez festival the mayor and his alternate arrived about this time.) They are not fed but are offered drinks. Everyone now starts to dance. Dancing and drinking continue until late at night.

The host, on the occasion observed, drank very little. The following day his relatives returned with bottles, saying now he had really to drink with them. He did, for about 3 days.

FIESTAS IN OTHER TOWNS

A few data collected on fiestas from other towns may be of interest here. None of the data are complete in any respect, but some similarities and differences are apparent. Properly, many of the fiestas described are part of Cherán culture, for many people from Cherán attend them either as visitors or as participants. The band, of course, goes to many fiestas. Other people go to sell goods, barbers often go to pick up some business, and so on.

Like most Tarascans, the people of Cherán pay special reverence to the miraculous Christ of San Juan Parangaricutiro, perhaps better known as San Juan de las Colchas, a former Tarascan town but now primarily a Mestizo village some 15 miles west of Uruapan. Many Cherán residents take vows to make pilgrimages to the saint on September 14 for various reasons, for example, if they are going on a long journey. The father of Agustín made such a vow when he went to the United States. When he returned safely 27 years later, he kept his vow at the first opportunity. Of course, as all thrifty Tarascans would, he also made the event a business occasion, taking advantage of the big market at San Juan on the day of the fiesta by carrying several burro loads of apples from Pichataro. The San Juan fiesta is the occasion of the major interchange of goods between the temperate region and the Balsas Basin.

Pilgrims to the San Juan fiesta come from a distance of as much as 22 days' journey, and obviously many of them are not Tarascans. Often individuals will take vows to go part way on their knees, wear a crown of thorns, carry a sack of cactus on their shoulders, or do other types of penance on the way. It is believed that invalids may be cured if they dance before the image in the church. Those who cannot dance may be cured by rubbing them with pieces of cotton passed over the "ulcers" on the Christ image. Many also dance from the edge of the town to the church when they first arrive. It is believed that anyone who laughs at the dancers will become paralyzed and must himself dance in order to be cured. Others say everyone must dance on entering the town or he will never be able to dance again.

The fiesta at nearby Paracho on October 20, that of Santa Ursala, offered some interesting points. Each side of the path through the atrium to the church was lined with posts covered with moss, paper flowers, and palm leaves. On two strings between the posts were hung paper flowers and paper candle lanterns in bright colors. The inside of the church was decorated with ropes of pine needles and candle lanterns also.

In the same town, for the fiesta of the patron saint, celebrated August 11, somewhat similar decorations were used. The front of the church was decorated with flowers. In the decorations there was much use of ropes of flowers from which various fruits and vegetables were suspended. The images of saints were placed in cloth-covered booths at the four corners of the atrium. On the following day, Monday, a group of little girls danced in the streets, dancing once in the office of the mayor about 11 o'clock. About noon a Mass was held, followed by a procession moving counterclockwise about the atrium and stopping before each saint's image. At each stop the priest prayed and there was an alms collection. A band played intermittently nearby, and while the procession moved it was accompanied by two *chirimías* and a drum. The dancers formed part of the procession, wearing heavy elaborate crowns.

On August 10, part of the fiesta was observed at San Lorenzo. There were four moros, the last one to enter the large atrium of the church being preceded by two *chirimía* players and a drum. After entering the atrium, the band played, and the horse of one moro, a beautiful animal, danced to the music. Groups of men carried *cuelgas* to the church. These were long ropes wrapped about with plants and hung with fruits and bread. Accompanying the *cuelgas* were women with cornstalks and elaborate paper decorations. At the church a minor crisis developed when one of the two priests, a young man, tried to prevent some of the men from entering because they were obviously very drunk. "God does not wish it, the Saint does not wish it, and I do not wish it," he exclaimed, quite unconscious apparently of the implications of the order of his statement. The groups barred from the church waited patiently outside until the Mass began and then went quietly in.

After Mass, the images of the patron saint, San Lorenzo, the Virgin, and Christ were brought from the church, decorated elaborately with the *cuelgas* and the cornstalks and paper ornaments. The moro dancers dismounted and paid their respects to the saints one at a time. Then they danced in pairs before the images, mostly walking back and forth in complex figures between the images and the big stone cross and clashing their spurs. Women threw handfuls of small candies over the dancers as they passed, and they shortly were wading thigh deep in small children scrambling for the candies.

The fiesta at Ahuíran, in September, was visited by many Cherán residents. Quantities of *atole de caña*, atole made with the juice from the stalks of green corn, is served. The principal item in the market is pottery, and it is believed in Cherán that pottery purchased in the market at Ahuíran does not break easily. It should be noted that Ahuíran does not make

pottery and the goods on sale are made at the same pottery-making villages that supply the other markets.

The fiesta at Cheranástico for the Assumption of the Virgin is considered a large and important one. Services are held in the church at Cherán on this day, and the date is also observed as a fast day by many Mestizos, in Uruapan, for example.

At Capacuaro the patron saint is San Mateo. Small jars of atole are offered for sale and are purchased, together with the containers, as offerings to the saint. At Capacuaro it is said that copal smoke is the food of God and that when He eats He smells the smoke. For this reason, it is said, the priests wave the censers when copal is burning.

The only town visited where no fiestas or *moyordomías* are celebrated is Urupichio. All the fiestas in this town had formerly been given by *cargueros* or *mayordomos*. People took their duties so seriously that many sold their lands in order to give the *mayordomías* properly. As a result, a few wealthy people came to own all the land. When the revolution came, the town became a supporter of Zapata and later an agrarian town. After the revolution the lands were seized and divided up and the *mayordomías* and fiestas were abolished. The church, which was burned down during the revolution along with the rest of the village, has never been rebuilt. Instead of a religious fiesta, Independence Day, September 16, is celebrated with bands and a *castillo*. The town is planning to have its own band. What the effects of this will be cannot be determined, but if the band is hired out to play at fiestas in other towns it may serve as the entering wedge for reviving the fiestas.

Data on the fiestas of a Mestizo town, Chilchota, are given in Appendix 2. They afford interesting comparative material.

MAYORDOMÍA ORGANIZATION AND THE CULT OF THE SAINTS

Approximately 13 saints exist in Cherán which belong to groups only indirectly or not at all connected with the church. Each of these saints is in charge of an individual known as a *carguero* or *mayordomo* during a year or more and is associated with special procedures and ceremonies. The ceremonies of the saints are sometimes called *mayordomías* as they are elsewhere in Mexico, although the term *cargo* is more common in Cherán. The elaborateness and expense of the ceremonies vary considerably. Some are virtually community functions or minor fiestas but held at the expense of the *carguero* or *mayordomo*. Others have very little expense attached to them. In many cases dance groups are associated with the *mayordomía*.

So far as could be learned, six of the saints and accompanying *mayordomías* "belong" to the *cabildo*. Four others are associated with particular professions (this is also true of some of the saints of the *cabildo*) and are "managed" by principals (*principales*). Another is managed by a group of principals but is not associated with a profession, while the final saint identified is owned by a private family. The saints belonging to the *cabildo* are San Isidro (of the farmers), San José (of the forest workers), Santa Inéz (of the cattle raisers), Santa Nieves or the Virgin of Snows, the Virgin of Guadalupe, and the Santo Niño or the Child Christ. Saints belonging to professions are San Antonio (of the *arrieros* or muleteers), San Rafael (of the merchants), San Anselmo (of the honey gatherers, with two separate images and ceremonies), and Santa Cecilia (of the musicians). Independent of any profession is the *mayordomía* of the Three Kings or Tres Reyes. The privately owned saint has no *mayordomía* properly speaking and is usually spoken of simply as the Miraculous Saint.

The *cabildo* is also known as the "ačes," meaning principal persons or things. In Spanish the *cabildo* is also known as the *principales*. The group consists of men who have occupied the offices of *colector* and *prioste* associated with the church. In the past the *cabildo* looked after many things connected with the church, including the collection and care of the tithes or gifts to the priest, cared for the saints in the church and the ornaments and decorations of the church, and brought the priests to Cherán during the period when religious functions were prohibited. Members also had charge of the *mayordomías* mentioned above, and considered the saints their property.

They decided who should receive the *mayordomía* each year.

The method of selecting the *mayordomos* was subject to dispute by various informants. The members of the *cabildo* insisted that the *mayordomías* were transferred in the order of application, although sometimes, if a person were too poor to care for the saint properly and live up to the obligations of the *mayordomía*, they would not permit him to have it. Lists of applicants were shown to verify this statement. Many people, however, claimed that it was necessary to give lavish presents to the *cabildo* over a period of 2 or 3 years before a *mayordomía* would be granted. One *mayordomo*, the *carguero* of the Santo Niño in 1940, claimed he had given many gifts of clothing, corn, wheat, *tortillas*, tamales, etc., to the *cabildo* at the previous Christmas ceremonies and in all had spent about $250 on them before he was granted the *mayordomía*. This man, however, was active in a campaign against the *cabildo* at the time. The *cabildo* members admitted receiving gifts, but claimed they were voluntary and in no way influenced the assignment of the *mayordomías*. It was customary, and the *cabildo* expected to be invited to the *mayordomía* and to be treated as guests of honor, receiving special large breads, atole, and gifts of food; the contradictions about gifts, however, seemed impossible to resolve, arising as they did out of a passionate controversy under way at the time.

The *cabildo* selects one of its number to act as head. In 1940 the head was Maximiliano Ortíz, a noted conservative. Ortíz was supposed to visit the church every day. Despite the quarrel, to be described, about the *cabildo*, Ortíz was elected alternate to one of the *regidores* or members of the *ayuntamiento* "so he would no longer be able to criticize." The *cabildo* also invites people to serve as *colector* and *prioste* and thus ultimately become members of the *cabildo* themselves. Others say these offices are sought. Such invitations could be refused. People were not invited to become *mayordomos* as there was usually a waiting list.

The office of *prioste* is occupied first. After one year, the person advances to the office of *colector*. The following year he becomes one of the *cabildo*. These two officials have the same duties, but the *colector* is the superior of the two. Their duties are to select and supervise the kéηi and the matters of the church. The day-to-day expenses involved they must pay out of their own pockets (despite the charges against the *cabildo* to be reviewed later, no one denied this expenditure by the *prioste* and *colector*). The two officers receive the gifts of maize and wheat made to the church and give them to the priest, who in turn entrusts them to the kéηi.

The kéηi is selected by the *colector*. For 1 year he lives in a house on the church grounds (probably formerly in the hospital before it fell to ruins), cares for the church property and the stores of the priest, rings the church bells every noon, runs errands for the *colector*, and does any odd jobs he may be assigned. After 1 year he does not become a member of the *cabildo* but retires to private life.

During his year of office, the *colector* has to provide the kéηi with the maize he needs for his family and some money for minor expenses. Usually the kéηi is a man who has a grown son or a brother to look after his affairs for the year. Among the public outside of the church group it is not regarded as a great thing to be a kéηi. The church group, on the other hand, make a good deal of the individual. Moreover, it is believed that the service is rendered to God and will bring recompense in the future life. The offices of kéηi, *prioste*, and *colector* change each year on December 8. The main ceremonies circle about the change of kéηi.

At one time the kéηi began in the month of November to visit the *cargueros* of the saints belonging to the *cabildo* every Saturday early in the morning, accompanied by musicians. The *cargueros* served *posole*. By December 8, the kéηi had visited all the saints, saying farewell to them. On this date a large lantern was suspended from a pole outside the house of the kéηi and remained until the ceremonies of changing the kéηi were concluded.

For the change of office, both the old kéηi and the new provide themselves with "old men" or *viejos*. These are men dressed in an overcoat and with a cane. They carry a little bell adorned with flowers, wear a small hat, and a wooden *viejo* mask (a wooden mask carved to represent an old man with a long white beard).

These are the speakers for the two kéηi. Each kéηi (in conjunction with the new and retiring *priostes*) has a band of music. Both the old and the new *prioste* invite friends and relatives to their houses for a meal. The *cabildo* goes to both places.

About 3 o'clock in the afternoon both parties go to the house occupied by the kéηi in the church grounds, still sometimes called the hospital despite the assertion of many that the kéηi never lived in the hospital. The new kéηi brings with him all the things he needs to set up housekeeping: new brooms, dishes, a *carga* of maize, the head of a beef, ax, metate, mats and clothes, all carried on burros. Arriving at the house, he finds all in disorder. The house is full of trash, the fireplace has been taken down, and everything has been left in the worst condition possible. The old kéηi carries away everything he has used. Even old brooms and broken pots are saved through the year to be carried away at this time.

The two *viejos* or old men now begin to argue. The *viejo* representing the incoming kéηi makes a long speech, criticising the administration of the outgoing kéηi. The other *viejo* then responds, defending the outgoing kéηi and explaining all the good things he has done. The two argue for some time. The music then plays a tune. First one and then the other dances; they endeavor to outdo one another, both in their ridiculous manner of dancing and in making jokes. Each is accompanied by a woman dressed as an old woman in a very much embroidered blouse and wearing a hat. Then the new officials inspect all the patio of the hospital; the new kéηi enters the kitchen and takes possession. The old kéηi goes out through the *zaguan* or gate with his belongings. The old kéηi goes to the house of the old *prioste* with his friends and they drink until night. The new kéηi and his *prioste* do the same in the hospital after the celebration of Mass.

Sometime during these events the *cabildo* elects the new *colector*. This official takes office on the 1st of January when he goes to church to celebrate the Circumcision. The new *colector* and his wife receive the benediction at the Mass. The wife of the *colector* carries with her an outfit of clothing for the Christ Child. After Mass the two go to the house of the new ké_ηi, who serves them *posole*. Afterward they return home. On this occasion, also, the *colector* is supposed to sponsor a dance called *los viejitos* in which five boys and five girls take part (some say six of each sex). The girls are said to be the future *uánánčes*.

Although the new *prioste* takes office on December 8, the duties of the *prioste* do not end until the *mayordomía* of the Holy Child, the Santo Niño. On this occasion he is obligated to accompany the *uánánčes* while they dance.[36]

The *uánánčes* mentioned above are a group of young girls selected by the *prioste*. (This is contradicted in a sense by the fact that some parents make a vow for their girls to serve as *uánánčes*, for example, if the girl is sick when small.) They act as servants of the *prioste*, going every day to the church (usually accompanied by their mothers). At church they sweep, bring flowers for the altars, and help keep things in order. At Christmas time they perform a sort of *pastorela* dance, aided by other girls. One of the girls is known as the šu_ηánda and is regarded as the first or leader. She is in charge of the incense, the "one who carries copal." The other girls have no special names.

Frequent references have been made to the quarrel between the *cabildo* and the new priest. The motivations and the exact events probably were not discovered. In any case, the roots of the quarrel go far back in time. Ostensibly, however, the fight started with the departure of the old priest.

So far as could be ascertained, the first overt act in the struggle was the calling of a *junta* on the matter. While the *junta* was called by the mayor, in this he was merely conforming to the custom of calling such a meeting whenever it was requested. The request was made by one David Guerrero, a somewhat surly and unapproachable person (so far as the staff of the study were concerned) who ran a small store and saloon (mostly the latter) not far from the plaza. Guerrero's motivations seem obscure. He was not particularly active in the church. Neither did he seem to belong to any

other group, although he was one of the few active supporters of Almazán in the previous presidential election. In the opinion of the best informants there had existed no movement against the *cabildo* until Guerrero undertook his campaign, although obviously the roots of the charges and bad feeling were already present.

At the *junta* between 75 and 100 persons were present. Guerrero spoke, charging the *cabildo* with demanding gifts from the *cargueros*, stealing from the church, driving out the previous priest, and being very drunken. The last charge was what many believed to have convinced the new priest so that he turned against the *cabildo*. An arrangement was reached in which the assignment of *mayordomías* would be taken from the *cabildo* and persons wishing to "take a saint" would ask it of the priest.

At the first *junta* everyone agreed with the charges. A second *junta* was called. In the meantime the *prioste*, one Magdaleno Guerrero (no relation to David) went to the Bishop in Zamora and secured a letter (which I saw) categorically stating that neither he nor anyone else had attempted to have the former priest removed. This letter was presented at the second *junta* by the *representante del pueblo*, who defended the *cabildo*. (The *cabildo* did not attend. Magdaleno Guerrero said for a while they were afraid they might be killed.) This made the people less bitter, but they still agreed to abolish the *cabildo*.

With regard to the other charges, the *prioste* asserted that all the work of the *cabildo* was voluntary, while his own expenses as *prioste* amounted to between $100 and $200 for the year. Among his duties was to pay for Masses on December 8 and December 25. Following the latter Mass, the *cabildo* met at the house of the *prioste* who served food. To this assembly came people who wished to ask for a saint. They brought presents of cigarettes, while the wives brought bread. These presents, the *prioste* asserted, were voluntary and were not demanded. The names of the persons were put down on lists in the order applications were received and each *mayordomía* was awarded to the person whose name headed the list.

---

[36] It should be noted that the above account is based on data from informants. Owing to the quarrel between the priest and the *cabildo* none of the ceremonies were performed in 1940. The data are from musicians who always attended and from members of the *cabildo*.

With regard to the charge of drunkeness, the *prioste* asserted that this had been true "in the time of our grandfathers" but it was not true today. What gave color to the charge, he said, was that people brought them many bottles of *charanda*. These the *cabildo* sold in the stores and returned the empty bottles to the donors.

It was quite evident that the *prioste* was filled with bitterness over the situation. The dance of the *pastorela*, he felt, was especially the dance of the *cabildo* and the *prioste* and one which gave much pleasure to the people, and now they would lose it. (Even our most anti-Church informants agreed that the dance was the best given in Cherán, partly because it was unaccompanied by the drunkenness and rowdiness associated with other dances.) The *prioste* also said that the *cabildo* was accepting the will of the people and was neither speaking nor making propaganda with anyone. After all, he pointed out, the *cabildo* gained, and especially the *prioste* and *colector* gained because they now did not have to spend their money. However, he had gone to the church and taken out the large candles and some small ones left by his wife. This, he said, was custom, for the old *prioste* always took the remains of the candles and the new *prioste* provided others. The priest had asked why he removed the candles and the *prioste* had explained the situation. The priest then asked if he was not disposed to leave the candles, but he refused. After this the *prioste* scarcely left the house, and never went either to the plaza or the church, partly because of fear, partly because in church he would have to see those who had thrown him out of office and this "caused him anger which it is better not to have before the Lord."

The *prioste* suggested that the leader of the opposition was an ambitious man who was furthering some devious and as yet undisclosed project to further his own interests. He also said the *cabildo* had made no move to seek a new *prioste* or kéηi, which they ordinarily did by August. He also said he had no idea whether the priest would appoint new officials to take the place of the *cabildo* or go on naming people to perform their duties from day to day as he was doing. Incidentally, he pointed out

that never before had the church been closed when the priest left town.

In addition to the above accounts, which seem reasonably correct as far as they go, there were floods of rumors and stories. At one time I was told authoritatively by several people that my landlord had been named the new chief of the *cabildo*. When I asked him about it, he was completely surprised and it finally appeared that no new *cabildo* was to be named.

With regard to the story told by the *prioste* of taking his candles from the church, a much more lurid version was circulated. One woman's account of the quarrel was as follows:

When the new priest came he asked one of the *cabildo* to bring him maize from the storehouse. The *cabildo* had taken all the maize from the storehouse but the man pretended not to know this. He went to the storehouse and returned, saying, "Father, there is no maize." "What has happened to it? There is supposed to be maize." The priest gave the man money to buy maize for that day. Next day the priest made inquiries. People told him the *cabildo* had stolen the maize. He called the *cabildo* together and accused them. They denied the theft. The priest said, "Do you want me to bring witnesses?" They conferred and said, "No. We took the maize." The father began to scold them, and they said, "What right have you to scold us? We collected the maize and we have a right to live." The priest became angry and told them they could no longer serve in the church. They went away. For 2 or 3 days they did nothing. Then they came in a body and began stripping the church of all the altar cloths, vases, and decorations. The priest interrupted them. They said, "These things are ours; we bought them. If we cannot serve here, we will take these away." They argued. The priest said, "These things belong to the community." But he realized it was not becoming for him to argue in this way and kept still. When they finished, he said, "Now have you everything belonging to you?" They thought and said, "Everything but the saints." At this the priest flew into a rage and said, "The saints belong to the community. Now take the other things and leave the church and do not let me ever see your faces again."

This is a very interesting tale, but it contains very little truth. The major fact which seems correct as compared with the *prioste's* tale is that the *cabildo* did actually remove all the vases, altar cloths, and other things they had bought.

One man, regarded as a fairly reliable source of information, stated that the *cabildo* had received the alms given at church but had formerly given them all to the priest. In recent years, he stated, the *cabildo* members began taking half for themselves. When the new priest came, people decided they no longer wished the *cabildo* and spoke to the priest. He abolished the *cabildo* and barred the members from the church so that alms would now be given directly to the priest.

Still another man, one who probably gave the best-informed statement, which gained weight because he was both an anti-Church and anti-*cabildo* man on general principles, pointed out some of the history of the affair. According to this informant, when the priests were forbidden to function in the church, the *cabildo* was responsible for bringing priests to town secretly and helping them to hold services in private houses. This involved very considerable expenses. (There seems little reason to doubt these statements, which were verified in other connections.) In the meantime, inasmuch as people believed it necessary to take seeds, i.e., maize and wheat, to the church, they continued their gifts, which were received and stored by the *cabildo*. This informant believed, however, that the quantities were probably less than usual inasmuch as there was no one to urge them. Out of this fact probably rose the real basis of the quarrel. When it began to appear that there was small likelihood of a resident priest returning, the *cabildo* began selling the accumulated grain, utilizing the profits to defray the considerable expenses of smuggling priests into the town. For the people it was difficult to tell whether the expenses claimed were correct or not. When a priest finally was reestablished in Cherán, the *cabildo* presented him with an account of their transactions. Many believed that this account was incorrect and that the *cabildo* had been guilty of defalcation. It was then that the idea began that the *cabildo* should be done away with. However, it is unlikely the *cabildo* received any profits after the return of the priests. The priest made an investigation of the affair and as a result the *cabildo* tried to force him to leave the town. (This last accusation seems adequately disposed of by the letter from the Bishop mentioned above.) When the new priest arrived in 1940, he announced his intention of reopening the investigation and stated that, as the *cabildo* would probably try to get rid of him, too, he had better get rid of the *cabildo* right away.

An aspect of the situation which had not been resolved at the termination of the study was the effect of the change upon the *mayordomías* formerly in the charge of the *cabildo*. It was the belief of many, including the priest, that applicants for a *mayordomía* would simply apply to him. The priest was quoted as saying that he had no intention of interfering with the local customs. None of the *cargueros* consulted seemed ever to have thought of the possibility of the change effecting the operation of the system. The *cabildo* nevertheless has a proprietary interest in the saints and there were some indications that the *cabildo* was willing to suppress some of the customs. The *uánánčes* did not perform the *pastorela* in 1940. The *prioste* refused to put up anything for the dance, or even participate when a cousin offered to pay all the expenses. The parents of all but one of the *uánánčes* also apparently welcomed the excuse for avoiding the expenses involved. The *cabildo* also attempted to forbid the *carguero* of the Holy Child to sponsor the performance of the *negrito* dance (described below) although this was a traditional duty of the *carguero*. As he was one of those who attacked the *cabildo* and claimed to have been forced to make heavy contributions in order to get the *mayordomía*, he sought the permission of the priest and held the dance despite the *cabildo's* objections.

The progressive element in the town was of the opinion that the demotion of the *cabildo* would mean the early disappearance of the *mayordomías*. However, this overlooked the several *mayordomías* which functioned outside the *cabildo* system, and it is doubtful if the disappearance of the *mayordomías* will be particularly accelerated by this change. There is some possibility of this, of course, and one of the curious features of the situation is that a priest who apparently is conservative and who does not wish to interfere with the local customs should have been responsible for this attack upon them and for alienating the most conservative Church group from his support.

MAYORDOMÍAS

Mayordomías are undertaken by families voluntarily. The word family is used advisedly, for it is doubtful if a man would ask for a *mayordomía* unless his wife was in full accord, for much of the successful carrying out of the duties depends on the cooperation of the wife. The motives are definitely religious and the persons taking *mayordomías* are always pious and loyal Catholics. In visiting the various *cargueros* and observing the images of the saints, almost every time the first question asked of my guide (in Tarascan) when I visited a house was whether I was one "who could see the saints," that is, was I for or against the saints and the *mayordomías*. However, certain of the *mayordomías* are restricted to specific occupations.

For the most part the *mayordomías* are undertaken to secure some future good or to give thanks for some past good. Undoubtedly *mayordomías* are sometimes undertaken to secure social prestige, but this appears to be a rare motive. Generally the *mayordomía* is sought as the result of a promise, *manda*. If a man has no sons, he may promise to seek a *mayordomía* if he should be favored with a male offspring. Sick persons, or families in which there are sickly children, may also make such a promise. On the other hand, one who has prospered greatly may seek a *mayordomía* to express his gratitude.

One family, as an example, had a sickly son. The parents obtained the *mayordomía* of the Holy Child, one of the most expensive. As the mother put it, "The child seemed comforted at the presence of the Holy Child in the house and improved." The following year the parents sought and obtained the *mayordomía* of the Three Kings. As improvement continued, they added several items to the celebration of the *mayordomía*, paying the expenses of the dance group, which up to that time had been independent.

Other types of promises are also made. Vows to make the pilgrimage to San Juan de las Colchas (Parangaricutiro) have already been mentioned, but shrines of other saints may also be visited. Usually some slight gift, a candle or a garment, is taken on the occasion of such pilgrimages.

MAYORDOMÍA OF THE SANTO NIÑO

The *mayordomía* of the Santo Niño or the Holy Child, celebrated December 25, is the most expensive of the *mayordomías* of the *cabildo*. More than any other it may be undertaken for motives of social prestige and ostentation. The *carguero* in 1940, according to his wife, did not take the post as result of a vow, but simply for pleasure, *"no mas por gusto."*

The new *carguero* assumes his duties on December 26. The previous day and night the image connected with the *mayordomía* is left in church. The new *carguero* takes the image from the church to his house. Previously, he prepares a special place for the image with the help of invited relatives and friends whom he feeds. Usually the place for the image is the *"troje."* Everything is removed from the room, a suitably decorated altar is prepared, and often an alcove is built up of boards and lined with colored paper. Strips of colored paper are hung from the ceiling and ornaments are sometimes suspended from the ceiling as well. Miniature objects—chairs, metates, dolls, etc.—are frequently hung from the ceiling also.

During the year, the *carguero* has few duties. He keeps the image in good condition and always ready for visits of persons who may wish to say prayers and who often leave a few alms or burn a candle in honor of it. The *carguero* also begins accumulating food and property for the ceremonies. He plants as much corn and wheat as possible and prepares animals for fattening. He also accumulates cash. If necessary, he may be helped by his brothers and cousins.

The first act of the *carguero* is to assemble dancers to perform the dance of the *negritos* (pl. 6, lower left). In this also he is helped by his brothers, who invite various young men to perform. The *carguero* also hires a teacher to teach the dancers their steps and their speaking parts, *relatos*. For about a week before December 25, the dancers rehearse in the house of the *carguero* and food is provided, at least in theory. In 1940 one of the assistants, Agustín, was a *negrito* dancer and commented that the *carguero* did not seem to wish to give even cigarettes. To which Pedro Chávez, our progressive and anti-Church assistant, replied sagely that this was because the *cabildo* had been abolished.

On the evening of December 24, candles are burned at night before the image in the house of the *carguero*, and he, his family and relatives, and the dancers and their relatives sit up with the image but do not participate in other activities of the *mayordomo*. The *uánánčes* are also present. All are given food by the *mayordomo* in the late afternoon before dark. About midnight the image is taken to visit the image of the Child Christ in church and a Mass is held at the expense of the *carguero*, who also provides special candles for the occasion. The image in the church is put in a reclining position in a crib where it remains until January 1.

After the Mass, whch does not end until nearly morning, the men go home, but return at an early hour to the house of the *carguero* for breakfast. The women remain in the *carguero's* house, assisting in preparing the meals for the dancers. After breakfast the men either return home or accompany the *carguero* as he cares for the dancers who now go out to dance in various houses. The dancers perform the days of the 25th, 26th, and 27th. During this time food is provided for them and many people assist in the food preparations. The dancers provide their own costumes for this affair, but the music, a band of wind instruments, is hired by the *carguero*. At the houses where the dancers perform they are given gifts of fruits and things that children would like (because it is a fiesta of the Child Christ).

In addition to the *negrito* and *pastorela* dances connected with the December 25 events, three other groups of dancers sometimes appear, the *melebris*. Neither they nor the *pastorela* are connected with the *mayordomía*. They are discussed in connection with the dances.

The expenses of this *mayordomía* are between $500 and $700. Music is hired for a week (for part of the practice as well as for the dancing), an expense of about $200. One or two beeves usually are killed and about three fattened pigs. As much as 15 *fanegas* of maize may be consumed. Quantities of bread are also purchased, and *charanda* forms a considerable

item of expense also. A midnight Mass and candles are paid for, as well as the dance instructor. Special foods are also prepared at this time, for example, *mole de pepita de calabaza molida*, mole of ground squash seeds, a very rich food prepared only on this occasion (see recipes, p. 53).

MAYORDOMÍA OF SANTA NIEVES

Santa Nieves, or the Virgin de las Nieves (Virgin of the Snows), was evidently once the Virgin associated with the hospital. The *carguero* in 1940, as was the case with the *carguero* of the Child Christ, had taken the post "for pleasure."

The *carguero* receives the saint August 5. He takes it to his home and places it in a specially prepared place. On the day of the saint, August 5, he is supposed to arrange a dance, the caballita uaɹáriča, dance of the little horses, and to provide a band. This was not done in 1940 because of the quarrel over the *cabildo*. The dancers perform on this one day only, visiting the houses of the *cabildo*. The *carguero* pays for a Mass in church to which he takes the image of the saint. The image is left in church for the new *carguero*.

MAYORDOMÍA OF GUADALUPE

The *mayordomía* of the Virgin of Guadalupe on December 12 is also a fiesta of the *cabildo*. The *carguero* gives food to his relatives in his house and they help him to decorate the church. The image of the Virgin is taken to church for the Mass and is left there for the new *carguero*. A long Mass is held. In 1940 there were three priests and the cost was $60. Eighteen large candles were provided, each with bows of red, green, and white made out of tin (because of a shortage, four candles had paper ornaments). The candles are carried to church in procession by the helpers (relatives) of the *carguero*. Behind is carried the Virgin's image, followed by the *carguero* and his wife. A dance is supposed to be held, but it was omitted in 1940.

MAYORDOMÍA OF SAN ISIDRO

The *mayordomía* of San Isidro is also connected with the *cabildo*. The date of the *mayordomía* is May 15. Information of this *mayordomía* was obtained from the *carguero's* wife, who was very suspicious and possibly ignorant. Consequently it is not wholly satisfactory.

The saint is the patron of those who cultivate the ground with oxen, but there is no evidence that only cultivators assume this *mayordomía*. The *carguero* pays for a Mass and probably for candles. Usually the relatives of the *carguero* and his wife are invited to eat at the house, but this is not obligatory and may be omitted if the *carguero* cannot afford it (the *carguero* in 1940 was obviously very poor). If the relatives are invited, the wife's female relatives aid in preparing the food. The saint's image is taken to church before the Mass and remains in church until the fiesta of Corpus, when it is removed by the new *carguero*. The *carguero* in 1940 had taken the saint because of a vow, but the wife said she did not know what the vow was.

MAYORDOMÍA OF SAN JOSÉ

San José is a patron of the shake makers and the plank makers. The *carguero* is usually of one of these occupations. He begins his service on the saint's day, March 19. At the fiesta of Corpus he takes the image to church and pays for candles. He also provides meals for the commissioners and musicians of the woodworkers at the fiesta (for the entire fiesta according to one informant, but this contradicts other information given in connection with the Corpus fiesta). In the following year on March 19 the *carguero* pays for a Mass, candles, and *cohetes*, taking the saint's image to the church where it is left for the new *carguero*. On the 19th, if the *carguero* wishes, he may invite his relatives to the house for food and have music, but this it not obligatory.

MAYORDOMÍA OF SANTA INÉZ

Santa Inéz, also a saint of the *cabildo*, is regarded as one of the virgins. She is patron of cattle and pigs. Formerly there were cows belonging to this saint, but they were lost. About 15 years ago a cow was presented to the saint. Now she possesses two cows, two bulls, and two young steers. The *carguero* looks after these animals. He may use the milk from the cows, but he is not supposed to sell any of the cattle.

The saint's image in this case was kept with special elegance in a large case with glass on the front and sides. Inside the box were small images of a cow, a steer, and a pig on the left side. The box stood on a table decorated with paper flowers and supporting an incense burner, a basket of copal gum, and a candle. The table in turn rested on a mat on the floor. The wall behind the box was decorated with colored papers and chains and paper cut-outs.

The new *carguero* receives the image of the saint on April 21. On Corpus the image is taken to church (and probably candles are burned). At the end of the year, on the following April 21, the relatives of the *carguero* visit him. He has musicians and food for them. The saint's image is taken to church for a Mass paid for by the *carguero* (probably with candles). Some *cargueros*, when they receive the image, give it a new outfit of clothing. The image is large and one of the best-dressed in Cherán. The dress is white with a blue cape. A gilt crown is on the head and a necklace of the red glass beads prized by Tarascan women is about the neck. The altar is decorated with many flowers and aromatic herbs.

MAYORDOMÍA OF SAN RAFAEL

The *mayordomía* of San Rafael is not connected with the *cabildo*. The saint is patron of the merchants, and apparently the *mayordomía* is administered by a principal or principals selected by the merchants. The principals decide who shall receive the *mayordomía* and pay an occasional visit to the *carguero's* house to see that all is kept in proper order. This seems to be the regular arrangement for all the independent saints connected with *mayordomías*, although specific information is lacking for some of them.

As patron of the merchants, the image of San Rafael carries a fish under the left arm and in his right hand bears a staff (actually a shepherd's crook). About his neck is a necklace of sea shells. In front of the altar are hung other sea shells and miniature fire fans, clay fruits, etc. The house and altar are well decorated with paper flowers and colored papers. Before the altar are candles and an incense burner. The merchants visit the saint's image and burn a candle before setting out on a journey.

The new *carguero* takes charge of the image the day before Corpus. He goes to the house of the old *carguero*, secures the image, and takes it to church. There it remains in a "box" during the week-long festivities of Corpus. On Monday afternoon of Corpus the musicians of the merchants come to the house of the *carguero* and make it their headquarters during the fiesta until Saturday noon. The musicians, the commissioners, and whatever people attach themselves to the group, breakfast and dine at the house of the *carguero* during the fiesta. If he cannot afford this, the commissioners provide the meals, three or four cooperating in providing each meal. The musicians of this group also greet the honey gatherers when they return from their stay in the woods collecting honeycombs for the fiesta (on Friday, according to the *carguero*; Tuesday, according to all others).

The day of the saint is October 24. The *carguero* pays for a Mass (and presumably candles). In 1940 the Mass was delayed because the priest was too busy and was out of town frequently.

The *carguero* ordinarily is a merchant, but in 1940 he was a fireworks maker. Because he traveled from town to town, the principals had decided he could qualify as *carguero* when he asked for the *mayordomía*. The *carguero* sought the responsibility "for pleasure" and not because of any vow. Incidentally, he is a native of Pichataro and speaks very little Spanish. His wife speaks even less. Perhaps because of this origin they were much the most open and cordial of the *cargueros*.[37]

MAYORDOMÍA OF SAN ANTONIO

San Antonio is patron of the muleteers, the *arrieros*. The new *carguero* receives the image on June 13, the day of the saint, and takes it to

his house. On Corpus he carries the image to church and spends money for candles. If he wishes he may have a fiesta with music and food at his house, but this is not obligatory.

A few notes on the history of San Antonio, obtained from one of the principals, are of interest. The original image was burned at the time the town was destroyed during the revolution. For a number of years the *mayordomía* was in abeyance. About a dozen years before the study, a young man in the house, a traveler, expressed an interest in having the saint. The principal borrowed a saint from somewhere, and they kept it in the house. The muleteers talked a good deal about the matter, but did nothing. Finally the principal placed an order for a new image. A principal of the old image of the saint, which had been destroyed, assisted, as he knew about such things, and solicited alms from the muleteers. In about 2 years they got the new image of the saint and then informed the priest. He came to the house to see it and commended them. Then he said they should seek godfathers for the image and have it blessed. This was done, and thus the *mayordomía* was revived. The old principal, the informant, and one other who had recently died had been the principals ever since. Persons wishing the *mayordomía* had to ask them for it. If more than one person asked, they were given it in order.

Although San Antonio is the patron of the muleteers, they do not visit the image before going on journeys. Persons not muleteers may also receive this *mayordomía*. In fact, the principal who served as informant is a mason who interested himself in the saint because of the youth living in his house (possibly his son, although he carefully avoided any suggestion of relationship).

Some persons not muleteers also make vows to the saint. The same informant cited the case of a man named Antonio who made a vow to take the *mayordomía* when there was an epidemic killing many pigs in Cherán. None of Don Antonio's pigs died. He sought the *mayordomía* and received it. Ever since, he fattens and kills a pig every year, sells the lard, and buys something for the saint with the proceeds.

[37] Those desiring the *mayordomía* of San Rafael apply to the principal. The holder of this office in 1940 had occupied it for 18 years, although he had several times tried to resign. Occasionally he calls meetings of the merchants to discuss some expense relative to the saint, such as new garments or altar table. Sometimes money is collected in the meeting in advance for such expenditures. On other occasions the principal spends money out of his pocket and takes up a collection at the meeting to reimburse himself. According to this principal, the new *carguero* goes to the priest during Corpus for benediction. Probably this is true of the other *mayordomías* but the point was not investigated.

THE MAYORDOMÍAS OF SAN ANSELMO

There are two *mayordomías* of San Anselmo, each with its saint's image. Both belong to the honey gatherers, the *panaleros*, and there is a certain amount of cooperation between the two *cargueros*. For example, they share the cost of the Mass on the saint's day. One of the *mayordomías* is always in *barrio* III or IV, the upper *barrios*, while the second is always in the lower *barrios*, that is, I and II. It is said that only honey gatherers can receive the *mayordomías*. Although honey gatherers apparently are not numerous, there are a good many men who occasionally follow the occupation. As it is highly dangerous, the aid of the saint is felt important and there usually are numerous persons willing to accept the *mayordomía*, especially as it is not a very expensive one.

The new *carguero* receives the saint at the church 8 days after the fiesta of Corpus. The new *carguero* presents the saint with a hat, blanket, palm fiber raincoat, and other miniature items. As the saint's image is small, everything connected with it is small. On April 22 the two *cargueros* jointly pay for a Mass, but it is said not to be such an important Mass as for other saints. The Mass follows that of Santa Inéz on April 21; it is said that as the *mayordomías* of this saint follow after Santa Inez, one should not spend as much as is spent for Santa Inéz. San Anselmo is more humble. The giving of a fiesta in the house on the saint's day is optional with the *carguero*.

Eight days before Corpus both images of the saint are taken to the mountains when the honey gatherers go out to seek honeycombs for the fiesta. The two images are taken to different places, and the men from the different *barrios* accompany the associated saint's image. The *carguero* supplies large quantities of *charanda* on this occasion. The men get drunk and dance every afternoon to guitar music. On Tuesday of Corpus the images are taken to church and left there until taken by the new *cargueros*.

The choice of the new *cargueros* is made by the priest from lists provided by the principals. According to the *carguero* for the two lower *barrios* in 1940, four principals named by the honey gatherers determine the list of candidates for the *mayordomía* at a meeting before Corpus. For the upper two *barrios*, only one principal was mentioned. In this case the principal was interviewed and asserted that all candidates for the *mayordomía* applied to him. The real *carguero* in the lower *barrios* in 1940 was the 4-year-old son of the household, according to his father. The *mayordomía* was sought because the boy was not growing normally.

On some occasions the principals of the lower *barrios* have some expenses. For example, one year the box in which the saint's image is taken to the mountains was partly burned through an accident. The principals ordered a new box at their expense.

MAYORDOMÍA OF THE THREE KINGS

The *mayordomía* of the Three Kings, Los Treyes Reyes, is celebrated on January 6, the new *carguero* taking the images the following day. The *mayordomía* is relatively new, and the present images were secured in 1940. The previous images were small and provisional. The *carguero* in 1940 had held the *mayordomía* of the Holy Child the previous year. In both cases the *mayordomía* was sought to aid the health of a sickly child. In addition, the parents had vowed the child to perform in the dance of the *viejos* every year.

It is obvious that the *carguero* in 1940 was well-to-do to be able to take two *mayordomías* on 2 successive years. Moreover, he introduced an innovation by taking over all the expenses of the dancers who perform in connection with the Day of the Kings. Previously the dance group had been entirely independent of the *mayordomía*, raising their own money for expenses and music.

The expenses of the *carguero* in 1940 were secured in some detail. They are as follows:

Musicians	$ 70.00
1 pig butchered (estimate)	25.00
1 ox butchered (estimate)	60.00
22 *fanegus* of maize at 3.75 to 4.00	80.00
40 sugar canes and 40 oranges for dancers	2.00
Bread for all (about 200 guests) at end of dance; three breakfasts for dancers	10.00

3 liters milk daily	
25 tablets chocolate daily	
3 or 4 centavos of bread each daily	15.00
Three breakfasts for musicians	
2 kilos of sugar	.70
3 bottles alcohol (estimate)	3.00
Coffee for musicians (estimate)	1.00
Total	$266.70

Ordinarily the new *carguero* seeks the *mayordomía* from the principals. The *carguero* in 1940 had some doubts as to what would be done because of the insistence of their priest that *mayordomías* should in future be asked of him. On the other hand, the principals had no doubt that the *mayordomía* was their special property.

The *mayordomía* of the Three Kings was definitely a new departure in Cherán. The dance group apparently had performed for many years.

According to the three principals, whom by good luck it was possible to interview together, until a few years ago only a group of dancers performed on the Day of Kings. The dancers were not organized but each year a group of volunteer performers got together informally. There were images of the Three Kings in church, but none were taken to private houses. One time the three principals were talking about the dance when "God sent them the idea" of creating a *mayordomía*. From some 15 or 18 others they collected some money. The principals, however, put in a good deal more than the others. Then they started with the three small images which one of them had in his house, in the meantime ordering the new images. One of the principals received the *mayordomía* first. The *carguero* in 1940 was the third and those for the following 2 years had already been appointed.

With regard to the position of the priest, the principals remarked that the saints belonged to them and neither the *cabildo* nor the priest nor anyone else had anything to say about the images. However, the priest, according to the principals, accepted this situation, for he had no cause to be angry with them.

MAYORDOMÍA OF SANTA CECILIA

Very few data were collected concerning this *mayordomía* which was not discovered until shortly before the close of the study. (It is quite probable that two or three *mayordomías* exist in Cherán which were not discovered at all; no one in the town appears to know all of them.) Santa Cecilia is patroness of the musicians, and the *carguero* is always a musician. In 1940 no one wished to "take the saint," so the image remained in the same house, a nephew of the former *carguero* who lived in the house taking the responsibility. The musicians all gather at the house of the *carguero* and play all day. (This is how the *mayordomía* was discovered; however, no outsiders were invited in, despite the most obvious hints.)

THE MIRACULOUS HOLY CHILD

This saint, El Milagroso Santo Niño, is not properly to be included among the *mayordomías*, as it is the property of a single family and does not circulate among other households. According to the story told by the owners, the saint was found by the man of the family some 18 years before, while he was cutting wheat below the town. Tiring, he sat down, and while picking idly at the dirt with his sickle he uncovered the image. He had the image fixed up (at present it looks entirely like the other saint's images with respect to the technique and painting). With the aid of others, a chapel was then built for the saint in the yard of the house. When the image was found it was only about 30 cm. high. It is claimed that it has grown steadily until it is now between 70 and 80 cm.

The saint first became known as a miraculous saint when a man from the ranchos (a group of small Mestizo settlements on the boundaries of Cherán in the mountains) cut his foot while alone in the woods. As he was bleeding to death, he recalled the saint, of which he had heard, and vowed to take it to his rancho accompanied by dancers. The bleeding stopped and he recovered.

Keeping his vow, the Mestizo brought dancers to Cherán and took the saint to the rancho. There other miracles occurred. For example, a child who could not walk and who was dumb had the crown of the saint put on him; he now walks and talks very well.

As a result of these experiences, the people

from the ranchos came every year with dancers. They spent 3 days in Cherán, dancing in the church and in the municipal building. Then they took the saint to the ranchos and it often was kept there many months. In 1940 the owners decided not to let the saint go any more because they wished to have it with them "as we have lost much time with it."

COMPARATIVE NOTES

Material collected from other towns suggests that other types of *mayordomía* organization exist. In Angáhuan, Rendón found an elaborate hierarchy of officials, evidently corresponding to the *cabildo* and the associated organization at Cherán. In Angáhuan, according to Rendón, the officials are ranked as follows: *Alcalde, regidor,* kámbiti, petájpe and biskál, *mayores,* kiéηi, anyítakua.

In addition, there is a group of elderly men, corresponding to the Cherán *cabildo,* who are known as *tarénpenya.* These are men who have served the above offices or part of them.

The *alcalde* and *regidor* correspond to the *prioste-colector* positions in Cherán apparently. The *alcalde* is in charge of the church for 1 year. During this time he has to hold six fiestas. The first is at New Year's, when he receives his post and when he must provide food and *aguardiente.* The second is carnival, when he is aided in the expenses by the *"cabildo"* (it is not clear from Rendón's notes whether this means the same as it does in Cherán). The third is the day of the Holy Cross when he must pay for two bands and there is the dance of the moors and soldiers. The *alcalde* provides food for the dancers. The latter dance in the houses of various functionaries. The fourth fiesta is Corpus, at which time all the members of the different occupations take miniatures of their products and dance with them before the church and also perform their offices. The fifth fiesta is that of Santiago (the patron saint), when there is music, dancers, and also bull riding. For this fiesta the *alcalde* pays for the Masses and gives food to the dancers. The final fiesta is the day on which the *alcalde* is chosen by the elders.

The *regidor* is the helper of the *alcalde* and aids him in every way possible. The relatives of the *alcalde* also assist him with food.

The duties of the kámbiti are to pay the expenses of the Holy Week festivities and to decorate the front of the main altar with fruits from the hot country, such as bananas, watermelons, mameys, coconuts, mangoes, and sugarcane. The fruits are suspended in small nets or are perforated and hung from strings. The ceremony is called uirímutakua, which means "to adorn the front of something."

On Holy Saturday the young people of the town divide in two groups and go through the town, the girls carrying an image of Mary Magdalene, the men one of Saint Joseph. At strategic points the two groups meet and have races with the images. Certain young girls also place themselves at the door of the church during Holy Week and offer the refreshments known as čarápes to all comers. These girls must change the flowers on the altars during the ensuing year and are known as cʌcʌki jaȼirati. All these ceremonies are regulated by the kámbiti.

The petájpe gathers the young men at his house in February and feeds them *"esquite,"* of the type known as kanita takunji. At this time he announces the date for cleaning the spring from which the town gets its water. The day the spring is cleaned, the petájpe provides music and rice, beans, and pork for the helpers at his house. At the spring, many families go along and take picnic food, singing and enjoying themselves while the young men clean the spring. When the spring is cleaned, they carry *ollas* of water to their houses, using it as drinking water in preference to water from the pipes until it is gone.

There are no data on the office of biskál. Rendón's notes suggest that the offices of petajpe and biskál are the same.

To reach the office of *mayor,* one must give a fiesta to the patron saint and appear as a moro dancer. The moros dance on December 25 and 26 in the houses of the elders. On the 24th they worship in the church. *Mayores* must aid their superiors with firewood and their wives grind and carry water when the *alcalde* or kámbiti or petájpe hold a fiesta.

The kiéηi has similar duties to the kéηi of Cherán. He is entrusted with the care of the church and follows the orders of the *alcalde* in cleaning and adorning the structure. He has under his orders the anyítakuas or "semaneros."

The latter are those in charge each week of the hospital or yuríšo. This duty rotates by street blocks. Each week seven or eight families must go to a house beside the church and one of the group prepares food for the remainder and for any sick persons in the town. This service occurs about every 3 months. Those whose service occurs the first 2 weeks in December must provide a group of pastorela dancers; those whose service is the second 2 weeks must provide a competing group. The dancers perform December 24, 25, 26, and 31. Dances of the "little old men," viejitos, are associated with the pastorelas.

See Appendix 2 for further comparative data.

DANCES

The dances performed at Cherán are all associated with some religious festival. Organization of the majority of them is part of the duties of the mayordomo, although the moros are connected with the fiesta, while a number of unorganized independent dances are given around December 25. At least three of the dances have spoken parts and are essentially dramatic performances. All center around the birth of Christ, December 25, and the visit of the Three Kings, January 6. The greatest public interest, however, seems to attach to the dance of the moros, connected with the fiesta of the patron saint. Participation in dances is voluntary, although vows may be taken by an individual, or a child may be promised to a dance by its parents.

THE MOROS

The dance of the moros (Moors) is widespread among the Tarascan towns and generally appears to be associated with the fiesta of the patron saint. Usually only four dancers appear. In Cherán, commissioners are named, each seeking a dancer and providing the costume and the horse ridden by the moro part of the time. Good horses are sought and one that will "dance" to the music is especially desirable.

The moros wear a pair of trousers extending part way down the calf of the leg and slashed to the knee on the outside. These trousers are usually of velvet with rich decoration in gold braid and ornaments. Underneath is worn an ordinary pair of cotton calzones. The lower part of the legs is wrapped in cloth to represent leggings. A richly decorated velvet cape is worn over the shoulders, with gold braid and fringe about the edges and gilt ornaments and often small mirrors scattered profusely over the rest of the cape. Underneath is worn a bright-colored rayon shirt.

The headdress is a complicated crown of split cane with a number of upright pieces a foot or more in height. The crown and uprights are decorated in brightly colored papers, feathers, and bright ornaments, including small mirrors. The face is almost covered with a bright rayon kerchief. Shoes are worn. A pair of spurs, with very large metal disks in place of the rowels, completes the costume. The trousers, cape, and headdress are usually rented for the occasion by the commissioner. The rest of the costume is purchased and presented to the dancer by the commissioner.

The moros parade about on their horses a good deal and also dance, especially at the stores and cantinas, where they are given small presents, cookies, cigarettes, money, or drinks. They usually dance singly or in pairs. The steps are simple shuffling steps designed to give as many opportunities to clash the spurs together as possible. The figures of the dance are not well defined but appear related to European country dances. Realizing from previous experience that without skill in choregraphic description (and being unable to witness the dances closely), attempts to record steps and figures are of little value, the writer made no effort to secure details.

THE NEGRITOS

The negritos, turí'a, appear in connection with the mayordomía of the Holy Child, December 25. The brothers and relatives of the carguero invite people to dance. Persons who accept give a promise and have to appear. Thirty to thirty-five unmarried young men or boys are sought, "alert people, good learners, who can read." Also, anyone who wishes may volunteer. In addition to the young men, four little girls participate. Each dancer picks a godmother, who is known as the koroníče.

Usually the dancer picks one of his existing godmothers whom he likes. The godmother dresses the dancer and takes care of his costume, keeping it in her house at night.

The *negritos* wear a regular "citified," *catrin* costume, that is, dark-colored trousers and a woolen sack coat and shoes. They wear a black wooden mask but with European type features. The mask is decorated with many silk ribbons fastened to the top of the mask and hanging down over the head and nearly to the ground behind the dancer. The ribbons are about 2 inches wide and are of many colors. As they are 7 meters long, each ribbon is looped down and back two or three times. There is some competition among the dancers to have the most ribbons, and wealthy young men may wear as many as 24. "Earrings" are suspended from the ears, and a number of strings of beads are worn. Gloves are worn (pl. 6, lower left).

other (fig. 16). Occasionally each pair of *negritos* will walk to the head of the line and back while the two recite their part of the *relato*.

The teaching of the *relato* and of the dance is done by a specialist hired for the occasion by the *carguero*. The best-known specialist is Gregorio Castillo, although he was not hired in 1940. Castillo also teaches the dance of the *viejos, Europeos* or *Españoles,* as he prefers to call it, and was hired to teach the group in 1941. He had been teaching the dances for 28 years (in 1940). His *relatos* he wrote himself. He secured many *relatos* locally and also sent to Mexico City and Guadalajara for others, but he liked none of them. (But several people said they were very tired of Castillo's *relatos,* which have been the same for 20 years and which they felt were not very good anyway.) Castillo feels that the *negrito* dance is especially fine and that the *negritos* of Cherán are

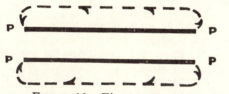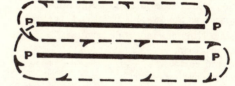

FIGURE 16.—Figures executed in the *negrito* dance. *P* indicates *pastores.*

The costume is provided by the dancer. Part is rented and part is purchased. In the case of one *negrito* dancer in 1940, the following expense was involved:

Mask (rent)	$0.50
Ribbons (rent)	8.50
Suit (rent)	6.00
Shirt (purchase)	5.00
Shoes (purchase)	9.50
Necktie (rent)	.50
Total	$30.00

The *negrito* dance, properly speaking, is not a dance at all. The group recites a *relato* or relation of some length, sings several songs, and walks through a number of not very complicated figures. Ordinarily, they are in two files, with one of the little girls at each end. From time to time, the two files will march forward or backward or each file will walk in a circle or one file will make a circle about the

superior to any he has seen in other towns. The only time he admits having seen a better dance than that of Cherán was once when Aranza borrowed his *relato* and had especially elaborate costumes. Nahuatzen *negritos* have a better dress than those of Cherán, but they are no longer trained.

Castillo, perhaps because it is not in his field, believes the *pastorela* to be a very inferior performance. It is, he says, merely a lot of children dressed up prettily but knowing neither their lines nor their dance. The *negrito,* on the other hand, is a nice clear *relato,* all divided into acts, and the performers are old enough to learn their parts.

Castillo's *relatos* are, naturally, part of his stock in trade. While he was cooperative and willing to permit them to be copied, he would do so only at a price commensurate with their value to him. This price seemed more than they would be worth as documents, particularly as it is evident that they contain much literary echo and perhaps are almost entirely derived from literary sources. As considerable portions of the *relatos* were secured from Agustín Rangel, assistant on the project, who participated in both dances in 1940–41, it was felt the expense of securing the complete *relatos* was not warranted.

The following is the *relato* of Agustín Rangel for the *negrito* dance (spelling as given, but punctuation added):

First act: Music, followed by a song

Tu tienes! oh! Niño, las adelfas y las Rosas,
Aun en boton, con purpura brillante.
Las Azuceñas puras y olorosas
Colores en su tallo vacilante,
Las amapolas frescas y pomposas,
Se Abren, Señor, bajo tu mano amante.
Y del tomillo en las pequeñas ramas
Mil flores hermosísimas derramas.

Second act: Music, followed by a song
Second caminata, or walking figure

(during which several speak; Agustin's part is as follows:)
Bellísimo Niño de amor y de ternura,
Divina criatura,
Te doy mi cariño . . .
(Second speaking part:)
Haces crecer el Cedro en las montañas
Y el sauce a la orrilla del torrente,
Do nacen los helechos y las cañas
Y las yervas mil en la estación ardiente
De la tierra fecundas las Entrañas
Con el Calor y el agua dulcemente
Y asi los campos de verdor revistas
Tornando alegres los que fueron tristes.

Third act: Music, followed by a song

Con gusto y con amor a ofrecer passemos
Felices ya seremos nacido el Salvador.

(*The following is sung as they pretend to make offerings*):

Ante tus plantas postrado
Te ofrece aqui este negrito
Recibe me niño amado
Este fino Silloncito.

Fourth act: A dance

Fifth act: Music, followed by a song and the "farewell"

Adios, Niño Santo,
Con suelo y amor;
Escucha mi canto
Niño Salvador.
Benedice toditos,
Divino Creador.
Se van los negritos
Y llevan tu amor.

TRANSLATION LINE BY LINE

Thou hast, oh Child, the rosebays and the roses,
Still in bud with brilliant purple.
The white lilies, pure and fragrant,
Colors in their waving stems,
The calm and pompous poppies,
They open, Lord, beneath Thy loving hand.
And from the small branches of the thyme
Scatterest Thou a thousand beautiful blossoms.

Act 2

Lovely Child of love and of tenderness,
Divine creature,
I give you my love.
Thou causest the cedar in the mountains to grow,
And the willow at the brink of the torrent,
Where the bracken and the canes grow,
And the thousand herbs of the warm season,
From the entrails of the fecund earth
With the heat and the sweet water,
And thus the fields you dress anew with verdure,
Turning gay those who were sad.

Act 3

With pleasure and with love we go to make offerings,
Happy that now the Savior has been born for us.
Prostrate before your feet
This *negrito* offers Thee,
Receive from me, beloved Child,
This fine little saddle.

Act 5

Farewell, Holy Child,
Comfort and love,
Hear my song,
Child Savior.
Bless everyone,
Divine Creator.
The *negritos* go
And take with them your love.

Fragments of other *relatos* remembered by Agustín are the following (given in English):

The Holy Child is born in a beautiful arcade in Bethlehem.
I have come to see your birth and to adore Thee.
Guided by a star, the *negritos* have come to witness the birth.

(Following this each told where he came from and the gift he brought: A little burro, a horse, a saddle, a dog, and different playthings.)

The main part of the *relato* is recited by a person known as *el letra* and another called *el segundo*. These two stand at the head of the two files, except for the little girls at that end of the lines. When the recitation begins, *el letra* steps forward alone and recites his part, returning to his place when finished. There is then a *caminata*, the files walking in a circle. *El segundo* then does the same, followed by a *caminata*.

The *negrito* dancers begin to learn their parts about a month before December 25. For several evenings before the date they meet in the house of the *carguero* and rehearse. The procedures beginning the night of December 24 are described as follows in an account written by Agustín Rangel:

The *negritos* started to dance about 9:00 p.m. at the *carguero's* house. There were lots of people and about 10:30 the candlemaker came to sell candles. The *negritos* finished dancing about 10:30 p.m. Then they were given supper and they sat around for a while. They were waiting for the bell to ring from the church. The bells were supposed to ring three times, first for the Holy Child to start for the church, second when the Holy Child was supposed to be half way from the *carguero's* house and the church, and third, when the Holy Child was at the door of the church to be blessed before going inside the church. There was a 12 a. m. Mass. The priest of the church came over to the *carguero's* house before the Holy Child left the house. The priest went with the Holy Child up to the church where he blessed the Holy Child before going inside the church. Lots of people went to the 12 a. m. Mass. [Note: There were several hundred persons in the procession, all with candles. The streets and houses were all lit up by the candles. In some towns it is said that pitch pine torches are carried and give even more light.]

December 25. Today the *negritos* started to dance about 9 o'clock in the morning. First they went to Mass and there they danced after the Mass. Then they came to the *carguero's* house to eat dinner. After dinner they went to church again to visit the Holy Child. Then they went home again to the *carguero's* house where they danced again. Then they went to the night Mass. After the night Mass they went inside the patio of the priest's house and danced before him. After they finished dancing, they danced in front of the municipal building before the mayor and officials. After they finished dancing there they went to the *carguero's* house to eat supper. They ate supper and every one of the *negritos* was free to go home.

December 26. Today the *negritos* started to dance first at the *carguero's* house after they had eaten breakfast. After they finished dancing at the *carguero's* house, they went to the Calvary, where they danced. After they finished there they went to Paricutin (*barrio IV*) where they danced at a house. I don't know what saint is there. Then they went to the house

of the *carguero* of the Three Kings, where they danced in the afternoon. Then they went to eat at the *carguero's* house. After they finished eating dinner, they danced and then went to the house of the new *carguero* for the Holy Child where they danced until the evening. Then they came back to the *carguero's* house to eat supper. Then they separated after supper.

December 27. This morning they danced at the *carguero's* house and then they went to the house of the *carguero* of San Isidro. From there they went to the house of [the *carguero* of] San Rafael. Then they went to the *carguero's* house for dinner, after which they danced. From there they went to the priest's house where they danced in front of the priest. Then they danced in front of Don Emilio's store where they were given fruit.

UNORGANIZED CHRISTMAS DANCES

A number of dance groups often appear at or before Christmas. Collectively they are known as the *melebris*, the masqueraders. Formerly, they appeared about 10 days before Christmas Eve and then appeared every third night until December 24. Of recent years they have been forbidden because the various groups often arrived at the same house and then they would fight. In 1940 a few masqueraders were out but they went mainly to houses in their own *barrio* for fear the police might catch them.

Three types of dancers appear. First are the čúrikua anápu tuɹíča or sʌkíč, "the negroes who go out at night." This group wears ordinary clothing but with the crown of the hat decorated with cut papers representing ribbons streaming out behind. Dancers of this group also wear paper ornaments on the front and back of their clothing. They have guitar and drum music and dance a *zapateada*, that is, a sort of *jarabe tapatio* dance.

The second group is the t'aɹé aríriča, the dancing old men. The word "aɹi" also means a person who talks too much and who certainly does not speak the truth. This group dresses like old men; the members wear a long overcoat and a black wooden mask with the beard represented. The masks are similar to those worn by the negroes of Uruapan. Some of the dancers are also dressed as women. They have five or six stringed instruments. No data were collected on the type of dance.

The third group is the apáčiča or the *salvajes* or *negritos salvajes* (Apaches, savages, or negro savages). They paint their faces to resemble the negrito masks but wear no masks. Rooster feathers are stuck in their hair, and they carry bows and arrows. Their dance is purely leaping about. They form a circle, leap about, shout, and make gestures with their bows and arrows. They never speak but make a sort of buzzing noise and make signs with an arrow to indicate what they want. They have guitar and drum music.

The three groups are said to signify that when the Christ Child was born, there appeared a star and various persons had to follow the star, performing their dances in various places. The three dances represent those of the tribes of the Three Kings who went in search of the Child. The Apaches were the last and were the most savage.

The various groups (and more than one group may appear for each dance) go about to various houses where there are unmarried girls or girls approaching marriageable age, and especially to houses where one of the boys has a sweetheart. Usually the girl is warned in advance (through the agency of some small boy) if she is to be visited. She prepares presents of balls of pinole and brown sugar, wrapped in maize husks, often elaborately painted. Sometimes some of these are made in the shape of a rooster or some animal. The girl gives these to the boy who has been courting her if she favors him, and the plain pinole balls to the others. They are also often given food. One of the surreptitious groups in 1940 at a well-to-do house were given coffee with *charanda* in it and boiled squash. When the dancers first enter the house yard, they shake hands with the girl. After eating, they dance a while. Then they say a word of thanks in Tarascan, shake hands with the girl again, and leave. "The idea," said unmarried Agustín, "is just to touch the girl's hand and see how neat her cooking and housework is." Obviously the dances are significant parts of the mating selection, for on almost no other occasion would a boy have a chance to see how a girl's house was run or have a chance to touch her hand openly.

According to one informant, a burlesque of the Mass is given by the dancers. This was not verified from any other source. It is the sort of thing which might sometimes have been done, but it seems foreign to the main purpose of the dances.

THE PASTORELA

The *pastorela*, or dance of the shepherds, is also performed at Christmas time. The dance is particularly connected with the *cabildo* and with the *prioste*. The leaders in the dance are the *uánánčes*, the four girls (six according to other accounts) who have taken incense and flowers to the church during the year and performed other services at the church. Generally they are about 10 years of age. Usually the girls have been vowed to the service by their parents as the result of illness or some other misfortune threatening the child. The time of the dance is sometimes called the fiesta of pajáču (meaning not secured).

The *uánánčes* invite a number of other girls to participate, 12 in all being needed. The girls invited by the *uánánčes* have no responsibilities other than dancing, but each of the *uánánčes* must feed the group for 1 day. The *uánánčes* also select adults to represent the parts of the devil and the hermit and also select the teacher. The girls (all the expenses, of course, are borne by their parents) also have music to accompany the dance.

For the dance the girls are dressed in the *catrin*, i.e. "citified," style, in white dresses with straw hats adorned with artificial flowers (actually the style is not citified, but is rural Mestizo). Owing to the quarrel between the priest and the *cabildo*, the *pastorela* was not performed in 1940 and the actual dance could not be observed. A *relato* (in this case known as the *coloquio*) is an important part of the performance. One of the songs collected (for the *pastorela* of Cheranástico) is as follows (spelling as given):

A que noche tan cremoza
Ensillad mi buen caballo
Que en Belen nos conbida de Salvador
Muy lejos tieras bengo
Agosar de una pasiada
Con gusta y contento
A juntar mi ganadito.

TRANSLATION

Ah, what a beautiful night.
Saddle my good horse,
For to Bethlehem the Savior invites us.
To very distant lands I will arrive.
I will enjoy a journey,
With pleasure and content
To bring together my cattle.

Usually the *pastorela* is given the night of December 24 and for 2 or 3 days afterward. The dancers perform first between the church and the municipal building. Then they visit the houses of the members of the *cabildo* and the various *cargueros*. At the houses they are usually given some fruit.

In 1940 considerable feeling was engendered by the collapse of the *pastorela*, which many believed to be the pleasantest of the various dances, the more moralistic because no one drank in connection with it. Don Inocencio, the father of the first *uanánče*, the šunánda or pári, wished to give the *pastorela* so that he could comply with the promise he had made when his daughter was sickly as a small child. He was somewhat incensed because the *prioste* had spoken to the other families first and told them they should not give the dance. When Don Inocencio visited the other parents he found them unwilling to go ahead and disgusted with the whole situation. Most extreme was Tomás Hernandez, who said he would not comply with the obligation, even though it should mean losing the 10 pesos he had advanced on behalf of the group to bring the band from Tanaco. Or, he added, he might be willing to bring the band, but he wouldn't give the dance; instead, he would give a big paránda or drinking party for the benefit of themselves and not for the town.

Don Inocencio expressed great distress at this attitude. He already had fattened two pigs and expressed himself frequently as willing to go ahead with the *pastorela* if others would help. He appealed to the staff of the investigation to speak to the mayor, asking him to compel the other families to comply with their obligation; or, failing that, for permission to take up a voluntary collection. Clearly, Don Inocencio felt that the families of the other *uanánčes* were taking advantage of the dismissal of the *cabildo* to avoid their just obligations.

This suspicion of Don Inocencio's was quite correct in some cases. One of the other family heads stated that the dismissal of the *cabildo* canceled the obligation. Although his daughter had become a *uanánče* in compliance with a vow, her father announced he would not help to give the *pastorela* even though others volun-tarily contributed to the expenses. One of the more cynical assistants in the investigation pointed out that the attitude was quite understandable, as the man owed a debt of $160 to a woman in the town, who was trying to force him to pay at least half of it.

The father of another of the *uanánčes* stated that with the dismissal of the *prioste* the custom of the *pastorela* had ended and that it was unnecessary to continue. Evidently he did not care for the custom and remarked, "To me it seems best that they dismissed the *prioste*."

Another case is of some interest. Although the girl was not a *uanánče*, her parents had made a vow that she should appear in the *pastorela*. The parents made an arrangement for her to participate in the *pastorela* of Cheranástico. The Cheranástico *pastorela* evidently is somewhat different from that of Cherán. The girl would wear a red dress, a silk handkerchief covering the lower part of her face, a man's hat, and shoes and would be known as a *rancherita*. She would dance opposite a small boy partner called a *ranchero* (rancher). The *pastorela* of Cheranástico is performed January 1.

DANCE OF THE *VIEJOS* OR *EUROPEOS*

The dance of the *viejos* or *Europeos* (old men or Europeans) appears in connection with the Three Kings, January 6. Previous to 1940 the dance had been given by a volunteer group. In the afternoons, as men lounged about the streets and talked after work, people would begin to mention that the time for the dance was approaching. Eventually a group would decide that they should organize the dance. They would collect money among themselves and others and hire musicians and a teacher. In 1940, however, the *carguero* of the Three Kings, announced that giving the dance was properly part of the *mayordomía* and undertook to organize the dancers, pay the teacher and musicians, and provide food for the dancers.

The group in 1940 consisted of 30 *viejos* (but not all of them appeared all the time), three kings, and five *pastorcitas* or shepherdesses. (There should have been only four shepherdesses; we were unable to learn the reason for the extra one. Possibly someone asked to participate after the four were chosen or there were reasons why the *carguero* felt it would be politic to ask five different families.) The *viejos* were mostly young men, but married men participated in this dance. They wore *vestido de catrín*, "city dress," including a long black overcoat for preference, a felt hat with a colored ribbon for the hat band and artificial flowers attached, a muffler, a handkerchief about the head, shoes, and a well-made white wooden mask with black or golden beard, the features being very European.

The kings also wore masks; one was white, one rose-colored, and one black (one of the images of the Three Kings is also black). They also wore a long white wig surmounted by a crown, each one different; a long, intentionally ragged cape of colored material (really a smock in 1940); petticoats or trousers of rayon with cotton trousers underneath; rose-colored cotton stockings; and shoes (although they could wear *huaraches* or sandals). The kings merely sit or stand and do not dance. The shepherdesses are dressed in the same fashion as those for the *negrito* dance.

The dancers provide their own costumes. The cost of a *viejo* costume is as follows:

Mask ($1.50 to 2.50, rent; $5, purchase)	$ 2.50
Hat	2.00
Overcoat	3.00
Pants and vest	2.50
Muffler	1.50
Incarche (hat band?)	.50
Flowers	1.50
Shoes	$6.00–$10.00
Shirt	5.00
Necktie	.50
Total (with shoes, $25–$29)	$19.00

All the items listed above are for rent except the shirt, which is purchased. If the dancer had no shoes, he normally bought a pair.

The local masks are expensive and are regarded as inferior. Those from Sevina and Cheranástico are said to be cheaper and better. The masks of the kings in 1940 were inferior local products; good masks had been ordered from Sevina but did not arrive in time.

The early part of the dance is really a recitation. The *viejos* form in two files, each with a shepherdess at each end (two at one end in 1940), with the three kings facing the files at

one end. First spoke a *letra* (in 1940 Agustín Rangel, assistant in the study), who gave an introduction (see below), walking up and down between the files and describing the events of the birth of Christ and the Three Kings. Then all made a circuit (fig. 17). After this, everyone (except the Three Kings but including the shepherdesses) stepped between the lines in

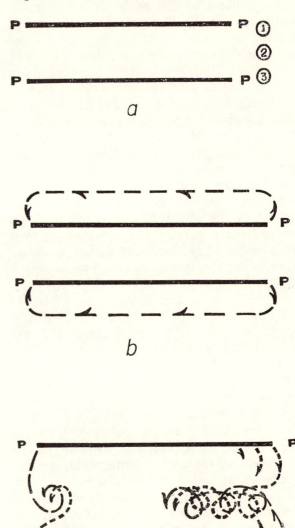

FIGURE 17.—Dance of the *Europeos*, showing various dance figures. *a*, Basic position at start of dance and in which all figures end. *b*, Circling movement. *c*, Movements of paired dancers, executed by each pair in turn, reversing the figure to return to their original position. *P* indicates the *pastores*; the numerals indicate the Three Kings.

pairs, speaking a *relato* referring to events that had happened in those days. Then they sang a song, making another circuit. After this, the Three Kings marched between the files to the opposite end, where they were met by one of the pairs, the shepherdesses first. The Kings returned to their position, followed by the pair of dancers. Each dancer then spoke a brief verse, telling what he had brought to the Christ Child. The Kings answered. The others sang without words during this event except while the dancers spoke. This was repeated for each pair of dancers.

A pair of dancers from each end of the line now passed down the files until they met one another. Each pair held hands and danced in a circle, then reversed to the original position. The pairs then returned to their position and were followed by the others until all had danced. The *letra* then spoke a closing piece, telling everyone they should be gay. After this, each pair in succession danced a *jarabe* between the files from one end to the other. If a dancer performed very well and with much spirit, the others cried out in a falsetto voice. Sometimes they did this anyway for pleasure.

The *relato* of the *letra* or leader in 1940 was that composed by Gregorio Castillo and went as follows (spelling and punctuation as given):

No duda, bien lo Sabeis
Mis respetables ancianos;
El 25 del mes.
De Diciembre en la locacion:
Bajo hay del alto cielo,
Han acer en esta suela
Nuestro Dios de predencia.
Al instante los pastores,
Sabidos del gran portento;
Salen preste en el momento,
A visitar el Señor.
Dejando el campo y ganado
Asi como sus cabañas;
Ven por bosques y montanas,
Y con crecido contento,
van a ver el nacimiento
Del Niño Jesus amado.
Cuando contaba ocho dias
De nacido el Niño Amado
Fue tambien cir convencido
El verdadero mezias.
Compañeros Veteranos,
Recordar el 6 de enero
Fiesta de la epiphania,
Fue de gloria el feliz dia;

Del bellisimo lucero,
Fue la manifestacion,
Del Niño Dios y Señor;
Por eso con todo amor,
Vamos a su adoracion.

Canto: 1ª caminata

Salid presuros,
Las glorias cantandos;
Al Nino en sal sando
Cantos de amor.

1° Relato

Tambien Los Reyes de Oriente,
Manchan en este momento;
De Dios Niño al Nacimiento,
A ver a mi portente.
Luz de vina los va guindo
Y van a la adoracion,
En tan feliz ocasion,
La gloria le van cantando.

Ofrecimiento—Canto

Pasad al monto,
Con gusto y amor,
Ofrecer al Niño,
Amor y consuelo.
Ofrece
Te veo en humildes pajitas,
Y me postre en el instante,
Yo te adoro Nino Amante,
Y te ofresco estas conchitas.
(Pide el baile al terminar los
ofrecimientos de todos.)

Baile

Pues todos nos complacemos
Yavimos tu Nacimiento
Y Todos con gusto estamos
Porque felices seremos;—
Niño Dios, bello portento,
En grupo todos nos vamos;
Al terminar la Vecita;
Mas en nuestros corazones;
Todos Fidos te llevarnos;
Jamas, jamas nos olvides,
Hoy te dicen toditos,
Hasta el año Venidero
Mas todos con Alegria
Vimos ya tus Maravillas:
!Oh! Ninito Salvador,
Permitanos gran Senor,
Que con gusta te bailemos
Unos alegres cuadrillas;
En tan felices momentos
Adios digo companeros,
Toquen ya los instrumentos
Y los sones abajemos—

Despues del Canto

Musica

Ya nos retiremos,
Del lugar Sagrado;
Llovando nos vamos,
!Oh! Jesus amado.

TRANSLATION

Do not doubt it, well you know it,
My respectable ancients,
The 25th of the month
Of December in the location
There below the high heavens
Has been born on this earth
Our Lord who takes precedence.
Instantly the shepherds,
Knowing of the great portent,
Started quickly at that moment
To visit the Lord.
Leaving the fields and the cattle
As well as their cabins;
They went through woods and mountains,
And with growing contentment,
Went to see the birth
Of the beloved Child Jesus.
When eight days were counted
From the birth of the beloved Child,
Likewise were made neighborly
The true union [meaning unclear].
Veteran comrades,
Remember the sixth of January
Feast of the Epiphany,
That happy day was glorious.
From the beautiful morning star
Came the manifestation
Of the Child, God and Lord;
For this with all love
We go to adore Him.

1st walking interval. Song

Go forth hastily
Singing the glories;
To the Child raising
Songs of love.

1st relation

Also the Kings of the East
March at this moment;
Of God the Child at the birthplace
To see my portent.
Divine Light guided them
And they went to the adoration,
On such a happy occasion,
They went singing the glories.

Offering—Song

Pass to the amount [meaning unclear]
With pleasure and love,
Offer to the Child
Love and consolation.

The Offering

I see Thee on humble straw
And I prostrate myself instantly,
I adore Thee, loving Child,
And I offer Thee these little shells.
(The dance is asked for when the
offerings are ended.)

Dance

Well, we all are pleased,
Now we have seen your birth,
And all are pleased
Because we will be happy.
Child God, beautiful portent,
Together we all go
To put an end to the visit.
Moreover in our hearts
All faithful we carry Thee.
Never, never forget us,
Today all tell Thee,
Until the coming year,
But all with joy,
Now we have seen your marvels;
Oh, little Child Savior,
Permit us great Lord,
That with pleasure we dance for Thee
Some joyous quadrilles.
In such happy moments,
I say "farewell companions."
Let the instruments play
And the lowland tunes . . . [Meaning
not clear—possibly *abajeños* is meant,
not *abajemos*, that is, "tunes of the
low country."]

After the song, music is played

Now we take ourselves away
From the Sacred place.
Weeping [?] we go,
Oh! beloved Jesus.

The style of delivery of these *relatos* was highly declamatory and monotonous. The words were spoken in a level tone without inflection or other interpretation of their meaning.

The sense of a few of the other individual *relatos* was secured. One dancer said he was very old, so old he couldn't walk on level ground. If he couldn't walk on level ground, how was he going to walk downhill? Nevertheless, he was going to the place of the Holy Child anyway. Another said that if he got tired walking, he would go on his knees to visit the Child, even though they were scratched. Yet another complained of his high squeaky voice, but even if his voice gave out, he still would go to the Holy

Child. The performer with the latter lines was the only one who managed to make the crowd laugh. The remainder were greeted in silence or by asides criticizing their performance, especially several who had not learned their lines very well.

The dancers practiced at the house of the *carguero* of the Three Kings on Thursday, Friday, and Saturday. The *carguero* provided food for all the performers. The ceremonies proper began on Sunday in the late afternoon. The following is the account of the proceedings as written by Agustín Rangel.

January 5, 1941. On Sunday we started for the Calvary from the house of the *carguero* at about 5 p. m. The Three Kings went on horseback. At the Calvary the Three Kings took the star (a star on the end of the pole). The King in the middle took the star and the Kings on either side took hold of a ribbon tied on each side. Then we started for the *carguero's* house where we were supposed to take the saint to the church. At the church we left the saint where a vespers was given for it. Then we started for the *carguero's* house where we danced. Then supper was served. Before we left, the *carguero* told us that on the next morning we had to be at his house about 6:30 a. m. [According to one informant, customarily the group should have danced at the church.]

January 6. I arrived at the *carguero's* house about 6:00 a. m. After a little, they told me to go around on some of the streets with the musicians and tell the other guys to hurry up and get over to the *carguero's* house. When the bell rang for the long Mass we all left for church. After the long Mass the priest told us we could not dance until after the Rosary. We then left for the *carguero's* house where we ate breakfast. After breakfast we danced at the *carguero's* house. We did nothing all day until after the Rosary. We went to the Rosary; after we came out we danced in the priest's house, then we danced in front of the church. After that we danced in front of the municipal building. From there we went to the house of the new *carguero* of the Holy Child where we danced and we were given oranges after we danced. Then we went home (to the *carguero's* house) where we danced before eating supper. Then we went home and were told to be at the *carguero's* house about 7:00 a. m.

January 7. On this morning we went to the church after the Mass. We were to take the Holy Kings to the house of the new *carguero*. We started from the church and we headed for the new *carguero's* house where we arrived and left it [the images] there. They told us to sit down and we were given *atole de cacao* (black atole). We danced before the atole was served and after that we left for the *carguero's* house to eat breakfast. After breafast we headed for the Calvary where we danced. Then we headed for Bruno Gaspar's house

where we danced and were given oranges. We then went to the house of [the *carguero* of] San Antonio, where we danced and were not given anything. From there we went to the store of Victoriano Turja where we danced and were given 1 liter of *aguardiente*. Then we left for the meat market of one of the *cargueros* of the Holy Kings [he means one of the principals], Don Ygnacio Duran, where we danced and recited the *relato*, the whole works, and were given oranges. From there we left for the house of [the *carguero* of] Santa Nieves, where we danced and were given money, 1 centavo apiece. From there we went to the house [of the *carguero* of] Our Lady of Guadalupe where we danced and were given limes. From there we came dancing what they call a *carnival* through the streets to the store of Don Hilario (Xhembe) where we were given sugarcane. Then we left for the *carguero's* house to eat supper. We were told to be early at his house the next morning.

January 8. The next morning we started to dance about 9 a. m. from the *carguero's* house. We went to the house of Rosalio [*representante* or representative of the town], where we danced and were given oranges. From there we went to the house of Crescencio Hernandez where they gave us a 50-centavo piece because she said [the mistress of the house] that they had not expected us to come and dance at the house. Then we went to a house on Galeana and Allende where we danced and where we were not given anything because he [the house owner] said he wasn't expecting us. Then we danced to one of the *carguero's* of the Holy Kings [meaning principal again] where we were given oranges. From there we went to the house of [the *carguero* of] San Isidro where we danced and were given oranges. Then we went to [the *barrio* of] Parícutin to the place of the Virgin Inéz; there we danced and were given oranges. Then from there we went to the house of the *carguero* of some saint near the barranca of Parícutin where we danced and were not given anything. Then we went to the house on the corner of Rayon and Comercio streets where we danced and were given oranges. Then we headed for the *carguero's* house to eat dinner. After dinner, we then went to the house of the Miraculous Holy Christ where we danced and were not given anything because we started to grab the oranges from the basket and the woman got sore and didn't give us anything. Then we left for the house of Don Jesús Velasquez (the main marriage manager), where we danced and were given oranges.. He had invited us to go over to his house and dance. From there we went to Ricardo Queriapa where the saint of San Anselmo is. There we danced and were given oranges. But this time some of the *viejos* had separated and some of them had gone to the plaza. After we finished dancing at that lady's house we then danced at the store of Alberto Muñoz where we were not given anything. Then the Doctor invited us over to dance in front of his office. After we got through, the Doctor flipped a peso to see who would get it. One of the *viejos* got it and got drunk with the peso. From the plaza we then went west over to the store of Don Emilio Rojas where we danced and were given a 50-centavo piece. From there we then came over to the house of Rafael Castillo, where we danced and were given two packages of cigarettes. From there we went over to the store of Benito Pahuamba, where we danced and were given a bottle of sherry. From there we went over to the *carguero's* house to eat supper, but before we ate we danced the whole works. Then we ate supper and after that they gave each of the *viejos* a loaf of white bread. But before, when we were dancing and reciting, the *carguero's* wife began to pass out sugarcane and oranges and then we went to eat. After supper we danced for a little while, up to about 11 p. m., and then we went home. We danced [this time] because that was the *combate* for this year's *mayordomía* for Don Aurelio. [The last sentence is obscure. Don Aurelio was the *carguero* for the succeeding year.]

Ordinarily the dancers appear again for 1 day at the time of Candelaria, February 2, reciting the same *relatos* but without the Three Kings. For 1941 one man had agreed to pay for the music and two others had agreed to provide food for the dancers, but for some reason the arrangement fell through. On the vespers of Candelaria, people burn pitch pine (ocote) in front of their lots.

OTHER DANCES

On January 1 a group of children, 6 to 8 years old, dances in the day time. Six boys and six girls participate and are called taré sapíratiča, or the "little old men." They go to church very early in the morning and change the image of the Holy Child, which had been placed in a reclining position in a crib on December 25, placing it in a sitting position. After the Mass the children go to the house of the *colector*, where they breakfast and dance. They then go to the house of the kéηi and dance. Later they go to some other houses to dance. At midday they eat at the house of the *colector* again. The dance is performed to music furnished by wind instruments. It apparently attracts little attention and often is not performed. A former *colector* stated the girls are the *uánánčes* for the ensuing year, but this fact seemed not to be generally known.

In connection with the *mayordomía* of Santa Nieves or the Virgin of the Snows, a group of girls performs a dance on August 5 for 1 day to music of wind instruments. The dance is known as the caballita uaɹáriča dance of the little horses. The figures of horses are made of withes from certain plants, with openings in the middle in which the girls stand. The head is made so it can move, and the dance consists mostly of the girls standing and moving the horses' heads in time to the music. Again, little attention is paid to the dance, and the *carguero* often does not arrange to have it performed.

In connection with the fiesta of the Virgin of Guadalupe, the *carguero* ordinarily arranges a dance known as the uáris. The dancers consist simply of unmarried girls and young women who dress in the traditional costume but perhaps with a few more ornaments than usual. They dance the usual Cherán fiesta dance in the streets.

DANCES IN OTHER TOWNS

Only a few dances were observed or learned of in other towns. The *pastorela* of Capacuaro was the most thoroughly studied, but the data remain superficial and unrelated to the ceremonial setting. The dancers are connected with the *carguero* for the December 25th ceremonies. A pole is erected in his patio with a large paper lantern suspended from the top (this is done by the kéηi at Cherán, but use of this term was denied at Capacuaro) and a stage is erected at one end of the patio on which some of the *relatos* are given. The house is also decorated with paper flowers and pine boughs. A table altar on the porch has a *creche* with miniature figures. The dancers appear for 3 days at Christmas and again on January 1. On Christmas Eve it is claimed that they perform a very long *colloquio*, lasting 18 hours without repetition, on the stage at the *carguero's* house. Doubt of this statement seems indicated.

The dancers consist of between 35 and 40 *rancheritas* and *rancheritos*, boys and girls of 8 to 12. In addition, there were two "hermits" or *hermitaños*, dressed as friars with gray robes and a conical cap. They wore a rosary and carried a whip, serving, among other functions, as police (pl. 6, upper right). Two *Europeos* were dressed in white wooden masks with long blonde wigs of goat hair, citified clothes, and boots (pl. 6, lower right). Three "devils" or "demons" were dressed in black, wearing a crown of feathers on the back of the head, with a black veil over most of the face. The devils bore such names as "cunning," *astucia*. Some of the dancers were dressed as ranchers. Two small boys represented angels (one, Michael, with a sword), but the majority were dressed in shepherd's costumes. The girls wore loose blouses, fairly long full skirts, straw hats with ribbons, and shoes. The boys wore satin blouses and bloomers, stockings, shoes, and straw hats. Pinks, blues, and whites predominated in the costumes. Both sexes carried shepherd's crooks, decorated with celluloid animals, ribbons, balls of yarn, and feathers.

The performance begins with a long *relato* by the devils in which they talk about a journey they are going to make, the curious things they are going to see, etc. Then a *ranchera* and a *ranchero* dance a *jarabe*. The other *rancheros* supervise the two files of children. Then there is a *relato* by the dancers. Then the dancers give their crooks to friends or relatives and dance. The *Europeos* dance about the files of children alone or occasionally with the hermits. The devils and the hermits, on the other hand, constantly engage in byplay, pursuing one another. Occasionally one or two of the devils will capture a hermit and force him to dance along with them. Also, from time to time the hermits use their whips to keep the children from crowding in too much on the dancers.

The *hermitaños* were special buffoons. One was seen "praying" before the church with his hands together but with both thumbs to his nose. Boys threw bits of stick or pebbles at them; the *hermitaños* would threaten the crowd with their whips or if they identified the offender, would pursue him with their whips— and sometimes used them if the stones had been too big.

The dances are performed first in front of the church before the saints' images, which are brought out of the church for this. Then the dancers eat in the house of the *carguero,* after which they dance. Then they go to various houses and dance. The householders give them fruit, sugarcane, peanuts, or other small gifts. Then they return to the house of the *carguero* to eat once more.

At primarily Mestizo San Juan Parangaricutiro on January 7 a dance of *Europeos* was observed. The two main dancers were a man and woman in burlesque of *catrin-ranchero* costumes (the "woman" was a man dressed in women's clothes). The woman wore a straw hat with artificial flowers, a well-made white wooden mask of a European woman's face, a cloth enveloping all of the head not covered by the mask, a yellow waist, and a black *ranchera's* skirt with a beautifully embroidered yellow silk apron, gloves, and a handbag. In her hands she carried a narrow woman's sash. The man wore a white wig with ribbons, white mask with black beard and attractive features, a sweater, a moro dancer's cape (but worn a little lower than the moro dancer does, so the mirror was over the man's buttocks), and several women's aprons of silk or rayon hung from about his neck. About his legs from the knees down were wrapped numerous women's belts and about his ankles were copper bells. Over one shoulder he carried a stick with one end carved into a burro's head, adorned with ribbons and with a bell hung from the neck of the burro.

The other dancers were dressed somewhat like the male leader, except the cape was black with an opening like that of a serape although worn as a cape. The lining of the cape was in brilliant colors of silk or rayon. Ornamentation of the cape was done with colored sequins. Otherwise the costume was the same, but no stick was carried.

The dance music varied according to various aspects of the dance, changes being indicated by the male leader ringing his bell. The dancers formed in two files, with the male leader at the head of one file, the woman leader at the head of the other. When the music began, the dancers leaped in the air several times and shouted in a high voice. Then the files performed several circuits; the one headed by the male making its circuit first, followed by the other. Following the circuits the dancers performed a sort of *jarabe*, but remained in one place. From time to time they leaped high in the air (individually), shouting in a falsetto voice. As they came down they spread their capes wide and, with hair and aprons flying in all directions, they resembled some impossible bird.

Following this performance, the "woman" danced alone between the files, taking very small steps and with her nose high in the air. The sash she carried in her two hands at about shoulder height, raising first one hand and then the other. With her handbag dangling from one wrist, she was the perfect caricature of a *nouveau riche* young lady parading down the street. Next, the man and woman leaders danced a *jarabe tapatio* very well (except they did not use the hat) although in very restrained and "correct" fashion. Meanwhile the others danced in their places and leaped in the air and cried out from time to time.

The dance is said to be held by the young men, who organize it themselves and provide the music and meals. It follows a traditional pattern, however, in that among the first places in which the dances were performed were the house of the priest and the offices of the *municipio*.

In Parícutin the dance of the fiesta of the patron saint is apparently called either sondado uarán or turiȼauarani. The dancers wear "citified" or *catrin* clothes with masks.

Dances are also reported from some of the Mestizo towns and the *ranchos* lying along the borders of Cherán. From Tingambato a dance was brought to the Eucharist Congress held in Uruapan which much resembles in costume the feather dances of Oaxaca. A deer dance is reported from La Mojonera and Las Canoas in which the dancers wear striped or checkered clothing and have the face covered by a mask of a deer with horns. The dance is performed to a tin rattle, violin, and guitar of the special type known as *panzón*, that is, one with a large sounding box. The actions of the animal are represented in the dance.

MUSICIANS

Frequent reference has been made elsewhere to the musicians. The organized bands are essentially parts of the ceremonial system; without them no fiesta would be complete, while they form a significant part of many *mayordomías* and dances. They appear for a great many individual functions also, such as weddings and house-roofing fiestas. As a public body they also play for some civic events, such as the installation of new officers, for which they receive no pay.

In addition to the organized bands, there are smaller and less well organized groups of musicians, mainly performers on stringed instruments such as violin, violincello, bass fiddle, and guitar, although a clarinetist may be included. Such groups meet and play together at one another's houses for their own pleasure. At times, however, they may be hired for *mayordomías* or household fiestas, especially if the sponsor cannot afford a full band. Such groups may also be asked to play at some public function. In 1940 one such group was asked by the mayor to play in the school in connection with the final oral examinations and closing exercises.

WITCHCRAFT

For many miles around, Cherán has the reputation of being the outstanding center for witchcraft among the Tarascans. As is often the case, however, it was extremely difficult to secure any information about witchcraft in the town. Enough was secured, however, and enough significant evasions encountered, to make it likely that the reputation is deserved. Even by the informants and assistants on the study, concealment was practiced, and at the very end of the study some data were obtained virtually by accident from Agustín, our United States born helper, which he obviously told with great reluctance.

Witches, sʌkuájpiri, are believed always to be women. In general, the name of witch is applied to all "women of the street," that is, women who live without men. Generally, these are either aged women without relatives or women, usually widows, who are believed to be prostitutes. No one would dare do anything against such women. Although these women may live in any part of the town, there is evidence that they are believed to live more in *barrio* I on the slopes of Santiákujákua, the hill on the northwest corner of the town. This hill is said to be full of witches and to be a very dangerous spot to go to at night. Passing along one of the uppermost streets on the hill one day, we were asked for a coin by an old woman. Agustín R. refused to let me give a coin and hurried us away, obviously much shaken by the experience and firmly convinced the woman was a witch.

Despite the fact that several persons stated all witches are women, a story was collected that witchcraft was started in Cherán by a man who found a book. Most power, though, is said to be obtained by a witch who goes alone to the summit of Kukundikáta, a volcanic cone a mile or two southeast of town and about a thousand feet in height. Here the witch calls the devil, "Sir devil, I ask a favor." A strong wind is felt or the sound of a strong wind is heard and the devil appears before the petitioner. The would-be witch then makes a contract for 20 years, at the end of which time he loses his life. In the meantime the witch may teach others, however, who do not have a contract unless the witch makes a subsidiary agreement with them. In any case they are not as powerful as the witch who secures power directly from the devil. (Note again in this account the implication that the witches are male.)

Witches operate in several ways. The most common is to secure some very personal object, a comb, piece of hair, piece of clothing, or even sweat from a coin (which is why Agustín refused to let me give a coin, as mentioned above). A doll of wax or clay is made to resemble the person and dressed in similar clothes. The article obtained is used in making or clothing the doll. If hair of the victim has been obtained, for example, it is placed on the head of the doll. Pins are then stuck in the joints and, if it is desired to kill the victim, in each temple. The doll is then taken to one of several places, things are recited in Tarascan, candles are burned, and each time the pins are pushed in a little farther.

The places visited are a spot in the *barranca* separating Parícutin from the other *barrios* or two caves on the slope of Kukundikáta. It was undesirable to attempt to locate the spot in the *barranca*, but the two caves were visited. Neither showed signs of much use. In one candles had evidently been burned. The second had been visited fairly recently. Far in the back of the cave a small trench crossed the steeply sloping floor and the rocks about it had been well swept. In a corner were twigs from an oak tree and at one side two crossed branches of oak. A cigarette butt and some fragments of pitch pine, apparently dropped casually, were the only other evidence of use.

It was reported that a good deal of witchcraft had been stamped out and that the municipal government, acting on orders from Morelia, had posted two armed guards at night in the *barranca* and one on Kukundikáta with orders to shoot to kill anyone they found practicing witchcraft. It is necessary to kill the witch, because if the witch escapes the magic will turn against the person interfering. Any attempt at verification of this report from the municipal officials met with such skillful evasive action that there may be a modicum of truth in it.

Another way of bewitching is to carry objects at night to the house of the victim. Bones of dead persons were mentioned as one of the objects. Pedro Chávez had also seen a candle with many holes in it and cut in many places which was hidden close to the house of an intended victim. Candles are used because they are associated with the dead. Earth from the floor of the jail is also very useful in such matters, and certain flowers may also be deposited.

One of the ways of leaving things or of obtaining a personal object is for the witch to change into some animal. Witches may change into cats, owls, dogs, roosters, or burros. In this guise they may hide something by the house of the victim or may steal some personal object. If a strange cat, or even a neighbor's cat which has never come around before, should come into the kitchen and play and try to snatch personal things it is probably a witch in disguise. If such a cat is caught by the tail and held in the smoke of an oak fire it will soon talk and answer any question asked, such as the name of the witch, the person sending the witch, and so on. A friend of Agustín R. caught a witch cat in this way. He threatened to kill it if he saw it again. When he released the animal, it simply vanished.

The animals may also talk softly to the victim at night. A woman heard a voice outside saying, "Sleep, *Doña* ———, sleep." She went to a good witch and after a period of treatment was not bothered again. Owls will get in trees outside the house and speak in this fashion. They do not have to be close by, however, for a large cherry tree south of town is said to be a favorite roosting place for owl-witches engaged in their occupations.

In addition to persons who come to believe they are bewitched, any sick person who does not recover after treatment is thought to be bewitched. The only remedy in cases of bewitchment is to seek the aid of a good witch. In some cases at least, the good witches are persons taught as other witches are but who refuse to use their knowledge to injure people. Obviously there is room for suspicion of such people. Agustín R. knows a woman who is a good witch (but he refused to introduce us to her or tell her name). The woman is reported to have been taught by her mother who was a bad witch. On her deathbed the mother made the daughter promise never to use her power to injure people. The witch is now teaching her own daughter.

Little is known about curing techniques. In the account secured, the good witch goes into an empty house, strikes the walls with a stick, and calls the bad witch. The latter can hear even though as far away as Paracho. The bad witch will come and the two fight. To those outside it sounds like thunder, and the walls shake so it seems they must fall down. But if one has the courage to look inside, everything is calm and peaceful. After a time the friendly witch comes out. If she says she lost the fight, then there is no hope for the patient.

In all probability an important reason for the departure of the Rangel family from Cherán for their long stay in the United States was because of bewitchment. Agustín's mother was bewitched before the family left. She had no specific ailments but felt bad all over and could not get up. Someone told her husband that a certain witch was working on her. Agustín's father then hid in the *barranca* until a woman came with a doll, which he recognized as his wife. He confronted her, but she did not speak. In some way, though, she agreed to give up the witchcraft. Agustín's father threatened to kill the woman if she tried bewitchment again. He took the doll and burned it. If he had merely thrown it away, the

magic would have worked against him. He was said not to have been bothered after this, but he warned Agustín in our presence against giving a coin to a stranger who seemed very friendly, as he might merely be wishing for sweat to bewitch him.

The reason Agustín's father could deal with witches so effectively was that he had been immunized against witches. A friendly witch had wrapped him from head to foot in string soaked in snake oil and other things. He wore the string for 2 days and then was told not to bathe for another week. Agustín knew no other details, but shortly before the study closed he admitted that immediately after his arrival in Cherán the family had hired a witch to immunize him. Beyond stating that it was only a temporary and simple immunization, Agustín would give no further details. Ultimately, it was intended that he have the more complete treatment.

The fact that the Rangel family left Cherán after the alleged bewitchment mentioned above and had the son immunized immediately after their return lends support to the belief that the family left town because of witchcraft.

Data are too scanty to form any reliable hypothesis about the effects of witchcraft in Cherán. Nevertheless, an attractive theory might be developed that witchcraft accounts for some of the personality traits in Cherán and more particularly for the prevalence of walled yards and the general unwillingness to invite strangers or little-known persons inside the yard gate. It should not be overlooked, though, that the exclusive character of the Cherán family or household grouping may also be accounted for in terms of the more urban character of the settlement.

Two other items should be added to this discussion. It was reported that some witches had a white powder which they threw into people's faces. The powder instantly disappears inside and the persons become ill. Good witches may cure this sickness.

Although not considered witches, there are women who tell fortunes with cards. One woman in *barrio* III is said to be able to tell **where lost cattle are and**, if they have been stolen, who the thief is.

WITCHCRAFT IN CAPACUARO

As is often the case, more specific details of witchcraft were secured in Capacuaro, which has no reputation for witchcraft, than in Cherán. In the course of a brief stay in Capacuaro, Rendón and Carrasco made the acquaintance of a delightful couple who openly admitted to being witches. The remaining members of the staff subsequently became fairly well acquainted with the couple. Their witchcraft seemed, on the whole, a relatively harmless and unmalicious variety, which may account for their willingness to admit to the practice. Perhaps the most entertaining incident was when the wife told Rendón under promise of secrecy that she had secured her husband through witchcraft and had been able to keep him only through the same means. The husband told Carrasco the same story about his wife!

The following are details, mostly collected by Rendón:

1. Method of winning the love of someone; of making a wife return to her husband; or of making a husband return to his wife; or causing someone who is impassioned without hope to obtain what he desires:

Secure five candles costing 5 centavos, three of paraffin and two of tallow. The practitioner must shut himself in a room without anyone seeing him, but if he has asked a witch to do the ceremony for him, he must be present. The candles are arranged in the following form:

```
    *           tallow candle
*   *   *       paraffin candles
    *           tallow candle
```

The paraffin candle in the center is known as the "Candle of the Heart." The candles must be in the center of the room and oriented to the cardinal directions.

Placing of the candles begins with the lower tallow candle. First the candle is turned between the fingers in a certain way, saying "so and so, come, come, come, come, come . . . " many times. Upon saying this the necessary number of times depends much of the success of the ceremony, but there are no rules; the witch simply feels when it has been enough. The candle is then lighted and put in position. The same is done with the other candles, but the order could not be given unless the investigator had hired the ceremony performed with serious purpose.

The center candle, the "Candle of the heart," is previously softened by exposure to the sunlight. Two fingers are then measured on the candle from the base

"for your guardian angel, two fingers for the Holy Spirit, and one finger for your name." At the point reached by the five fingers measurement, the candle is opened and a flower called the "flower of thought" is placed inside, and the wax is replaced carefully as though the candle had not been opened.

The center candle is now lighted at the butt end and placed in position upside down. Great care must be exercised, however, not to permit the candle to burn past the point where the flower is located. If it did, the bewitched person would die and the person performing the incantation would go to the inferno and suffer throughout eternity.

This ceremony may be performed in any position of the moon and by either day or night. Nevertheless, Wednesday is the best day, and night is the best time. The indispensable prerequisite is that no one see the ceremony except the person on whose behalf it is performed. Any other person, even though equally interested in the success of the procedure, would interfere with the result, while a hostile person who knew, could intercept the "labor" and even do injury to the witch.

Despite this prohibition in ordinary cases, there are some circumstances in which several witches or women "initiated in remedies," even though they did not know how to officiate, might perform this ceremony together. The informant, however, refused to tell how the ceremony was performed in this case or the object of the ceremony.

After the ceremony has been performed, the subject is observed for several days or a week. If no improvement in attitude is noticeable, the bewitchment continues in the following form:

Candles are burned again as described above. In addition, the witch procures a meter of black belting material, a small stamp of Saint Judas, a bit of red paper, "flowers of thought," dahlias or other red flowers, and a collection of as many kinds of flowers as can be found. The Saint Judas is wrapped carefully and thoroughly in the black belt. The bundle is then wrapped in the red paper and laid on a cross made of the miscellaneous flowers at the "head" of the candles with the saint's face down. On the bundle is placed the red flower and the "flowers of thought." Then the witch says, "Saint Judas, bring me so and so, for I have you there prisoner and if you do not hurry I will burn you." A "prayer" is then said in Tarascan which the informant refused to divulge. The witch remains in a kneeling position and recites seven credos until the "Candle of the Heart" reaches the point past which it must not burn. (In order to have the candles burn an equal amount, it is necessary to put out the others when they reach the same level.)

2. To make someone hate another person; to make a husband leave his wife or a wife leave her husband; to make children desert their parents or parents abandon their children; to make a person feel repulsion for others:

The witch or the person who wishes to accomplish the result secures excrement of the person who is to be hated. The excrement is dried in the sun from 12 until 3, being careful not to expose it at other hours. When dry, the excrement is ground to a powder. Each day at sundown a little of the powder is burned and clothing of the person who is to hate the other is passed through the smoke. Thus a witch who wished another woman's husband secured some of the woman's excrement and passed a pair of trousers and shirt of the man through the smoke. The very next day the man left his wife and came to live with the witch (and is now her husband). The deserted wife immediately went with another man and her first husband "danced with pleasure."

3. To make mischief so that something goes badly with a person—so that his animals will die, so his harvest will fail, so he will fall in jail, so he and all his family will weaken and catch diseases:

Take about a quarter-liter bottle of alcohol. Mix this with earth taken from a spot where there was a quarrel to the death, or where someone had an accident and died, or where there is a burial of a person who did not die in Christian fashion, or from the illegal grave of some recently born child whose parents did not notify the authorities and buried it surreptitiously. If no serious injury is to be caused it will be sufficient to take earth where there has been a quarrel and bloodshed, even though there was no death. This earth, after mixing with alcohol, is allowed to dry thoroughly and is kept in a bottle until it is needed. When the opportunity offers, a little of the earth is sprinkled on the back of the person it is desired to injure, at the same time saying in one's mind the kind of injury one wishes will occur.

4. To cause suppurating sores on the genitals of a person one hates:

Buy oil for lamps and let it burn several days before a holy image. Take what is left and mix it with a bit of earth recently stepped on by the person it is desired to injure, or put in the oil something of the victim, such as hair, fingernails, or some piece of used clothing, and burn the oil, saying "So and so, you must have sores on such and such a part of the body." In addition, if the person is a man, he must be given a glass of *aguardiente* in which an herb from the hot country has infused a number of days; and if the person is a woman, a *gorda* made from maize dough or nixtamal in which the same herb is mixed. (The informant refused to name the herb, claiming she identified it only by sight when the herb sellers came around.)

5. So that a man or woman will "become tame" and do what one wishes, including making a husband permit his wife sexual relations with another man or a wife permit her husband sexual relations with another woman, and, in addition, aiding the adulterers to meet:

Buy a new small pottery vessel (*ollita*); it is best to buy it direct from the kiln to make sure it has not been used for anything else. Fill the vessel with holy water, first fastening a new 20 centavo piece to the bottom, inside, with campeche wax. Into the water put a large paraffin candle which has been cut into many small pieces. Each piece represents part of the strength (*fuerza*) of the individual while the holy water signifies that the strength is broken. In order that the results will be "good," put in a piece of cane from the mountains known as *otate del leon* and a very resinous splinter of pitch pine. Then cover the top of the vessel with a thick cap of campeche wax so that no air may enter. The vessel is then buried beneath the spot where the person to be bewitched sleeps, if this person is a spouse. If not, the vessel is buried in the patio of the house of the person.

6. To make a man lose his sexual vigor so that he will recover it only with the woman who has had the magic done:

The witch must first seek a small grass known as *pito de toro* and place it in *aguardiente* to infuse. The man should drink a little of this *aguardiente* every day for 8 days. If he is not a drinking man, then it must be given in coffee or atole or in some other manner so that he will not be aware that he is being given something. After 8 days the woman spies on the man until he goes to urinate, when she must recover a bit of the moist earth or, if he has not urinated on the earth, place earth in the receptacle. The urine-moistened earth is placed inside a *chile ancho* of the largest size it is possible to secure. The *chile* is then sewed up with needle and thread so none of the earth can escape and placed below the spot where the man sleeps with someone, or, if he is unmarried, it is buried in his patio as close as possible to the place where he sleeps. With this, the man remains incapacitated from having sexual relations with any woman except the one who has performed the rite.

7. To make a person suffer so that he will be sad and feel sick, although it will be imagination and not in reality; so that he will feel he is going to die; so that everything is revolting; and so that he will be unable to find tranquillity at any moment because it will seem something is about to happen:

Make a small doll resembling the human figure out of campeche wax and clothing used by the person. It is important that the clothing used should not have been washed, but be soiled from wearing. When the doll is made, stick pins in it all along the part of the spinal column, one in the crown of the head, two in the temples, two in the throat on each side, two in the nape of the neck, two in the umbilicus, and seven on the breast (in an arrangement the informant did not wish to explain). Now place the doll in a cooking pot with oil for lamps. In front of the figure put a tallow candle and burn it but not down to the point the flame touches the oil.

In addition to the above methods of bewitchment, powders brought from the region of the ocean are extensively used for love potions. The powders are brought by muleteers from the hot country and are said to be made by grinding a tree which grows there. A pinch of these is taken between thumb and forefinger and rubbed on the clothing, face, or hair of the desired person without his knowledge.

Methods of prevention and cure against witchcraft were also provided by the same informant. The following method will immunize a person against witchcraft and also cure certain types of sorcery:

Materials needed are oil from a certain poisonous snake, grease from a certain species of scorpion, oil of San Ignacio, oil of Vicente, oil of San Aparicio, a little dry marihuana, and small balls of two herbs sold by the herb vendors at Uruapan. The marihuana and the balls are ground and then carefully mixed with the oils and greases. The witch then anoints the patient's body with the mixture.

A person ill of sores (granos) may be cured by catching certain poisonous snakes, killing them, taking out the oil, and placing the flesh to dry. The flesh, when dry, is reduced to a powder and mixed with the oil. The genital organs of the patient are then anointed with the mixture until he has recovered.

Marihuana and toloache (Datura, sp.?) made into a powder and dissolved in aguardiente serves to cure witchcraft, taking a little every morning. Marihuana also aids one to "dream beautifully."

To clean someone who is dying of witchcraft, take fresh toloache, jediondilla (unidentified), an egg, and jara (cistus or rockrose). Mixing all this together, clean the patient's body, repeating the cure as many times as is necessary and not permitting him to go outside in the air. It is also possible to cure without breaking the egg, but passing it entire over the whole body. (Probably there is more to the latter method than was told.)

A few general points appear from the data on witchcraft. It is interesting to note that in most of the important "recipes" the informant refused to tell some part; probably omissions were made in the others as well. It is also clear that with almost no exception, the witchcraft is wholly European in origin. This is true of both the data from Cherán and from Capacuaro. Despite the fragmentary data from Cherán, a number of correspondences with the Capacuaro data are evident. For example, Agustín mentioned only snake oil for the immunization to witchcraft, Capacuaro data show snake oil as well as other items. While the data are too scanty to afford generalizations, erotic interests and anxieties are suggested much more strongly by the Capacuaro witchcraft data than by data secured from any other source.

In Mestizo Chilchota exists belief in witches disguised as owls. The owls call for the death of their victim, and death takes the call of the owl as a signal. Such owls cannot be killed by bullets or rocks, which simply pass through the bird without making it even change its place. The only manner in which such an owl may be driven away is for a woman not wearing underwear to throw her skirts over her head in front of it; at this the owl flees and never returns to the house.

MISCELLANEOUS BELIEFS

Relatively few superstitions and beliefs in the supernatural outside of the various aspects of Christianity and witchcraft were encountered in Cherán. Most common, apparently, is the belief in the miríŋgua, a malevolent spirit which, according to some, lives in the barrio of Parícutin. At night, in the fields, woods, or in the town itself, a person will think he is going a certain way and will recognize various places, and then, if the experience is a mild one, he finds suddenly that he is in some place quite different. Or the person may be carried off by the miríŋgua. The most common place about town for the miríŋgua to ambush its victims is in the barranca between Parícutin and the rest of the town.

One young man of 25 years recounted his experience to Rendón as follows: One dusk he was returning from the fields to his house and thought he was following the proper road but he felt very unusual (in a manner he was unable to explain because of his faulty Spanish). Finally he felt that someone pulled on him without his being able to see who it was. Then he became frightened and ran toward his house (as he thought), but instead he ran faster and faster in the opposite direction. Eventually he became terrorized and ran, falling and bumping into things, for it was getting increasingly darker, until he arrived at a place he did not recognize. He ran through many nettles which struck him like pack straps, drawing blood all over his body. Finally he found a cave and took refuge in it, where he struggled all night with something that tried to strangle him. He was found in the morning by a search party which had been hunting him all night. He was 17 when this occurred.

On another occasion a woman was found dead in a sand cave without any tracks except her own footprints. She showed all the signs of strangulation. Before her death this woman had told her relatives and friends that frequently she would think she was on her way home and would find herself in the *barranca*. She would sit down awhile and make the sign of the cross and pray. With this, things would become clear to her and she could retrace her road.

A youth returning from his field to his house, felt something pull him strongly toward the *barranca* as he crossed the bridge. He resisted, and then it seemed to him he was going toward home when suddenly he lost his footing and began to fall in space. As he fell he had the impression he was entering his house. He was found next day in the *barranca,* half dead, and was unable to speak for 8 days. He stammers still as the result of his fright.

Another story tells of a man who had attended a wedding in Parícutin. After the wedding the group went through the streets with the music, dancing and drinking. As they crossed the bridge to Parícutin the man said something was pulling at him. He began to gesticulate as if he was fighting something, but his friends, having drunk a great deal, paid no attention. He began to run but fell from the bridge. His body was found down the *barranca* (as the water evidently was high) after considerable search.

This spirit is known at Capacuaro as mirinyin, mirinchin, or miringin. The spirit appears sometimes as a *bulto* (indistinct form) which whistles to people and gets them to follow it until they are lost in the woods. One informant, named Juan, said he had been seized in the Cerro del Aire and was able to escape only by recommending himself to the patron saint, San Juan. Otherwise he would have fallen in a cave where the devil could have seized him.

In Urén in La Cañada it is said that the miriŋgua appears where money has been hidden. If someone gets rich suddenly it is said that "he has encountered the miriŋgua." The miriŋgua is also said to appear in the shape of dog or cat, but these are really disguised witches.

When houses are repaired or reconditioned, it is customary to hang up flowers, usually fastening the flowers to strings which are looped over doorways and windows. The practice was said to be customary and no beliefs concerning it could be discovered.

When the rains are late in coming in May, the image of one of the saints is taken to the top of the Sierra San Marcos, south of town. There the image is raised up and down several times and *cohetes* are fired. Even sceptics admit it usually rains soon after this; some of the naive attribute the rain to the *cohetes,* others to the proximity of the rainy season.

When the mountain of Pilón, east of town, has mist on top, it is going to rain, say many. The early rains come from the direction of Pilón, the later from the direction of San Marcos.

If people are seated and a dog comes and howls, some misfortune may befall the people.

The coyote has magical power over animals. If he just gives himself a shake, the chickens will walk over to him and let themselves be eaten.

A person who finds a dead deer in the mountains which he has not killed will have some misfortune befall his family. A son, brother, parent, etc., will certainly die, and there is no way of averting the misfortune.

If a coyote crosses the road in front of one, it is a sign some misfortune will occur.

A blue-bellied lizard found occasionally in Cherán is believed to be able to jump on a person's back without his knowing it and burrow inside. It leaves a blue lizard mark on the back where it enters, but no further beliefs could be discovered.

An animal said to be unique in Cherán is the *hachoque* or ečékurita. It resembles a lizard and is spotted black and white. It lives in corners, inside the walls of houses, or in the stone pillars. It does not bite or injure people, but it is believed to suckle the breasts of nursing mothers while they are sleeping, taking all the milk. The animal cannot be killed with blows or by cutting it up, for the pieces reunite. Only by burning it with coals can it be killed.

A very clever man once went up on San Marcos and struck the mountain. Water poured out, creating a *barranca,* and continued for several days until the plain west of town was covered several feet deep. The priest then went up the mountain and ordered the water to stop, which it did.

Against hurricanes and hail, a cross is made in the patio or the street, of ashes, taken from the household fireplace. Salt is not put in the fire for this purpose.

The crosses put on top of houses are to protect them from lightning or whirlwinds.

If people swim in Las Pilas, a small pond northeast of town, they will sink after swimming out a certain distance. Horses will drown there also.

Eclipses are thought the work of some higher power and that nothing can be done about them. There is no fear of eclipses, though, except in connection with childbirth. Some believe eclipses result from struggles between sun, moon, and earth. The defeated element is said to devour part of the foetus, causing adhesions between various parts and the womb and making birth difficult. No beliefs could be discovered about the stars. Indeed, informants insisted that there were no names for the stars and that people did not distinguish one from the other. This is unusual if true.

Mention should be made here of beliefs in the evil eye and in *los aires,* "the airs or winds." They will be discussed in connection with disease concepts and curing.

THE INDIVIDUAL AND THE CULTURE

In the preceding sections the culture of Cherán has been treated primarily from its technological and institutional aspects. The position of individuals and their activities have been discussed, it is true, but the orientation has been toward generalized and institutionalized activities. In the following pages will be discussed the activities which are more directly individual in character. This is not to say that many of these activities are not institutionalized; certainly the wedding ceremonies, for example, are quite as institutionalized in character as the *mayordomía.* Nevertheless, the wedding is more closely related to the development of individual personal relationships. Emphasis in succeeding pages will be upon the crisis periods in the individual and upon the developmental and behavioral patterns in the intervals between crises.

It will be obvious in the following discussion that treatment of the role of the individual in the culture and the impact of the culture upon the individual is very incomplete. Particular weaknesses are apparent in the discussion of infancy and childhood and in the part of women. These lacks are inevitable, not only from the shortness of the study, but from the special attitudes in Cherán which closed so many avenues of approach to male investigators. Material collected by Rendón is very helpful, but it is fragmentary and insufficient. It does show, though, that women investigators could secure many data otherwise difficult to collect.

BIRTH

Children are generally desired in Cherán, and motherhood is regarded as normal and expectable. There is a clear idea of the physiological causation of pregnancy, and normally no means are taken to avoid it. Men are said to prefer boys and women to prefer girls, but whatever the sex, both parents usually welcome the child and wish many, and childbirth appears to cause minimal emotional disturbances, although they are not lacking. Although no accurate data were available, informants did not believe there were more than six or eight women in Cherán who had not borne children. Some said that no remedies are taken for barrenness. Others reported that women speak to the professional midwives, who give them herbal remedies, anoint the abdomen with mountain lion grease, or give stew made of mountain lion meat. However, none of the midwives reported any such practices.

Despite these attitudes, belief exists that pregnancy can be prevented or abortion caused. It is believed by some that only families of poor economic standing who already have two to four children attempt to use these methods. Others suggest absence of love in the home as a reason; some women carrying on illicit affairs are believed to practice abortion. A good many people seem to know of the existence of abortion and to have knowledge of the herbs used. Consequently attempted abortion probably is more frequent than people wish to admit. The ideal of Cherán is the large family; people prefer not to talk about those who do not share the ideal and some refuse to talk about it. It is also said that the municipal officials are vigilant in punishing such cases, but as the penalty is said to be a fine of $1.00 or $1.50 or a night in jail after recovery, this probably would not be a great deterrent even if the danger of detection were great.

Four plants are named as being taken to cause abortion. One, *artamisa*, taken with plenty of salt, was mentioned by one of the midwives. Another admitted to using iris root for this purpose, although generally the midwives claim to be opposed to abortion. The two plants most used, however, are *ruda* and *gobernadorcillo*, kuʌsʌ. It is possible that these are the same plants; at least descriptions of their use appear to be the same. If they are effective (and local medical men are sharply contradictory in their opinions), many unintentional abortions are probably caused, for *ruda* is a regular remedy for stomach pains. It is not taken, except intentionally, when pregnancy has occurred, as the herb is widely known as producing abortion. The herb is also believed to be helpful to women who have been unable to have children.

Much the same accounts were given of *gobernadorcillo*. To have children, the herb is cooked with a tablet of chocolate and taken just before the menstrual period is expected.

To cause abortion, the root is mashed to obtain the juice. The latter is strained and taken mixed in a liter of water. *Gobernadorcillo* is also taken to accelerate the birth if it should be slow.

One midwife purges barren women with the bulb of the white lily. Two or three bulbs are used; they are cooked and strained, and the juice given. Three days after the purge, the patient is bathed and "given a sweat" with cooking oil and ground salt rubbed all over the body. This cure is given during the time of menstruation to "clear" the blood. This cures the "coldnesses" of the patient or causes the harmful elements to be discharged. One patient now has four children. Another, barren 10 years before treatment, now has two children.

Involuntary abortions also occur. Pregnant mothers are often fearful of this and sometimes will not go to curers when they are ill for fear they will be given a medicine which will cause abortion. A woman in her eighth month of pregnancy who was suffering fever and spitting blood refused to go to the curer for fear of being given abortive drugs. Drinking is believed to cause many abortions, and heavy work, such as lifting a log while helping to build a fence, is recognized as a possible cause of abortion. If the mother "likes something too much," for example, a horse or a kind of food, the child may be born prematurely, but apparently may live. Solar eclipses are likewise believed to cause early births. The midwife is sometimes called if abortion is feared. One midwife anoints the coccyx and abdomen with the white of an egg (which has been beaten on the ground) and also with lard and oil. Another midwife gives the flower of maize, tomato peel, a shoot of verbena, and a potsherd of Guadalajara ware. The potsherd is ground and the whole made into an infusion. This is taken twice and the coccyx and abdomen are rubbed with the white of an egg beaten on the ground.

Some people believe that the first child takes 9 months to mature, while the subsequent children take only 8 months. While women do not keep exact count of the period between menstruations, they have a pretty accurate idea of the proper interval, and pregnancy is recognized when menstruation fails to occur. Lassitude, heaviness, and loss of appetite are considered frequent symptoms also. Sometimes in the early months women are sick at their stomachs and vomit in the mornings.

Usually a midwife is sought early in pregnancy and pays frequent visits to the enceinte woman. The midwife massages the woman with lard or cooking oil "to make sure the foetus is in the right position" and generally keeps an eye on the patient's health. Sometimes the midwife locates the head of the child during the massage. A fee of 10 centavos is charged for each visit.

A pregnant woman should not do much work, should not lift heavy things, and should take frequent baths in cold water in the house. She continues to grind corn and carry water; young mothers, indeed, are encouraged to keep active by older women, who believe some exercise helps the mother. She does not cook tortillas if she can avoid it, because the fire might "cook" the foetus. Toward the end of pregnancy some women are "delicate" and eat very little. At Capacuaro this is customary in the last days of pregnancy. Otherwise there are no prenatal food taboos.

An eclipse during pregnancy may cause something bad to happen to the child. To prevent the effects, a red belt is worn underneath the several belts worn by women who dress in traditional costume. If Mestizo costume is worn, red underwear is used. Women should do nothing during an eclipse. The occurrence of Mongoloid spot is reported. It is believed that this is caused by the woman carrying her coins in the customary fashion in her belt during pregnancy.

Women should not tie any animals during pregnancy, as this may cause the child to be strangled by the umbilical cord during birth. If the mother urinates where some animal has urinated, the child may be born with some part of the animal. Reports were given by midwives of children having been born with a pig face or a goat face and tail because the mother urinated where these animals had urinated. In the latter part of pregnancy a woman should always remove the lid from a vessel before lifting it from the fire; if she fails to observe this rule, the child may be born dumb. Clubfoot is caused by the mother not taking proper care of herself.

Wrong positions, especially breech presentations, may result from several causes. The mother may have moved around too much and worked too hard, hit a dog with her foot, put the "foot" of a stick of wood in the fire first, failed to remove the *comal* from the fire immediately after finishing the cooking of tortillas, eaten toasted tortillas, or eaten off the metate (the latter taboo was explained on the basis that the metate has only three legs). Children are born blind only because "God wills it."

Witches may interfere with pregnancy and make the child arrive dead. The preventive remedy is to cook tomato peeling and a potsherd of Guadalajara ware together and drink the liquid.

Fathers are also under some restrictions during the period of pregnancy. Whenever a load of wood is brought to the house it must be untied immediately or the child may be strangled by the umbilical cord. Also, the father must not kill lizards or snakes during the pregnancy, or touch resin or turpentine, or they will enter into the child. Some say the father should not kill any kind of an animal, from a snail to an ox. If he does so, the animal will enter into the child through the mouth or nose and the child will be born dead. One midwife thought the father should not have relations with his wife after the third or fourth month of pregnancy for reasons of cleanliness, but some say difficult birth or wrong positions may result from continued intercourse. The father should not work on the day of birth.

No distinction is made between first and subsequent births. Midwives varied in their ideas as to the frequency of births. Some believed that women had children from 1 to 1½ years apart, others said from 8 months to 3 years. One midwife explained that the number of children and the frequency of births were determined by something resembling links in the uterus. These could be counted by the midwife, who could tell how many children the woman would have and, by the spacing, what the interval between births would be. Some women might be capable of as many as 25 pregnancies.

All births are attended by midwives, who form a professional group, although without organization. It is believed all the midwives in Cherán were interviewed by the staff. Most of them are elderly women past childbearing age. Some 4 or 5 years before the study, all of the midwives apparently had received instruction from a doctor called in by the priest. This is reflected to some extent in the methods used, particularly in some efforts at asepsis and the use of antiseptics. The following biographical data were secured from the midwives, the individuals being referred to by number.

No. 1. About 55 years of age; 4 years' experience. Formerly was a curer. No one in her family had been a midwife; she entered the profession "by accident" and "knew how" by the grace of the Holy Virgin.

No. 2. Age unknown, but has had 20 years' experience. Her mother was a midwife and urged her to become one also. She became a midwife because her small business was not enough to keep her alive. She had been married and had one daughter in 6 years of marriage, apparently taking up midwifery after loss of her husband.

No. 3. About 55 years of age, 4 years' experience. Learned by observing a grandmother who was a midwife. Other "grandparents" also tried to teach her. She believes, in addition, she possesses a special "virtue" for such work. Before becoming a midwife she was a curer, devoting herself especially to women who suffered abdominal pains from overwork, using massage. She still does curing, but since her husband died, 5 years before, has been a midwife. She likes the work. She says the Virgin of Monserrato is the patroness of the midwives.

No. 4. New to the profession. Has attended only two births; one of the patients accused her at the court of causing swelling of the organs because of inexperience and refused to pay her fee.

No. 5. Has been midwife 5 years. No further data.

No. 6. Has been a midwife 30 years. Was assistant to another midwife for a long time. One day a child was being born dead; the subject took cotton and put a medicine she knew on the head of the mother and the child was born successfully. There was a quarrel, but finally the midwife, who was very old, began to teach her; "but God gave me the power to know medicines to aid births." Is from Nahautzen. Is scornful of the local midwives, and is sometimes called into consultation in cases of difficult births.

For other midwives, no personal data were secured.

Midwives receive a fee for each prenatal visit, as has been mentioned. For their aid at births, they receive from $1.50 to $2.50. One midwife charges $2 for a first birth, subsequent charges being $1.50. Sometimes the parents cannot pay even the $1.50, according to the midwives, or do not pay for some time. Quarrels may result from failure to pay.

According to some midwives, if there is time, the midwife goes to church before the delivery, saying prayers to the Virgin of Guadalupe, Our Lady of Monserrato, and Santo Roberto, asking help. Others say this is not done because there is never time. Another carries with her a picture of Santa Rita de Imposible and says a prayer to her just before the delivery. Midwives do not bathe in advance, but some are careful to wash their hands in tepid water and rub them with rafino, considered an antiseptic, before the delivery. The midwife should not smoke or drink alcohol before the delivery. Midwives usually have as helper the mother or mother-in-law of the patient.

One midwife thought the mother should stay in bed for 1 to 3 days before the delivery, but others did not think so. Before going to bed, a prayer to the Virgin is said by some mothers, promising to bring the child up correctly. Midwives also differed on the delivery position. One said the position is always flat in bed, the others said a kneeling position is common. One midwife said both positions are used "according to circumstances." The mother decides the position, not the midwife. If the birth is in kneeling position, the patient may hold on to the metate in the position assumed in grinding maize. Alternatively, two loops of rope may be suspended from a house beam by which the mother supports herself. Sometimes the husband is seated on a low chair and supports the patient's shoulders, applying pressure to the sides of the abdomen with his knees. Normally, however, men are not present.

Sometimes, when the pains first start, the patient is laid on a blanket which is then lifted by four persons, one at each corner. The mother is then turned around gently for 15 or 20 minutes. This is believed to hasten the birth and aid the child to get into the proper position. The midwife may also walk from one side to another, saying, "I am coming," to hurry the child.

Most midwives specify certain materials which should be provided by the family in advance. These things include scissors, cooking oil, lard, cotton, and silk thread. Parents provide clothing for the child; the midwife does not specify anything for the infant.

Some midwives, when the birth pains begin, give the mother *gobernadorcillo* or possibly other plants to accelerate the birth. In any case it is asserted that the same herbs believed to cause abortion are administered at this time, usually with sugar or brown sugar. One herb (unidentified) is called zihuapaxtle, a Nahua name. There is no use of wheat rust, however. When the crown of the head of the child is visible, the midwife tries to hurry through the rest of the birth so that there will be less danger of the child being born dead.

It is said that many normal births take only about 15 minutes. This can hardly be counted from the time the first labor pains are felt but is possibly from the time the labor becomes intense. Many mothers in Cherán, however, seem to have fairly difficult births. Cases of labor lasting as much as 6 or 7 hours are reported.

In case the labor is difficult and prolonged, remedies of various sorts are used. The helpers apply pressure to the abdomen. One midwife boils a bezoar, the calcareous secretion from the intestines of some ruminant, brought from the hot country, and has the patient drink the water. Another gives the mother hot chocolate made with water and sugar, and massages the abdomen. Another covers the patient with a blanket and has her breathe the fumes from sugar or some sweet thing burned in a brazier. One midwife stated that when the patient is very "dry," that is, there is no discharge of blood and no breaking of the amniotic membrane, a bit of *nopal* (prickly pear) leaf is roasted in the fire, opened and rubbed with oil, and placed on the abdomen and coccyx of the patient.

Some midwives say the influence of the phases of the moon determines the length of labor. Eclipses also affect the labors. Witchcraft or improper care by the mother may be a cause of prolonged labor. If much silky white liquid is discharged in a difficult birth, it is said the mother did not bathe herself and keep clean or that she had relations with her husband after she should have ceased.

Breech presentations and other abnormal positions are known, although one midwife had not seen one in 5 years of practice. When they occur the midwife must be adept at manipulating the child. She puts lard on her hands and works the legs out first. The arms of the foetus must be kept at its sides and the chin down to prevent strangulation. According to one account of a breech presentation, several midwives were called in and an attempt was made to get the doctor from Paracho. One midwife (by her own account, at least) used a wooden bowl to distend the cervix, reached in and turned the child and delivered it successfully before the doctor arrived. In difficult births the child is sometimes born dead. The midwife touches his belly to see if he is still breathing; if he is, she lights a cigarette and puffs the smoke in his face "to wake him up."

Twins are relatively rare, but are known to a number of midwives, who do not report special trouble with them. One remarked that they came "like two cherries on branching stems." The Mongoloid spot is described as occurring occasionally.

Numerous abnormalities in birth are reported. Some are undoubtedly due to venereal diseases, about which the Cherán people know very little. Even our most sophisticated informant was a little dubious of just what gonorrhea and syphilis were. Some abnormalities, almost ceretainly due to syphilis, are attributed to the father having worked in turpentine. One midwife reported a case where the father persisted in working in turpentine, which foams when being boiled. When the child started to arrive, the mother nearly suffocated. All she could smell was turpentine. The child's arm emerged first; it was black and when the midwife touched it the skin broke and the inside was foam like the boiling turpentine. By giving the mother medicines the delivery succeeded, but the child's skin broke easily and inside was foam. The more bizarre aspects of this account may be discounted, but some factual basis probably existed.

Another case reported was a child born with the "head all hollow." Yet another had eyes "as though gouged out with a knife" and only the rudiments of a nose. Both children were born dead. The phenomena were attributed to an eclipse. Few cases occur in which the mother has died without delivery being accomplished, but still-births are more frequent. Strangling with the cord is said to occur in some cases. Birth of children with clubfoot (said to be caused by the mother not taking care of herself) and blind children (caused by God's will) are both known. No hunchbacks were reported. One other case where the child's arm emerged first was reported; the child died but the mother lived. Animal births are mentioned also. Only one case accompanied by severe hemorrhage was reported.

Children born in May are said to be mischievous and courageous, those born in February to be half crazy.

After the birth of the child the mother stays in bed from 8 to 15 days. At the conclusion of this time she bathes and gets up, but remains under food taboos and spends some time reclining during the next 5 days, when she bathes again and may go out of the house. The midwife visits the mother daily until she gets out of bed, massaging her. When the mother can walk, she begins to do small tasks. Full resumption of tasks is not undertaken until the termination of the food restrictions, about 40 days after birth. Some women do not go out of the house until 3 weeks have passed. After the mother has gotten out of bed, the midwife may still massage her with unguents, either coconut oil or white lily. During the period the mother should not be left alone, so she will not be frightened or visited by an evil spirit. Usually the mother is cared for after birth by the husband's mother, by her own mother, or some female relative. Wealthier families, though, may hire someone to assist.

One case of what was probably a postparturient infection was recorded. The midwife bathed the infected parts with *yerba de cáncer*. The entire herb was boiled and then hydrogen peroxide was added to the brew. Two treatments daily for 2 months finally cured the patient.

Husband and wife do not resume sexual relations until at least 35 days after the birth; in most cases the period is 40 days. Husbands are sometimes said to behave badly in connection with the first pregnancy; they have "whims" and "weariness," probably a polite way of saying that they resent the loss of sexual privileges and the lessened attentions of their wives. Some go with other women.

Shortly after the delivery the mother is given her first food. This may be chocolate, milk, and a bit of bread. Some midwives give the mother *rafino* or coffee but others prefer white atole "because it strengthens the blood." A chicken may be killed the same day and put on to cook to make broth to be served to the mother the following day. Oatmeal is also a favorite food for the mother in the early days. Broth from beef is prohibited but broth from mutton is permitted during the first week. The second week, additional foods may be taken, but nothing "cold." Tortillas may be eaten after the second day. In general, pork, chile, fish, and beans are forbidden for from 3 weeks to 40 days. Fruit and vegetable greens must be eaten sparingly in the latter part of the period, not at all in the early part. There is no restriction on salt. Beef is apparently forbidden only in the first week; cheese is mentioned as a permitted food by some. In some cases the mother is fed the atole known as kágwash kamáta for several days after birth. In view of the general agreement that chile is forbidden, probably this ingredient is left out when the atole is made for mothers. According to some, the midwife stays on the same diet as the mother until the time of the mother's first bath.

Fathers have virtually no restrictions. The only one discovered is that he should not kill poisonous snakes. If he does, the newborn infant may have bloody discharges from nose and mouth. The cure is to catch a rat, remove the intestines, add to them some *rosas de castilla* and a few grains of *tequisquite* and place on the child's stomach.

According to Rendón, women in Mestizo Chilchota observe no special diet before delivery. Births are attended by midwives, who charge $2. A mixture of egg and flower is sometimes rubbed on the abdomen to lessen labor pains if these are severe. Massage and irrigations with water and soap are used to accelerate birth. After delivery the diet is based on chocolate and atole. After a few days, chicken broth and chicken are added but beef and beans are not eaten for 72 days. The atole is called púkua and is made of maize cooked without lime, ground on the metate, and cooked in water without sugar. If there are hemorrhages the patient is given rubbed (shredded?) parsley in water. The mother stays in bed for a week. On the eighth day she bathes.

Rendón reports a mild couvade in La Cañada pueblos. The mother does not eat salt after the birth, eats atole of the same type as at Chilchota, and cooked greens. The fathers stay in the house several days without working.

INFANCY

When the birth is in kneeling position, as is most common, a mat and clean cloth are placed on the floor to receive the child. The cord is not cut until the afterbirth is delivered. If this is slow, the mother's knees are massaged. The cord is then tied with thread and cut with scissors (a knife may not be used). According to some the cord is cut about a span length from the umbilicus (thumb to forefinger with both extended). Others say this is the length for girls and that the length for boys is a *cuarto* (this cannot mean a quarter as most are agreed that the length for a boy is greater than for a girl). Some families ask that the cord be cut longer "so the child will relax easily." Cotton is applied, sometimes preceded by anointment with oil, and a band fastened about the abdomen. Some say if this is not done the boys would not have strength and the girls would be "goers," *andulantes*, that is, they would probably have affairs with men. Some wipe out the child's eyes with cotton, and others drop a little lemon juice in the eyes. Some oppose this and do nothing unless a gummy secretion appears, when the eyes are treated with flowers of Castile and San Juan.

The child is then wiped off with a clean cloth and oiled but not bathed. Clothing prepared in advance is put on the child. It is said that the midwife tells parents in advance whether to prepare clothing for a boy or a girl and that they seldom make a mistake. But as no difference could be found in the clothing and, indeed, the child is usually wrapped just in some clean rags, the statement has little significance. Sometimes the child is given tea of Castile roses or a bit of edible oil, but most midwives thought nothing should be given the first day.

The child is nursed the second day. Rarely does the mother not have milk. Should this happen, the aid of some nursing mother is sought or the child is given cow or goat milk. The latter is not diluted, but it is boiled before using, often being flavored with a bit of yerba buena or cinnamon. Special drinks are given the mother to induce milk flow if it is inadequate. Brews of flaxseed (?) were mentioned.

The afterbirth is buried, sometimes beside the fireplace, sometimes under it. If this is not done, it is believed the mother would become "cold," but one midwife stated the cord is preserved and used for remedies. The cord of Agustín Rangel's father was taken to the shrine of the Virgin of Guadalupe at Tepeyac and left.

Midwives continue to visit the house to attend to the mother and child. The bandage over the umbilicus is removed every 2 or 3 days. The cord drops off between the second and eighth days (the longer period apparently being unusual). The umbilicus is then anointed with iodine or powder made from tules. Sometimes small hernias are cured with a small ball of sosa (an herb) or a green tomato. Hernias result from carelessness or "coldness." Infections of the umbilicus result from carelessness in bathing the child. One midwife reported curing them with face powder!

The child is normally bathed by the midwife on the third, sixth, and ninth days (according to one midwife, immediately after birth also "if that is the custom of the house"). Warm water is used for the bath.

Some idea that children resemble parents seems to be prevalent and to be attributed to hereditary mechanisms (although in this informants may have been sophisticated). An instance cited was that of a man with a very linear body build which was repeated in the children, "who looked as though a wind would blow them away," yet otherwise seemed healthy. As an exception, there was cited the case of two girls with red hair and blue eyes in one family. The children were not seen and might have been albinos, but the large number of persons who have visited the United States suggests other explanations. Another case was cited in which the parents had black hair and the fairly dark skin common among Tarascans. Three sons all had dark-red or auburn hair, and the skin, although equally dark, showed also darker spots resembling freckles. In later years the freckles spread until the skin became a solid color, darker than that of either parent.

Occasional examples occur of children apparently deficient in mentality. Some continue to show childish reactions and behaviors, laugh a great deal without occasion, do not care for their clothing, eat badly, and do not seem to understand well even when approaching adult years. Nevertheless, no adults were encountered who seemed to exhibit insanity or feeble-mindedness.

Few special attentions to infants are recorded. There is no use of ashes or leaving of corn ears or fire pokers with infants when they are left alone, but a broom of straw may be left at the head of the child's bed for protection against evil if the mother wishes to leave it for a few minutes. Children are nursed freely whenever they desire the breast. Although some evidence of shyness was evident, for example, some mothers draped their *rebozo* over the breast, nursing takes place in a variety of public circumstances, on the streets or on the roads, and even while riding on a burro. Through the first year or so the child sleeps with the nipple of the mother's breast in its mouth at night. Perhaps as a result of this there is a virtually complete absence of thumb sucking at all ages.

Infants are ordinarily carried by their mothers, almost invariably wrapped in the *rebozo*. Even if the child is carried in the arm, the *rebozo* is slung around the child and over the shoulders to take part of the weight. Ordinarily a small child is slung more or less horizontally in the *rebozo* on the mother's back. One end of the *rebozo* goes under the left arm, the other over the right shoulder, the two ends

crossing on the chest and being either tied or tucked under the opposite arms. When a little older the child kneels on the top of the *rollo* or thick pleats at the top of the skirt or sits on the *rollo* with legs on either side of the mother's waist. In either case the child is held in place by the *rebozo*. Men often carry infants in their arms, while small girls frequently carry their younger brothers and sisters in the same way as their mothers. The infants seem to interfere with the older child's activities very little.

Occasionally a boy will be seen carrying an infant in a *rebozo*. While this is not common, the boys seemed entirely unself-conscious and were not teased at all. Almost never is an infant put down until it is able to walk. As indicated above, it sleeps with the mother and is permitted to nurse at any time, often sleeping at the breast.

Children are not weaned until 18 to 24 months; rare cases are reported of children nursing to the age of 3 or 4. Weaning is aided by anointing the nipple with some bitter or piquant material, for example, chile. Weaning is done because of belief the child needs to have better nourishment, not because of boredom or feeling that the mother may suffer from prolonged nursing. Solid food is given the infant as early as 3 or 4 months, when a little fruit may be offered, such as banana. Tortillas are not given until 8 months. Milk, soup, and mild foods are first given the child. Cooked vegetables are fed at about 3 or 4 years. Chile is not fed children until they are well-grown, or adult, according to one informant.

Although children are rarely put down, after they are several months old they may occasionally be placed on the ground and permitted to crawl for brief periods. Occasionally children walk on all fours rather than on their knees. They are not permitted to try to walk, even though they wish to, until they are judged old enough to do so without causing curvature of the legs.

When children are permitted to attempt walking, a wooden bar is hung from two ropes, which in turn fasten to a single rope suspended from a tree or beam. The child is stood up and persuaded to hold the bar, which moves and forces the child to walk. Some children walk as early as 8 months, but most later, and some not until 2 years.

It is said that children begin to speak between the ages of 18 and 24 months. The parents pronounce words for the child, encouraging it to repeat them. The first words are said to be papá, mamá, ueksínga ("I want"), and auáka ("eat").

The teeth normally appear about the time tortillas are first fed, that is at about 8 months.

Toilet training is not rigorous and little is done until the child is able to walk. Up to this time the infant is usually kept in a diaperlike piece of cloth which is changed when soiled. A shirtlike garment and, at an early age, a small straw hat are the usual clothing. Occasionally children learn toilet control before they walk. Probably this is due to training by the mother, but informants were unaware of any efforts in this direction. Even when the infant walks, training is evidently indirect. If the child persists in urinating, after a time the mother cuts down its liquid intake and refuses to change it immediately when its garments are wet. Small children evacuate the bowels normally once in the day and once at night if they have learned some control; when a little larger, they evacuate once a day. The only control recognized by informants was through fixed feeding schedules. Undoubtedly there is more than this, but there were few opportunities of observation and much of the control apparently was so commonplace that informants (who had to be mainly men) were unaware of it. It was felt, however, that in the occasional cases where a child had not learned control at the proper age it was because of carelessness on the part of the mother. In general, however, there seems little stress or emotional overtones about the training problem.

As soon as children begin to walk, they are dressed in miniature replicas of adult garments. In all cases observed, imitations of the traditional garb were worn, Little girls wore a tiny *rollo*, while boys wore cotton trousers and shirt. At the age of 2 or 3 the ears of little girls are pierced by their mothers, using a needle. A bit of straw is used to keep the openings clear until earrings are provided, which is usually done very soon afterward. The operation is purely for beauty and is not regarded as necessary for any other reason, nor are there any beliefs about the operation.

The infant is ordinarily baptized between 10 days and 2 months after birth. The tendency in recent years is for the period to lengthen. Selecting godparents is important, for the care of the child in the event of death of the parents may devolve on the godparents, and intimate relations will exist in any event. For this reason people will often refuse to accept the responsibility or do so only after repeated invitations. Normally a married couple are sought to act as godparents but sometimes an unmarried man serves as godfather. In this case, when he marries, his wife will automatically become godmother. More rarely an unmarried man and unmarried woman are asked to serve as godparents. Agustín R. acted as godparent one time and had never met the woman who served as godmother.

Most commonly the godfather takes the child to church for baptism unaccompanied by the godmother, but sometimes the godmother goes along and carries the child. The godfather pays the priest the fee for baptism, $2.50. In the case of Agustín R., mentioned above, he was accompanied by his mother who supplied the information the priest needed to enter the baptism in the parochial register.

When the godfather returns the child to its parents, the godmother goes to the house of the parents for food. She takes with her 2 to 5 cakes of chocolate, 2 bars of soap to wash the child, and 3 to 5 pieces of bread worth 10 centavos each. If the godfather is unmarried, he gives money to some woman to buy these things and take them to the child's parents.

The parents of the child prepare beef cooked in broth (čurípo), tamales, tortillas, and sometimes other things. The godmother eats at the parents' house, and sometimes they invite others. The godfather cannot eat at the parents' house, but they send food to him at his own house, which he eats by himself or he may invite a few of his friends in to help him. In the case of Agustín, he was sent 2 chickens cooked in mole sauce, a big pan of rice, a large basket of tortillas and some tamales. He ate most of the food by himself, his parents refusing to partake of it.

The godfather is supposed to supervise the growing up of the child. He should see that his godchild "grows straight like a tree" and is properly trained and clothed, and he should make presents of clothing from time to time and remedy any deficiencies in the parents. Should the parents die, the godfather is responsible for rearing the child.

The name is usually selected by the parents. There are four ways of naming a child: using the name of the saint on whose day the child was born; the name of some distinguished person; a name selected by the godfather; the name of some relative, such as the grandparent or sibling of the parents. In the case of persons named for San Juan, San José, San Pedro, San Pablo, or San Francisco there are special observances in connection with their name day throughout the rest of their lives. Early in the morning, people visit persons of these names on their name day; often they will be strangers, for it suffices if one member of the party knows the person. The guests merely say "Good-morning" to the person visited and then are given *posole*. They may then stay around and talk a bit or may leave immediately, merely saying "Thank you" in the ordinary way. Sometimes the band starts at midnight, going around to various persons' houses and playing. In some cases the band members appear to be paid and to come by invitation, but in others they seem merely to be following the usual custom.

Persons with other names are also expected to show hospitality on their name day. When one of the schoolmasters, who is a native of the town but is stingy and not well liked, celebrated his name day, the town officials thought it would be a good joke to invite themselves to his house for dinner and did so. Meeting members of the staff of the study on the street, the mayor and secretary promptly invited them along. As the invitation was not seconded by the rather surly school teacher, who showed considerable signs of distress already, the invitation was not accepted.

Infants are subject to a number of diseases, but there are few special treatments for them. Only the evil eye must be guarded against especially, for it is usually fatal for infants of a year or less. This illness is especially insidious as it is usually caused inadvertently, that is, the person with power to cause the evil eye does not know it and is apt especially to cause it to attack a child that is particularly liked or admired by the person. As a preventive a "deer eye" is hung from the neck or wrist, or a little sack filled with cooked black chile, lime, and salt is suspended from the neck. Additional data are given under sickness and curing.

In La Cañada the infant's name is said to be chosen at a council of the adult relatives who pick a name from among the deceased relatives, never the saint's day, as is the case among the Mestizos at Chilchota. Neither does the godfather ever choose a name. The godmother presents the parents with a basket of bread, a package of chocolate, 30 centavos of soap, and 1 or 2 kilos of sugar. The other items may vary, but bread and chocolate must be included in the gifts. The parents of the child give the godparents a meal. A year or less after the baptism the godfather takes musicians to the child's house and presents the infant with some clothing. With invited relatives and friends, the godfather holds a day of fiesta. The parents provide atole, *aguardiente*, nacatamales or tamales made with flour. It is to be noted that here the emphasis in choosing godparents is on selecting the proper godmother and that the godfather's personality is of less importance.

At Huánsito in La Cañada, infants are fed atole, bread or tortillas, bean broth, cooked rice, and similar bland foods, beginning when they are less than a year old. Older children are fed whenever they are hungry and may eat numerous times during the day. Normally a child of 6 years will eat bread or tortillas and black coffee or cinnamon tea in the morning. At 10 o'clock in the morning he will eat tortillas, čurípo, and perhaps beans with the elders. In the middle of the day he will eat tortillas and some other item (the adults will not eat at this time). In the evening about 6 o'clock will be the main meal, perhaps broiled or fried meat, broth, and beans with tortillas.

At Ichán in La Cañada, Rendón noted the practice of children taking the baptismal name of their fathers as their surname. For example, the son of Diego is known as Juan Diego, the child of the latter being known as Pablo Juan or Luisa Juan, etc.

CHILDHOOD

Small children are usually clothed today. Occasionally a small boy is seen wearing nothing but a shirt, but this is uncommon, while girls able to walk always have a blouse and a skirt. In early childhood there is a good deal of affection between parents and children. Adults of both sexes play with the children and carry them about a great deal. Small children are kissed by both parents. Fear of strangers is absent. While opportunities for observation were limited, on several occasions when I had opportunity to be with children while talking with parents, they responded immediately to any caress on my part, often promptly climbing into my lap, or seizing hold of my clothing if I were standing. At this age there is evidently little correction. Some children cry and whimper a good deal and are reproved for it or told to hush, but nothing is done if the child continues.

As the child grows a little older, it evidently goes through a somewhat trying period of readjustment. This probably coincides with the coming of another child and also with the increasing care of the child by older brothers and sisters. At this period some rough treatment is given by the parents. Several times children were seen to stumble and fall on the street. When the child began to cry, the father either smacked it on the rump or kicked it along, gently it is true.

A boy about 4 was observed in a temper tantrum on the Cherán plaza. The tantrum began when the mother took a large piece of sugarcane held by the child, broke it, prepared the smaller piece, and gave it to the child. The child began to scream and weep, demanding the larger piece back. The mother laughed good-naturedly and told him to come along. He refused, and finally the mother gave the boy a gentle tap on the rump with her piece of sugarcane. The child screamed and beat at the mother with his cane. She continued to laugh, made some comments to others passing by and gradually got the child moved along, but he continued screaming as long as he was within earshot. In this case the mother showed more forebearance than seems likely to be usual. Possibly her behavior was inhibited by awareness that I was watching.

In another instance, a group of small boys were playing marbles. The mother of one of them, a boy probably not over 7, came up behind him, kicked him rather smartly, and scolded him shrewishly for crawling around on his knees and destroying his trousers. The boy was obviously furious but made no reply; when his mother was out of sight he resumed his game—and the crawling. The opportunities for observation of the treatment of small children were far too few to be certain the foregoing cases are typical.

Other situations are handled without stress. Masturbation by small boys is simply ignored by everyone even though it be in public. There seem to be no efforts to inculcate fears in the children or to control them by fear. Children showed some curiosity but certainly no fear of members of the staff. In one instance a mother trying to get a small boy to come to her remarked that I might carry him off. He looked me over calmly and was sufficiently perturbed to make a start in his mother's direction, but he certainly did not take the possibility very seriously. It may be of significance that the mother spoke to the small boy in Spanish.

Being an orphan is regarded as a grave misfortune, even though a child may be helped by its godfather. A child whose father has left the mother or died is also spoken of as an orphan. A common figure of speech in Cherán when a person wishes to emphasize how he has had to struggle is to compare himself to an orphan or to say his parents were so indifferent that he felt himself an orphan.

About 25 percent of the boys go to school at ages between 6 and 8. None of the girls are ever sent to school. Generally by 5 or 6 there is some start toward participation in adult activities. Boys may be sent on errands, while girls begin to play at adult activities.

Actual participation in adult work begins at about 8 years for boys. At this age they accompany their fathers to the woods and help carry back firewood. In the fields they may do no more than guard the father's blanket, but they are given a sense of participation. They may also help drive animals or care for them. By

10 they may guide the plow and do other field work, for short times. By as early an age as 15, boys may be working for wages. When a boy begins to accompany his father and to aid in his work, he no longer plays with girls. There seems no rule about this, but about this time, when a boy is not working, he goes into the streets and plays with other boys of his own age, while the girl no longer plays outside but always stays near her mother unless sent on an errand. On rare occasions, if a child is disobedient, he may be struck once or twice with a rope or switch.

At a little more than 6 or 7 a girl may be carrying about a younger child and caring for it much of the time. Soon after this she begins to grind on the metate, not as a help, but simply to learn how. The mother also gets a small water jar, and at an early age the girl accompanies her mother to get water. Girls observe the mother in the kitchen and gradually begin to take part in the activities. By the age of 8 a girl may be going alone to the mill with maize. If disobedient, girls may be punished in the same way as boys. In general, it is the opinion in Cherán, and this was borne out by all observations, there is very little disobedience or punishment at this time and the relations between father and son and mother and daughter are close and affectionate once the child begins active participation in the adult activities. The period of conflict, then, seems a rather limited one, between the time when a child is no longer carried about and the time when it begins to participate in the adult life. These remarks again are based on very inadequate data and observation.

Some time between the ages of 6 and 10, usually toward the upper limits of the age period, the child is usually confirmed. There is very little ceremony involved, but when a visit from the Bishop is expected there will be a period of some weeks beforehand when children will be instructed and adults will confess so they may receive communion. For the event a new pair of godparents is sought. These godparents in theory assume the same responsibility as do the godparents of baptism. Actually the bonds seem to be much less close and the duties much less.

Boys and girls play together a good deal until aged 8 or 10. Varieties of tag games are common. Boys also play among themselves frequently. For small boys at present, small home-made wagons with four wheels, usually with no method of steering, are one of the more popular playthings. Older males in the household make the wagons. Balls made of rags are also used. They are thrown and, at times, are used with a hockeylike game in which the ball is hit with curved wooden sticks. The street is used as a field and the object is to hit the ball past opponents (Beals and Carrasco, 1944). January is a favorite time for this game. Small boys amuse themselves by roping pigs, and about the time of the fiesta of the patron saint they may attempt to ride the pigs.

The most popular boys' game probably is marbles. The common marble game is "follow the leader." It is sometimes played for centavos. The rainy season is the most popular time, because the rain lays the dust and provides clean, hard surfaces. Quite popular is top spinning, which is most played in June and July. Top fighting is a common form. The first player throws his top at a ring. If he misses, his opponent attempts to hit the top with his own. He may split the first top, for the points are sharpened, or win it.

Stilts are made, especially in October and November. They are small, peeled pine trees with one of the branches left projecting near the bottom. This is almost exclusively a boy's amusement, but one girl was seen walking on stilts. Hunting birds with sling shots (mostly of the rubber-band type) is most common in May and June. A ring and pin game, made of wood in Paracho, is played by all ages.

A favorite sport from March through May is kite flying. Kites of small boys are about 7 by 9 inches; those of larger boys are about 2 by 3 feet. They are six-stick kites made with sticks all the same length and requiring a tail. They are commonly in bright colors. Big boys tie razor blades on the tails of their kites and fight each other. They try to maneuver their kites into the top position where they can be dropped and cut the strings of the other kites. There is a slight element of danger in this; one boy got his cheek laid open in 1940.

Small girls and sometimes small boys play with swings in the house yards. These are merely larger versions of the swings used to teach infants to walk. Girls also play running games in the streets with small boys and play "keep away" and other games with rag balls. Girls are shy and always stopped playing when they were observed.

In general, girls ape adult activities much more than do boys. Girls pretend to mill maize, using a board for a metate, a rock for the mano, and mud for the maize dough. They play at being street vendors, using flower petals for merchandise. Sometimes they have dolls made of rags, but not very often. More common is it for several girls to get some boards or branches and make a house in which they will play at housekeeping with their fireplaces, grinding stones, dishes, etc. After several weddings had been held in close succession, a group of girls were observed playing at having a wedding. Flowers were put in the hair of the "godmothers" and leaves of maize were tied in the hair to represent the ribbons used in real weddings.

Education for life in Cherán is completely on an informal and unconscious level. Children learn first by imitating and then by doing while assisting their parents. The social and religious structure they learn little by little through observation first of parents', and later of relatives', reactions to various individuals and situations and by listening to conversations. Only to a very small extent do children learn by being told. Again, observations are too few to generalize extensively, but apparently children are counseled and advised only when they begin to be old enough to undertake adult responsibilities. When they mention that they may do a certain act, the parents may discuss the advisability with them. In small matters of etiquette, parents may prompt children of any age. Formal training, though, seems to play little part in education for life as it is lived in Cherán.

Formal education for about 25 percent of the boys is received in school. Those who continue throughout the available course receive four years of school education. They learn to read and write and do a little simple arithmetic. They learn very little history or geography.

They learn something of natural history, such as major classifications of things in the animal, mineral, and vegetable kingdoms.

A few ambitious families send one or more of their children to high school in Morelia or to an agricultural school. Some are sent to the boarding school at Paracho, where they receive some education in a trade and in farming. A few also may go to Mexico City, and a case or two were discovered of children studying law or medicine. However, it is doubtful whether 2 dozen families in Cherán have sent their children on to advanced school training.

With all due acknowledgement of the effort and sincerity involved in the school system, the Cherán schools do not train children in any real sense for life in Cherán. The average Cherán resident completing the school training has little advantage over his unschooled fellows in following the farming routines of the community. If he can read and write he perhaps has some less chance of being swindled in business transactions and more opportunity of rising to some municipal office. If his education is effective, however, and is put to use, it is by moving out of the basic pattern of Cherán. Such a person may become a storekeeper or a mill operator, where his education will be of some slight service to him. The major advantage of school training is to better equip some individuals to cope with the Mestizo world which impinges on Cherán to some extent. Even so, the school child acquires little knowledge of rights and responsibilities in a larger world. Insofar as the education is effective and is utilized—and this is even more markedly true of those going on for more advanced education—the effect is to move the individual out of the culture of Cherán. If he stays in Cherán he tends to become an exploiter rather than a producer, or to occupy a position where he furnishes some liason between the rest of the population and the Mestizo world. Or, more commonly, he moves out of the Cherán culture completely, residing in some other part of Mexico. Only to a very small extent and in a very limited number of cases does an individual become a better producer, that is, a better farmer; or practice a trade learned through schools; or become a force and example guiding the community to better housing, reformed diets, better health practices, or higher standards of community organization. Formal education is still not geared to the needs and problems of Cherán life and is and will remain relatively ineffective until it becomes of obvious utility to the average Cherán resident. In other words, until the educational process is conceived of first of all from the standpoint of Cherán culture, instead of from the standpoint of national needs or theories, it will not be effective. And when education becomes geared to Cherán needs, paradoxically, it can then be effectively geared to national objectives.

YOUTH

The period of youth is very short in Cherán for most persons and there is no clearly defined lower limit to it. Boys seem to be regarded as youths when they are able to do a man's work or to be self-supporting but have not yet married. Marriage puts a termination to the period, although the young married man may still be under the tutelage of his parents. Still, after marriage a boy will be consulted in all family affairs; before marriage he normally will not be consulted unless he is much older than the age at which most Cherán youths are married. By 15 practically every Cherán youth is either earning his own living in part by working for wages or is working regularly on the family estate, taking a full man's share of the labors. In individual cases this may be true of youths as young as 12. Unmarried youths of 16 to 18 do not spend much of their free time at home; indeed, they may not even eat at home regularly. They tend to hang around the streets in gangs in their spare time. They spend a good deal of time in one of the two billiard parlors which modern civilization has brought to Cherán, where they may gamble on billiards at 50 centavos a game, or may be drawn into card games, or may begin drinking. However, few of the youngsters go around the saloons very much, nor are many of them prone to drink excessively. In such groups will be concerted many of the "stealings" which are the preliminaries to marriage. At this period boys in general are rather antisocial and appear to have some conflict with their parents. They feel they are growing up very fast and are impressed by the age gap which separates them

from their parents. In an overheard conversation, two young men commented at length on how fast people got old at their ages, while people over 30 did not seem to age at all.

The transition for girls is even less clearly defined than that for boys. As girls are sometimes married even before their first menstruation, this physiological transition hardly seems to mark a status change. From the age of 6 or 8, girls essentially perform adult labors in assisting their mothers. Youth is essentially a transition to adulthood and marriage. As a general thing, girls are married soon after the first menstruation.

Informants were agreed that most girls experience the first menses at about 14 years of age; whether this is the ideal age or the actual age could not be determined. No cases of failure to menstruate were known. Menstrual disorders apparently do occur sometimes and the aid of midwives is sought in such cases, but no details could be secured. Men, at least, believe that girls are generally ignorant of the menstrual period until they experience the first occurrence, and this belief coincides with a few statements by women. Some girls are said to be a little depressed or frightened, but the experience is not severe. Mothers explain to their daughters that the phenomenon is perfectly natural, and girls never become ill.

The mother always informs her husband when the first menstruation occurs. At this time the father increases his admonitions to his wife to watch over the girl. Careful mothers from now on do not let the girls go alone for water or to church or walk about the streets. Care is taken that girls do not see "bad" things. Well-brought-up girls, in fact, are hardly allowed out of the house until they are married, but if this ideal were really lived up to, it is difficult to see how either marriages could be arranged or "stealing" occur. Cherán, though, feels its standards are much above those of other towns and people mention some of La Cañada towns, especially Tacura, as being very bad. The latter town is said even to have many cases of sexual relations between father and daughter, which is said never to happen in Cherán.

Most women early become regular in their menstrual periods. No devices for keeping track of the periods are used but some account is kept of the phase of the moon and an approximate idea formed. The normal menstruation is regarded as lasting 3 or 4 days. Slight or excessive flows during the period are believed to be bad. No special garments are worn, but the ordinary underwear is carefully washed after the flow ends.

Women should not have relations with men during the menstrual period, and most women do not resume relations with their husbands until they have bathed, although some do so as soon as menstruation ends. Violation of this rule is believed to be bad for the men and to cause them to contract a disease with ulcers. Women may prepare food for themselves and others, but they must not eat certain foods. These include "cold" things, such as avocados or prickly pears. Beans, if eaten, must be consumed with quantities of onions. Rice, pork, and preserved chiles (because the liquid is very "cool") are also believed to be bad. Dried chiles may be eaten. *Aguardiente* is also avoided, although a little in coffee or orange-leaf tea is believed to be helpful. The majority, if possible, drink chocolate in the mornings even though they may not normally do so or may even dislike it. In connection with the concept of "coldness" it should be noted that this refers to the supposed effects on the person, not to the quality of the thing itself. Cold water, for example, may be consumed freely. Aside from sexual restrictions, men have no special rules to observe when their wives menstruate.

MARRIAGE AND SEX RELATIONSHIPS

Marriage is the normal state of the Cherán adult and unmarried persons are relatively rare, except among the aged. Although sexual inverts were reported, in every case they had married. One woman is known to be an invert and is called *toro-vaca*. As a girl she attempted to seduce other girls, and a woman told Rendón that in her childhood the individual in question once tried to drag her into a vacant lot, stopping her mouth with a *rebozo*, but she tore loose and screamed and was rescued by her father. Various charges were also made against the woman in court, but nothing was ever done.

The individual in question was also said once to have lived with another woman who did the work in the household while the former acted like a man. It is also believed that she is a "man" during one month and a "woman" the next, the change being regulated by changes in the moon. During the month she is a "man" she is said to go through the streets at night, trying to entice girls to her house, or else she stands at the door of her house and offers presents to girls who will come in. At one time the woman married and had two children but later was widowed. That the individual is emotionally unstable is indicated by her claim to have once "died" and come to life again, after which she brought many people messages from their dead relatives whom she had encountered in the other world.

No cases of men dressing as women or men who had homosexual relations were encountered, but there evidently are occasional instances. The only specific reports encountered were of subadolescent boys who showed a preference for doing women's work. One example cited was of a boy who washed dishes, swept, made tortillas, and did other housework. His voice was high-pitched and he refused to fight. Later, however, the boy's voice changed and he married.

Some prostitution exists in Cherán. There are several houses of assignation operated by elderly women who know the accessible women. Men go to these houses and the old woman then takes a message to some girl or woman. The younger women are often the daughters of older women who have taken this way of life, but sometimes the girls from other families will visit such houses clandestinely. Such girls become known among the unmarried men and usually have difficulty in marrying. Often they attempt to force boys to marry them by claiming to have been "stolen" by a boy and lodging complaints with the mayor, often abetted by their parents. If the girl's reputation is bad, the boy may be put in jail as a discouragement to boys who might be tempted to steal a girl without marrying her, but the boy will not be forced to marry.

The patrons of such houses are usually bachelors and older unmarried youths. Some whose wives are pregnant also visit such houses occasionally. Payment, usually 50 centavos, is given to the girls prostituting themselves, part of which is given to the woman who lends her house for the purpose and arranges the meeting.

Despite the existence of prostitution, it is claimed that most young people before marriage have no sexual experience. Girls particularly are believed to be relatively innocent, although obviously all have knowledge of the nature of the sexual act in a setting as full of animals as is Cherán. Boys are believed to be somewhat more sophisticated because, even though they may not have visited houses of prostitution, details are talked about among them. After marriage, aside from the prohibitions on intercourse during pregnancy and confinement and during menstruation, there are no restrictions on sexual relations between husband and wife. There seem to be no ideas about a fixed interval or ideal interval between sexual relations and informants thought relations were "frequent" but would not suggest any time periods. In general, the subject of sex relations proved embarrassing and informants seemed purposely to avoid definite statements.

The customary preliminary to marriage is for the groom to "steal" (robar) his bride. Virtually everyone of the older and the more articulate men in town deprecate the custom and many assert that it is a recent development. Nevertheless, no one could name a time when the custom was not practiced. Moreover, it is to be found in many other Tarascan towns, perhaps in all of them, and is regarded as an old form at Mestizo Chilchota, where most marriages also begin by stealing. Although occasionally the groom asks for the bride instead of stealing her, such cases are exceptional and seem more likely to be the innovation than does the stealing of the bride.

Only on very rare occasions is the bride stolen without her consent. Generally the entire performance, including setting the time and place, has been arranged beforehand between the bride and groom, although it is good form for the girl to struggle or at least to pretend to do so. The groom enlists the cooperation of some of his age mates and they assist in carrying off the girl and in blocking pursuit. The usual time for carrying off a girl is on a Sunday when she comes out of church after the Rosary and when she is usually accompanied only by female relatives. The relatives scream and create a disturbance. The male relatives are summoned at once, either by the female relatives or by any bystander who may be interested enough to do so. The male relatives go in pursuit of the girl and the groom's friends interfere with the chase although they must not use force. They try to block the streets, and sometimes push or trip the male relatives, but they do not hold on to them or strike any blows. If the male relatives of the girl catch the groom before he has gotten the girl to the house of one of his relatives, he must not resist, even though the girl's relatives may abuse him or beat him.

Opportunities for courting and for making arrangements are few. The boy may visit the girl's house only on rare occasions, such as the *melebris* before Christmas, although he may occasionally have accompanied his parents on a visit. He also may speak to the girl at the door of her courtyard or exchange a word or two when she is on the streets with her mother carrying water. The best opportunities are the rare occasions when the girl may be allowed on the streets alone in the daytime to visit a relative or to run an errand nearby and especially when she has been allowed to go somewhere with other girls. Sunday afternoon is the main time for courting. A boy uses a special whistle to attract the attention of a girl. If she is with other girls, all stop, and the boy uses signs to indicate which one he wishes to talk to. The other girls go on slowly and the indicated one, if she is interested, lingers behind for a few minutes' conversation.

The standards for choice of spouse by a boy are several. A boy wants an attractive-looking girl who is fairly tall and of medium build and who also is industrious and of good family. This means her family is not completely poverty-stricken, her father not a drunkard, and her mother not "perverse" (apparently meaning "immoral"). Also, the girl should be either the same age or a year or two younger than the boy. In a few instances the girl is a year or two older. No cases were reported of widows marrying younger men, but sometimes a widower marries a younger woman. One case cited is a man of over 65 who has a wife aged 20. The instance is regarded as exceptional and as undesirable. As a rule, the boy discusses his choice with his parents or with one of his uncles. Although no specific data could be secured on the subject, from the facts that boys at this age seem to be shy with their parents and that the bride is usually taken to the house of an uncle, it seems likely that uncles are consulted on matters of marriage more commonly than are the parents. Some stated there is no preference for maternal or paternal uncles in this connection; others said the girl is taken to a paternal uncle or, lacking an uncle, a paternal aunt.

After a girl is stolen, only on rare occasions does the marriage not follow. Her parents, however much opposed they may be, must always give their consent, for it is very difficult for girls to get married if they have been stolen and then returned home. As Agustín put it, "they have to wait for a sucker" in order to get married. A youth marrying such a girl is the butt of teasing by all his age mates, even by persons who do not even know his name. In the one case known of a young man who married a girl who had previously been stolen by someone else, the youth is subjected to so much teasing that he is virtually a recluse, either staying in his house when home or working by himself in the woods.

It is generally felt that the municipal authorities should force a youth to marry a girl after he has stolen her. If they do not, the authorities are always suspected of receiving bribes to overlook the case. Informants best acquainted with customary viewpoints, though, stated that the municipal authorities are not required to act unless the parents of the groom make the first formal visit to the girl's parents. In this case the municipal authorities are expected to force completion of the marriage. In actual fact the municipal authorities bring some pressure to bear on youths if the girl's parents lodge a complaint.

The following accounts of stealing girls give additional light on the procedures. The first account was written by Agustín Rangel.

When I first met the groom it was about 2 p.m. (on a Sunday) at the corner of Damas Gambe's store. We walked around for a while and when we were coming down the highway he told me he was going to steal a girl that afternoon after the Rosario. The corner of Morelos and Galeana was where the boy and girl had the place arranged for the stealing. When we knew that the Rosario was just about to be finished, we came down the highway to the plaza where we sat down at the municipal offices. Then the people began to come out from the Rosario and were called back by the priest to move the rocks in back of the priest's house. The girl's father called us to help move the rocks but instead we moved over to the corner of Morelos and Ocampo where we sat and waited until they finished.

After a little the girl came by and she looked at us. As she turned the corner up Morelos, she got ahead of her folks about 10 feet and just stood there. Then she turned back and looked at us to see if we were going to do anything. She was with five women. Knowing that we were not going to do anything, she evened up with the rest of her folks. Then we followed her; we went straight and she turned the corner of Morelos and Galeana. Then we ran so that we could beat her to the corner of Hidalgo and Arista and we stood there until she came.

When she came, the groom stood in the middle of the street and two of us stood on each side of the street and the other stood a little ways from the corner. When the girl passed us, the groom grabbed her by the arm and I took the other arm on the other side. The mother just said, "Maria Purisima, where do you take my daughter? Why do you take her and who are you?" We just ran to beat everything. When we were crossing the bridge (to Parícutin), one of the kids hollered, "Hurry up, because the father is just in back of you."

When I turned to look back the girl's father was just about half a block behind us. Then we separated at the street junction across the bridge. The boy and girl took the upper road and we went on the lower road. We just walked a little ways to where it was dark and changed blankets. Then we walked back as if we were innocent bystanders. We saw the girl's father after the boy and girl. We just made out we didn't know anything and said, "I wonder who was the kid who took the girl." Then we said, "Let's follow them," and we did. When we reached the corner of Madero and Salazar the girl's father was madder than a wet hen. He was saying, "If I ever catch the guys who did it, I will kill them," swearing to beat anything. Then he left and we followed him up Salazar and past the calvary to his house.

His wife was waiting for him in the doorway. His wife then said, "Didn't you catch the boys who stole my daughter?" He answered, "No, I didn't catch them. How do you expect me to catch them when I didn't know who they were?" They argued for a while in the doorway and then went inside. We came back to the saloon and when we got back they were already drunk (the groom and another helper). Then we went home. We were just afraid that if the father knew who we were he might call us in at the mayor's office and get us put in jail overnight.

The boy and girl had agreed to go out together since the last time they talked together. The father was chasing us because he was trying to get the girl before she had reached the boy's house. The girl was not taken to the house of the boy when we stole her but to the house of one of his relatives. If the father caught up with us, we would have to take what was coming to us and not fight back. Some boys tried to make a blockade on the road when the father was chasing. He had three friends with him and so he got by.

The following day Agustín's fears were realized; he was summoned to the mayor's office and shut up in jail from about 5 until 8 o'clock. Then, since it was a first offense, he was let out (although he had helped steal a number of other girls) with the warning that next time it would be a couple of days. The mayor also scolded the boys severely, pointing out that several people had been killed stealing girls; in fact, the implication was that he had put them in jail for their own protection, not because there was anything wrong with stealing the girl. As during the winter scarcely a Sunday passes without a girl being stolen in the plaza, the mayor's shock could not have been great.

Another less typical case involved a girl who had three suitors. The three suitors agreed to steal her and make her choose between them. If she refused to choose, then one of them, José H———, was to take her. The aid of three other youths was enlisted to guard all the approaches to the plaza in case the girl tried to flee. The plan fell through, because the girl did not come to church as she had promised.

The following week José made signals to a girl in Parícutin that he wanted to talk with her. She was with two other girls, carrying water. She stood and talked for a while and José then started home. After a block or two he discovered the girl following him. He made a circuit beside the *barranca*, but she still followed. He waited for her and asked where she was going. She replied, "I am going with you." On this, José ran down into the *barranca*, followed it down to the plain, and after a very long circuit, returned home. He had scarcely arrived when the police summoned him to the mayor's office. There was the father of the girl, accusing José of stealing his daughter. José denied the accusation and explained, but he had no witnesses and the girl insisted. The mayor ordered José to marry the girl; he refused, as he was interested in the girl he had hoped to steal the previous Sunday and the present girl he knew visited one of the houses of assignation. José was then put in jail, but when his mother stood responsible for him he was let out in a couple of days. The girl's mother went around town talking about the wrong that had been done, while José went around town telling everyone bad things about the girl. Eventually José had to run away and no one knew where he had gone.

Normally, sexual relations are begun between the bride and groom soon after she is stolen. Permission of the girl's baptismal godfather (and perhaps the godfather of confirmation) should be sought and is usually given; to refuse might cause hard feeling. Cases were cited where the godfather and the boy's parents became very angry with each other over a refusal. On the other hand, evidently the boy is stimulated to accumulate the property necessary to hold the wedding if sex relations are not permitted.

The stealing of a girl sets in motion a complex series of events constituting perhaps the most complicated aspect of Cherán culture.

The following account of marriage is one written by Pedro Chávez. Parts in brackets represent additional comments made by Sr. Chávez on other occasions or data gathered from other sources. All the features of the wedding were verified by observation and utilization of other sources of information.

A TARASCAN WEDDING

Marriage among the Tarascans of the town of Cherán embraces many points of great importance. In the first place, it is now a custom that the groom, when he desires to enter into marriage, steals the girl. This theft consists of catching her and carrying her off forcibly or, sometimes, willingly without force. But in either case, as much in the first instance as in the second, the bride goes in accordance with an agreement made in advance and the action is merely feigned by the two.

When the theft of the bride is completed [by taking the girl to the house of an uncle or other relative or, more rarely, to the house of the groom], the parents of the groom proceed to the house of the bride and appear before her parents. This act is called the puátperankua or "the pardon." It should be taken into account that in order to present themselves before the parents of the bride, the parents of the groom must take a person called t'aɹepiti diósʌ uandári [who is a professional marriage manager]. The first act of this person is to arrive at the house of the parents of the bride, saluting them very respectfully, and immediately falling on his knees, accompanied by the parents of the groom and various other persons most near to the father [especially the brothers and sisters of the groom's father]. Then the marriage manager says a Catholic prayer, making reference to the marriage of Joseph and Mary, how it was, and that thus it is necessary to effect the marriage they propose to bring about. This act completed, he offers a cigarette to the offended party [that is, the father of the bride]. If the latter receives the cigarette, it is an indication that he does not find the marriage undesirable. If he does not receive it, it is an indication that he wishes to be begged with many favors to give his consent, but finally he always gives his consent. [Because if he did not, the girl would be returned to her parents and no one would marry her. The girl's father is often very annoyed. He may scold his wife for letting the daughter be stolen and he often refuses to receive the boy's relatives for several days, going off and hiding in the mountains in order to show his anger and to cool down a bit.] Immediately [on giving his consent] the father of the bride calls together all his neighbors and principal relatives, others coming by themselves later. This reunion is with the object of drinking with the bride's father, for the parents and companions of the groom have brought a quantity of liquor, until all are very drunk, which concludes the first ceremony. The marriage manager reminds everyone to await them again within 8 days, that is to say, that they [the groom's relatives] will return within 8 days.

Eight days after the first ceremony, both the father of the bride and the father of the groom assemble all their relatives. Four or five days before they are notified so that the relatives of the groom will each prepare a quantity of bread costing not less than 1 peso and not more than 5 pesos, while the relatives of the bride make tamales with chile and meat of the kind we call nákatamali. Once the day arrives, all assemble in the house of the parents of the bride and begin to exchange. The parents and relatives of the groom give 4 or 5 pieces of bread to all those of the other group. The latter in their turn give 6 or 8 tamales, continuing until all the bread and tamales have been given away. [Each relative of the groom gives bread to one or more of the relatives of the bride in accordance with his wishes.] This affair also ends in drunkenness. During all this time the bride has been left at the house of the relative in whom the groom has most confidence, but this day she is brought to be present at the function.

The following day after the function referred to, the couple present themselves at the civil registry to make their application to marry, accompanied by the closer relatives. The authorities notify them to present themselves within 8 days to effect the civil marriage. [This represents an ideal case. Often the application for marriage and the civil marriage may not occur for weeks or even months. In at least one case the religious marriage took place before the civil marriage, although on the same day. However, the priest normally refuses to perform the service unless the certificate of civil marriage is presented. The relatives accompanying the couple are parents, uncles and male first cousins of the groom, the parents and close relatives of the bride, and the godmothers of the groom and the godmother for the wedding. The latter stands by the couple when the legal formula is read by the secretary or the mayor. All the relatives sign the papers as witnesses. Sometimes the secretary or mayor makes a little speech, pointing out to the husband that now he has to support his bride and can not expect her father to go on supporting her. He also may deliver a homily on behavior, pointing out that a married man shouldn't have two women or a married woman two men, warning them to avoid divorce, etc.]

After following the course indicated by the authorities, the proper steps are taken for the religious marriage. On the vespers of the day of the marriage they celebrate the t'irénkua or the dance. For this the parents of the bride hire a band with the object of going to the house of the groom with the music to take him the clothing called Aríperata, or gifts, which consist of a pair of shoes, two or three pairs of trousers (calzones), three shirts, and a hat. The cost of this is divided by the godparents and relatives of the bride in this way: one pair of trousers, a shirt, and a sash from each of the two godfathers of the bride and the rest from her father. The groom is dressed in this clothing by the grandfathers, grandmothers, siblings, and first cousins of the bride. [One of the latter actually dresses the groom. The groom is called tembuča and his siblings and cousins of both sexes are called tembučas. Similarly, the bride is called tembunga and her siblings and cousins are called tembungas. The female tembučas give the female tembungas narrow colored ribbons or bands to wear in their hair.] Immediately the dressing is completed, the musicians play some regional tune and the groom has to dance, with which ends the affair of the gifts of the groom. [Atole is sometimes brought to this function also. The custom seems to be decaying.]

On the day of the wedding the parents and godparents of the groom, together with the grandfathers, uncles and cousins, are those charged with going to the house of the bride very early in the morning when the bells ring the first call to Mass to take her clothing also, that is to say, the Aríperata. [The bride has returned to her own house a few days before the wedding. During this time the groom may visit her freely.] This consists of three rebozos, a shirt and blouse, earrings, corales (red glass beads), sash, and a pair of shoes. The cost of these is divided as follows: one rebozo from each godfather, these being the blue rebozos of Paracho, and the father of the groom a very fine white rebozo [it is not actually white but one of the remarkably fine mixed color rebozos from Tangancicuaro, costing anywhere from 20 to 80 pesos] and all the other articles. When the bride is dressed [she wears all three of the new rebozos], the parents of the couple and the principal godparents and relatives, together with the musicians brought by the parents of the groom, accompany the couple to the church to effectuate the marriage before the priest. [During the Mass a ring is placed on a finger of the bride. The groom can bring his own ring, but if he has not done so, a ring lent by the priest is used. The priest also puts silver money in the hands of the groom who in turn places it in the hands of the bride. If the groom has not brought money, the priest lends it to him. However, it is believed that the groom should bring the money and that the more he brings the greater the benediction for their life and the more fortunate the couple will be. There is said to be no use of the collar, chain, or ribbon used in some churches in Oaxaca.]

After the wedding, all leave the Mass and go to the house of the bride's parents, where she and all her relatives are left, the rest of the party going to the house of the groom's parents. Later, in about an hour, all return to the house of the bride's father [first calling for the bride's godparents to invite them] to escort the bride and all her relatives to breakfast [at the house of the groom's father] which consists only of a piece of bread and small cup of chocolate. On arriving at the house of the groom's father, the [male] guests seat themselves in a place previously prepared. The preparation consists of placing some logs of wood for seats [in two rows with others sometimes arranged as a table between the rows at a somewhat higher level] and at one of the ends they place the image of some saint of the Catholic religion [most commonly a picture of the saint] before which is a lighted candle and flowers [and sometimes an incense burner with copal incense]. Before the guests are served, it is the duty of the marriage manager to say a prayer in thanks. It should be noted that the first places [before the altar] are reserved for the marriage manager and the godfathers of both bride and groom and that only the men sit on these seats, the women being seated apart. The godmothers also sit apart [usually on mats in the center of the courtyard], the godmother of the groom being distinguished by ribbons tied in her hair. These ribbons are given and tied on the hair by the godmother's *comadres*, granddaughters and sisters-in-law. [Ribbons are tied in the hair of all the godmothers of the groom, and of the godmother of the wedding.]

Upon completing the breakfast, all the relatives of the bride return to her house, taking the bride with them again and not being accompanied by the relatives of the groom. In the meantime the musicians play in the house of the groom. This is usually between 10 and 11 of the morning. [Meantime many guests may drop in and will be fed, being seated in a different place from the relatives. Everyone is welcome because the more who attend, the more prestige attaches to the wedding. As outsiders, the members of the staff were usually especially welcome, as apparently we gave special *eclat* to the function.] Meantime all the sib-

lings and cousins and grandparents of the groom together have hired another band and at this time they separate themselves from the rest of the groom's relatives. [They go through the streets with the musicians, ultimately going to the house of one of the groom's uncles where they eat dinner. The remainder of the groom's relatives and the guests eat at the house of the groom. Tortillas, kurúndas (tamales), and čurípo (beef broth with cabbage, chile, and chunks of beef) are served.]

After the dinner is served, the party is prepared to go for the bride. This is called the p'ipejperakua. The party consists of the parents of the groom and their brothers and all the friends of the parents. [Actually not all go; those who are invited to go on the party are given iris leaves which they carry with them. Staff members at weddings were frequently given invitations to accompany the party in this same form.] The same relatives of the bride are all assembled at her house, ready, as are the friends of the parents. [The party of the groom's relatives is accompanied by musicians. The party goes first to the house of the godparents of the bride. They serenade the house outside and then the closer relatives enter the house. They form a circle before the godfather and the godmother of the bride. The marriage manager makes a long but informal speech, asking permission to take the bride. The godfather replies, giving his permission. All present then shake hands with the godfather and godmother, making a movement simulating kissing the hand. The group leaves the house, accompanied by the godparents.] Arriving at the house of the bride's parents, the groom's relatives immediately ask for the bride. [Actually, only the closer relatives again go inside, accompanied by the musicians. The marriage manager again asks for the bride.] When consent is granted, they start for the groom's house, carrying with them the clothing they have ready. [For a big wedding a procession of a hundred or more people may have formed by the time the group returns to the groom's house.] In the meantime the other relatives of the boy [the siblings, cousins, and grandparents] arrive with their musicians and do the same [that is, they take off the siblings, cousins, and grandparents of the bride] who carry quantities of clothing. This consists of shirts for men and women, trousers for men, jackets for men and women, sashes for women, and bags, and tortilla cloths, the latter two objects to be given the groom at the time all the others are changing clothing and bread. In the house of the groom's father the guests are all seated as before. [The godmothers are again seated on mats in the center and the bride sits for a time beside the godmother of baptism. Guests continue to arrive and additional ribbons are tied in the hair of the godmothers and long and elaborate paper ornaments fastened to sticks are placed in the hair. All the relatives of the groom give cigarettes to the groom's father when they arrive in the courtyard for the first time and also give cigarettes to the godfathers of the groom. To the mother and the godmothers of the groom are given 5 or 10 centavos each. The form of presentation is always the same; the money is placed in a china plate covered with a cloth. The recipient tips the plate so the money slides into her hand without the amount being visible to anyone else. The recipient shakes the hand of the donor and in the case of the mother, who is standing, curtseys. Sometimes money is given to the males in lieu of cigarettes. If the family is large, the godmothers and the mother may receive from 8 to 15 pesos. Shortly after the arrival of the bride's party, the parents and uncles of the bride and groom, and sometimes other relatives, all enter the kitchen. There the marriage manager performs a ceremony (described on p. 103) by which all become *compadres*.]

The father of the groom now orders the distribution to all the relatives of the bride [and in observed weddings, to everyone present] of one piece of bread each. The bread was prepared in advance and is an obligation of the father. This is called the ¢ʌ¢ʌ́ki t'irén¢kua. Ordinarily these pieces are in the form of a crown which we call kanákua. [The *compadres* or brothers of the groom's father help him with the distribution, handing him a piece of bread which the father himself usually hands to each guest on a lacquered tray (pl. 7, upper right). The order of events in the account here does not coincide with any wedding witnessed. The distribution of bread usually came after the exchange of clothing and bread described below. Only if there were to be little or no clothing exchange or dancing would the distribution of bread be this early in the proceedings. The time of distribution is regarded as indicating the probable length of the wedding; the later it is distributed, the longer the wedding will last. In the case of the latest distribution observed, the wedding lasted 3 days. Similarly, the beginning of the drinking usually did not take place until the clothing and bread exchange was well under way.]

When this act [the distribution of the bread] was finished, they begin to bring out the bottles of *charanda* and all begin to drink until they are quite drunk. It should be noted that only the relatives of the groom have the right to buy and carry liquor, the relatives of the bride drinking what is offered them [which is abundant. The person who produces a bottle drinks from it first.] While they are drinking, at the same time they are making the exchange of the clothing and bread in the following form.

All of the women relatives of the bride such as the maternal and paternal aunts give clothing to the uncles and aunts and other relatives (of the groom) as well as the parents, who are those who receive the best clothing. These in their turn in recompense return bread in a quantity not more than $1.50 and not less than $1.00, while the musicians are playing regional tunes and *jarabes* and others are dancing. [For a somewhat different sequence of events with some additional details, see the account of the Sánchez wedding below.] In a word, there is a very great movement.

[Each person giving a garment presents it to a relative of the groom who had given bread to the person at the ceremony 8 days after the pardon.] In another locality the same acts are being performed by the others who have a separate group of musicians. These are the brothers and grandparents of the bride and groom. Comes a moment when the groom is taken by the arms and they hang about his neck bags and tortilla cloths (*servilletas*). The groom is made to dance to two tunes. With this he leaves [the brothers, cousins and grandparents] and the remainder continue drinking and dancing until it is late and time to leave, only the bride remaining in the house of the groom, with which ends the events of the day of the wedding.

The following day is another small fiesta called the kauíjan¢kua. On this day it is an obligation of the parents of the groom to go to give thanks to the godparents of baptism and of the marriage in their houses, accompanied by their closer relatives, making their thanks concrete by all getting drunk in the house of these godparents. On the other hand the brothers, sisters, cousins of both sexes, and grandparents of the bride and groom hire musicians and go to the house of the groom to wash all the pots used the previous day, which is an obligation of the bride, although actually it does not result this way as they arrange to drink *charanda* and very few pots are washed. When they are all good and drunk again, celebrating this drunkenness among the cousins, brothers, and grandparents of the bride and groom, the marriage events end. As a regular thing there has been an expenditure of between 200 and 300 pesos for all the parts of the marriage ceremony, which must be paid by the father of the groom. [Written by P. Chávez, Cherán, Michoacán, October 10, 1940.]

The foregoing account represents the thoughtful view of a Cherán wedding as seen by an intelligent and well-informed native resident of the town. As is to be expected, certain aspects of the celebration are overlooked. Some of these have been inserted in brackets in the account given above; others will be added below. The Chávez account also presents a slightly different order from that observed at several weddings. In all probability the Chávez account is in part somewhat inaccurate in its order; very likely it also represents an expression of one of several possible arrangements. Some weddings are much more elaborate than the generalized description, while others are much simpler.

The most elaborate wedding during the time of the study was that of Samuel Sánchez, son of Antonio Sánchez, a well-to-do farmer with a large number of relatives (pl. 6, left, center). The most significant points are discussed below. Samuel stole his bride about the middle of July, and the wedding occurred on August 17. On August 16 the women of the household, aided by relatives, soaked and washed between 5 and 6 *fanegas* of maize for tamales and tortillas. Also, a beef was killed, cut up, and placed in the storage loft. The evening of the same day new clothing was taken to the groom by the bride's relatives, and he was dressed, everything but his pants being changed in the patio. The groom's house, where breakfast was served. The godmother of baptism and the godmother of the wedding were seated on mats in the patio with the bride at the right hand of the godmother of baptism (pl. 7, right, center; fig. 18). Both received gifts of ribbons and coins, but only the godmother of the wedding had the paper ornaments on sticks placed in her hair (pl. 7, lower right). When breakfast was

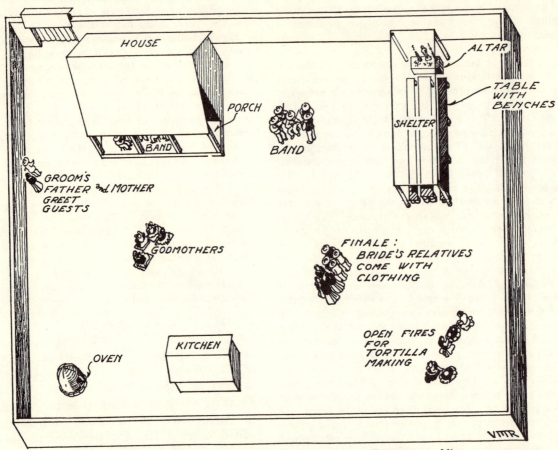

FIGURE 18.—Arrangement of the principal actors in a Tarascan wedding.

dressing should be done by a male first cousin of the bride. (Agustín, for example, dressed the groom when the daughter of his mother's sister was married.)

The wedding in church took place at about 4 a. m. So early a wedding is unusual, partly because it costs more, but the Sánchez family obviously planned to make the most of the wedding. The bride was dressed in new clothing before the wedding. After the wedding the bride and her party went to her parents' house. Between 10 and 11 o'clock they returned to the finished, the bride and her relatives returned to her house.

A group went out with the musicians and brought back a large quantity of bread. On such trips with the musicians a direct route is never followed, particularly on the return, but a circuitous route is taken to display the bread and the crowd to as many as possible. As soon as the bride's relatives had left, dinner began to be served to the relatives of the groom, the men eating under the shed separately from the women. The bread was put on a table decorated with ferns. The serving of food to the men was done by brothers-in-law of the groom's father. Cigarettes were passed around by one of the groom's uncles.

About 12:45 p. m. a second band arrived. While the mother was not occupied she sat on a mat in front of the house where she received coins from guests. The father received cigarettes, which were placed beside the altar under the shed until needed, when they were passed about to the guests. After eating, many went to the house of one of the other relatives of the groom where they ate again. The bride's relatives were given dinner at her home by her parents.

Iris leaves were distributed to the men selected to go for the bride, and they left with the band hired by the groom's father. The godmothers moved under the house porch where they sat on mats. A procession of women came in bearing lacquered trays on their heads filled with fruit and bottles of soda pop. These women were female relatives of the groom who had not helped in the kitchen work. The soda pop was given to the men who had been assisting, while the fruit was given to the women assistants. Some of the men fastened quantities of breads and cookies to strings suspended from the roof of the shed where the bride's male relatives would sit again on their return.

A number of women bearing cornstalks and flowers (cannas, dahlias, and calla lilies) left with the second band and some of the men, including the groom's father. They were going to get bread.

In the meantime the bride and her relatives arrived. The bride's male relatives went to the shed where they all grabbed at the breads and cookies, each trying to get the most. The female relatives sat in a group in another place (see fig. 18) with the clothing before them arranged to make the greatest possible display. The bride sat beside the godmothers. She was barefoot and accompanied by a small girl.

The first lot of bread was brought in. The godmothers with the first band, which had returned with the bride, went out into the street to meet the bread. About 15 minutes after this the bride went into the house where she stayed the remainder of the ceremony, accompained by a number of younger girls.

The exchange of clothing for bread now began. The father and mother of the groom were the object of most attention and every effort was made to keep giving them clothing too rapidly for them to remove it. Each donor placed the garment on the recipient. Occasionally the father would succeed in getting away and dash into the house where he would remove it all. Despite this, at one time he wore about six shirts and four or five pairs of extra *calzones* (trousers). Three or four times during this procedure, the groom came hastily into the courtyard and entered the house to leave the bags (*morales*) and tortilla cloths he had been given.

After some exchange had gone on and part of the repayment in bread had been accomplished, a group brought in seven more large baskets of bread. Some of the older women accompanying the party brought breads made in the shape of bulls. They rushed about holding the breads between their two hands and pretended to gore others until other women finally seized them and broke them to pieces. These breads in the form of bulls (and sometimes other animals) are provided by the grandparents of the groom but are used only in the period from January until after Carnival according to some informants. However, this was August, so the informants must have been in error.

Before the exchange of clothing and bread was completed, the godmothers began the dancing. No one was supposed to dance until the godmothers began. All the early dancers were women, mostly elderly, dancing by themselves or in pairs. When the music began to play for a second dance, elderly women with more breads in the shape of bulls began running at various persons standing around and pretending to gore them with the animal until they began to dance.

The dancing was interrupted at this point by the eruption of a group of men and women into the courtyard carrying baskets, cooking pots, *comals*, water buckets, etc. Two men carried on a pole a huge copper pot in which tamales had been cooked. This group began to dance and everyone cleared a place, primarily because the pots were black. After a time the dancers began to wipe their hands on the sooty bottoms of the pots and to rub their hands on each other's faces, with other horseplay.

This group included the men and the women who had been working in the kitchen. It is said the custom of the kitchen staff dancing with the kitchen utensils is an old one which is rarely observed now. A number of informants had not seen it for many years, and it was not practiced in other weddings observed. The custom is believed to be peculiar to Cherán.

The godmothers, in the meantime, had been seated again. The groom's father gave them each a small pop bottle of *charanda* with a package of Tigres cigarettes tied with gay ribbons to the neck of the bottle. These are provided by grandchildren of the godmothers. The father also gave each grandmother a small green glazed pottery "barrel" with a tiny spout on top and a cup fitting over the spout; these were also filled with *charanda* and the godmothers ceremonially drank a drop or two from the cup and then began pressing it on others. Each person offered a drink took a drop or two. When most of the small supply of *charanda* in the barrels was gone, large bottles were produced and began to circulate in the crowd. The first large bottle was taken to the shed where the bride's male relatives sat.

The dancing now became general, although for a time the elderly women with breads rushed about charging into people who were not dancing and forcing them to dance. Drinking also became general, and numbers soon showed the effects of the liquor. Several expeditions went out for more bread, accompanied now by the godmothers, who danced rather drunkenly in the streets at the head of the processions. Many women accompanying the procession also danced, but the younger women, especially those carrying babies, merely walked along the sides of the street.

The following day the male first cousins took atole to the groom. The atole was made by the youths' mothers, but the boys had to take the maize to the mill to have it ground and get the ingredients for the atole.

The wedding of Samuel Sánchez, described above in somewhat abbreviated form, was one of the extremes of Cherán marriage. At the other end of the scale was the wedding of a niece of Agustín's. The groom, Juan Gerónimo,

was a widower but still young. The girl lived with an aunt, for her mother had become a woman of loose morals after having an affair with a worker on the highway and at the moment was in jail in Uruapan for disorderly conduct. The bride's father was dead. Another aunt refused to attend the wedding because she did not approve of the girl's marrying a widower.

In this instance the groom had not stolen the girl but had asked for her, taking bread to the house of the aunt, accompanied by musicians. Agustín, with other relatives of the girl, took her to church for the civil wedding, where she was delivered to the groom's father. She was not returned to her own home and there was no breakfast. As the groom's father was poor, there was no celebration in his house, but at noon the girl's aunt did the best she could to rectify the matter by serving a dinner in her house.

At another simple wedding attended, the general forms were gone through in truncated fashion. The dinner was over before 12 o'clock, and immediately following it the groom's father distributed the special breads in the form of crowns. This early distribution indicated that there would be no exchange of clothing on a large scale (although there was a little) and no drinking. There were no music and no dancing, and the affair was over by about 2 p. m.

Another of the weddings observed in some detail presents a number of interesting features. This was the wedding of Samuel Santa Clara, son of the widow, Doña Feliciana, principal informant regarding herbs.

Again, as the families knew each other well and it was certain that the girl's mother, also a widow, would consent, the girl was not stolen. Indeed, Doña Feliciana and her "brothers" went to the girl's house on a Thursday evening and asked for her. There were no music and no marriage manager on this occasion. The following Monday, September 9, Doña Feliciana and all the groom's relatives ate at her house and then went to the bride's house, starting about 2:30 p. m. This hour is early and was arranged for my special benefit so I would be sure to see everything. Unfortunately, I had not been advised of the plan and was not in Cherán that day, but Agustín, who as usual turned out to be a relative, was a member of the party.

Because of the early hour, the marriage manager had not arrived. The party all waited outside until the manager was found and came. The manager prayed, and then the men were given tamales to eat. The women then began exchanging bread and tamales at about 5:30. Later they drank all night and sat around and talked. They would have danced, but Doña Feliciana had provided no music.

On November 9 the groom was learning the prayers and it was intended to hold the wedding soon, but it was postponed until January because the priest said that no one could marry until after Christmas *por los velados*. As Doña Feliciana remarked, "No one knows what these are. This priest is very capricious. We have had various priests here, but never one like this."

During the interval of waiting, Doña Feliciana made it plain that, as she was a widow, she had no intention of holding a large wedding. The mother of the bride, however, was affronted and sent word that with all the Santa Claras in the town it was a shame they would not do anything. She also announced that although she also was a widow, she intended to pay for a band herself. When word of this got around, the Santa Claras became ashamed and bestirred themselves to see what could be done. Soon Agustín's father was remarking that the Santa Claras had gotten the better of the Rangéls, and perhaps they should do something. When the wedding finally was held by the Santa Claras it turned out to be, if anything, more elaborate than that given by Antonio Sánchez, described above.

The distribution of expenses, as it finally turned out, was approximately as follows:

Breakfast for the women—Erino Santa Clara, a "grandfather."
Breakfast for the men—provided by a cousin, a Santa Clara.
Dinner and bread—Emilio Santa Clara, a "grandfather."
One band—Doña Feliciana, the cousins, and uncles (Agustín paid a contribution for this).
Second band—brothers, sisters, and cousins of the groom, "grandfathers" of both bride and groom. (Agustín's father paid a contribution for this.)
Civil wedding—Domingo Hernández, a "grandfather."
Church wedding—Doña Feliciana.

According to report, Doña Feliciana provided only a new *rebozo* for the bride in the way of clothing, but this was not verified. No data were secured on who paid for the liquor.

The church wedding took place about 7 a. m. on January 9, this being the cheaper hour. The bride was returned to her home, then brought with her relatives to the groom's mother's house for breakfast. After breakfast, the party went to the municipal offices for the civil registry. This order was quite incorrect, as customarily the civil registry should precede the religious ceremony, usually by about a week. After this, matters proceeded as usual with the dinner. The older brother of the groom functioned as the male head of the household. Had the groom had no older brother, Doña Feliciana would have had to discharge the functions of the male head; none of her brothers or those of her deceased husband would have taken this position.

Late in the afternoon a number of poles were brought into the courtyard. Stuck in holes in these poles were many small sticks to which were attached small flaglike ornaments of paper of many colors which were divided among the women and children with a great deal of shouting and disorder (pl. 7, lower left). These banners are not produced at any other time than the period preceding Carnival.

The crownlike breads were not produced until quite late, about 4:30 p. m., and were not distributed until some time later (pl. 7, upper right). In turn, the dancing was late in starting in the groom's house, although it began some time earlier in the house of the grandfather entertaining that group.

Just before dusk the priest arrived and scolded the party for getting drunk. One of the men who took this to heart started home; he was shot and killed while crossing the bridge to Parícutin by an unknown enemy, but none of these events stopped the wedding, which turned into one of the most prolonged large-scale drinking bouts occurring during the time of the study. Atole was served at midnight, while between 4 and 6 a. m. and again at 8 a. m. *posole* was served. The atole was provided by

Antonio Sánchez (whose son's wedding is the first described) and his brother. The *posole* was provided by the cousins of the groom.

At 10 o'clock the following morning, water for dish washing was carried through the streets accompanied by a band. At 11:30 additional maize was taken to the mill, again accompanied by a band. On both occasions numerous people were dancing with the procession. Several other processions occurred during this and the following day when the wedding finally terminated.

Doña Feliciana estimated the expenses for the wedding to be about $100 for food and bread, paid for by the relatives. Doña Feliciana supplied 9 *fanegas* of maize, worth $36, and paid $25 to one of the bands, and she still owed $20. She also killed a cow with an estimated value of $60. The second band, which did not stay the entire time, was paid $20 by the relatives. This makes a total expense of $261, not counting the fees for the civil registry and the priest. Neither does it include the very considerable quantities of liquor consumed. Doña Feliciana collected $21 in gifts given by her female relatives.

The wedding of Samuel Sánchez mentioned above cost his father $150. In addition, Don Antonio's brothers spent at least $50. Don Antonio also killed a beef, and 7½ *fanegas* of maize was consumed. The civil registry cost $6 and the Mass $13, a total expenditure of approximately $309 exclusive of the liquor.

Alfredo Romero, pointing out that even poor families had to make every effort to give a proper wedding so the parents of the girl would be satisfied, reported that his wedding cost $135, 5½ *fanegas* of maize, and some beans, "and it did not last more than 3 days" (but his group of relatives is smaller and there were fewer guests than at some of the other weddings). He had to buy a beef "which hardly lasted" and there was expense for musicians, bread, lard, salt, onions "and who knows what else." Romero was forced to sell a lot in Parícutin and two small pieces of land, despite aid given him by his relatives.

In general, the attitude of disapproval voiced in the previous paragraph is not shared in Cherán. Although accounts of expense were given with a good deal of headshaking, obviously the majority of persons were rather proud of the amount they had spent. Unquestionably, a wedding is the most extensive and ostentatious display of wealth and social position that exists in Cherán. Attempts in the past by outsiders to suppress the *costumbres* are almost always taken as attempts to suppress the weddings first of all and are met by sullen and dogged resistance. The reaction of Emilio Rojas, godfather of the bride in the Samuel Santa Clara wedding, is fairly typical:

> The custom here is pleasant, except people get very drunk. Well, not everyone, but some. It is good to take something, but not to the point of drunkenness. It is good to dance and be gay. Besides, I like weddings because I always sell something in the way of clothing. [Don Emilio is a storekeeper.]

The social prestige factors involved in weddings revolve about several aspects of the ceremonies. One is the sheer factor of display already mentioned. Whenever any group of people goes through the streets in connection with the wedding, it is accompanied by a band. Furthermore, a direct route is rarely followed. Often a circuitous route two or three times as long as the direct route is used.

Another aspect is the display and exchange of clothing and bread. Every effort is made to show the amount of bread being brought and the quantity of clothing to be exchanged. The clothing is carried on trays, usually lacquered, or in baskets either in the arms or on the head. The majority of the participants bearing clothing come in a single large procession which always makes a special effort to traverse as much of the town as is possible without making the ostentation too evident. The women bearing clothing all sit together for a time after arriving at the groom's house and spread out their clothing to make it look as impressive as possible.

The clothing exchange also has an economic aspect, for the investment involved is very considerable. To some extent, though, the gifts are formalized. Clothing for wedding gifts is usually not as well made as regular clothing. Furthermore, a large part of it is kept for exchange in future weddings. Only if a family does not expect to have any relatives marry for some time to come will it actually use the clothing, unless it is very poor and in need of the garments. Alternatively, some of the clothing may be sold if it is not apt to be needed for gifts. Informants estimated that each garment was exchanged two or three times; probably the estimate is conservative.

The third aspect of the wedding display involves the number of persons who attend. Every relative must attend a wedding if he does not wish to create hard feeling. Should a relative fail to appear, his own functions such as weddings, house movings, house roofings, or *mayordomías* would be boycotted by the persons he had affronted. At the wedding of the daughter of such a person as Rosalio Sánchez, representative of the town, very large numbers of nonrelatives attended in order to show their liking or admiration for the father. Friendship is likewise clearly demonstrated by attending the wedding of a nonrelative.

Resentment and avoidance seem to be the only methods of retaliation for neglect at Cherán. In many other towns there are probably more direct methods. In Charapan, at least, relatives who do not attend a wedding are sought out by their fellows and forcibly brought to the wedding where they have to parade through the kitchen bearing a water bucket.

Essential to every wedding, even the simplest, is the marriage manager. In a larger wedding the arrangements are too complex to be known properly to most people and the successful carrying out of the wedding depends on his ability. A fee is paid the marriage manager for his services; the amount apparently was not ascertained, for it does not appear in the notes, but it probably is fairly generous, for the most active of the few marriage managers, Gregorio Castillo, is a fairly prosperous individual.

As a neutral third party, the marriage manager also smooths over differences of opinion more successfully than the principals could ordinarily do face to face. This is especially marked when the bride's father is annoyed with the theft of his daughter. For example, at one "pardon," the father had left for the mountains and only an uncle of the girl was in the house. He claimed to be sick and refused to come out of the house for some time. When he did, he gave evidence of anger. Then Don Gregorio

said, "Well, it is custom. The girl was not forced but went willingly. There is no reason to be angry about this, nor with me, for I am not concerned in the matter but come to speak for the parents of the groom. They have come as is proper to arrange the affair." Late in the evening the father returned and agreed to the marriage, but he said little and clearly was angry.

One aspect of the marriage ceremonies not sufficiently emphasized in the preceding accounts is important: the new marriage means that the two families, in the most extended sense, will constantly cooperate in all sorts of ceremonial occasions. Thus, the groom's male relatives will help to move a house or roof a house, while the bride's female relatives will be called on to work in the kitchen on the same occasions. Both families will likewise be concerned with all the subsequent crisis periods in varying degree, especially when a grandchild marries at some future date.

The function of the wedding as an occasion for celebration, the release of tensions through drinking, the provision of diversion with the dancing, and the general stimulus through extensive social interaction is very considerable. For the participants, weddings probably rank as high or higher than fiestas as occasions for social contacts and amusement.

A feature most clearly demonstrated in the weddings is the much greater participation of the older women. Young women with children usually do not take a very active part in the kitchen work, nor are they leaders in the exchange of clothing. The old women, on the other hand, are in the forefront of all activities. Essentially the wedding is a woman's affair in many respects. Old women are the most active in the kitchen. They are the first to start drinking, although they rarely drink to the excess common among the men, and they are the first to dance. Indeed, on older women the playing of dance music has an almost compulsive effect. Time and again, when dance music is being played, even though it is not time for dancing, some of the old women will be seen quietly dancing by themselves in a corner.

Although the ceremonies of marriage are most elaborate in the case of first marriages, often marriages of widows or widowers are almost as complex, particularly if it is the first marriage of one of the parties. A widow or widower is not expected to marry for 6 months after the death of his or her spouse, but marriage usually occurs soon after that time. Marriage is regarded as the normal state for an adult, and one who does not marry is thought to be queer. "Here they believe that a man without a woman or a woman without a man cannot be either man or woman and they are not respected." Moreover, life is very difficult for the widow or widower. The woman has difficulty getting her fields properly cultivated, even though she may own sufficient property. A man, unless he has relatives who will take him in, also has great difficulty in getting food, for no man knows how to cook. Women do not wish to take a widower as a boarder, fearing either that he will make some attempt on their virtue or that their reputation will suffer. Husbands are also much opposed to such an arrangement, so the widower must marry, if he is to eat decently.

In Mestizo Chilchota, Rendón found many similarities with the Cherán wedding customs. The bride is sometimes stolen, sometimes not. If stolen and then not married, the girl finds marriage difficult, and mothers will not let their daughters talk to such a girl. Chilchota residents assert that in the Tarascan villages of La Cañada this is not the case, but such evidence from Mestizos is notoriously unreliable.

Generally the bride is stolen. In Chilchota, Rendón definitely secured the impression that this custom is older than asking for the bride. The bride is taken to the house of a friend or to the godparent of baptism of the bride. According to some women marrying in this way, the marriage was not consummated until after the wedding ceremonies; others said they had relations with their husbands the day they were stolen. If the girl is asked for, rather than stolen, the relatives of the groom take mescal and cigarettes when they visit the bride's parents. They are accompanied by an old man skilled in such matters.

The wedding takes place traditionally in the house of the groom, but among the "snobs" it takes place in the house of the bride. Guests take a kilo of salt, a kilo of chiles (preferably dry chiles which are more expensive), several kilos of rice, and a basket of corn or beans. The male relatives of the bride supply one or two loads of wood and also present to the groom agricultural tools if he is a farmer or utensils of his trade if he has some other occupation. The male and female relatives of the groom also dress the bride in a complete new outfit and present her with clothing and household and kitchen equipment. Gifts received by the bride and groom are divided with their respective relatives. The sisters of the groom carry rosaries made of *amole* tubers to indicate that they should wash with this and not with soap. (This statement is ambiguous and needs further investigation; possibly it refers to bathing the bride.)

The church wedding takes place in the early hours of the morning and is followed by a breakfast in the house where the celebration is to be held. Invariably the breakfast consists of bread and chocolate. After breakfast there is a dance, which continues through the day except for intervals in which to eat. The food is *mole* of chicken or turkey, fried rice, beans, and tortillas. After the meal a drink made of pulque and called *charape* is served. If it is not the season for pulque, the *charape* is made of a wild plant resembling the maguey and called timbiriče.

After dancing a while following the dinner, the bride is taken to the house of the godparents of the groom, in case she has been stolen, or to her own parents' house, if she has been asked for. The bride spends the night at this house without her husband. Some time during the day the sisters of the groom wash the bride and dress her.

The following day the godparents of the wedding hold a fiesta in their house similar to that on the preceding day but with some additional features. Early in the morning, when the invited guests arrive, they are served breakfast of bread and chocolate made with water. Then there is dancing. At midday a dinner is served, consisting of many of the typical Tarascan foods such as čurípo (beef broth with cabbage, chile, and meat), kurúndas (yellow tamales), chayote, and cooked squash (*chilacayote*).

About 3 o'clock in the afternoon, while the dancing goes on in the house of the godparents of the wedding, the godparents of baptism of both the bride and groom organize a group to carry the atole. A large *olla* is filled with atole. The *olla* is decorated with green branches, flowers, and paper streamers. A carrying basket full of bread and bottles of *aguardiente* is also carried. The atole can be of whatever type is usual at the season of the year, while the bread must be of the type known as *pan grueso*, "thick bread." Various members of the group take turns carrying the bread and atole. At each corner the person carrying the bread or atole dances, while his companions circle about him.

A group of relatives by marriage of the groom known as the "cats" now attempt to take away the *olla* of atole. They carry bundles of nettles and similar plants and strike the bearers of the atole until they succeed in getting it away. They carry it to a store and "sell" it for *aguardiente* or cigarettes.

Another group, known as the sisters, *hermanas,* composed of consanguineal relatives of the groom, attempt to defend the *olla* of atole. When it is finally stolen, they must "buy" it back from the storekeeper for the value of the goods given to the "cats." This is repeated several times before the atole is finally brought to the house of the godparents about sundown.

The godparents of the wedding meantime have strung a rope across the street and receive the group with the atole with lighted splinters of pitch pine to symbolize their late arrival. For a time the party with the atole are not allowed to pass the rope, but eventually they climb over or under it and get into the house.

The godparents of baptism now give the godparents of the marriage *charape*, mescal, and cigarettes. In return they receive presents of clothing and mescal. In the Tarascan villages of La Cañada it is said the exchange of clothing is much more extensive. A supper is served of tamales, *bunuelos* (a sort of fried bread dough dipped in sugar), and *charape,* and there is more dancing. Later the bride is carried to the house of the parents or relatives of the groom. The relatives of the bride are present. Female relatives of the bride toast chiles on a *comal*, and the groom has to enter the smoke to prove that he is a man. The bride is now given to the groom.

The following day there is a ritual meal in the house of the bride to which come the bride's relatives and many friends. The women of Chilchota often dress in traditional Tarascan costume for this meal, wearing the *rollo* or pleated skirt. They also wear straw hats much decorated with flowers and paper streamers. Men dress in *calzones* or trousers of Indian style. If they have money, a band is hired and the group dances at every corner. The meal served consists of boiled cabbage (without meat or meat broth) and beef tripe cooked with herbs and chile.

Soon after the wedding, the groom takes the bride's parents one or two large baskets of bread, chocolate, sugar, and from $10 to $100 (depending on his economic status) to show his thanks. There is some sort of ceremony in the house of the bride's parents.

In San Juan Parangaricutiro, also primarily a Mestizo town, the male and female relatives of the bride dance in the streets on the day of the wedding. The group has a band and dances at each street intersection in the town, the men in one file, and the women in another. The men make a circuit of the women's file and return to their places. The women do the same and then the group moves to another corner. The persons in the files are arranged according to their stature. A sister of the bride accompanies the group, and represents her. The night after the wedding the relatives of the groom do the same, lighting their way with pitch pine torches.

A dozen or more families in Cherán live in "free union," that is, a couple lives together without marriage. In most cases one or both parties to the arrangement have been married previously and divorced according to Cherán standards but not according to law. The majority of such free unions are said to result in successful households, and children of such unions suffer no stigma. Children of free unions inherit from their parents in the same fashion as children of legal or church marriages. This type of union is said to be fairly recent, and at first persons living in this fashion were not permitted by the priest to hold any church office or to act as godparents. Children of free unions were also refused baptism. In recent years it is said that these restrictions have disappeared.

One reason for the free union is the difficulty of securing a legal divorce. Such a divorce can be granted only by a court of first instance (*juzgado de primer instancia*). The nearest court of this kind is in Uruapan, and to secure a divorce requires many trips to Uruapan and an outlay of more money than most Cherán residents can afford. Moreover, most people do not understand the needed steps.

Causes of divorce are drunkenness, wife beating, failure to support the family, or abandoning the family for another woman on the part of the man. On the part of the woman, infidelity is an important cause. Lack of children is rarely if ever the direct cause of divorce, and is not recognized as a sufficient reason. Incompatibility evidently may play a part also. Uncles and grandfathers of the married couple and the godparents of the marriage intervene if a marriage is not going smoothly, and attempt to persuade the couple to change their habits.

In all cases of divorce for whatever cause, the officials of the *municipio* investigate. If they find the divorce not justified, the officials may force the couple to continue living together. If the causes are deemed sufficient, the officials do not interfere, although they may supervise disposition of children so that they will have the best care. If children are less than 6 or 7 they are usually put in charge of the mother. Over that age they are usually given to the parent best able to rear them properly. If the mother is industrious and the father a drunkard, the children will be given to the mother, but if the mother is careless of her obligations, the father will receive the children. Dislike or quarrels rarely arise between relatives of a divorced couple. In free unions, as in marriages of widows or widowers, sometimes a parent is jealous of the spouse's children by a previous marriage, sometimes not.

ADULT LIFE

Entry into adult status is closely associated with marriage. Normally a child is not consulted in family affairs until he is married; the only exceptions are a few families where youths have not married at the customary ages. Usu-

ally by the time of marriage, individuals of both sexes have mastered the essential technologies for carrying on life.

Nevertheless, marriage rarely if ever means complete independence for either sex. The couple almost invariably lives with the groom's parents after the marriage, usually for a year or longer. Even if the husband has enough resources to set up a separate establishment, he will rarely do so until after the first child is born and often he will not do so for several years.

For the wife, this appears to be a somewhat difficult time. She is definitely under the thumb of her mother-in-law and for the first month after the wedding she is supposed to get up before daylight and make atole for everyone living in her new home. She is sent on errands and given orders constantly. Nevertheless, the difficulties can easily be overemphasized by a person from outside the culture. The bride is called "daughter" by her mother-in-law and in large measure is treated exactly as a daughter would be. In the relatively few instances in which it was possible to observe behaviors, outwardly a friendly and perhaps even affectionate relationship existed between mother and daughter-in-law, although one woman said she greatly feared her parents-in-law, who were very hard on her.

Although the daughter-in-law appears to be imposed upon by her mother-in-law to some extent, in some sense this is part of the process of gaining adult status and of the retirement of the parents to a less active life. The father does less work in the fields and leaves more and more of the harder labor and more and more of the responsibility to his son. In the same way, the mother leaves more and more of the running of the house to her daughter-in-law. If the parents have worked hard and have accumulated a reasonable amount of property, some of which they have probably expended in giving their children a proper marriage, it is considered right and proper that they should begin to work less hard.

After a year or more of marriage, or after the birth of the first child, some change of status will begin to occur. In a minority of cases, a new kitchen will be prepared and the young couple will move out of the "*troje*" where they have lived thus far. In the few cases where this is done, eventually several brothers and their wives may live in adjoining kitchens and the economic enterprises of the family will be carried on as a unit under the direction of the father. In such cases a joint purse will be kept by the parents or one of the older brothers. All important activities will be subject of discussion and consultation, particularly such matters as buying or selling land, building a new house, etc. In time, the direction of affairs will pass to the younger men, usually the older brother directing and giving final decisions. The extent to which the father will be consulted as he grows old will depend in part on his individual merits.

More commonly a joint family will not be established even though the son and his wife may remain living in the family residence. If the parents can afford it, they may give the son a lot or even a house and lot where he can live. Lacking parental aid, the son will do everything he can to acquire a new house and lot. Or his wife may own a house and lot which she has inherited and in which the couple will live.

Much the same situation will obtain regarding farm lands. A father may give his son some farm lands when he has shown he is able to manage his affairs properly. Or the son may work for others and save money to begin acquiring his own land. And in a considerable proportion of cases the wife will own lands which the husband will farm. In some cases, even though a joint family is not established, a son will take over management of the farm lands.

Lacking farm lands, the man will work for others as a laborer, become a trader going down to the hot country, work in the forest cutting ties, shakes, or lumber, or work at some trade if he knows one. In any case he may do some of these things on a part-time basis to supplement his income.

In addition to acquiring a house and lands, the couple needs to assemble the proper tools and furnishings. Although none of these are expensive, in the aggregate they require a bit of time, either to earn money to buy them or to make them. A census of the things found in a house, kitchen, and yard gives some idea of the amount of accumulation required.

Objects found in a house or "*troje*":

Sleeping mats
Small table
Chairs, either low chairs, regular size chairs, or stools, one for each man in the household and usually two or three for guests.
Serape, worn by the man during the day and serving as a blanket for man and wife at night. A second *serape* will often be found if there are children.
Chest, box, or trunk for extra clothes
Saint's picture
Candle and candle holder
Flower holder
Ladder for getting to loft
Gun (sometimes)
Cross beam suspended from the ceiling on which are hung clothing, blankets, etc.

Objects found in the kitchen:

Wooden hooks for hanging up "anything"
Stump and flat stone for burning pitch pine for light
Corn husk mats for holding up pots (at least three)
Large comal
3 "frying pans" of Patamban pottery for cooking meat
1 "frying pan" of Patamban pottery for cooking eggs
Several round and oblong wooden bowls
Grass-root pot brush
Atole strainer
4 cane splint baskets of various sizes
2 pottery jars
Broom for sweeping yard (of brush)
Broom for sweeping house (of broom straw)
Paring knife
Bowls of Quiroga ware or Guanajuato ware for serving broth and meat on special occasions
Charcoal-burning flat iron
Gourd canteens for use at harvest time or in woods
½ dozen china plates
½ dozen china cups
Tea pot
China bowls
½ dozen wooden spoons of various sizes
Tin can for dipper to fill water jars
Chocolate beater
Tortilla baskets
2 water ollas
1 small pitcher
5 large 2-handled pots
8 smaller 1-handled pots
Clay fireplace
Firefan
Small metate for chiles
Large metate for maize

Table
3 chairs (usually small low style)
Machete
½ dozen spoons
2 table forks (rare)
1 table knife (rare)
1 can opener (rare)

Objects found in a lot:
Pear picker (if there is fruit on the lot)
Hollowed logs for water and feeding pigs
Smooth rock and wooden paddle for washing
    clothes
Wooden pitchfork
Wooden hook
Carrying crate with tumpline (occasional)
Frame for carrying water *ollas* on donkeyback
    (occasional)
Clay oven with shovel and broom (occasional)
Hoe

In addition to these items there are the tools of work to be acquired. A farmer needs a plow, yoke, goad, oxen, carrying nets, weeding machete, and perhaps other items. A forest worker needs an ax, a hafted blade for splitting shakes, a wooden mallet, oak wedges, a 2-man crosscut saw about 8 feet long, and an oil can (to oil the saw). A mason will need a trowel, hammer, sledge hammer, and string for guide and plumb lines. A traveling merchant will need burros, pack saddles, and halters.

Clothing must also be secured. The man will own *huaraches*, or sandals, two or three pairs of *calzones*, or cotton trousers, often a pair of overalls, a pair of shoes, shirts, knitted cotton undershirts, a blanket or poncho, belt, straw hat, straw or rubber raincoat, a rubber cover for the hat, and a Catholic amulet. In addition, many will own a jacket or coat and pair of trousers of "citified" style to wear when going to Uruapan.

The wife will need a skirt, petticoat, blouse, sashes, jacket, shawl or *rebozo*, bead ornaments, and shoes for special occasions. For working about the house she may have a few cheap cotton dresses of Mestizo style.

As children arrive, clothing must also be provided. Boys usually own *calzones* or cotton trousers with a strap fastening, straw hat, small blanket, shirt, sandals, and perhaps an amulet. Girls will have skirt, petticoat, blouse, jacket, sashes, *rebozo*, and sometimes shoes.

Not everyone will have the above things, but some will have more. The lists given are based on actual inventories of a few middle-class homes and persons.

In addition to a house and kitchen, which constitute the Cherán minimum of decent housing, there are also many other structures to be built, mostly by the man himself. If he has burros or cattle, he will have a shed used as a stable when the animals are kept at the house. A pigpen is usually built of small poles, often with a shake roof over all or part of it and an opening to the street. Additional storage space for fodder or straw is often provided, usually a pole construction roofed with shakes. The lot needs to be fenced with poles and the street side preferably should have a wall of stone or stone topped with adobe bricks. A substantial gate with a sheltering roof is regarded as a virtual necessity.

Most of the family life goes on in the kitchen. Cooking, eating, and sleeping all take place in the one structure. In fine weather, people may sit outside or sit on the porch of the house. Guests may sleep in the house, and when a son marries he and his bride will occupy the house for a year or more. Much of the business of living takes place in the lot, in the fields and mountains, and in the streets of the town.

When children come, the acquisitive activities of the family become even more important. Now, not only is there a desire to secure the minimum of housing, food, and clothing, as well as the property to make these things possible, but there is the urge to obtain resources with which to start the children out in life. Efforts are made to obtain additional fields and to buy lots so that when the children marry they can immediately have their own home and their own means of subsistence in what Cherán residents regard as the most satisfactory way, that is, by possessing sufficient farm lands.

As solid citizens the family members will also have additional responsibilities. At least one out of four families will hold a *mayordomía* at some time. The father will also serve as *comisionado* for various fiestas, perform some community labor, and serve on the night watch. He may also take some position in the church organization or occupy some office in the municipal government. If he can read and write he almost certainly will at some time be chosen for an office.

Ideally, the objectives of the family are achieved by joint and harmonious cooperation between husband and wife. As in other cultures, there exist households in which there are continual quarreling and dislike between husband and wife, sometimes culminating in divorce. More common seem to be harmonious households in which at least mutual understanding and toleration are achieved; probably in the majority of cases there are also affection and trust. In harmonious households, all activities and plans are discussed by husband and wife. Even though a piece of land is owned by the man, he will consult with his wife before selling it and she will do the same with reference to her property. Important purchases are usually made only after consultation, also. In most cases where trust exists between husband and wife, it is the wife who holds the purse. That is, most actual cash is given to the wife. On her devolves the responsibility for spending the money wisely in small affairs and in accumulating the savings necessary for buying new lands or houses.

In general, the man is definitely the head of the family, but the manner of wielding authority and the degree of authority vary with the personalities of the married couple. If the man owns considerable property and the woman comes from a poor family, the man may enforce his authority by reminding her that she has nothing. There are also cases where the woman owns practically everything and uses the fact to dominate her husband. Ideally, and probably actually in a great many cases, the couple treat their property as being owned in common. In any case, both parents seem to wield about equal authority over the children. Women may give orders to their sons until they marry, just as much as may the men. Girls, on the other hand, are more directly dominated by their mothers, and the father expresses his opinions concerning their upbringing to the mother.

Within the household certain routines and habits are common. Labor is rather strictly divided along sexual lines also. For example, the family usually rises about 5 o'clock in the morning, breakfasts about 8, lunches or dines at 1, and sups at 7:30 or 8, but the hours tend to vary from family to family. The family usually sleeps on mats in the kitchen, husband and wife on one mat with a single blanket. Small children under 9 or 10 years old sleep with the parents; above that age they sleep on separate mats and have a separate blanket.

The general weekly routine of the family of a farmer or of a forest worker, who represent the typical Cherán families, is about as follows. On Sunday most of the women go to Mass at 6:30 or 7. The men may go at this time or wait until the 8 o'clock Mass, or may stay home and sweep the courtyard and street in front of the house. Children usually go to the 8 o'clock Mass. Most people do not eat until after Mass.

After Mass, men stand around the church and plaza or on the streets talking to their friends before going home for breakfast. After breakfasting, the young men get towels and go to the bathing place in one of the *barrancas* (about a mile from town) and bathe. The older men go out and loaf about the streets all morning, talking to friends and acquaintances. Older men bathe less often, but also usually bathe on Sunday. Between 11 and 12 the younger men return home, eat again, pick up their blankets (it is more apt to be windy or rainy in the afternoons) and go out on the streets to meet their friends again. Women may go out after dinner and visit neighbors. Small children, it might be noted, do not go to Mass but play around the house and nearby streets all day. A young unmarried man may hang around the corner near the house of some girl in whom he is interested. If the girl is also interested, she will go out after water several times during the day and the two will talk on the streets. If they are clever and the girl's family is either not very strict or not very suspicious, they may manage to talk together several hours.

At 5 p.m. is the *Rosario*, attended by many women, some men, and many of the young people. After the *Rosario* is the favorite time for stealing a girl for a wedding and, especially in the fall, the young man may be involved in helping his friends. Or he may simply walk along in the direction his girl is going in the hope of having a chance to talk to her. Alternatively, he may talk on the streets with friends or go to one of the billiard parlors. Although people eat later than usual on Sundays, the young unmarried men may not come home until 9 or 10 o'clock, when the family is in bed, and they feed themselves with cold food left for them.

On Monday the men and young men go to the fields or to the mountains between 7 and 9 o'clock, after eating a breakfast which always includes tortillas and chile and likely includes remnants of the previous day's meal such as *sopa de tortilla*. If the men are going out all day and the place is distant, they take a lunch. If the place is nearby, wives carry lunch to their menfolk. Women will take maize to the mill and carry whatever water is needed during the morning. They may also buy some vegetables at the market, although most will have done this at the Saturday market. They may shop for meat and other needed items at the store. The main housework will be sweeping and putting the sleeping mats in the *"troje."* Then the woman will start work on the midday meal for herself and children (earlier if she is to take dinner to the fields, which she will do if her husband is working within an hour's walk). This meal is apt to be quite simple if the husband is not home. Some women make tortillas before dinner and again before supper. Others will eat warmed up tortillas for dinner. After dinner, following about an hour's rest, these women will make up a supply of tortillas sufficient to last 24 hours. An older daughter may be set at this work. In any case, probably 2 hours will be put in making tortillas and preparing supper. Men who went for firewood will probably be home as early as 4 o'clock, others not until 5 or 5:30, while those who had to look for a strayed animal or who are delayed for other reasons may come in after dark. The men of the family will eat together; the women and children usually eat together but after the men. Before he eats, a man may have to water and feed his animals, unless there is a small boy who can do it.

After supper a man will often go out on the street for about an hour to loaf and talk to friends. Young men will go out and stay longer; they are usually the last to bed. Small children are put in bed about 8 o'clock.

Some families vary the schedule given above. In a fair number of cases the men of the family rise before the women and go to the fields without breakfast. The woman in this case usually takes the maize to the mill or grinds it herself, in the meantime making atole. The men return about 10 for breakfast (*almuerzo*). Usually the women and children already have eaten, but some women wait until their husbands have eaten.

Tuesday, men go out as on Monday. Women may wash clothes on Tuesday, in which case they leave home at 8 and do not return until about 2. There is no regular wash day for all of Cherán, but each woman usually has a regular wash day. Customarily women bathe when they wash clothes.

Subsequent days of the week until Saturday are much the same, the main variation being in the time of washing. Some younger girls and boys go to church between 11:30 and 1 o'clock for doctrinal training from Monday through Friday. About a fourth of the younger boys also go to school.

Saturday the men come home early, usually by 3:30. They loaf about street corners, the plaza, billiard parlors, and saloons. There is a small market in the plaza and women shop and talk there between about 5 and 7. Sometimes a man sees his wife at the plaza and goes home with her, or seeing her leave he may follow a few minutes later. Saturday night supper is the best meal of the week. It features fish, if possible, and there may be special treats such as fruit, peanuts, cherimoyas, sugarcane, avocados, or other items, depending on the season. Supper is late, often between 8 and 10, and the family goes to bed soon afterward.

In some ways the activities of men are less varied and complex than those of the women. A man works at his fields or his trade as it is necessary. When slack time occurs, he goes for firewood or does odd jobs about the house. He serves on the *ronda* or night watch and does other municipal jobs when called upon to do so. In his free time he may sit about home or go out on the streets or to the plaza.

It would be a mistake to assume, however, that the man's life is an unending cycle of labor, broken only by Saturday afternoons and Sundays. Young men, of course, spend more time in recreation than do older people. Agustín Rangel, who probably represents a somewhat extreme case, remembered the following activities:

Agustín arrived in Cherán from the United States on January 25, 1940. For 17 days he did not eat at home. There were no fiestas but he was "taken around." He was brought chocolate and bread before he got up. February 5 there was a wedding, which he attended for a while in the evening and part of the next day. February 6 was Carnival and he went on horseback to Nahuatzen, where he followed the music about for a time. In March, during Holy Week, he went to church Thursday, Friday, and Saturday. He spent some time watching the *Judíos* chase small boys with their spears. The boys blew whistles to annoy them. Between Carnival and Holy Week there were several weddings, but he did not attend any of them for more than an hour or two. At the fiesta of the Octava following Holy Week he spent 4 days going about with the musicians. He spent 3 days at a fiesta in Nahuatzen, coming home each night. At Corpus he spent 4 days, following the music and visiting various parties. He spent 1 day at the *carguero's* house on the day of San José, April 10. After Corpus he spent a whole day at one wedding and an hour or two at another. On San Juan's day, June 24, he spent the whole day watching the horse racing and other activities. On the day of San Pedro in June he ate posole at various houses and walked around all day. In August he spent 2 more days at another fiesta in Nahuatzen and spent an evening and a day in connection with the *mayordomía* of Santa Nieves. He also attended three weddings, spending an entire day at each. In September he visited the Ahuiran fiesta for 1 day. In October he spent 4 days at the fiesta of the patron saint in Cherán. A half day was spent at the Huansito fiesta in La Cañada. The Day of the Dead was almost all spent at the graveyard and at people's homes. In December he danced with the *negrito* dancers for 4 days and in January danced with the *viejos* or *Europeos* for 4 days (he did not count any of the practice time which was in the evenings). In January he spent 1 day at a wedding.

Another informant, between 40 and 50 years of age, spent the following time in fiestas:

Carnival, 2–3 hours
Wedding, 1 day
Holy Week, 3 days at church
Octava, 4 days
Corpus, 4 days
Nahuatzen fiesta, 1 day (got drunk)
San Juan, 1 day
San Pedro, 1 day (wife's father had a little fiesta; got drunk)
Nahuatzen fiesta, 1 day
San Francisco fiesta, Cherán, 4 days
Wedding, 1 day
Wedding, 1 day
Negrito dancers, watched 1 day
Wedding, 1 day
Funerals, remembers two, but not certain.

Aside from the funerals, this informant remembers spending over 24 days in entertainment during the year. Agustín, on the other hand, spent 41 days (aside from the time after he first arrived in town), at least 6 days being spent at weddings and 8 days in dancing. From various information collected, it seems reasonable to believe that most men spend at least 20 days in weddings, fiestas, and similar entertainment, while young men probably exceed this figure.

Women, in general, work longer hours at more varied tasks and with numerous interruptions. While women also attend fiestas and weddings in Cherán, they are less apt to go elsewhere. Moreover, even on fiesta days there are meals to prepare and water to carry. Women's work, however, is essentially more social. Water carrying is almost a ritual, as is going to the mill with the maize. Water is almost always carried in special decorated and polished ollas used for no other purpose. Water is dipped out of the fountain in the plaza, the tank at the end of the pipe line, or out of the hollow logs of the aqueduct. The ollas are always carried on the left shoulder on top of the *rebozo*, which forms a sort of pad. Women often go in groups after water and the task is frequently an occasion for meeting friends and talking. Taking maize to the mill is less formalized behavior, but it, too, is a social occasion, which may take 15 minutes and may take an hour, depending on the time of day and the number of friends encountered. Most women prefer to go at a rush hour when they have to stand in line, because they meet so many friends.

The best picture of women's activities may be presented by giving a number of actual cases. Women's work varies greatly with the size of the family and the age of the children. Most women had no clear idea of the time spent, and the following figures are guesses given under some pressure.

CASE 1

(3 adults in family.)

	Hours
Going to mill	½
Carrying water (3 ollas in morning, 2 in afternoon)	1 or 2
Making tortillas	1 or 2
Other food preparation	2 or 3
Washing clothes and taking bath on Wednesdays	5
Sweeping (not every day)	½ to 1
Marketing	½
Shelling corn:	
Green	¼
Dry	½
Visiting neighbors	Variable
Resting	Variable
Minimum daily schedule	6
Total waking hours	13

CASE 2

(Family of 8; two girls, one about 8, one about 13. Woman helps in store owned by family in spare time but both girls help, take maize to the mill, etc. Following is estimate of the day preceding the interview.)

	Hours
Going to mill	¼
Shelling corn	2
Making tortillas	2
Carrying water (met friends)	2
Washing clothes (Friday)	2
Sweeping (daily)	¼
Marketing (longer if she meets friends)	½
Food preparation	3
Care of children	No idea
Visiting friends—does not go out, friends visit her in store	None
Estimated total on ordinary days (not including work in store and caring for children)	10

CASE 3

(Family of 6; 4 children, all big enough to care for themselves; woman also helps in store.)

	Hours
Mill	½ to 1
Making tortillas	4
Carrying water (3 or 4 ollas)	1
Ironing (Friday or Saturday)	2
Sweeping (daily)	½
Marketing	½
Food preparation	3
Daily minimum, about	10

In addition to above, washes 1 day a week, 7 hours. Also goes occasionally to Parícutin for an hour to interview a debtor.

Waking hours, about	15

CASE 4

(A widow. Several adults in family; woman assisted by daughter-in-law.)

	Hours
Making tortillas	½
Carrying water (10 ollas with assistance of daughter-in-law)	½
Cooking	1½
Sweeping (twice a week)	¼
Marketing (average)	½
Shelling corn	½
Daily minimum	4 to 5

In addition, washing and bathing on Wednesday consume 6 to 7 hours. On Thursdays the informant goes to the Paraje to gather herbs, about a 2-hour trip each way. From Saturday to Monday the informant is in Uruapan selling the herbs.

CASE 5

(3 adults in family.)

	Hours
Water carrying, 5 to 7 ollas morning and afternoon (estimate)	1
Tortillas, morning and afternoon (total)	2
Shelling corn—buys it shelled	....
Going to mill	5/12 to 1
Marketing	½
Food preparation	½ to 1
Sweeping (once a week)	½
Washing and bathing every Thursday, about	5
Daily minimum, about	5

Despite the few hours appearing in the statement, the informant said she had little time to rest.

CASE 6

(3 people in family.)

	Hours
3 ollas of water, morning and afternoon	½ to 1
Tortillas	1
Going to mill	½ to 1
Shelling corn	½
Sweeping	¼
Food preparation	1
Marketing	½ to 1
Resting	1 to 2
Daily minimum (exclusive of rest period) about	5¼

Visits neighbors a little.
Clothes washing 8 a. m. to 1 p. m., Tuesdays.

CASE 7
(3 people in family.)

	Hours
Tortillas (½ hour morning and afternoon)	1
Going to mill	½
Carrying water, 3 ollas, twice a day	⅔
Preparing food	⁷⁄₁₂
Marketing	½
Sweeping	¼
Shelling corn	½
Visiting mother daily	1
Care of child	2 to 3
Resting	½
Daily minimum (exclusive of rest periods) about	5

Washing and bath, Fridays, about 4 hours.

CASE 8
(4 people in family.)

	Hours
Tortillas, morning and afternoon, total	1½
Going to mill	¼ to ¾
Carrying water (5 to 7 ollas daily)	⅔
Preparing food	⅔
Sweeping (twice a week)	½
Marketing	⅓
Shelling corn	⅔
Resting	½ to 1
Visiting, not every day	1
Daily minimum (exclusive of resting and visiting)	5½

Washing and bath, Wednesdays, 9 a. m. to 1 or 2 p. m.

None of the women interviewed were too poor to pay for having their maize ground. If they had ground their own maize on the metate, the hours of labor would have been materially increased.

In addition to learning the techniques of earning a living and acquiring the necessary sense of responsibility to manage one's affairs, adult life usually requires the learning of a number of rules of behavior. Adults should know that it is never proper to enter a house yard without an invitation, even though it be unfenced. Visitors knock on the gate or call out until an invitation is given. Usually someone comes to the gate to inquire what is wanted, unless the person is very well known. Men are never invited in unless the man of the household is present. If one calls on a person about business, one always stands and talks about other things for a bit first.

When one meets friends of the same sex, one says "Good day," "Good afternoon," or "With God" (*Buenos días, buenos tardes, adiós*). If persons stop to talk, they touch hands in greeting and on farewell. A person of opposite sex, if well known, will be greeted in the same way verbally, but the hands will not be touched and, unless the persons are relatives or *compadres*, they will not stop and talk.

If a man visits a friend in his field or his *solar* when he is working, he always helps a bit. A woman calling at the house will help a little with any work going on. If one sees a stray animal and knows the owner, it is good manners to take it to him; if the owner is unknown, the animal should be taken to the municipal building. If one is in a group and people become angry, efforts should be made to dissuade them from fighting unless they are drunk. It is all right to drive another person's dog away (although usually people just give strange dogs a wide berth), but a pig should never be molested unless it is trespassing. It is not proper to punish another person's child, but if he throws a rock, for example, it is all right to throw rocks back.

If you hear a piece of land is for sale and do not know the owner, you get all the information you can about the land and then send the person giving the information to talk to the owner. If you know the owner you go yourself. Most commonly the owner will come to you. It is proper to stand and talk about other things for a while and then make an appointment to go to see the land. On the trip, the final arrangements about the price are usually thrashed out if you decide to buy the land. Then you go together to the municipal building and have a bill of sale made out, for which you pay.

At meals the oldest man present is served first, unless there is a male guest present. Then the other men are served and then the women and children. Of course, there are always the small children who come about pestering their mothers for a tortilla and, as Agustín remarked, "Of course you want to get rid of those guys first." When water is passed around and one drinks out of a common pitcher, it is polite to pour a little water on the ground, over the part of the rim the lips have touched, before passing the pitcher on.

Adults bathe fairly regularly on their own initiative. Young men and women usually bathe at least once a week; older men may not bathe more than once a month. Most people go to a special bathing place, Uékuaro, a waterfall in one of the *barrancas* beyond Parícutin, but women sometimes bathe at home. The bathing place at Uékuaro is reserved for men on Saturday, Sunday, and Monday; for women the rest of the week. Most people soap themselves freely and shampoo the hair thoroughly. Young men seemed a bit shy when bathing, often covering the genitals with the hand when turning toward others, but older men and boys seemed to have no self-consciousness.

Head lice afflict many if not all Cherán residents, especially children. Delousing is a common occupation when women are visiting or resting with the children about. Men also delouse the children, but a man was never seen being deloused. Sunny days when people sit about the house yards are a favorite time, but delousing was never seen on the streets.

Most adults possess a fairly common set of likes and dislikes, some of which have been developed during childhood, others acquired as adults. Perhaps the strongest likes are for the fiestas, *mayordomías*, and weddings. These are the core of the *costumbres* and Cherán people are as passionately attached to the body of practices they call customs as are most Mexican Indian groups. Most people are also fond of flowers, and almost every house has a little flower garden. Shasta daisies, dahlias, iris, larkspurs, marigolds, geraniums, calla lilies, roses, and gladiolus are the most popular plants. Fancy pottery, especially the green glazed ware of Patambán and La Cañada, the brown or black glazed ware of Santa Fe and Quiroga, and the colored glazed wares of Guanajuato and, to a lesser extent, Guadalajara, are all prized and accumulated for special occasions. Lacquered plates and gourds are also liked. Many have a real passion for collecting miniatures of the material artifacts of Tarascan life. Miniatures are found on sale in abundance at every fiesta and might be mistaken for playthings, but they are all bought by adults who hang them up in the kitchen and the *"troje."* Both sexes like

drinking *charanda*, but only men get drunk outside the fiestas and weddings.

Music is liked by both sexes. All ages will gather to hear a phonograph, regardless of what it plays. Boys gather to play the harmonica and sing, often dancing the *jarabe tapatío*. Older men often play instruments and will gather together in their spare time simply to play for the fun of it. Women never play instruments, although they may sing.

Fireworks, magicians, and ventriloquists will always draw crowds at fiestas. Several years before the study some of the "progressive" families had social dances in their houses, with ballroom dancing. The leaders were a group of sisters who had lived outside the town. They later married and left the town, and the practice ceased.

Women visit and talk together a good deal. Much of the embroidery and crocheting done is for amusement as well as for sale.

Some men like gambling for small sums. Gambling devices at fiestas are always well patronized. A few years ago card games, especially poker, were introduced by men who had been in the United States. Games are played at the billiard parlors, mostly by younger men. The billiard games are also patronized primarily by the young men. Perhaps 4 or 5 men in town smoke marihuana, growing it in their lots. Cigarettes are the common smoke of the majority; most adult males, and many adult women, smoke. Cheap "tailor-made" cigarettes are smoked, usually a brand known as Tigres.

Tastes are fixed even in some matters of dress. Men in Cherán all wear dark serapes and blue sashes. The bright rose and blue serapes of Capacuaro are never seen, nor are the red or white sashes of other towns. Some say the dark colors are faster, others say the bright colors are only for boys, and a few say that the dark colors were more "civilized." As Miguel O. de Mendizabal pointed out in conversation, the first mark of urban influence in Mexico is usually the disappearance of the brighter serapes.

Women have similar habits, although perhaps they are more traditional. Of the several belts worn by women in the traditional costume, unmarried girls put the brightest outside; married women wear the darkest outside.

Undoubtedly the greatest amusement in Cherán is simply talking. Both men and women gather in their spare time and talk by the hour. Most of the talk is gossip. Who has recently done what, the price of corn, the condition of the crops, the change in the weather, forthcoming events, the problems of the church, the progress of the war, what one would do if the Germans came to Cherán—all the everyday things of life and a great deal of speculation about the unknown form subjects of conversation. The North American members of the staff found two questions most common in 1940 and 1941—what were the chances of getting work if one went to the United States, especially since the rearmament program, and what did we think of the progress of the war. Particularly on the subject of the war and its economic repercussions for Cherán did men seem surprisingly well-informed, considering the few who read and the scarcity of newspapers.

With all the talk that goes on in Cherán for amusement's sake, one would expect to find an important repertory of tales. This is not the case. No doubt one could collect a body of tales if one cultivated the older people assiduously. The tales that were found were few, and the majority of them circled about hidden treasure. In addition, there were a few dealing with supernatural happenings and some fragments about the founding of Cherán. Even these prosaic stories had to be sought for diligently and were told badly and in obviously incomplete form. Most persons questioned could not recall any specific occasion on which tales had been told, nor did they know any stories themselves. Story telling is not a significant part of the culture of Cherán.

OLD AGE

The transition from adult to old age is not a clear one in Cherán. In general, parents whose children are all grown up, married, and moved away from home are not necessarily "old" by Cherán standards. At least one individual apparently over 80 years old was encountered who still did his own farm work, was completely self-supporting, and an inde-

fatigable dancer at fiestas. By any standard this man is old, but he certainly shows no sign of senescence, although it is unlikely he is still sexually potent. Similarly, women obviously far past child-bearing age are often the most active workers at fiestas and the most eager dancers, in contrast to the often lackadaisical attitudes of young mothers who dance not at all.

For women the menopause comes between 40 and 50. Information from women on sexual subjects is difficult to secure even by women, and the scanty information is quite unsatisfactory.[38]

Some women appear to be more or less spiritless and sad after the menopause, while others seem to be quite gay. In some cases this difference may have psychological basis or may reflect the presence or absence of physiological difficulties. Indifference of husbands, the sexual potency of husbands, and the continuance of sexual relations may also have some bearing on individual cases. At least one woman expressed herself as pleased to have passed the menopause because "now she was free" and was not dependent upon men. Further study of the problem is needed but would require considerable time and tact on the part of women investigators.

In general, whether old age is depressing and unhappy or not seems to depend upon the continuance of a successful marital relationship and the possession of adequate economic resources. The only really unhappy old people seem to be elderly women without children or husbands who eke out a miserable existence in ways that could not be discovered. They dwell in hovels and lean-tos of brush and boards, carry their own wood, and to some extent live on charity. Those with reasonable health and either dutiful children or enough property to insure care on the part of the children seem to lead a fairly satisfactory life. Often nephews and nieces also help care for old people; again, possession of property probably aids in securing

[35] Early in the study Mrs. Ruth W. Beebe, of New York, aided by the nurse from the boarding school at Paracho and by a Mestizo girl from Paracho, tried to fill out comprehensive questionnaires on sexual subjects, directed primarily toward gaining insight into the psychological problems related to the menopause. She was able to secure only three reasonably complete schedules and even these probably contain evasions and some unanswered questions. I am indebted to Mrs. Beebe for copies of the schedules and have drawn upon them slightly for these remarks.

proper care.   But helpless old people are few in Cherán.   Most old people, even though they may not perform an equal share of the labor, keep fairly active and useful.

SICKNESS AND ITS CURE

Ideas about sickness and its cure are in a state of transition in Cherán.   The list of diseases is a combination of standard medical terms, sometimes misapplied, and names from traditional sources.   Treatment of disease is likewise changing rapidly.   Some people in town will go to a clinic in Parácho and in serious cases will send for the doctor there. For part of the time of the study a *practicante* in medicine was resident in the town (a *practicante* is a medical student who has completed all his work but has to spend 8 months in a town without a doctor and write a report on medical and health conditions before receiving his final credentials).   Very few people evince any dislike for doctors; if they shun doctors it is because of the expense involved. On the other hand, most of the local curers are reticent and uncommunicative, although many of them make use of remedies purchased in the drug stores of nearby towns (Cherán has no drug store).

All the curers (*curanderas*—šuríjki; in other towns *ɸinájpiri*) located in the town were women.   Usually they are middle-aged or old. In those cases where biographical data could be secured, the majority were daughters or granddaughters of curers.   In some cases they had been taught, but apparently few of them used their knowledge until they became of mature years.   Very few curers profess to cure all illnesses; usually they claim to cure two or three and in some cases only one.   Twenty-five centavos is the usual charge for curing, whether the patient comes to the curer's house or the curer visits the patient.   One curer visited had the reputation of being a "bad" witch, another a "good" witch, but generally the curers are not witches.   Some rejected indignantly the idea of having anything to do with witchcraft, denying even ability to cure witchcraft.   Anything to do with witchcraft is a *maloficio* and not to be touched by ordinary persons.

Ideas of sickness are varied.   Injuries, such as broken bones, dislocated joints, and wounds, are recognized as of mechanical origin.   Some diseases are vaguely regarded as of natural causation and as possibly contagious; others are clearly of supernatural character even though curable by natural means, although the line between the two is not sharp.   In either case, herbs, unguents, and drugs are believed capable of helping the sickness.   To utilize these methods of curing requires no special ability but merely knowledge.   Many minor ailments are treated at home; the curer is merely a person of greater knowledge who is called in when home remedies fail or the case is obviously beyond the knowledge of the household. Similarly, the doctor at Parácho is called only when the curer fails or the case is believed beyond the curer's powers.   Obviously, this situation has not greatly enhanced the reputation of the doctor, for most of his patients are nearly moribund some hours before he can reach them.

Curers usually make a diagnosis first.   No information on methods could be secured.   It appears that a visual inspection and questioning of the patients are parts of the diagnosis, and possibly the only diagnosis.   Once the diagnosis is made, the curer decides what steps to take to cure the patient.   Often herbs kept on hand can be used; others, however, must be specially sought because they must be collected either fresh or at certain hours of the day.

In general, sickness by some is related to the strength of the blood which resides below the nape of the neck.   This is also the location of the individual's life.   Persons with much blood are healthy.   When persons are seriously ill, it is because their blood is scanty; when there is insufficient to nourish the "seat of life," the person dies.   There are also vague concepts of sickness being caused by "heat" or "cold," (sophisticated Agustín attributed a cold to drinking water while sweating) "airs" (which may also be either hot or cold), fright (*espanto*), and, much more specific, evil eye.

Broken bones are treated by specialists, who may also be curers of diseases or, in one case at least, midwives.   The bones are manipulated into place and bound to splints without other treatment.

Dislocations are massaged repeatedly with olive oil until the bones are back in place.   They are then covered with belladonna leaves. Bruises are sometimes cured by splitting a lizard and applying it to the injured place.

Hernia is recognized as being from natural causes through lifting heavy weights. One curer treats the ailments with massage with oils. The patient also takes medicine made by collecting all the kinds of alcoholic drinks the curer can find, such as *charanda,* sherry, etc., and mixing them together. The patient takes a third to a half cup of the mixture every morning before breakfast.

Headache, ép'ameráni, is extremely common and is ordinarily treated with home remedies. A patch of some herb (or of adhesive plaster or court plaster bought in the stores) is applied to each temple. Some people wear these patches almost constantly, especially some women.

Bilis, bile, is one of the commonest diseases, especially among children; it also is one of the most difficult to define. Often the vaguest of symptoms are attributed to *bilis.* Lassitude, especially in young persons, often is diagnosed as *bilis.* According to one curer, however, the patient turns yellow, seems tired, and develops sores similar to those of smallpox. Three causes are given for *bilis,* air in the stomach from waiting too long for a meal, not getting enough to eat and so getting air in the stomach, and getting air in the stomach from any other cause. Children are sometimes born with *bilis* and are thought to become infected in the womb. Treatments of *bilis* are vague. *Flor de pila* well cooked with cinnamon, and given by the teaspoon as a tonic, and an infusion of *simonillo* are two remedies. *Amargo* (see below) is another remedy.

Stomach pains are also regarded as being caused by air, either hot or cold. *Basa,* a pain on either side, is also caused by air, or by drinking too much water. *Espinocilla,* a red-flowered plant, is good for both these afflictions. Nopal leaves are put on the soles of the feet for too much heat in the stomach. (See below for account of a cure of one of the members of the staff.)

Itch or mange, *sarna,* súta, is treated with unguents purchased in the drug store, polvo Juan and mercuric ointment.

Heart trouble, *latido de corazón,* is recognized from pains in the heart and by palpita-

tions. There is a high fever, a cough, and sometimes the patient spits blood. The patient is rubbed with oil of seven different flowers, bought in the drug store, and given an infusion of sunflowers, spines from the tejecote tree, prickly pear, chayote, and dry white and red maize leaves. The infusion is taken several times a day in place of. water. The disease may be caused if the person arrives somewhere very agitated and drinks cold water or something cold, *fresca.* One informant thought eating lice was good for heart trouble.

Piles, *almorranas,* are cured with a remedy made with copper sulfate and lard washed with vinegar, unguent of serato, and drying salve (*pomada secante*). One of the assistants was told confidentially, and as a thing not to be passed on, that cauterization with a hot iron was also employed.

Erysipelas, čarápiti, appears with a high fever, which increases. There is angry red swelling and much pain. The cause given is allowing the clothing to dry on the body if one becomes soaked; the disease is also an accompaniment of wounds. The patient is given a cooked infusion of *yerba de cancer* and asked to eat only milk, sago, and orange-leaf tea.

Salmoneda is a disease of small children; they fall down in fits. The cause is fright, *espanto,* and the disease is cured by burning copal and having the child inhale the smoke.

Smallpox, kuarósikua, occurs every March. There are 3 days of fever, 3 days of cough and .fever accompanied by breaking out of the pustules, 3 days of feeding to regain strength. After the sixth day the pustules begin to dry up. Possibility of contagion from using the same cup, spoon, etc., is recognized. The stage accompanied by the cough is treated with burro's milk (application not clear) and a common herb occurring on the streets, ¢ákua perénš. The latter is boiled and drunk instead of water.

Sarampión, measles, usually occurs in March also and is regarded as much more dangerous than smallpox (although this may be true, it seems more likely that the identification of diseases is faulty). The patients get a red rash, fever, and colds. An infusion of grapefruit (?) is used to bring out the rash; if the rash does not come out the patient may not recover. Some curers wash their hands in alcohol when treating *sarampión* to prevent catching the infection.

Whooping cough, perénsjuk (*tosferina*), is a very common disease, with a high mortality rate among children. Burro's milk, turpentine, copal, and *yerba buena* are used in treatment.

Syphilis, gonorrhea, diphtheria, and tuberculosis are either unknown or their existence in Cherán is denied. Most of the previously described diseases are recognized as infections by some curers; other diseases are not so considered.

Toothache seems always to be treated by patent medicines bought in drug stores at Uruapan or Purépero. One man said he had heard that letting of blood from the gums was done in the past, but the practice has been abandoned.

Goiter, ku¢ékua, is fairly common in Cherán, especially among females. It is regarded as a disease. Patients are bathed up to the knees with hot water to make the "heat" come down. Alcohol is then applied to the bottoms of the feet to make the "heat" stay down.

An extremely common disease, especially for children in the dry season, is dysentery, *posición*, usually accompanied by high fever. Lard is washed with clean water. When the water is evaporated, a half centavo of sodium bicarbonate is mixed with the lard and the stomach is rubbed with the mixture.

Fevers are said to be very common, but there are few standard treatments. A well-known herb, *romero*, is much used. A blue-flowered plant called *sadadrón* is also employed. Pneumonia and rheumatism are recognized, but, again, there are no standard treatments. Typhus in mild form has occurred in epidemics, but no treatment could be learned.

Pains are regarded as a class of illness. When children have pains, *dolores*, the mother anoints the seat of the pain with saliva mixed with ashes. The water in which maize has been cooked, *nejallote*, is also given in small quantities. This water is also used as a remedy whenever anything "fresh" (*fresco*) is needed. Women after birth are especially subject to pains of the breast, k'uaningiota. The pains may be in the breast, about the stomach region, or anywhere about the ribs. Sometimes

swellings occur in the breast, ribs, or back. A curer specializing in this ailment discovers the seat of the pain by feeling with her fingers. She then anoints the area with unguents purchased in the stores. If the first ones do not work, she then tries others.

The blood of animals is generally regarded as bad and dangerous. The black blood from a butchered animal will cause ulcers if it falls on the skin. The cure is to cauterize the ulcers with a hot iron. The danger from animal blood is said to be the reason many people will not use meat until several days after butchering.

There are a number of treatments of illness which are quite generalized, that is, they may be used on a variety of occasions. For example, *amargo*, is taken in the morning before eating to cure rheumatism, *bilis*, and "fright." *Amargo* is *aguardiente* in which cinnamon bark, sugar, lemon juice, and lemon rind have been steeped for 2 or 3 days. Roses of castile, made into infusions, may be used for any sort of pain or sickness. Persons on the verge of death may sometimes be brought back by putting an onion under their nose or blowing tobacco smoke in their face. A mild diet is frequently used regardless of the illness. Milk and oatmeal gruel are the two most preferred items. Nuríte, a common herb used in cooking, is also widely used for stomach disorders and colics. *Romero*, *quién sabe*, and *yerba buena* are also widely used herbs. Additional herbal remedies have been collected, but the plants have not yet been identified.

Of considerable interest is a class of diseases and ailments which seem to be of supernatural causation. Witchcraft, which has already been discussed (p. 156), is an important cause of illness and death. Others are č'érpiri or jándaku íri ("fright," *espanto*), tariáta pákata ("wind," *aire* or *viento*), and éskukata (evil eye or *mal de ojo*).

Some informants believed that "fright" was something attacking only drunkards and persons who went about at night, and considered it merely seeing ghosts or similar imaginary supernatural things. A curer, however, described to Rendón an elaborate treatment for the disease. The curer puts a bit of cotton over the end of the index finger of her right hand. Over this she puts a green tomato, preferably slightly broiled, on which is sprinkled a little salt. The patient's mouth is opened and the tomato is pressed upward against the soft palate while with the left hand the curer pushes down on the crown of the patient's head. After doing this for some minutes, the tomato is removed from the finger, opened, and rubbed on the crown of the patient's head, on the wrists, and on the joints of the arms. Following this, the patient's head is massaged with gentle pressure, with special attention to the face, the cheek bones, forehead, temples, and occiput. This is called "raising the crown of the head." The treatment is given to both adults and children.

Few data were secured on "wind" or "air." People with the sickness are sometimes said to have been "taken by the wind." In some cases "air" attacks the stomach; some data on treatment have been given above.

The "evil eye" is a very dangerous matter because it attacks mainly small children who are often unable to resist the sickness. Moreover, the power of the evil eye may be possessed by anyone without the knowledge of the possessor. Most commonly persons with the power of the evil eye will afflict individuals of whom they are especially fond. Children who are very pretty or clean and with neatly combed hair are particularly subject to the evil eye. When two persons desire very much to see each other and cannot do so, one is apt to afflict the other with the evil eye; for example, lovers who wish very much to see each other. The evil eye is always believed to be caused unconsciously and without malice.

Symptoms of the evil eye among children are weakness, pale or yellowish complexion, and a tendency to cry a great deal. Adults feel disconsolate; are unable to sleep or, when they do sleep, dream constantly of the person causing the disease, dream someone is calling or talking; or while awake, they think constantly of the person causing the sickness, with feelings of sorrow and pain. In either case, if a cure is not effected, the person dies with vomiting and fever.

In order to cure infants of the evil eye, mothers take their children to a street intersection. All passersby are asked to "clean" the child with their clothing. As everyone knows what is involved, they accede without asking questions. They take one of the garments they have on, such as the end of a *rebozo* or a blanket, and pass it over the infant's body, pretending to rub the child, although actually they often do not touch it. According to Rendón's information, as they "clean" the child each person says "číta ká'ka" (meaning not learned), repeating the phrase three or more times. The person cleaning the child then raises its shirt and either spits on the child over the heart, or pretends to do so. All persons, regardless of age, are asked to "clean" the child, for the evil eye may be caused by a child as well as an adult. This statement would seem to imply that the performance is conducted with the hope that the person causing the attack will be one of those to "clean" the victim; this is borne out by other information that if the person causing the evil eye is known, anyone can effect a cure by "cleaning" the victim with a piece of worn, soiled clothing lent by the causer.

Another method of curing the evil eye is to "clean" the patient with certain grasses or animals. The animals used are pigeons, black cats, and dogs. The entire body of the patient is rubbed with the animal, which is then released. By using only the pigeon or both the cat and dog, a child may be cured, but adults require rubbing with all three. If the evil eye is very strong, the pigeons may die, but the other two animals apparently are uninjured.

In order to prevent the evil eye, "deer eyes" are tied to the wrist or about the neck, or a little sack filled with salt, lime, and black chile is hung about the neck. Adults wear a scapular with a stamp of some saint inside as a preventive.

McCorkle made several efforts to be "cured" in order to secure additional data, but in only one instance was he taken seriously. Even this case is open to suspicion that the curer decided there was a possible gold mine in the situation and tried to exploit it to the limit. The curer in this instance also has the reputation of being a witch and able to turn herself into an owl at night. She refused to talk until her husband arrived, and he actually did most of the talking. They were very suspicious, asking if there were not doctors in Uruapan or in California. This was the usual reaction of other curers who, although less suspicious and more good-natured, simply refused to go further, advising McCorkle to go to a Mexican doctor.

When McCorkle insisted doctors had done him no good and that he had a persistent pain in the stomach, the curer suggested it was indigestion and would go away, asking Agustín privately if McCorkle was not making fun of them. Agustín replied that the curer knew how to tell fortunes so why did she not discover for herself whether McCorkle was sincere. The customary fee of 25 centavos was now offered and the curer and her husband at this point evidently decided that McCorkle could be exploited.

The symptoms recounted to the curer were a sudden pain in the stomach, sometimes after meals, sometimes before breakfast or at other odd times, and poor sleep. The curer asked how long the patient had been in Mexico and where he had slept the first night in Mexico. The curer now unwrapped a deck of cards from a dirty cloth. She shuffled the cards, picked out one, and declared the disease was *maloficina,* an affliction not reported by any other source. Someone had given the patient something to drink so he would have a stomach ache all the time.

The remedy suggested was to take a purge to be bought at the drug store. When asked to recommend a purge, the curer and her husband decided they could capitalize on the situation and said they could get a very superior purge at an old drug store in Purépero for $5.00. When this price was demurred at, the curer finally decided that if the patient was not difficult to purge, $2.50 would secure enough of the purge. The first day after taking the purge, the patient was to stay in bed, as he would sweat; the second day he could get out of bed but should not do heavy work and should eat only toasted white bread and milk. The third day the patient should stay home and on the fourth day come back to the curer and be massaged. During this time the patient could smoke but not drink liquor. A case was cited of a man who violated this prohibition and died shortly afterward.

On McCorkle's return to get the purge, an effort was made to raise the price. When this had been successfully countered, McCorkle asked if the curer could find out who caused the pains. This was said to be difficult because McCorkle had stopped in a hotel instead of with friends on his first night in Mexico. Finally, after consultation of the cards, it was stated that a tall woman with blue eyes had caused the illness "just for fun." This was a person whom McCorkle had "liked very much" in the hotel. At this point they asked Agustín in an aside if McCorkle was "church married" to his wife.

The purge proved to be a packet of herbs and a bottle of oil. New directions were now given for the treatment. Half the tea was to be boiled, sugar added, and the mixture allowed to become lukewarm. The oil, about an ounce and a half, was all to be taken, then the tea. The patient would purge about five times. He should not eat meat, chile, or beans, but could eat cheese, milk, and toasted white bread. The medicine should be taken in the morning and the patient should stay in bed 3 days and not drink water. The patient should not bathe for 6 days. The instructions were somewhat confused because the curer and her husband sometimes simultaneously produced variant instructions, for example, one stating that the patient should return in 4 days, while the other said 6.

A few notes were secured by Rendón in other towns. In San Juan Parangaricutiro the fat of animals mixed with ground river crawfish is rubbed on the body to cause a sweat in cases of pneumonia. Headaches are treated with "patches" covered with melted copal, kurikⱡunda, placed on the temples.

In nearby Parícutin the leaves of the *floripondio* (*Datura* sp.?) are placed on the body to cure pains.

In Capacuaro attacks of "air" may be either hot or cold. If cold, the urine of the patient is mixed with *aguardiente* and rubbed on the joints. When the "air" is hot, the joints are rubbed with ashes. Pains are cured by rubbing the joints with edible oil. Another treatment used in a variety of illnesses is to "take out," *sacudir.* The patient's arms are placed behind his neck and two persons pull on them "until the veins thunder." This is done when the person feels pain over the entire body. The *zorilla* (a wild animal, perhaps a small fox) is used in ways not specified to cure skin diseases with small ulcers or pimples, illnesses of the blood, and pneumonia. Buzzards are also used in some cures, while spiders and snakes are employed in curing *mal oficio* or witchcraft. Green tomatoes are used as food in illness; they are also rubbed over the chest when there is pain, to "freshen it."

The majority of Capacuaro residents have goiter. This is said often to result from drinking from a spring of bad water. The spring is said to be bad because many humming birds drink there. Evidently only acute goiter is believed to be a disease, as the majority of people in Capacuaro consider a certain amount of swelling of the neck to be natural, so common is the affliction. If the goiter becomes too large, a knife is passed over it as though the goiter were being cut out. This is believed to stop its growth. A string about the neck is also thought to stop the goiter from growing (the same belief exists in Cherán) or, when the moon is in the first phase, someone pretends to take bites out of the swelling.

The power of the evil eye belongs only to certain persons in Capacuaro. The face of the person afflicted is suddenly twisted, he feels burning in the face and body and "wishes to take out his heart." The first step in the cure is to cause the patient to sweat freely. The body is "cleaned" with tules; the curer (apparently a man) also rubs the patient with his (the curer's) trousers.

The following remedies are reported by Rendón from Chilchota in La Cañada:

For pains, stitches, or palpitations of the heart:

1. Place on the chest a piece of red Chinese paper cut in a square and previously dipped in tepid alcohol. Over this sprinkle lemon juice and then cover the patient warmly.

2. Give tea of cooked magnolia petals with cinnamon.

3. Give tea from cooked branches of "asparagus" (of a type not eaten).

4. Give hot fresh deer blood as it comes from the animal or dried deer blood dissolved in hot water.

For "attacks," give the patient water which has been heated and into which the nostrils of a recently killed coyote have been placed just before the water reaches the boiling point.

Scorpion stings are treated by giving the patient immediately a drink made by boiling *casaguate* with salt. Another treatment is to give powder produced by rubbing two stones together. The powder is dissolved in water. The wound is also rubbed with lemon juice.

Rabies is treated by giving water in which has been macerated a ball of the male ash tree (male and female trees are distinguished).

Sickly children are treated by bathing them with turtle blood. After a sufficient number of fresh water turtles are collected, they are made to put out the head by putting coals on the shell. The neck is then severed with a single blow of a machete, and the turtle is suspended over the head of the child (who is standing naked) so the blood streams down from head to foot.

DEATH

Death is regarded as a normal event in Cherán and mourning is restrained and, in the main, private. Somewhat more grief is shown when the deceased is a child or a person still vigorous. An old person, who has begun to lose some of his vigor, is often spoken of as only half alive. Similarly, very small children are often regarded as not fully alive. For persons already regarded as not fully members of the community of the living, no great emotional response to death may be expected.

Ideas about death and afterlife are essentially Catholic. Small children who die are believed to go directly to heaven, while adults must pass some time in purgatory. The dead are not particularly feared, nor is it believed that they ordinarily return. However, if a person dreams frequently of a dead relative it is believed that the deceased individual has returned for a member of his family and that one of the household will certainly die. There is no remedy for such a situation.

Because of the different beliefs regarding the afterlife of children and adults, there are some differences in funerals for the two age groups.

In the case of a child, the godfather of baptism provides the burial dress, which is placed on the body by the godmother or the mother, or by the sisters of the mother. The body is not washed. If the deceased is a girl, the dress is a long gown of white with a sort of long cape of blue. The corpse of a boy is dressed in the same way except the inner garment is yellow and the cape is green. In both cases a crown of cardboard, covered with silver paper and decorated with paper flowers, is placed on the head.

The body is placed on a table. Arches of flexible wood, wrapped in paper and decorated with paper flowers, are placed over the body.

A bunch of flowers with a candle in the middle is placed in the hands of the corpse. Preparation of the flowers is done by girls related to the deceased. The body is watched during the night and candles are burned. A "prayer," uandátsikuritíč (*rezador*), is asked to come and pray. He is paid from $0.75 to $1.50 for his service.

In the morning all the relatives assemble and are fed. The food is provided by the parents, but the relatives of the mother aid in its preparation. Opinion is divided regarding aid given the parents. Some say that persons attending the death watch during the night bring *aguardiente* and that all those visiting the house make a present of a few centavos to aid in the expenses. Others denied this custom and claimed the parents must stand all the expense even though they have to sell some property. However, everyone who visits the house brings a candle, which is burned for the deceased.

The body is usually taken to the graveyard sometime during the afternoon. Formerly the body of a child was often accompanied by musicians, but this practice seems to have entirely disappeared, or nearly so. Each family has a plot or section in the graveyard and three or four male relatives prepare the grave in advance of the burial. Four girls, who are relatives of the deceased, carry the body to the graveyard on the table on which it has rested. Often only a few of the closer relatives will go to the graveyard, but the godparents are always present.

At the graveyard the body is removed from the table and placed in a wooden box or coffin. This is lowered into the grave without ceremony by relatives who also fill the grave with earth. Sometimes some of the women will sprinkle a handful of earth on the coffin in the form of the cross before the grave is filled. The arches decorating the table are placed over the grave. There are no prayers or other ceremonies and the party leaves immediately after the grave is filled.

The body of an adult is watched through the night with candles; this night watch is attended by many more people than in the case of an infant and atole made of rice and brown sugar is served at midnight. The corpse is dressed in black clothing of the type worn in life. Nothing is placed on the head. A candle is placed in the hand of the corpse but no flowers. The clothing is prepared by the nearest relatives, the godparents taking no part in the funeral of a person over about 14 years of age.

In the morning the visitors and mourners are served beans and tortillas. At noon it is obligatory to serve broth, čurípo, and white tamales, kuŕúndas (although these are regarded as injurious to the digestion). The food is all prepared by relatives of the wife. The body is taken to the graveyard in a wooden coffin and is carried by four male relatives. A few people take the body first to the church, but generally it is taken directly to the graveyard. In any case, there are never any prayers at the graveyard. As in the case of a child, all the prayers are in the house, usually with the aid of a professional "prayer" or *rezador*. The priest is never asked to officiate, although he may have been summoned while the person was dying. The body is buried in the family plot (but a woman is buried in the plot of her husband's family). In the case of both adults and children a small stoppered *olla* of water is placed at the head of the corpse but outside the coffin. There are no flowers, but each mourner carries a candle.

One evident contradiction between theory and practice was observed. Numerous informants insisted that there was never any music for funerals of adults at any time. In actual fact, several funerals were observed in which music played in the house almost the entire day of the funeral.

In some cases, the interment ends all mourning. In others, the family hires a *rezador* to come to the house every afternoon for 9 days to pray. The members of the family join in these prayers, but it is not necessary for other relatives to do so. However, if a relative attends the first day, he is obligated to continue the entire 9 days. On the ninth day, the *novena* is sometimes observed with prayers in the house. There is no purification or burning of incense or other materials in the house.

After the funeral, the parents or the surviving spouse may remain very sad. If it appears they may be made ill of "sadness," the relatives visit the survivors frequently, talking to them of things which they think may alleviate their condition and giving consolation. If this does not improve matters, they seek a curer who gives medicines.

A very few families pay for Masses for the deceased. More commonly, members of the family of the deceased will visit the church from time to time and burn candles and pray for the dead.

A few additional observations may be of interest. It is said that formerly the bells were tolled 10 or 12 times in the morning and afternoon when someone had died. This is not done now. The graveyard is on the lower edge of town and is surrounded by an adobe wall. In some cases the graves are paved with cobblestones or more elaborate masonry pavements. On rare occasions a tomb or head stone is erected, but in the majority of cases only a wooden cross is put up. The age of the present graveyard is unknown; the oldest date found on a grave was 1883. There is no evidence of offerings (except in connection with the Day of the Dead), although the graveyard is apparently visited at night by some people to judge by the presence of numerous partially burned pitch pine splinters about the entrance. All informants denied knowledge of such visits, however.

The major mourning ceremony is the Day of the Dead, November 2. Several days before this date the graveyard is divided in four sections and the young men from each *barrio* are required by the municipal officials to clear the brush and weeds away from the entire cemetery. On November 1 everyone prepares quantities of nákatamales, a small tamale filled with beef in chile sauce and wrapped in husks rather than maize leaves. Fruit is also purchased and bread is made. A few make tamales for sale, but most people make their own.

The night of November 1, a Mass is celebrated in church. In 1941 the priest spoke to the people against taking candles or food to the graveyard, telling them instead to bring candles to the church. Another Mass is held the morning of the 2d, after which people go to the graveyard. There is no organized procession, nor does everyone arrive at the same time. In many cases only the women and children attend, although usually the men drop in for a short time and some stay for several hours. Indeed, the function is said to be a woman's affair and men may not carry candles or even take part if they have no women folk.

Generally, the first thing the visitors do is to more thoroughly clean the graves of their dead. Often the ground is dug up and the mounds are built up and shaped. The graves of the more recent dead (children, parents, and siblings) are then decorated with flowers and pine boughs. Often pine boughs are set up at each corner of a grave or group of graves. Each grave mound has flowers sprinkled over it, mostly yellow marigolds and purple orchids. In some cases part of the flowers are finely shredded and sprinkled over the grave and crosses are sometimes marked out in flowers. Pine needles are also sprinkled over some graves and sometimes baskets of food placed on the graves. Food is placed at the foot of the grave in all cases and candles are burned, despite the admonitions of the priest.

After the grave is decorated, the family sits around and chats. There are few evidences of sorrow; one or two people remark that the day is "very sad," but most people seem cheerful in a quiet way and there is even some subdued laughter. the *rezadores* or "prayers" go around from group to group and say lengthy prayers using a rosary. Everyone in the group kneels while the prayers are said. Fruit, bread, and tamales are given the *rezador* for his prayers.

In 1941 the priest came and said prayers. He charged a *real*, 12½ centavos for each prayer. His prayers were shorter than those of the *rezador* and he and those with him remained standing, but he sprinkled the grave with holy water. He also scolded people for having candles and food offerings, so most people hid them when the priest approached, placing them out again when he moved on. The *rezadores* continued, but kept unobtrusive in another part of the graveyard from the section where the priest was functioning. Most people had both priest and *rezador*.

About noon or shortly afterward most people eat lunch consisting of nákatamales, bread, and fruit. Friends and acquaintances who stop to chat are usually given two tamales, which they eat at the time. After 3 or 4 hours at the graveyard, people return home. Few people do any but the most necessary work on this day.

Sometime during the day, either before going to the graveyard or after returning, most people hang strings of yellow flowers over the frames of the house doors. Yellow is regarded as the color of mourning still, as it is in many parts of Indian Mexico. In view of reports of more elaborate ceremonies in other Tarascan towns, it should be recorded that no one at Cherán spends the night in the cemetery.

CONCLUSION AND FURTHER PROBLEMS

Of immediate concern in dealing with a group as large as the Tarascans is the question whether Cherán is adequately representative of the group as a whole. Certainly Cherán is not typical in its size and this difference alone makes it probable that it is not entirely representative of other Tarascan towns. A complete answer to the question raised must await more extensive investigation, but the staff of the present study visited or investigated enough other communities to indicate that, in a broad sense, Cherán is probably fairly typical. From a narrower viewpoint it is certain that many detailed differences exist. Strong indications also exist that there are some regional differences which have already been mentioned. The villages about Lake Pátzcuaro, through their partial dependence upon fishing and closer contacts with Mestizo culture, necessarily must be somewhat different. The villages about La Cañada likewise seem distinguishable as a group. Probably the Sierra communities may be set apart as a regional unit, although it is possible that the Sierra group may ultimately be found to consist of two or more sections. Finally, a number of marginal towns assimilated to some degree into Mestizo culture present special problems.

Final resolution of the question raised seems to call for at least two further steps in the study of the Tarascans. First, at least two or three additional community studies are needed, one in the Lake Pátzcuaro region, and another in La Cañada. Very probably another Sierra town should also be studied, preferably one at considerable distance from Cherán and with a significant manufacturing industry supplementing its agriculture. The second step would be an intensive but rapid survey of a large number of communities, perhaps by a trait-list technique, to discover the extent of local and regional variation. Quite possibly such a survey would reveal additional types of communities meriting study. For certain types of problems, of course, the marginal, more acculturated communities require study, but a fairly complete knowledge of typical Tarascan culture seems the first need.

The present study of Cherán reveals a number of points of considerable interest. Perhaps the most striking fact about Cherán is the essentially European origin of most of the culture and the relatively small number of traits of native provenience. Most of the material culture of Cherán is probably European, although obviously some of the plants, including the major crop, maize, is native. Farming techniques, implements, housing, men's clothing (and possibly women's clothing) are Indian only to a slight degree. The economic specialization and trade patterns may be based upon aboriginal conditions, yet they are known to have been formalized by Europeans. Political and ceremonial organization are also European, although in part their origins represent Bishop Vasco de Quiroga's interpretation of Thomas More's "Utopia" (1923). The extensive *compadre* system is but an enlargement upon European ideas. The origin of the Tarascan wedding ceremony alone remains obscure and may have important native antecedents. Concepts of the supernatural, both in formal religion and in witchcraft, are certainly almost wholly European.

Despite the European origins of Tarascan culture, it obviously represents something different from the European-originated Mestizo culture. Neither is it a mere survival of sixteenth century conditions. If Vasco de Quiroga or any other sixteenth century European were to return to Cherán, he no doubt would find it as strange as any lay visitor from modern European culture. Nor would this strangeness be wholly or even primarily due to the infiltration of later European ideas.

The uniqueness of Cherán culture, whether viewed from the standpoint of the sixteenth century or from that of today, lies in the extensive reworking of its European materials. For example, the *cabildo* system seems almost certainly related to the organization of the hospitals introduced by Quiroga, yet the good Bishop might have to do considerable research to recognize the relationship. Such reworking may be due to the patterning influence of native ideas rather than to a spontaneous evolution of a purely European culture in the partial isolation of the late Colonial period. The character of such things as family life and attitudes and the real educative forces affecting the thinking and personality of Cherán inhabitants may have been relatively unchanged, despite the modifications in material culture and social organization.

A subject meriting more thorough investigation in Cherán is the persistence of the mixed culture of Cherán. The fierce attachment to *costumbres* is part of the acceptance of a way of life by most members of the community, even the most progressive. This attachment persists despite the fact that Cherán culture not only changes visibly but that such change is accepted and even desired by a large part of the population. The limits of acceptable change, however, need further definition. The impression of the staff of the present study is that change is accepted rather readily in those things relating to material welfare and perhaps health. Cherán residents are not averse to changes leading to more money, food, medical service (if it does not cost too much), or elements increasing comfort, such as a larger and better distributed water supply. The introduction of industries giving employment at

better wages would meet no opposition. Probably political reforms would have support if they clearly would provide more effective and representative self-government. Nevertheless, it seems probable that extensive changes in these fields would still leave Cherán life with a highly distinctive flavor. No matter how long Cherán residents have lived away from the community, and even if they have been born out of the community, they seem to accept a pattern of attitudes and behaviors which have not been successfully identified and analyzed in the present study.

In some measure a dichotomy of Cherán culture is implied in the foregoing remarks. The areas in which change is permissible and accepted may be identified as "secular" in the sense Robert Redfield (1941) has used the term in his studies of Yucatan culture change. Such a characterization might be misleading, however, for it seems doubtful if the term "sacred" can be applied equally well to the sectors of the culture where change is rejected. Certainly a Cherán resident would be nonplussed at the application of the term "sacred" to weddings and the obligations of kinship (although he might consider it properly applied to the *compadre* obligations). Primarily the sacred in Cherán is closely associated with the affairs of the Church, a view that is perhaps best high-lighted by the fact that those progressives who are most anticlerical (a position to be kept clearly distant from "anti-Catholic") are not opponents of the *costumbres*.

Cherán, like many Indian communities of Mexico, is increasingly influenced by the town and the city. Nevertheless, the processes again seem significantly different from those hitherto described by Redfield. In Cherán there is no distinction of *los tontos* and *los correctos*, Mestizo and *indio*, or *ladino* and *indio*, although such may exist in some Tarascan towns with an appreciable Mestizo population. Nor does the neat diminishing order of city, town, and village of Yucatan hold in this area. Cherán is probably more influenced by Gary (Indiana, U. S. A.), Mexico City, and Morelia (possibly in diminishing order) than it is by Uruapan and Pátzcuaro. Indeed, it is quite probable that fundamentally Cherán is more progressive, more in touch with the modern world, than is

Mestizo Pátzcuaro with its conscious idealization of a Colonial past. (Pátzcuaro has not been studied but apparently the social structure is fairly rigidly fixed in terms of the families whose signatures occur on last Colonial charter of the town with relatively little modification by present economic or occupational conditions.)

As indicated in the introduction, the study of Cherán thus far has been conducted in a single time dimension. Ultimately, considerable light can be shed on the present culture by relating it to its historical background. Tarascan culture seems not to have been static in pre-European times and to have changed greatly both during and after the Colonial period. Materials are probably sufficiently abundant to permit study of change in enough detail to give some knowledge of processes. Of particular interest would be a study of contemporary culture in the light of the utopian ideas of Quiroga, ideas that to a considerable degree seem to have been translated into a functioning system.

Many problems related to the individual in Cherán need further attention. The role of women in Cherán could not be adequately studied for reasons already explained; it would not be too much to say that the present study gives merely the masculine culture of Cherán. Such problems as the significance of witchcraft and its relation to personality structure and emigration should be fruitful. The pattern of growth and development and child rearing undoubtedly has bearing on this point. Similarly rewarding should be a deeper investigation of the curious contradiction between the normal concealment or denial of wealth and its ostentatious display in connection with the wedding ceremonies. The characteristics of Cherán culture and Cherán personalities which seem to make it possible for individuals to adapt readily to the outside world, spend years in the heart of industrialized civilization, yet be reabsorbed wholly into the local situation on their return should offer fruitful problems for investigation. Likewise the influence of the returning emigrant on present conditions in Cherán should be more thoroughly understood.

Most of the foregoing suggestions for study involve the role of the individual and the relationship between the individual and culture. To this field of investigation also are related

many of the practical administrative problems connected with Cherán. In the last analysis, the success of programs on behalf of the Indian undertaken by governmental agencies boils down to the problem of getting individuals to accept change.

In the field of practical administration, it should be evident that best results will be obtained if the area of culture recognized by Cherán residents as *los costumbres* is not disturbed. Officially expressed administrative aims lie primarily in the fields of economics, technology, education, and political life. Extensive modifications seem possible in these fields without tampering with the *costumbres*.

The most effective administrative measures, if it be conceded that the *costumbres* be not disturbed, seem to call for reducing the general objectives of governmental programs into specific objectives for the community of Cherán. Greater effectiveness seems likely to result if such objectives be very concrete, strictly limited initially, and held as consistently as possible. What is needed would appear to be a determination of what the desirable and practical objectives are in improving such things as farming techniques, introducing manufacturing techniques, and modifying housing. If the national objective of greater industrialization is to be realized, a clear corollary program should be developed to determine what types of industrial products Cherán residents are to be stimulated to desire. Mechanisms to protect the group initially from exploitation, both as buyers and sellers, might be desirable. In the educational field, decisions must be made and maintained over a reasonable time as to the purpose of Cherán education. Fundamentally, the problem is whether the people of Cherán are to be educated to live in Cherán or whether they are to be educated to leave Cherán. In the political field, it must be determined whether Cherán is to be self-governing and is to participate freely in a larger national democratic life. If the decision is affirmative, administrators must realize that the best school of democracy is practice in democracy and that the cure for errors is not less but more democracy.

Only when these and similar objectives are concretely framed and the necessary decisions made can a practical program be formulated for Cherán. Anthropological studies by themselves offer no easy and golden pathway to the solution of Indian problems. The most thorough study of the Tarascans must be ineffective practically if the necessary administrative objectives are not clearly defined. The data of an anthropological study such as this can do no more than offer hints as to the "soft" spots of the culture, the areas in which change can most easily be introduced, as well as the *costumbres*, the points of resistance, such as ceremonies (not necessarily including religion), dress, dances, weddings, and death customs. The study can likewise indicate some of the major problems of Cherán, such as the underproductivity of the soil and agricultural technology, the inadequate mechanization, the probable existence of an overly large population to permit any marked rise in economic status, the need of creating new attitudes in spending (for Cherán could finance many public improvements itself), the inadequacy of the water supply, the lack of public health facilities, and the shortcomings of the educational system.

In relation to these problems, further studies are needed in which the anthropologist is aided by technicians in soil use, farming, forestry, and animal husbandry techniques. Scientific-

ally, such studies should be of great aid also, permitting better understanding of the fundamental limitations on Cherán culture.

Once a set of definite objectives has been established, the data of the anthropological study will be of considerable use in formulating a concrete program and in developing Tarascan cooperation. Moreover, the introduction of a program in itself, creates changes in the cultural situation. The dynamic quality of culture makes it important that administrative programs be accompanied by further study and be flexible enough to adapt to the changing situation.

Despite these remarks on the practical problems of government in the Tarascan area, it should be emphasized that the present study is primarily concerned with scientific objectives. These objectives happen to be closely related to practical considerations, for administrative objectives in Mexico call for culture change in some measure. Cultural processes and the function and interrelation of the parts of a culture emerge most clearly from dynamic situations rather than from static studies without temporal extension. Not only practical but scientific objectives can be served by the study of Cherán culture in transition.

APPENDIX 1

DATA ON FOOD PLANTS AND FOOD FROM LA CAÑADA

The following data were collected by Silvia Rendón in the pueblos of La Cañada, the next valley to the north of Cherán. As the valley is at a lower elevation than is Cherán, some differences are noticeable in techniques and in plants grown. Unless otherwise specified, the data are from Chilchota; although far from complete, they are included here because they afford some interesting comparisons, the more so in that Chilchota is a Mestizo town today.

Plants cultivated: All of the plants cultivated in Cherán as well as many others, are found in La Cañada. Black maize is grown in the fields, rather than in the house lots, but, as in Cherán, it is kept separate in storage and is used only for certain types of tamales and

atoles. Wheat is sown twice a year; one planting is in June and it is harvested in December; the second is in November, in the house lots, and it is harvested in May. Beans are grown more extensively than at Cherán; the harvest is exclusively by women.

Among the plants generally grown in Chilchota is amaranth (*bledos*). The cultivation is not commercialized, each family growing a little for its own use. Amaranth is used by Indians of La Cañada for making sweets; in Chilchota it is employed in sweets, certain atoles, and in an uncooked tamale resembling a tortilla which is sold in Capacuaro.

A considerable number of fruits are cultivated in Chilchota. Mangoes of the *criollo* and

Manila varieties are grown extensively for export. Scarcely a house lacks a sweet lemon tree. The fruit is sold in bulk to dealers before it is ripe. Bitter limes are sold the same way; the prices are less than for sweet limes, but people in Chilchota say they are more pleasant in flavor. Oranges are also grown extensively in orchards. Two varieties of guavas are utilized. The type known as *corriente* grows wild and is used only by poor people who cook the fruit in honey. The "fine" type is cultivated and sold. A few bananas are grown of the type known in Mexico City as *platano bolso* and in Uruapan as *corriente*. The local name is *Costarica*. A "fine" and an "ordinary" variety of peaches are grown; the entire crop is exported. Cherimoyas occur in most orchards, but not in such quantity as in the Tarascan towns of La Cañada. The product is all consumed locally. Some *zapote blanco* is cultivated in Chilchota; more is grown among the Tarascan towns. Cherries grow half-wild, being planted but not tended. The fruit is eaten raw or made into confections. A fruit known as juakinicuiles (in Mexico City, jinicuiles) is planted but not cultivated; it is much prized. Citron is grown in some orchards; all the product is sold. The tejocote is not used at all in Chilchota, and some people even were amazed at the idea it should be eaten.

Coffee is extensively cultivated, sharing with lemons the major place in the orchards. Almost all the coffee is sold in the bean in Zamora, and the coffee consumed locally is brought from Zamora.

Three varieties of squash are cultivated. Calabaza Tarasca is grown in the fields and is all consumed in the town, either boiled or roasted in hot ashes. Calabaza de Castilla is grown in two varieties, one with hard shell and one with soft. Both are exported. A variety called sopoma grows in the fields and is all used in the town, either to make sweets or as greens for broth or stew.

The principal wild plant used for food in Chilchota is a species of prickly pear (*tuna*), known as jococoxtle. It is used in certain of the beef stews or is ground with chile to make a sauce placed on the table.

Meat is mostly butchered on Saturday and Sunday, and the main sales take place on Sunday. The places where meat is sold are called "*despachos*" and are announced by hanging out a red flag on a standard. Four or five places sell meat remaining from Sunday through most of the week. No distinction is made in price between meat with bone and meat without bone, but on request one will be served only meat; in the Tarascan towns the buyer has to take what is cut. Pork is preferred to beef. Beef hides are sold to dealers; those of swine either are made into cracklings or are pickled in vinegar after rubbing with chile, onion, garlic, and fragrant herbs.

Some fish are caught with nets in the river passing Chilchota. The fishermen are only semiprofessional, fishing when they have time and selling the catch only if they have more than can be consumed at home. At least one man, a farmer, hunts deer in his spare time. He sells the flesh retail like beef. The dried deer blood, hoofs, and hair are sold for magical or medicinal uses.

Black maize is used primarily to make *chapatas*, tamales of black or red maize, sweetened with brown sugar and mixed with black or red amaranth. It is also used to make *atole de cascara de cacao* (atole of chocolate hulls) and *ponteduros*, which are toasted immature corn ground and mixed with brown sugar sirup.

Greens (*quelites*) of wheat are made from a wild plant or weed which grows among the wheat and are greatly liked in Chilchota. A curious custom exists in that anyone may help himself to these greens, entering into wheat fields belonging to others either with or without permission. Anyone objecting would be severely censored in Chilchota. Pozole is also made from green wheat toasted, ground, and mixed with chile, salt, and "*epazote*." The time for this is May at the harvest; it is "hot" food.

A food made from the chayote root is *sagú*. The skin is removed from the tubers and the pulp ground to a sort of flour. The flour is placed in water for 2 or 3 days, being stirred frequently. The flour is then allowed to settle, the water drained off, and the flour dried. Although it is used in various dishes, the main use is to feed small children and women recently delivered, when it is cooked in water, either plain or sweetened with honey. The plain boiled chayote root, uarás in Tarascan, is sold extensively in all La Cañada towns and is much liked.

One of the favorite meat dishes in Chilchota is not unlike the čurípo of the Tarascans and is called *"espinazo."* It is a broth made from the backbone of the pig, flavored with chile and including cooked bitter prickly pears known as jococoxtles. The broth is usually accompanied by boiled rice.

Not much sausage is made in Chilchota, but the blood of the pig is greatly liked, both in Chilchota and the Tarascan towns of La Cañada. The blood is placed in the cleaned entrails, together with other visceral parts of the animal, which have been cut into small pieces, *silantro,* chile, and onion. At some point the mixture is cooked. By the time the product is sold, the blood has solidfied. The purchasers remove the mixture from the casings, mill it on the metate with water, and fry it with lard.

Bread of the type known in Tarascan towns as *pan grueso* is made in Chilchota. Most bread, however, is brought from the larger neighboring town of Tangancícuaro.

APPENDIX 2

THE CEREMONIAL ORGANIZATION OF CHILCHOTA

The following information on the ceremonial organization of Chilchota was collected by Pedro Carrasco. Due to political struggles, the ceremonial organization was not in existence from 1932 to 1940. The data given are representative of conditions as they existed before 1932, amplified by data on the partial revival of the ceremonial life of the town in 1940 (the differences are indicated by past and present tenses). The organization and the observances present many interesting parallels and differences from Cherán, particularly in view of the fact that Chilchota is a Mestizo town today. Carrasco found only one man of about 90 who had been reared in a Tarascan-speaking family; nevertheless, culturally Chilchota evidently is still somewhat of a Tarascan town. Many Tarascan words survive and such old institutions as the hospital are better preserved than in many Tarascan towns.

The ceremonial organization is linked with division of the town into *barrios* of San Juan and San Pedro. Two other *barrios* exist, Uren and Chapala, but they appear to be recent additions and, unless otherwise specified, only the first two *barrios* are referred to. The principal ceremonial offices and their relation to the *barrios* are as follows:

Office	*Barrio*
Mayordomo of the Hospital	One year from San Juan, the next from San Pedro

Office	*Barrio*
Mayordomo of the patron saint, Santiago	One year from San Juan, the next from San Pedro
Carguero of San Roque or Karačakape	*Barrio* of San Juan
Carguero of San Nicolás	*Barrio* of San Pedro
Two *vaqueros*	One from each *barrio*
Four *roseras*[1] or uánančatis	Two from each *barrio*
Two *regidores*	One from each *barrio*

[1] One of the *roseras* is called *pendompari,* and one *capitamoro.* They are always of different *barrios,* the positions alternating from one *barrio* to the other each year.

All these individuals are called *cargueros.* It is they who bear the expense of all religious festivals.

Unlike Cherán, this group of *cargueros* forms a hierarchy through which individuals pass, ultimately to become one of the *viejos principales* (principal old men) or tarépiti. The sequence is as given, the first position being that of *mayordomo* of the hospital, then *mayordomo* of Santiago, then either *carguero* of San Roque or of San Nicolás, depending on the *carguero's barrio,* then *vaquero* (while female members of his family serve as *roseras*), and finally *regidor.* After this the *carguero* is an "old man," a principal. The old men and the *cargueros* who have occupied the positions of both *mayordomo* of the hospital and *mayordomo* of Santiago form the group known as the *cabildo.*

In addition to the hierarchical offices, there are a number of minor positions, the most important being that of the čičiua. A *fiscal* looks after cattle belonging to the Virgin of the hospital and acts as a sacristan. A topil (a Maya word) rings the church bells and does errands for the *mayordomo* of the hospital. The *regidores* each have two messengers, the *mayor* or petajpi and the katapi. One of the duties of the latter is to chase dogs away during the fiestas, for which reason he is known as the "dog frightener," uičariri.

A person wishing to take a ceremonial office makes his petition to the *regidor* (of his *barrio?*), taking bread, chocolate, and liquor. The *regidor* consults with the *cabildo* regarding the matter, but he cannot accept the gifts unless the person receives the office. Apparently the *regidores* function primarily as the administrative officials of the *cabildo*. They are said also to have functions with respect to the Indian population in La Cañada. Indians visiting Chilchota on business often consult with the *regidores* and, if the matter is one involving the court or *juzgado*, the *regidor* acts as intermediary and advocate of the Indian's cause.

Decision regarding the offices is reached by the *cabildo* before December 12. On this day the new *cargueros* assemble at the hospital where the wife of the mayordomo places a crown on each one; this ceremony installs them in office, although some apparently do not take up their duties until later.

The most important meeting of the *cabildo* is on the day of Candelaria (February 2). The principals and the *cargueros*, old and new, who have passed the office of *mayordomo* of Santiago, meet about 10 o'clock in the morning in the patio outside the chapel of the hospital. Men and women (wives of the men?) form two groups. The men are seated on chairs along the sides of a table covered with mats of tule. The *regidores* take seats at each end. The women are arranged in similar fashion but kneeling on mats on each side of a row of tule mats placed on the ground. The *regidores* evidently take their places first. As each person arrives, he kisses a cross placed in a little shelter before the chapel. He then goes to the *regidores*, crosses himself, and kisses the staffs of the *regidores*. He then takes his place.

Each of the *roseras* must bring two sugarcanes for each person and a bottle of liquor for each *regidor*. Each *regidor* makes a speech in Tarascan, called uandakua, after which they begin to drink čarape and to receive blessed wax. For lunch they eat *menudo*, while for dinner they eat čurípo and nákatamales. They continue drinking until about 5 o'clock, when they go to the house of the new *mayordomo* of Santiago and continue drinking until night.

Two days after Candelaria the *roseras* ring bells in the hospital to call the boys and girls of the town to get firewood for the hospital. The boys and girls go to the mountains for a week, chaperoned by the *roseras*, and accumulate enough wood for the needs of the hospital for a year.

On Monday of Carnival the images of San Nicholás are taken from the houses of the old *cargueros* to the houses of the new. Similar fiestas are held in each case. The evening before, the new *carguero* assembles boys to go to the place called Cerro Viejo to get flowers known as kanínšikuas. The boys are fed tortillas with pork and beans. They are also given liquor to drink on the trip. When the boys return they are met with music, and *cohetes* are fired off. Three cane arches are decorated with the flowers, one for the gate, one for the door of the room occupied by the image of the saint, and one over the image inside the room.

On Tuesday are changed the four *vaqueritas* ("little cow girls"), two virgin girls from each *barrio*, who are overseen by the *vaqueros*. On the roof of the houses of old and new *vaqueros* are placed banners with red figures. Boys climb up and remove the banners, giving them to the house owners, who give the boys a bottle of *aguardiente*. (According to another informant, the banners are placed in a tree 8 days in advance.) The boys later make bulls of mats and hides and play at bull fighting in the streets. Each *barrio* has two "bulls," with musicians accompanying them. The boys give presents of sugarcane to the girls, who, in return, give them čapatas. In the evening there is a concert in the plaza and much breaking of confetti-filled eggshells. Arches with the kanínšikua flowers are made for the *vaqueritas*.

At a period believed to be before 1900, actual bull fights were held. Women called *vaqueras*, who were hired by the *roseras*, did the bull fighting (of which no further details were learned). Some women appeared every year. They wore dresses of red bayeta, a white kerchief on the head, and a felt hat. Two kerchiefs were crossed on the body (breast?) and another was used to tease the bull. A machete was carried on the shoulder.

On these occasions the image of the Virgin of the hospital was taken out and handfuls of tiny confections, of the size of silantro seeds, were scattered. The boys and girls broke many eggshells filled with confetti. The boys struck the girls with sugarcanes when possible and the girls retaliated with čapatas wrapped in napkins.

On Ash Wednesday the *cargueros* assembled in the houses of the *vaquero* and karačakape. Piles of oranges, limes, ashes, and earth were placed in the yards, and men and women fought. The oranges and limes were blackened with charcoal and thrown, as were ashes and earth. When the game became violent, a woman struck a shake with a stick and called "peace, peace." The game then stopped.

The passion of Christ was once represented. On Thursday of Holy Week, the imprisonment of Christ was represented, many youths dressing as Jews and soldiers. Friday the image was taken in procession, decorated with laurel, roses, bananas, čapatas, and flour tamales.

Normally processions were held three times a year, Holy Thursday, the Friday of Sorrows, and Corpus. The same images were used each time. The image of Jesus the Nazarene was dressed in dark tunic, a cord at the belt, and the stretcher decorated with field flowers. Boys carried the stretcher. Anyone wishing to participate dressed himself in a black tunic and bonnet and went out to gather flowers. The boys were called Judas. The images of Mary Magdalene and the Virgin were also taken in the procession. The image of the Virgin was in the special charge of the *roseras*, who dressed it and prepared the stretcher with flowers. The *pendompari* carried a standard (*pendon*), from which her name is derived, while the *capitamoro* carried a spray of flowers. Both went ahead of the Virgin. The *fiscal* carried an incense burner at the head of the procession. Twelve boys dressed in red tunics represented the Twelve Apostles.

On Palm Sunday palms brought from the hot country are taken to the church to be blessed. Formerly a more elaborate observance was held. An image representing Christ was mounted on the image of a burro called San Ramos. The images were carried on a stretcher to the spring supplying water and were put in a little shrine made of flowers. To this spot came youths who had left 2 weeks earlier to secure palms. The youths came down to the spring from a place called La Mesa, wearing carnations and little gourds about their necks and cracking their whips. The girls brought music for dancing and also provided čurípo and kurúndas. About 5 o'clock in the afternoon all went with the palms to the church.

On Holy Thursday there formerly was a market at which the principal goods sold were clothing and fruit from the hot country. People purchased the latter to make offerings to the church for the decoration of the altar.

Holy Saturday the girls carried small, highly decorated jars of water to be blessed. These were used later to cure the sick and to protect from "fright" (*espanto*). When the church bells ring, children and fruit trees are shaken so that they will grow more rapidly. Images of Judas are burned on the street corners at this moment also. They are provided by anyone who feels like doing so.

In April the *regidor* notifies the youths to clean the spring. The boys provide music and the girls bring them čurípo and kurúndas.

The day of the Assumption, most people go to the fiesta at the town of Huáncito. On their return, the wild honey collectors go through the streets announcing the fiesta of Corpus. They play the *chirimía* and make a special cry called pitakuri.

Two days before the fiesta of Corpus, bread is made in all the houses. The night before Corpus, each *barrio* hires musicians to play. On the day of Corpus the girls bathe at the spring. On their return they dress for church. In the afternoon, boys and girls gather and present each other with fruit and trinkets.

The following day there is a large fiesta in the plaza. The ox drivers bring out their oxen with the yokes decorated with silk kerchiefs, ribbons, and flowers. The drivers also decorate their hats with flowers and their goads with ribbons and flowers at the points. Persons of other occupations also appear similarly decorated. All throw objects at the onlookers. The ox drivers scatter seeds, the muleteers throw flour and bran, the breadmakers throw bread, the overseers scatter ink. The honey gatherers collect many honeycombs from the mountains to sell and give away. One is placed at a corner of the plaza on a greased pole. The leader of the honey gatherers on this day is called kurindure. The butchers station themselves in one of the arcades of the plaza and butcher a goat, whose blood is thrown at the people. One of the butchers disguises himself as a coyote and steals a piece of meat; the others pursue him about the plaza.

On the day of San Juan, June 24, both sexes bathe early in the morning. The youths provide musicians, who play while the girls are bathing. In the houses where there is a person named Juan, a roll is placed between small boards tied with a cord. Youths on horseback try to seize the roll with their hands. The cord is jerked as they ride past, in order to make the task harder. The same is done on the day of San Pedro in the houses where there is someone named Pedro.

On the day of Santiago, *moros* and soldiers dance. The *moros* always come from the *barrio* of the *mayordomo*, while the soldiers come from the other *barrio*. They dance on the 25th and 26th, first in the chapel of the hospital, then in the priest's residence, then in the house of the mayor of the town, and then in private houses where they are given presents of fruit. Each group has a first and second captain. Each pays for 1 day of the music and serves a meal in his house. The *mayordomo* of Santiago has no expense except the Mass and another group of musicians who play at the church. The dancers gather to practice the evening before the day of Santiago at the house of the *regidor*. The *roseras* give a supper of curípo and kurúndas. The fiesta is called tzíndakua.

On the day of the Conception, youths and girls take musicians to the Virgin and sing *las mañanitas* to her in the church.

On December 12 the image of the Virgin in the hospital is removed from the altar and placed in the middle of the chapel. Girls and boys become "brothers and sisters" by crossing

themselves, kissing the image, and wearing a crown for a few minutes. Alms are given and the boy and girl are then "*hermanos*." During the day girls put on the dress of the Tarascan girl, uári, and go about to the stores offering tamales for sale in the manner of the Indians. Boys sing *pastores* in private houses and are given *aguardiente*.

The day of Christmas Eve, the *pendompari* goes about with musicians singing *pastores* (pastorals) to the houses of the *cabildo*, where she makes presents of *buñuelos*. In return each gives the *pendompari* 50 centavos and charape. With the money the *pendompari* pays for the Mass said on Holy Thursday.

One month before Christmas Eve the čičiua prepares figures representing the birth of Christ in his house. These are taken to the image of the Holy Child. The day of Christmas Eve, people watch and burn candles before the image until 11 p. m. Quantities of *buñuelos* and nákatamales are made for the *cabildo*. At 11 o'clock, the image of the Holy Child (which apparently is in a private house) is taken to the church accompanied by a band. Powder is burned at the street corners. In the church the Infant is placed in a reclining position. Moss for preparing the bed is brought from Cerro Viejo by youths in the same fashion flowers are brought for Carnival.

In addition to these observances, fiestas called *niños gorderos* are celebrated in private houses. A scene representing the birth of Christ is prepared. The Infant is "raised" sometime before Candelaria, and the scene is removed on the 3d of February.

Pastorelas are also celebrated on Christmas Eve. The *roseras* pay the teacher to instruct the dancers, and provide them with čurípo and tamales. Each dancer provides his own costume. The group consists of 5 girl and 5 boy shepherds, 3 devils, 2 old men, 2 *negros*, 2 hermits, 1 male and 1 female rancher. They appear to conduct the image of the Holy Child to church, and they also appear on the two following nights.

On January 6 the new čičiua goes to church with music and "raises" the Holy Child. The priest takes up the image and gives it to the čičiua to dress. He kisses the image and gives it to others to kiss. Afterward all go through the streets with the musicians to the house of the čičiua, who serves nákatamales, *buñuelos*, and čápata, the men and women of the *cabildo* eating first. During the night there is much dancing of *jarabes*, first women dancing with

women and later men dancing with women. The latter enter into contests with others. *Pastores* are also sung all night, verses taken from printed pamphlets from Mexico. This is continued every night until Candelaria.

APPENDIX 3

REPORT ON MAIZE FROM CHERÁN

By Edgar Anderson

Missouri Botanical Garden and Washington University, St. Louis

Fifty-five ears of maize were received from Dr. Ralph L. Beals, in lots numbered from 1 to 43, there being two ears each of most of the numbers above 30. The ears were photographed, grain samples were taken, and the ears returned to Dr. Beals. In the summer of 1942, 10 plants from each lot were grown at the Blandy Experimental Farm, of the University of Virginia,[39] Boyce, Va. Although the planting as a whole was badly infested with smut, at least one good tassel specimen was obtained from each lot and herbarium specimens were also made of leaves and seedlings. Notes on plant color, pubescence, etc., were taken in the field, and the internode pattern of one plant of each lot was recorded. Five plants from the entire lot were investigated in detail, cytologically, and the knob number and knob positions of their chromosomes were determined.

As a whole, the corn belongs to the race recently termed "Mexican Pyramidal" by Anderson and Cutler (1942). Many of the ears and the plants grown from them are indistinguishable (for all practical purposes) from collections made in the vicinity of Mexico City. However, there are certain average differences which seem to be significant, and a few of the numbers are unlike anything we have yet examined from Mexico, D. F. Plants are medium to tall, mostly with conspicuous sun red (occasionally purple) plant color. Tillers are few or absent. The leaves are broad but break easily in the wind, giving the collection a very bedraggled appearance, which is heightened by the susceptibility to smut. The tas-

sels are large and coarse but there are few tassel branches. The ears are short, though the husks are often very long. The ear branches vary greatly in length, the most extreme being 3 or 4 feet long, with numerous secondary ears. This is partly due to culture in a region of different day length (i. e., Virginia vs. Mexico). The ears are prevailingly broad at the base, tapering sharply and evenly. The kernels are mostly hard and flinty but are nearly all more or less dented. There is great variation in kernel size and shape, not only from plant to plant but also on each ear, since, owing to the position of the husks, the grains at the tip of the ear are under strong compression, whereas those at the base have plenty of room. It is not unusual to see an ear with the basal kernels deeply dented but with no perceptible denting in any of the kernels at the tip.

Two main types were well represented in the collections (table 18). There were the so-called "Black" maize from Cherán (Nos. 31–37) and from Nahuatzen (Nos. 38–43) and "Tulukénio" (Nos. 1–26), a mountain type grown only above 8,500 feet (pl. 8). A third type, "Trimásion," is grown on the plain below 8,500 feet. It is said to be later maturing, larger-eared, and larger-grained. This was apparently confirmed by our collections, but since there were only two numbers (29 and 30) no averages have been prepared.

The collections of Black maize stood out sharply both in the field and in the collection of ears. The latter were around 15 cm. in length, nearly all of them with dark (blue or purple) kernels which were deeply to lightly dented and were rounded (i. e., not pointed). Purple cob

[39] For laboratory space and many other courtesies, we are indebted to the Director, Dr. O. E. White.

TABLE 18.—Characteristics of Cherán maize

Lot No. of maize	Race of maize	Locality	Plant color	Cob color	Silk color	Seed coat color (S = stained or streaked)	Aleurone	Tillers (Number)	Tassel branch (Number)	Row (Number)	Glume length (Mm.)	Condensed inter-nodes (Percent)	Sessile upper spikelets (Percent)	Kernel	Knob (Number)
1	Tulukénio	Cherán	Sun red	White	Red	Red S	White	0–3	3–6	8	11	0	20	Pointed, flinty	
2	do	do	do	do	Pink	do	do	0–1	4–11	14	12	20	90	Pointed, flinty, semident.	
3	do	do	do	do		do	do	0–2	4	12	12	20	20	do	
4	do	do	do	do	Pink	do	do	0–1	4–15	18	9	0	20	do	4
5	do	do	do	do	Green	None	Yellow	0–1	12	16	11	50	90	Subpointed, flinty, semident.	
6	do	do	do	do	Pink	S	do	0–4	3–6	14	12	20	100	Rounded, flinty	
7	do	do	do	do	Pale purple	Pink S	do	0–2	4–12	14	15	20	40	Subpointed, flinty, semident.	
8	do	do	do	do	Pink	Red S	do	0	1–10	12	18	0	80	Subpointed, flinty	
9	do	do	do	do	Pale purple	None	do	0	7	14	12	20	100	Subpointed, flinty, semident.	
10	do	do	do	do	do	do	do	1	6–14	14	10	30	40	Rounded, flinty, semident.	4
11	do	do	do	do	Green	Red S	do	0–2	6–10	14	14	40	20	Subpointed, flinty	
12	do	do	do	do	Pink	S	do	0	3–15	12	12	0	100	Pointed, flinty	
13	do	do	do	do	do	Red S	do	0	3–14	12	13	40	100	Pointed, flinty, semident.	
14	do	do	Purple	do	Green	None	White	0	4–9	12	11	0	100	do	
15	do	do	Sun red	do	Pink	Red S	do	0		14	11	20	100	do	
16	do	do	do	do	do	do	do	0	12	12	11	40	100	do	
17	do	do	do	Salmon	do	do	do	0–2	16	12	10	80	100	do	
18	do	do	do	White	do	Mixed	Yellow	0	6	12	10	10	10	do	
19	do	do	do	do	do	S	do	0	4–9	14			60	Subpointed, flinty, semident.	7
20	do	do	do	do	do	Red S	do	1–3	3–11	14	13	30	100	Pointed, flinty, semident.	
21	do	do	do	do	Green	do	White	0	4–7	16	11	30	100	do	
22	do	do	do	Purplish	do	do	do	0–1	7	14	13	50	20	Subpointed, semident.	
23	do	do	Green	Salmon	do	Terra cotta	Tan	0–2	18	16	12	20	50	Subpointed, flinty, semident.	
24	do	do	Sun red	White	do	Ivory	White	1–2	5	14	11	0	10	Rounded, rough, semident.	
25	do	do	do	do	Pink	Tan S	Yellow	0–2	5	12	10	50	100	Subpointed, semident.	
26	do	do	do	Red	Green	Tan	White	0	12	16	12	40	70	Rounded, semident.	
27	do	do	do	White	do	Terra cotta	Orange	0	6	12	11	10	80	Rounded, dent.	
28	Trimasion	do	do	Purplish	Pink	None S	Purple	0	6	14	16	0	0	do	
29	do	do	Purple	do	Red	None S	do	0	5	16	17	0	80	Rounded, semident.	
30	Black	do	do	do	Pink	do	Blue	0	3–5	12	13	30	40	do	
31a	do	do	do	White	do	do	Purple	0	3–8	12	15	10	40	do	5
31b	do	do	Purple	Purplish	Pink	do	do	0	1–7	12	15	10	30	do	
32	do	do	do	do	do	Mixed	Purple	0–1	6	16	13	40	90	do	
33a	do	do	Purple	do	Red	do	Blue	0	2–8	10	11	0	50	do	
33b	do	do	do	Purple	do	Purple S	Purple	0	7–9	14	11	0	40	Rounded, dent.	
34a	do	do	do	do	do	do	do	0	8–9	14	12	0	50	do	
34b	do	do	do	White	do	Purple S	do	0	11–3	14	11	0	90	do	
35a	Nahuatzen	do	Sun red	do	do	Ivory	Blue	0	2–3	12	12	40	80	do	
35b	do	do	Purple	Purple	Pink	Purple S	White	0	6	16	14	10	90	do	
36a	do	do	Sun red	do	Red	Purple	Purple	0–1	8	14	12	0	100	Rounded, semident.	
36b	do	do	Purple	Purplish	do	Purple	do	0	6	16	10	0	0	Rounded, dent.	
37a	do	do	Sun red	White	Pink	None	Blue	0	5	12	13	10	30	Rounded, semident.	
37b	do	do	Purple	Purple	Red	do	do	0	8	14	12	20	80	do	
43a	Sun red	do	do	White	Green	Purple S	Purple	0	5	14	11	0	40	do	
43b	do	do	Purple	Purplish	Pink	None	Blue	0	6	14	12	40	100	do	6

color was frequent, and many of the lighter cobs were flushed with purple or red. Many of the specimens belong to the color type called "cherry" by geneticists. In the field the purple plant color of a good many of the plants was conspicuous as well as the almost complete absence of tillers, which were frequent enough in the Tulukénio collections to produce a mass effect and make the field look thicker below row No. 30 than it was above that number. A summary of the records shows that on the average the plants of Black maize were taller, that their leaves were a little less pubescent, and that they averaged 5 instead of 7 tassel branches. The differences between Black maize from Cherán and from Nahuatzen were minor, the chief one being more color in the seed coat itself in addition to the prevailingly dark aleurone color. On the whole, the plants from Cherán were a little more variable and were about what might have been expected if varieties from Nahuatzen were grown in close proximity to other varieties from Cherán.

While the Black maize of Cherán and Nahuatzen is in general very similar to Mexican Pyramidal corn from around Mexico City, its broadish, rounded grains, its less condensed tassels, and its tendency to purple plant color are atypical for that region.

Much of the Tulukénio maize is quite like the corn from Mexico City. Nearly all the ears had more or less pointed kernels (characteristically with a dent behind the point) and those which did not have them produced plants with pointed kernels. While there was great variation, most of the varieties were small-grained (7 mm. wide or less). Unlike the Black varieties (whose endosperm was invariably white) about half had yellow endosperm. While the Tulukénio maize varied greatly in the color of the grains, it was prevailingly light and much of it had a rather streaky, irregularly developed pinkish purple in the seed coat. The colored portions were not sharply defined as in variegated maize, but gave rather the effect of a colorless ear which had been lightly brushed with some such dye as eosin. It is apparently due to allelomorphs of the 'P' series. While a few of the ears were straight-rowed, on the whole they were very irregular, at least on a portion of the cob.

Three of the Tulukénio collections (Nos. 1, 9, and 12, table 18) were of particular interest since they are unlike any corn from Mexico City which we have so far examined and since resemblances to them were apparent in several other collections (e. g. Nos. 16 and 17). They are small-cobbed, very flinty, with no trace of denting, and the cobs are cylindrical rather than tapering. That they are not merely poorly developed ears is proved by the fact that the plants grown from them were somewhat distinctive. They were short, one of them had more tillers than any other plant in the field, and their internode patterns revealed a strong tendency toward the Pima-Papago pattern rather than the Mexican Pyramidal pattern.

We do not yet have enough data about the kinds of maize to appraise the significance of these extreme variants of Tulukénio maize. It may be they are inferior types which have, through inbreeding, segregated out of better varieties. Since these mountain varieties are grown in isolated plots and since each family carefully preserves its own strain, this is quite likely. Even so, their morphology may be a significant throw-back to a type of corn once grown in this region, or in some region from which the Tarascan maize was derived. Since in most of their peculiarities they suggest Pima-Papago maize, which is known to be similar to the prehistoric Basket Maker maize (Anderson and Blanchard, 1942), it is possible that they are evidence of a primitive small-cobbed maize.

A cytological study was made of five different plants, by means of pachytene smears.

TABLE 19.—*Summary showing knob of each chromosome for 5 collections of maize from Cherán*

Chromosome No.	Knob number in collections of—					
	Tulukénio maize			Black maize		Average
	Be4.	Be11.	Be22.	Be34b.	Be43b.	
1	0	0	0	0	0	0
2	1	0	1	1	S	1
3	0	0	1	0	S	0
4	0	0	1	S	1+S	S
5	0	1	1	0	0	0
6	S	0	0	0	0	0
7	1	1	1	1	1	1
8	1	1	1	1	1	1
9	0	T	T	T	TS	T
10	0	0	0	0	0	0
Total	4	4	7	5	6	5
Supernumerary ('B' chromosomes)	0	1	1	0	0	0

S = Small knob.
T = Terminal knob.

Two of these plants had supernumerary or 'B' type chromosomes. The numbers and positions of the knobs on the 10 normal chromosomes are summarized in table 19. These facts will ultimately be significant when we have more data on knob numbers and positions from other types of maize (Mangelsdorf and Cameron, 1942). For the present we can say only that the knob numbers are intermediate between the high knob numbers of Western Mexico and the low numbers of the Mexico City–Toluca region.

The more significant measurements and observations made on the collection are summarized in table 18. Average values for the four most useful criteria of tassel morphology are shown graphically in figure 19, where they are compared with similar averages made on collections from pueblo-dwelling Indians in Arizona and New Mexico; from Pima, Papago,

and allied tribes; and from Mexican Pyramidal varieties collected near Mexico City.

It will be seen that insofar as their tassels are concerned both the Tulukénio varieties and the Black maize varieties are intermediate between the Mexican Pyramidal and the Pima-Papago. On tassel morphology alone they are even closer to the latter than to the former. Since, so far as we can tell from the ears, Pima-Papago maize is very similar to that of the prehistoric Basket Makers (Anderson and Blanchard, 1942), this strengthens the suggestion made above that one element in the ancestry of this Tarascan maize may have been a primitive small-cobbed race somewhat like that of the Basket Makers. A diagram based on ear and kernel morphology would also demonstrate that both of these Tarascan types are intermediate between Mexican Pyramidal and Pima-Papago, but it would not indicate as close a resemblance to the latter as is given by the tassel morphology alone.

SUMMARY

The maize varieties from two adjacent Tarascan villages are described and their characteristics are recorded in detail. While as a whole they are more or less similar to collections of Mexican Pyramidal maize from Mexico, D. F., they can be divided into at least three subraces. For two of these, the "Tulukénio" and the "Black" maize, there is enough material to define the central core of their variation. Black maize is grown in gardens below 8,500 feet. Characteristically it has large, dark, smoothly dented kernels on a tapering ear about 15 cm. long. While it has certain technical resemblances to Pima-Papago maize (low percentage of condensed internodes in tassel, length of glume, etc.,) it differs only slightly from Mexican Pyramidal. Tulukénio varieties are grown above 8,500 feet in small isolated plots in the mountains. They are even more like Pima-Papago; their tassels technically are closer to the latter than to Mexican Pyramidal. They vary greatly in color, size and shape, the largest ears being about the size of Black maize. The kernels tend to be small, more or less pointed, semidented; their seed coats lightly stained or streaked with red. The extreme variants of Tulukénio are small-cobbed,

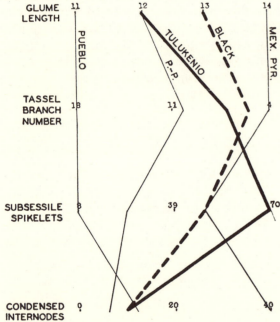

FIGURE 19.—Average values for four characters of the male inflorescence (the tassel) of Beals' collections of Tulukénio maize and Black maize. Narrow lines show averages of other collections for comparison: Mex. Pyr., Mexican Pyramidal from Mexico City; P.-P., Pima-Papago; Pueblo (Carter, Anderson, Cutler collections). The four scales used from top to bottom are glume length in millimeters, tassel branch number (values run from right to left for this scale), percentage of subsessile upper spiklets on tassel branches and percentage of condensed internodes on tassel branches.

nontapering, early-seasoned, undented, and many-tillered varieties. They may possibly reflect a primitive small-cobbed race somewhat like the maize of the Basket Makers. If so, it was one element in the ancestry of Tarascan maize.

Taken in conjunction with Mangelsdorf and Cameron's recent (1942) analysis of knob number in Guatemalan maize, these results demonstrate the importance of considering altitude above sea level in interpreting the history and development of *Zea mays*.

BIBLIOGRAPHY

ANDERSON, EDGAR, and BLANCHARD, FREDERICK D.
 1942. Prehistoric maize from Cañon del Muerto. Amer. Journ. Botany, vol. 29, pp. 832–835.

ANDERSON, EDGAR, and CUTLER, HUGH C.
 1942. Races of *Zea mays*: I. Their recognition and classification. Mo. Bot. Gard. Ann., vol. 29, pp. 69–88.

ARRIAGA, ANTONIO.
 1938. Organización Social de los Tarascos. Morelia, Mexico.

BEALS, RALPH L., and HATCHER, EVELYN PAYNE.
 1943. The diet of a Sierra Tarascan community. American Indígena, vol. 3, No. 4, pp. 295–304.

BEALS, RALPH L., and CARRASCO, PEDRO.
 1944. Games of the Mountain Tarascans. Amer. Anthrop., vol. 46, pp. 516–522.

BEALS, RALPH L., CARRASCO, PEDRO, and McCORKLE, THOMAS.
 1944. Houses and house use of the Sierra Tarascans. Institute of Social Anthropology, Smithsonian Institution, Publ. No. 1.

MANGELSDORF, PAUL C., and CAMERON, JAMES W.
 1942. Western Guatemala a secondary center of origin of cultivated maize varieties. Bot. Mus. Leaflets, Harvard Univ., vol. 10, pp. 217–252.

MORE, SIR THOMAS.
 1923. The Utopia of Sir Thomas More. Translation by Ralph Robinson. Edited by George Sampson. Everyman's edition. London.

MURDOCK, GEORGE P., and OTHERS.
 1938. Outline of cultural materials. Yale Univ., New Haven.

REDFIELD, ROBERT.
 1941. The folk culture of Yucatan. Chicago.

RUBIN DE LA BORBOLLA, D. F., and BEALS, RALPH L.
 1940. The Tarasca Project: A cooperative enterprise of the National Polytechnic Institute, Mexican Bureau of Indian Affairs, and the University of California. Amer. Anthrop., n. s., vol. 42, pp. 708–712.

SPICER, EDWARD H.
 1940. Pascua: A Yaqui village in Arizona. Chicago.

SWADESH, MORRIS.
 1940. Orientaciones Lingüísticas para maestros en zonas indígenas. Mexico.

ZAVALA, SILVIO ARTURO.
 1937. La "Utopia" de Tomás Moro en la Nueva España, y otros estudios. Mexico.

GLOSSARY

The following list includes Spanish and Tarascan terms frequently used in the text. Words used only once or twice and defined at the time are not included in the glossary. Spanish words are given the local Tarascan usage, which is often different from either customary Mexican or standard Spanish usage. Tarascan words are followed by "T".

Ačes (T), the *cabildo*, or chiefs of the ceremonial organization.

Agave, a genus of plants, often called the *maguey*. In the United States, called the century plant.

Agua miel, the unfermented juice of the *agave*.

Aguardiente, normally a liquor distilled from sugarcane; in the Tarascan area, often called *charanda*.

Almud, a dry measure of about 0.8 of a liter.

Arriero, a muleteer.

Arroba, a measure of weight, slightly less than 25 pounds.

Atapákua (T), squash blossoms and immature squash cooked together.

Atole, a thin gruel, usually made of ground maize with various flavorings.

Ayuntamiento, the civil government of a *municipio*.

Barranca, a steep-sided canyon or gully.

Barrio, a ward or division of a town.

Bilis, a word used to cover a variety of sicknesses.

Cabecera, the largest town and administrative center of a *municipio*.

Cabildo, the group in charge of the ceremonial organization; the ačes.

Calzones, cotton trousers of unbleached muslin, worn by men for work and, by conservatives, for everyday wear.

Cantina, a saloon.

Čápata, a tamale made from amaranth.

Čarales, a small dried fish.

Carga, a somewhat indefinite measure, often a burro load.

Carguero, a *mayordomo*, a person who has taken responsibility for a saint's image for a year.

Castillo, a set piece of fireworks on a tall pole.

Catrin, urban or citified, particularly applied to clothes.

Centavo, a cent, or one-hundredth of a peso.

Centimeter, one-hundredth of a meter.

Charanda, a drink distilled from sugarcane.

Charape, a ceremonial drink, usually made of *pulque*.

Chayote, a lush-growing vine and the edible fruit it bears.

Chilecayote, a type of squash.

Cherimoya, the anona, a fruit.

Cohete, an explosive rocket used in fiestas.

Cohetero, fireworks maker.

Comadre, the godmother of one's child.

Comal, a lenticular dish used for baking tortillas.

Comisionado, a person who has been commissioned by the authorities to perform some task in connection with municipal affairs or a fiesta. May also be named by the priest or by ceremonial organizations.

Compadrazgo, the system of relationships set up through the godparent custom.

Compadre, godfather of one's child.

Copal, the gum of the long-needled tropical pine (*Pinus montezumae*).

Corales, tubular red glass beads worn by every woman in native costume.

Cuartel, a *barrio*, or division of a town.

Cuelgas, ornaments hung from ropes, poles, or about the neck of participants in some ceremonies.

Curato, the residence of the priest.

Čurípo (T), a highly seasoned broth containing cabbage and chunks of boiled beef.

Fanega, a Spanish dry measure which has various values in different parts of Mexico. In Cherán, the fanega appears to equal 90.8 dry quarts.

Garabanzos, chickpeas.

Gordos, flat thickish cakes fried in lard, usually of ground corn but sometimes of wheat flour.

Guaraches, sandals.

Guavas, a fruit.

Habas, the broadbean.

Hectarea, a land measure of 2.47 acres, or 10,000 square meters.

Jefe de defensa, chief of the local militia.

Junta, any meeting of a town or organized body.

Kéηi (T), an official connected with the *cabildo* and the church who does errands and looks after the church and church properties.

Kurúnda (T), a tamale made of steamed *nixtamal* wrapped in maize leaves.

Litro, a liter, a liquid measure.

Maestro, a school teacher; a lay reader.

Maguey, the *agave* plant.

Malpais, an old lava flow.

Mano, the smaller milling stone held in the hands.

Manta, cheap unbleached muslin.

Manzana, a block or square in a town.

Mayordomía, the entire process of caring for a saint's image, arranging for the Mass and other ceremonies involved by tradition.

Mayordomo, *carguero*; a person who is responsible for the care of a saint's image for a year.

Metate, the lower or stationary milling stone.

Meter, a measure of 39.37 inches.

Mole, a common highly seasoned and complicated sauce used on meat; also a meat dish served in mole sauce.

Moro, a type of dancer common in Michoacán.

Municipe, a *regidor* or city councilman.

Municipio, an administrative area somewhat like a county or parish.

Negritos, dancers wearing black wooden masks who appear at Christmas.

Nixtamal, dough made by grinding maize after it is soaked in lye.

Nopal, the prickly pear cactus plant.

Očépos (T), a sweet tamale.

Olla, water jar of pottery.

Panalero, a person who collects wild honey.

Pan dulce, wheat-flour bread with sweetening added.

Papaya, a subtropical fruit.

Peso, a Mexican silver coin.

Pinole, flour made by grinding parched maize.

Plan, plain; a large level cultivated area.

Portales, covered sidewalks, the outer edge of the roof supported by pillars.

Posole, maize soaked in lye and then cracked into small pieces.

Pulque, fermented juice of the *agave*, or *maguey*. (See *Agave*.)

Raíz de paja, a root which is dried and used to make scrubbing brushes.

Ramada, a rectangular unwalled structure primarily for the purpose of affording shade.

Rebozo, a shawl worn by women.

Regidor, a member of the city council.

Relato, the text which is recited at a dance.

Representante del pueblo, an official who looks after community property in lands and forests.

Reserva, an authorized armed militia.

Rezador, a person who recites prayers for a small fee.

Riata, a long rope used in handling horses and cattle.

Rollo, the native skirt with the thick band of pleats across the back.

Ronda, the night watch, or volunteer police.

Secretario, the town clerk or secretary.

Serape, a blanket, usually ornamented, and with an opening so that it may be worn over the head as a poncho.

Solar, a town lot.

Suplente, the alternate for an office in the government.

Tabla, a plank.

Tamale, a food made of maize, often mixed with other ingredients, wrapped in maize leaves or maize husks, and steamed.

Tejamanil, wooden shakes.

Tejocote, a tree bearing a sloelike fruit much like a crab apple; the fruit of such a tree.

Tenencia, a settlement of some size which is administered by a representative of the *municipio*.

Tortillas, thin flat cakes of maize dough baked on an ungreased griddle, or *comal*.

Troje, the Tarascan storehouse, the largest structure in a Tarascan house group, as a rule.

Tuna, the fruit of the *nopal* cactus, or prickly pear.

Velorio, a religious celebration at which candles are burned.

Viajero, a traveling merchant.

Zapote, a tropical fruit resembling a plum.

CHERÁN LANDSCAPES AND METHODS OF CARRYING OBJECTS.

Upper (left): The plains below Cherán, the major agricultural area, about 7,000 feet elevation, viewed from the highway, near southeast corner of the town. Darker portions are plowed fields; the remainder not yet plowed. *Upper (right):* Women carrying water in typical manner, with the usual Cherán water jar. A method of wearing the *rebozo* is shown. The church and priest's residence are in background. *Lower (left):* The northwest *barrio* of Cherán. The new highway curves along the edge of the barranca. Typical cultivated fields slope gently up to the cinder cone, which rises 1,000 feet above the town. *Lower (right):* Carrying bowls of masa (corn ground for tortillas) from the mill. Carrying on the head is unusual, but the method used by the girl is common for small objects. The woman's skirt has the thick pleat or rollo.

WOMEN, CARRYING METHODS, AND HAIR GROOMING.

Upper (left): Woman bargaining for tomatoes, showing typical method of carrying burdens on the back, i. e., by a sling of sacking which supports a basket and passes around the shoulders and across the chest. Her rollo is clearly visible. The man in the short poncho is probably a Mestizo attending the fiesta. *Upper (right):* Woman using *rebozo* in carrying a child. Musicians in background. *Lower (left):* Unmarried young woman of San Lorenzo with rayon apron and light *rebozo* for a fiesta. *Lower (right):* Mother combs her daughter's hair and anoints it with oil or lemon juice (in bowl) to give it a sheen.

CHERÁN AQUEDUCTS, BOARD SAWING, SHAKE SPLITTING, AND WHEAT WINNOWING.

Upper (*left*): The Cherán aqueducts, east of town. *Upper* (*right*): Sawing planks with sawpit.   Often, the timber is raised on a pole framework instead of being placed over a pit. *Lower* (*left*): Splitting off a shake with a rajador. *Lower* (*right*): Starting to split a shake with a machete struck with a wooden mallet. *Center:* Cherán man winnowing wheat.

PLOWING, DITCHES TO PROTECT FIELDS, LOG HEWING, AND CHERÁN PLAZA DURING FIESTA.

Upper (left): Plowing on the plain.   Augustín, at the plow, wears felt hat, shirt, trousers, belt, and shoes; workman at left, less acculturated, wears straw hat, sandals, and mechanic's overalls.   *Upper (right):* Squaring a log with an ax before sawing it into planks.
Lower (left): A hill-slope field, with new ditch (center) and overgrown bank surmounted with thorny brush (foreground) to protect
it from animals.   Agaves are planted on right of ditch.   *Lower (right):* Portion of Cherán plaza during the fiesta of the patron
saint.

MARKET AND BULL FIGHTING DURING FESTIVAL.

Upper (left): Pottery before being unpacked for the market.   *Upper (right):* Riding a bucking bull, the man with cape diverting it from the horses.   *Lower (left):* Cowboys (*vaqueros*) throw the bull in the bull ring, then tie a rope around its forequarters.   *Lower (right):* Bull riding.   *Inset:* Construction of bull ring fence; post on right has holes cut with ax to receive the logs forming the gate.

CASTILLO, PASTORELA, NEGRITO DANCERS, AND WEDDING.

Upper (*left*): Portion of the fireworks set (*castillo*) nearly completed. The fireworks maker is on the right. *Upper* (*right*): *Pastorela* at Capacuaro; at left is one of the "hermits." *Left* (*middle*): Large wedding in the patio in front of the house. The kitchen is at left, the temporary cooking shed in the center. The woman at left bears a cloth-covered dish with an offering for one of the godmothers. *Lower* (*left*): *Negrito* dancers performing at private house. The ribbons hang down to their heels. The "pin cushions" (foreground) are the dancers' head decorations. *Lower* (*right*): *Pastorela* at Capacuaro, with "*Europeo*" in foreground.

ROOFING FIESTA AND WEDDING.

Upper (*left*): Men eating at a house-roofing fiesta; baskets of tortillas, jars of water, and dishes of salt lie on the ground.   Remaining photographs, a Cherán wedding.   *Upper* (*right*): Preparing to distribute bread, while one of the godmothers oversees the work. *Lower* (*left*): Bringing in paper ornaments for distribution.   *Right* (*middle*): The godmothers and close relatives of the groom. *Lower* (*right*): Tying a ribbon in a godmother's hair.

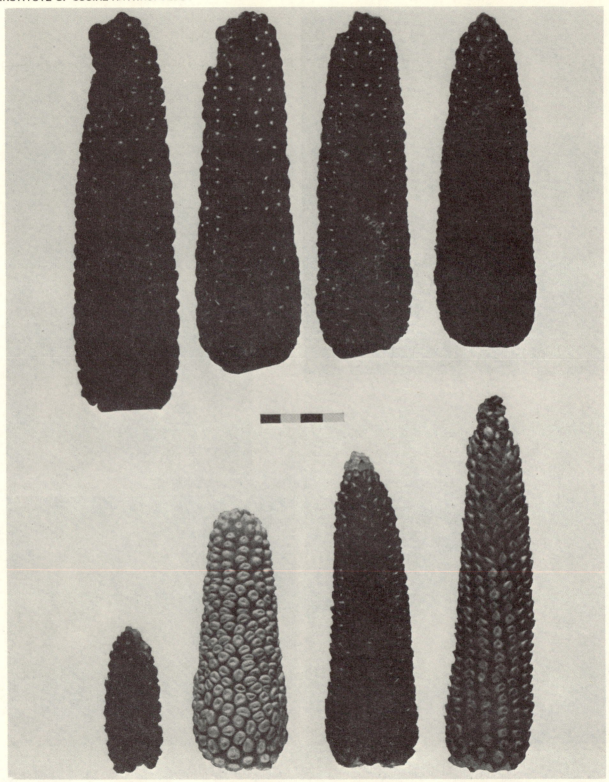

SPECIMENS OF MAIZE EARS.

Four specimen ears of Black maize (*above*) and Tulukénio (*below*), representing extremes of size. Two of the Black ears are from Cherán, two from the neighboring village of Nahuatzen; all the Tulukénio ears are from Cherán. Scale in center is approximately 4 cm. long.